JOHN DONNE: THE CRITICAL HERITAGE

THE CRITICAL HERITAGE SERIES

GENERAL EDITOR: B. C. SOUTHAM, M.A., B.LITT. (OXON.)
Formerly Department of English, Westfield College, University of London

For a list of books in the series see the back end paper

JOHN DONNE

THE CRITICAL HERITAGE

Edited by
A. J. SMITH
Professor of English
University of Southampton

ROUTLEDGE & KEGAN PAUL: LONDON AND BOSTON

First published in 1975
by Routledge & Kegan Paul Ltd
Broadway House, 68–74 Carter Lane,
London EC4V 5EL and
9 Park Street,
Boston, Mass. 02108, USA
© A. J. Smith 1975

ISBN 0 7100 8242 8

Set in 'Monotype' Bembo
and printed in Great Britain by
W & J Mackay Limited, Chatham

General Editor's Preface

The reception given to a writer by his contemporaries and near-contemporaries is evidence of considerable value to the student of literature. On one side we learn a great deal about the state of criticism at large and in particular about the development of critical attitudes towards a single writer; at the same time, through private comments in letters, journals or marginalia, we gain an insight upon the tastes and literary thought of individual readers of the period. Evidence of this kind helps us to understand the writer's historical situation, the nature of his immediate reading-public, and his response to these pressures.

The separate volumes in the *Critical Heritage Series* present a record of this early criticism. Clearly, for many of the highly productive and lengthily reviewed nineteenth- and twentieth-century writers, there exists an enormous body of material; and in these cases the volume editors have made a selection of the most important views, significant for their intrinsic critical worth or for their representative quality—perhaps even registering incomprehension!

For earlier writers, notably pre-eighteenth century, the materials are much scarcer and the historical period has been extended, sometimes far beyond the writer's lifetime, in order to show the inception and growth of critical views which were initially slow to appear.

In each volume the documents are headed by an Introduction, discussing the material assembled and relating the early stages of the author's reception to what we have come to identify as the critical tradition. The volumes will make available much material which would otherwise be difficult of access and it is hoped that the modern reader will be thereby helped towards an informed understanding of the ways in which literature has been read and judged.

B.C.S.

Contents

The eighteenth century

The nineteenth century

CONTENTS

Preface

An account of our heritage of Donne criticism must cover a whole cycle
of his fortunes, bringing together opinions of his poetry from its earliest
days to recent times. The present volume collects the known evidence
of Donne's reputation as a poet, and of the reputation of his poems,
down to the 1880s. It admits comments on his prose writings only
when they bear upon the poetry too. General discussions of metaphysical poetry are not included unless they directly refer to Donne. This
record of Donne's reputation breaks off just before his poetry returned
to general esteem and a modern view of it began to emerge. In some
ways the most striking of all developments in Donne criticism came
about between the 1890s and the 1920s. But to cover that period a
further volume of extracts would be needed.

Few of the items given here have critical value in themselves or offer
fresh insights into the poems. The book is simply intended to show what
people have made of Donne's poetry over several hundred years and
how opinions of it have shifted in that time; though it naturally reflects the tastes or canons of the commentators and the way tastes and
canons change. Donne has challenged his critics from the first, so that
the successive revaluations of him tend to mirror changing critical
assumptions.

Completeness is too much to hope for. But I have not knowingly
omitted any germane comment on Donne's poetry in the period; and
the volume records the comments which have so far come to light. Of
the many scholars who have located references I am particularly indebted to Sir Geoffrey Keynes, A. H. Nethercott, Professor W. Milgate,
Professor R. G. Howarth, Professor K. Tillotson, Professor J. E.
Duncan.

A.J.S.

Acknowledgments

For allowing me to print passages from materials in their custody, or copyright, I am obliged to the Director of the Houghton Library of Harvard University and to the Director of the Duke University Press. I acknowledge help given me by the staffs of libraries in Britain and America, and especially the university libraries at Swansea and Keele. The University College of Swansea and the University of Keele have assisted me with research grants, for which I am grateful. My particular thanks are owed to the following people who supplied me with references or material: Mr A. P. Burton, Assistant Keeper of the Library of the Victoria and Albert Museum, Mr W. P. Ingoldsby of the Huntington Library, California, Dr Peter King, Mr J. L. Hermans, Mr Tom Davies, Mr Kevin Barry, Mr Michael Munday, Professor S. Schoenbaum, my erstwhile colleague Mr F. M. Doherty, and Mrs Mabel Potter.

Introduction

I

As late as the 1880s Swinburne in England and Lowell in America independently wondered at the arbitrariness of literary reputation when they found so magnificent a poet as Donne still widely unacknowledged. That a great poet should cease to be recognised as such and for donkeys' years go belittled or neglected is a phenomenon that needs explaining. Was there a general aberration of taste? Did his times and concerns peculiarly cut him off from the eras that followed? The myth of Donne the modern has long been the received answer to these questions. It was a conscious modernism, partly defining itself by Donne, which credited Grierson and Eliot with the rediscovery of his poetry and hailed his return as the recovery of a lost mode of sensibility, or the harbinger of an intellectual revolution like the one he himself s supposed to have led. People still make it an article of faith that Donne's poems had a fashion in his own day and just after, then fell wholly into neglect until recent times when our like predicament showed us ourselves in them. We may acknowledge that our times have their distinctive view of Donne and yet require these assumptions to submit to the facts.

What admits no dispute is that Donne's poetry has come back into a general esteem in the present century such as it had not enjoyed since the time of Charles I—that his fame came full circle from Carew's day to Eliot's. But general esteem isn't all that matters, or even what matters most. The truth about Donne's reputation, as one finds it in particular responses to the poems, is far from simple. Such sharp differences of attitude as appear in the documents that follow don't form a single pattern, and often seem to have more to do with Donne's peculiar demands upon his readers than with the temper of an age or a condition of sensibility. They are interesting for what they tell us of the assumptions which people brought to Donne at various times, and then for what they show us of our own assumptions. Those patterns which really are to be seen in the way Donne's readers have spoken of him over some three centuries tend to define themselves clearly enough, not only because there were quite abrupt shifts of attitude and favour but because some features of the poems have continued to divide opinion in exemplary ways. It goes without saying, though, that the one distinction which matters is that between readers who have made good sense of Donne and readers who haven't, those who speak to the point about his poetry and those who travesty it or just patter off a formula.

II

The faith that Donne was a popular poet in his own day makes a good counter to romantic fairy tales of artists despised by their contemporaries, but hasn't much solid ground. Turning from myth to history we may well wonder where the evidence of Donne's popularity is to be found in an age that doesn't seem to have had much to say even of the greatest of all its poets. The reputation of Donne's poetry as the seventeenth century went on i sanother matter. That may be judged not only in direct comments on his writings or his merits but from an impressive variety of other testimony, such as the familiar quotation or adaptation of his lines, the appearance of his poems in manuscript collections, the record of published poems and editions.

None of this supports the idea that Donne led a new poetic movement in the early seventeenth century or even suggests as much as that his poetry had a revolutionary impact while he was still writing. But then the peculiar circumstances in which he wrote and was read specifically exclude that possibility for his poems were not, and could not have been, widely known in his own day. No more than five of them and some bits of another three were printed in his lifetime and no collected edition appeared until two years after his death, so that his contemporaries could have read most of his work only in manuscript.

For some time they would not have found it easy to come by even in manuscript copies. Donne must not have relished the prospect that anyone and everyone might read his poems for he at once regretted the appearance in print of the few pieces whose publication he had sanctioned:[1]

Of my *Anniversaries*, the fault that I acknowledge in myself is to have descended to print anything in verse, which though it have excuse even in our times by men who profess and practice much gravity; yet I confess I wonder how I declined to it, and do not pardon myself: . . .

The vehemence of this distaste for an indiscriminate audience is matched by Drayton's indignation in the opposite causes:[2]

In publishing this Essay of my Poeme, there is this great disadvantage against me; that it commeth out at this time, when Verses are wholly deduc't to Chambers, and nothing esteem'd in this lunatique Age, but what is kept in Cabinets, and must only passe by Transcription.

If these were the consciously opposed attitudes of gentleman-wit and professional poet there is little doubt how Donne saw himself. He appears to have kept a fastidiously exclusive idea of his audience, attempting to limit the availability of his poems by passing copies of them only to a few close friends whom he could trust to let them go no further:[3]

Yet Sir though I know there low price, except I receive by your next letter an assurance upon the religion of your friendship that no coppy shall bee taken for any respect of these or any other my compositions sent to you, I shall sinn against my conscience if I send you any more. . . . I am desirous to hyde them with out any over reconing of them or there maker.

But it was inevitable that copies would be made of copies and that their circulation should escape the poet's control in the end.

The earliest comments on Donne's poetry are based on the reading of poems in manuscript, often rather few poems, or amount to hearsay opinion unsupported by close acquaintance with the writings themselves. Five of the poems were published between 1609 and 1613 (which was quite late in Donne's poetic career) and had a wider fame open to them; in particular the two *Anniversaries* were several times reissued in Donne's lifetime and inspired an impressive body of quotation, imitation, adaptation, and remark. But direct comment on the bulk of Donne's poetry is limited by the circumstances to the testimony of acquaintances and of members of his own or cognate literary circles.

Our immediate witnesses of how Donne's poems were esteemed in his day and shortly after are thus the contemporary manuscripts themselves. Surviving manuscripts show that his poems, as those of other poets, were copied out by enthusiasts or their scribes and the copies themselves passed around for further copying. So that these documents may tell us how interested contemporary readers were in Donne's poetry, the kind of people who showed real interest in it, and which poems or groups of poems were popular. Since many of these manuscripts can be dated, however approximately, they also give us some idea when particular poems and kinds of poems began to be well known and well liked. This manuscript evidence changes its value after 1633 when Donne's poems became available in print.[4]

Two distinct kinds of manuscript compilation must be considered

3

since they offer somewhat different kinds of evidence. Some forty surviving manuscripts bring together substantial collections of Donne's poems. But as well as these we have over a hundred manuscripts of poetical miscellanies which contain poems by Donne scattered among poems by other authors. Few of the manuscripts, collections or miscellanies, tell us anything of Donne's reputation while he was still regularly writing verse. Most of the large collections of Donne's poems appear to have been made in the 1620s and early 1630s; of the forty extant perhaps a dozen were made before 1615 and no more than five of those before 1605. The miscellanies are generally of later date; many were made after Donne's death and even after the publication of his poems in 1633. But some twenty-eight of the hundred were probably compiled before 1625, and two of those may be earlier than 1605.

This profusion of surviving copies suggests that Donne had a devoted following during his lifetime and that some of his poetry became very popular from the 1620s on. But the scarcity of early manuscripts must mean that very few people could have read any of Donne's poems during the greater part of his poetic career. Indeed, the brief list of known readers confirms that Donne kept his verse close for they are almost all associates or correspondents of his: Goodyer, Wotton, Rowland Woodward, Hoskins, Christopher and Samuel Brooke, Thomas and John Roe, Jonson, Mrs Herbert, the Earl of Dorset, Everard Guilpin, Joseph Hall. Evidently it was well into the second decade of the seventeenth century before the bulk of the poems began to circulate much at all, and only in the 1620s did copies become more freely available; possibly Donne had himself by then made manuscript collections of his poems which were copied entire. As late as 1630 Constantine Huygens complained that amateurs of verse were only just beginning to distribute copies of Donne's poems, having kept them to themselves for years:[5]

Many rich fruits from the green branches of his wit have lain mellowing among the lovers of art, which now, when nearly rotten with age, they are distributing.

All in all, it is likely that no more than a few of Donne's poems reached a large audience until he was already celebrated as a divine who had long abandoned poetry.

The compiling of a manuscript collection of a body of verse as large as Donne's, or even a section of it, is a large undertaking and testifies in itself to a serious concern with his work. What kind of people were these first students of Donne who put the manuscript compilations together or had them made for their use? Many of the manuscripts appear to have been copied by scribes for particular employers, while others were evidently written out by private persons for their own satisfaction and study. Of the known first owners of extant manuscript collections some were noblemen, some were Donne's associates, and others were students, members of the universities or the Inns of Court. The Bridgewater manuscript belonged to John Egerton, first Earl of Bridgewater, son of Donne's sometime employer Sir Thomas Egerton. The Leconfield manuscript probably belonged to Donne's close associate Henry Percy, ninth Earl of Northumberland; and a fragmentary copy of this manuscript belonged to Edward, second Viscount Conway. The manuscript now known as *H 49* (British Museum, Harleian MS. 4955) probably belonged to William Cavendish, first Duke of Newcastle. *A 18* (British Museum, Add. MS. 18647) may have belonged to members of the family of the earls of Denbigh. The manuscript now in Trinity College, Cambridge (MS.R 312) may have belonged to Sir Thomas Puckering, son of Lord Keeper Puckering. The Westmoreland manuscript is in the hand of Donne's close friend Rowland Woodward, who probably copied it straight from Donne's holograph. The Dyce manuscript (Victoria and Albert Museum, Dyce Collection, MS.D 25 F 17) bears the signature of John Nedlam, Lincoln College, Oxford, and is dated 31 March 1625. The Dolaucothi manuscript is signed by one Richard Lloyde, possibly the Lloyde who studied at the Inner Temple in the 1620s and went on to become a royalist attorney and judge.

Many more readers would have known Donne only as the writer of satires, or elegies, or verse letters to noble persons. For the big manuscript collections on which all published editions of the poems are based were made by the bringing together of smaller collections or sets of particular kinds of poem, some of which must have been circulating quite early on. Of the five extant collections of Donne's verse which are likely to have been made before 1605 three are manuscripts of the *Satyres* and two of the *Metempsychosis*. 'The Storme' and 'The Calme' were probably quite early in circulation too, as were the *Epigrams* and the *Elegies*, some of which may well have circulated singly as well as in their sets. Later, the *Holy Sonnets* and *La Corona* must have made up a set which circulated among a small group of Donne's associates. Some of the *Songs and Sonnets* may have circulated independently or in small groups of poems. But there is no evidence that the love lyrics circulated as a separate set, and not much sign that people even thought of them as a single body of poems; though the compiler of the recently discovered Dolaucothi manuscript must have regarded them so for he grouped them together and marked 'The eand of the Songes' to distinguish them from the following poems. They were not brought together as a body in the edition of 1633 but scattered through the volume, presumably just as the editor encountered them in the manuscripts before him. It was the editor of the 1635 edition who first gathered them in under the single heading of *Songs and Sonets*.

The poetical miscellanies in manuscript show us a different kind of contemporary interest in Donne. Compilers of miscellanies collected together poems which struck their fancy or were popular at the time. So the surviving body of miscellanies can give us at least an idea of what poems were well known at particular times and how popular they were. R. A. Bryan and Alan MacColl have separately analysed these manuscript miscellanies and counted how often particular poems by Donne occur in them. Overall, Mr MacColl finds that in the twenty-eight surviving miscellanies probably compiled before 1625 about seventy different poems by Donne occur, some of them several times; and in all the surviving miscellanies compiled before 1650 about ninety different poems by Donne occur, some of them many times. One must bear in mind that few of Donne's poems could have reached a wide audience until the 1620s, but also that Donne wrote nearly two hundred poems, so that all the miscellanies quite ignore more than half of his poetic output. None the less some of his poems were among the commonest items in the manuscript miscellanies from 1625 to 1645 and they were especially common between 1633 and 1643. Toward 1650, in Mr MacColl's words, 'the flood dwindles to a trickle.'[6]

Here are some lists showing which poems occur most often in the manuscript miscellanies we have. The figures in brackets show the number of times a poem occurs in these surviving miscellanies:

(i) In miscellanies probably compiled before 1625

Elegies

> 'The Anagram' (7)
> 'The Perfume' (5)
> 'The Bracelet' (4)
> 'The Autumnall' (4)

Songs and Sonnets

Many of the slighter lyrics generally considered to be early occur several times each, with the following the most frequent:

'Breake of Day' (5)
'The Message' (4)
'Song. Sweetest love' (4)

Some of the weightier lyrics (those Helen Gardner dates after 1602) are not represented at all. But the following do appear:

'A Valediction: forbidding Mourning' (4)
'Twicknam Garden' (4)
'A Feaver' (2)
'The Good-morrow' (2)
'The Sunne Rising' (2)
'The Dreame' (2)
'Loves Growth' (1)
'Loves Alchymie' (1)

Other kinds (appearing once each)
Six epigrams
Twelve verse letters
The three epithalamions
Six funeral poems
Seven divine poems

(ii) In the miscellanies altogether

Elegie 'The Anagram' (25)
Elegie 'To his Mistris Going to Bed' (25)
'Breake of Day' (17)
Elegie 'The Bracelet' (16)
'A Valediction: forbidding Mourning' (16)
Epigram 'A Lame Begger' (14)
'The Message' (13)
'The Baite' (12)
'The Apparition' (12)
Elegie 'The Perfume' (11)
Epigram 'A Licentious Person' (11)
Elegie 'The Autumnall' (10)
'Loves Diet' (10)
'Song. Sweetest love' (10)
'Song. Goe, and catche' (8)
'The Legacie' (8)
'The Broken Heart' (8)
'The Flea' (8)

7

'The Will' (8)
'Twicknam Garden' (8)
Elegie 'Loves Warre' (7)
'A Hymne to God the Father' (7)
'Elegie on the Lady Marckham' (6)
Epitaph 'On himselfe' (6)
Elegie 'The Comparison' (5)
Elegie 'Natures lay Ideot' (5)
Elegie 'On his Mistris' (5)
Elegie 'His Picture' (5)
'The Good-morrow' (5)
Verse letter 'To the Lady Bedford' ('You that are she and
   you') (5)
Epithalamion . . . *St Valentines day* (5)
'An hymne to the Saints, and to Marquesse Hamylton' (5)
'The Crosse' (5)

Such figures are reassuringly concrete but tell us only so much about
the taste of the times; less, one imagines, than an outsider might learn
about our own estimation of (say) Auden's work from a count of the
tired old circus horses which drag the rounds of our modern anthologies. It doesn't follow that poems appear most often in miscellanies because they appealed to most people at the time, or appealed most to
some people, or that poems which don't appear at all weren't what
interested people then. All sorts of things might affect a miscellanist's
choice of poems, not least the fact that he didn't have the run of a poet's
work but had to take what he could readily get. Several of the lyrics
which occur most often had already been set to music and become public
property; those which don't appear at all are the more personal of the
Songs and Sonnets such as 'Aire and Angels', 'The Anniversarie', 'The
Exstasie'. Again, the only two of the *Divine Poems* which recur at all
frequently are 'The Crosse' and 'A Hymne to God the Father', the one
dealing with a public issue of the day and the other having a well-
known musical setting which was 'often sung to the Organ by Choristers of St Paul's Church' according to Walton. Yet the figures do suggest that some groups of poems, such as the *Elegies*, circulated more
freely than others and that some poems didn't reach the circles where
miscellanies were compiled because they hadn't become widely available.
   All we can conclude from the fact that some poems by Donne occur
quite often in seventeenth-century manuscripts is that those poems were

available and popular. It would be pompous to announce on such evidence that this or that aspect of his poetry is what interested contemporary readers most. Nor can we reasonably go as far as to say that it was 'Donne the vivid realist and the witty and humorous satirist' who appealed most to his contemporaries,[7] or that Ben Jonson represented his times in preferring 'the epigrammatic, the satiric, the rhetorical and witty' aspects of Donne's verse.[8] Whatever Jonson's tastes may have been, Donne didn't become a 'popular' poet at all, even by the standard of the day, until quite late in his life. None the less some poems do turn up in the miscellanies convincingly often—a number of the *Elegies*, and a few *Songs and Sonnets* such as 'A Valediction: forbidding Mourning'. Of the miscellanists' choice of *Elegies* Mr MacColl remarks that it shows 'a marked preference for the witty or erotic; serious love elegies like "His Picture" were less popular'.[9] That is as far as we can go; and only if we find a 'popular' preference for witty or erotic poems remarkable, then or now, will we want to make much of it.

If we turn to the printed books of the time we find little sign that Donne's poems made their mark early on and nothing to suggest that Donne was well known at all, much less as a poet, until he was in his middle years. Sir Geoffrey Keynes has pointed out that the Vice-Chancellor of the University of Cambridge appeared to know little of Donne when he admitted him (perforce) to a D.D. in 1615, and that Donne first made a name for himself when he published his *Devotions* and sermons in the 1620s.[10] As far as we know, no one mentions or quotes in print a single poem of Donne's until 1598, when he was already twenty-six years old, and there is nothing after that until 1607 when he was thirty-five years old. Even Ben Jonson's splendid acknowledgment of Donne's mentorship in 1610 wasn't a public avowal like Eliot's deference to Pound but the seal of a small circle of associates; and Jonson takes it for granted that the appeal of Donne's verse is esoteric:

> Who shall doubt, *Donne*, where I a *Poet* bee,
> When I dare send my *Epigrammes* to thee?
> That so alone canst judge, so'alone do'st make:
> And, in thy censures, evenly, dost take
> As free simplicity, to dis-avow,
> As thou hast best authority, t'allow.
> Read all I send: and, if I finde but one
> Mark'd by thy hand, and with the better stone,
> My title's seal'd. Those that for claps doe write,
> Let punees, porters, players praise delight,

> And, till they burst, their backs, like asses load:
> A man should seek great glory, and not broad.

In 1620 John Cave still made Donne the type of the true poet who doesn't care for popular fame but seeks an elect following:

> Oh how it joys me that this quick brain'd Age
> can nere reach thee (Donn) though it should engage
> at once all its whole stock of witt to find
> out of thy well plac'd words thy more pure minde.
> Noe, wee are bastard Aeglets all; our eyes
> could not endure the splendor that would rise
> from hence like rays from out a cloud. . . .

By the second decade of the seventeenth century Donne's poems were being cited or quoted more often, though only the same few of them: the *Satyres*, some *Elegies*, a few *Epigrams* (especially 'A Lame Begger'), 'The Storme', and 'The Calme'. Writers drew on the *Anniversaries* fairly freely after those poems were published in 1611 and 1612, and the poem 'Upon Mr Thomas Coryats *Crudities*' (published 1611) was sometimes cited too, as were the *Metempsychosis*, some *Epicedes*, and a few verse letters. But it was still possible for Freeman to commend Donne to the public in 1614 as a poet lately launched who should now set himself to write something bigger than 'The Storme'; Freeman's epigram may well have been written well before 1614 but it appeared when Donne was in his forties, with most of his poetic career already behind him.

The *Songs and Sonnets* were not mentioned in print until 1613 when Donne was forty-one, and then only as 'Jhone Dones lyriques'; and not before 1616 did someone show that he had read any of them. Drummond extolled the 'Anacreontick lyricks' about 1616 in terms which became common later, but there is not the slightest sign that Donne gained wide recognition as a love poet until the poems were published in 1633. Only in 1638–9, years after Donne's death, do we find someone quoting familiarly from the *Songs and Sonnets* and attributing the conceit to Donne.

In the same way no one as much as mentioned Donne's religious poetry until 1628, when Donne was fifty-six. Walton first named particular *Divine Poems* in his elegy for Donne in the 1633 edition. No writer quoted a *Divine Poem*, as far as we know, until 1635 when James Howell took up some ideas and phrases from 'Goodfriday, 1613. Riding Westward' in his *Epistolae Ho-Elianae*.

Donne was unquestionably a very well-known Dean of St Paul's, and devout writer, of whom Huygens could justly report in 1630 that 'he is more famous than anyone'. Huygens tells us that it was this general esteem which at last led Donne's friends to distribute his poems in manuscript. But whatever Donne's fame in his later years, as poet or as preacher, such evidence as we have indicates that most of his poetry was not widely known before it was published in 1633. A very few pieces had a certain currency and fame in themselves but even some of the poems thus acknowledged were known because they had been published or set to music. The cult of Donne the master-poet is no invention, but it is a phenomenon of the mid-seventeenth century when Donne was long dead.

The first publication of Donne's collected poems in 1633, two years after his death, represented a considerable effort of garnering and assembly on the part of the unknown editor, whose printer offered them to the world with a flourish as writings of secure—indeed unparalleled—reputation: 'the best judgments . . . take it for granted' that Donne's poems are 'the best in this kinde, that ever this kingdome hath yet seene'. Both the number and the quality of the tributes to Donne assembled in the volume indicate that the publication was no ordinary event; though rather few of his elegists actually mention his poetry, let alone praise particular poems, and only one of them presents him as something other than a great divine who expressed his piety in verse.

Further editions of the poems quickly followed as publishers sought to meet a persisting demand. There were three editions within eight years of Donne's death, a further three editions in the following fifteen years, then a fifteen-year gap before the edition of 1669; and it was fifty years before another edition appeared, in 1719, the last true edition of the poems for nearly a century and a half.

By the mid-1630s poets were familiarly drawing on the *Songs and Sonnets*, and quotations from them or adaptations of them continued in a flood through the middle of the century; in fact people went on quoting Donne or referring to his lines down to the end of the century. Carew's elegy in the 1633 edition specifically celebrated Donne's poetic achievement, hailing Donne above all as a great poet who had decisively influenced English poetry. For more than thirty years following the first publication of his poems Donne's supremacy among English poets was generally acknowledged. Carew's acclaim of 'a King, that rul'd as hee thought fit/ The universall Monarchy of wit' set the accepted attitude of homage. Donne's achievements as a poet were fulsomely recognised, his unique standing and stature proclaimed, not least by the poets and poetasters who succeeded him. In another poem Carew places Donne beyond Virgil, Lucan, and Tasso, in some respects; Suckling writes of Donne as 'the great lord' of pure wit whom no man ever matched in his own line and whose death left an unfillable void in English letters; and a host of small versifiers speak of him with awe as one who gave English poetry its bearings and its star. Moseley in 1651 describes Donne as 'The highest Poet our language can boast of', and there is no discernible abatement of this understanding down into the 1660s. Donne's *Poems* appear in the *Catalogue of the Most Vendible Books* issued by W. London in 1657. For Shipman in 1667 Donne was one of the three monarchs of the Muses' Empire, a triumvirate in which Donne and Cowley appear to play Antony and Caesar to Waller's Lepidus. The effect of Donne's insights and attitudes on English sensibilities down to the time of Rochester and the Restoration dramatists is demonstrable in the writings of that era.

The first signs we have of the turn against Donne appear quite suddenly in the late 1660s. In 1668 Dryden preferred Donne's *Satyres* to Cleveland's on the ground that Donne gives us 'deep thoughts in common language, though rough cadence'; and this 'rough cadence' served then for a hundred and fifty years as a stick to beat Donne. Mrs Evelyn commented disparagingly on Donne's poetry in the same year, or at least implied that it was generally disparaged; and down through the 1670s a series of small sideswipes and digs shows that Donne was no longer the acknowledged lord of wit. Walton added the 'Valediction: forbidding Mourning' in the final version of his *Life of Donne*, 1675, thirty-five years after the first version; but his famous celebration of it then rings quite out of key with the times like a last valedictory flourish of the old order in the face of plain indifference or growing distaste. Yet in 1693 Dunton still recommended Donne in a list of poets to be read by the young.

It is plain that by the last three decades of the century Donne's poetry had become a mere curiosity which the amateur might indifferently patronise or discount. In 1675 Rochester presented Donne as nothing more than a quaint old antique while Edward Phillips, picking up Dryden's judgment, reported that Donne is commended for height of fancy and acuteness of conceit though not for the smoothness of his verse. Donne's versification was condemned outright in 1685, and attacked again in 1690, both times in terms that imply a wholesale dismissal of his poetry. In 1689 John Evelyn, listing the British poets, didn't as much as mention Donne; and within sixty years of Donne's death a student might have concluded that Chaucer, Spenser, Jonson, Shakespeare, Beaumont and Fletcher would endure, but Donne would not.

Dryden's definitive placing of Donne in 1692, 'the greatest Wit, though not the best Poet of our Nation', makes a distinction that only a few later critics observed or took seriously, Pope being one who did. Walsh found a bizarre way of putting it a year later when he allowed Donne the love poet a very great wit, a copious fancy and the like, but no such softness, tenderness, violence of passion as one finds in the poetry of the ancients. Dryden had already said of Donne that he 'perplexes the Minds of the Fair Sex with nice Speculations of Philosophy, when he shou'd ingage their hearts, and entertain them with the softnesses of Love'. Thus with the great age of wit and reason coming on we find people censuring Donne for putting wit before passion. That line of criticism, too, would persist and get a final reductive formulation in Johnson's *Cowley* essay.

Dryden was far from dismissing Donne at any time, having opened his poetic career as Donne's disciple and continued to imitate him. He speaks of Donne's surpassing talent and repeatedly singles him out for wit from all other English poets. Here is admiring acknowledgment of what he plainly took to be great qualities and achievement. But in the course of subsequent criticism the good qualities sank out of sight or were distorted and the features Dryden reprobates were taken for the whole of Donne.

III

By the early eighteenth century Donne was a dead issue, a historical specimen only, and no dramatic fluctuations of his fortune were remotely in prospect. All the century has to show is a steady division between those critics who (on the whole) speak up for Donne and those who condemn him utterly, with a few judicious souls in between who attempt to weigh his good and bad qualities. Not that this was a void in Donne criticism. In fact many eighteenth-century writers have something to say of Donne; but the scatter of references to the poetry is thin, and few people actually quote his lines. The commentators of the time often seem to be speaking of writings they scarcely know, and they don't so much criticise the poems as strike attitudes to the poet. Donne was chiefly known by his satires, following the publication of Pope's 'versions' of *Satyres ii* and *iv*. Very few people in the eighteenth century seem to have encountered anything else of his, or to realize that he was more than a satirist; and many of the references to his poetry come from the mid-century discussions of Pope. Repeatedly, the people who say that Donne's poetry is rough, lacking numbers and the like turn out to be speaking of the *Satyres* alone. As late as 1787 Headley classes Donne solely as a satiric writer; Kippis in 1793 says flatly that none of Donne's works are known at present except his satires, which Pope printed opposite his own versions of them.

What seems clear is that Donne's poetry wasn't familiar in the eighteenth century because most readers didn't encounter it, couldn't easily get hold of it even if (like Cowper) they wished to. Tonson's edition of 1719 dropped out of sight and was hard to come by; the reprints of 1779 and 1793, very small items in the vast *omnia* of Bell and Anderson, made no impression until late in the century and, as Coleridge recognised, were so full of errors that whole poems became unintelligible. Few eighteenth-century men of letters seem to have had a copy of Donne's poems in their library however well stocked their shelves may have been with the English and European poets; there was none in the magnificent collection of Spence, sometime Professor of Poetry at Oxford, when it was sold in 1769, and Sterne, Mrs Thrale, and Gray among others owned no text of Donne at the time of their deaths. But *Satyres ii* and *iv* were available in all the editions of Pope's *Works*. And after Johnson's *Cowley* essay readers at least knew Donne by those fragments of him Johnson quoted, scraps selected to illustrate a particular view of the metaphysical poets and giving no impression of whole poems against which Johnson's assertions might be tested. It is striking enough that even after Bell's reprint came out Donne doesn't appear in his own right in Ritson's *Select Collection of English Songs*, 1783; there is only an unascribed, untitled, prettified version of 'The Message'.

Pope, who read and used Donne, took up Dryden's idea of him with something of Dryden's warm esteem. Donne had great wit, 'as much . . . as any writer can possibly have', though little skill in versification; hence he was not so great a poet as a wit: 'Davenant a better poet than Donne'. No following commentator found anything to say for Donne's versification. Even his few champions conceded that Donne was barbarously rough and that his 'rhyme was prose'. But the surprising thing in this age of wit is that his very wit had become a charge against him as Dryden's dictum hardened into a cruder antithesis: Donne had much wit but wasn't a poet at all.

Steele, in 1713, thought Donne's and Cowley's lyrics the most defective of all English songs because of their surplus of wit. Following critics developed the point with less restraint and dismissed Donne out of hand, ironically or savagely as the mood took them. We hear of his confounding metaphysics with love and losing himself in his own subtleties and extravagances; of his blatant disregard of 'Nature' in favour of spurious ornaments, outlandish effects, cold and childish quibbles, an ostentatiously affected learning; of his failure to be just, simple, obvious; of his vicious manners and disastrous corruption of taste; of his general disagreeableness which soon produces disgust in the reader; of his puerility, triviality, and, in short, total lack of any poetic merit.

So strong and persistent a distaste can't be mere obtuseness. One senses something of the deeper impulses which are operating here in Hume's remark that the celebrated English writers of the two preceding centuries possessed great genius but no taste. Hume had a particular view of historical change in mind which he brings out by a model from antiquity, the degeneration of oratory between Greek times and Roman. He contrasts the admirable simplicity of Greek oratory with the false ornaments and conceits of the later Roman rhetoric. The Greeks, he argued, had a language which permitted an easy unforced strain of sentiment and was fit to express genuine movements of nature and passion; but in Roman times the neglect of nature and good sense brought about a total degeneracy of style and language which opened the way to ignorant barbarism. These are the common terms and antitheses of attacks on Donne for a century and a half. Writers from Spence to Taine mark this progression from natural simplicity to decadence when they speak of Donne's over-refinement of wit, corrupt taste and the like. They perpetuate the theory of cultural evolution formulated by Vasari in his *Lives* when he describes how primitive manners mature into the natural style, the natural becomes the artificial then declines into decadence, and barbarism reassumes its reign until a conscious renaissance of manners dispels it once more. People felt abhorrence for Donne in the eighteenth century because they associated him with the decline of manners which brought on the barbarism of the Civil War, and thought they found the evidence of corruptness in his poetry.

Johnson's account of the metaphysical poets, by whom he meant Donne, Cleveland, and Cowley, offers a coherent critique and is altogether more trenchant and judicious than the views of his predecessors. But its tenor doesn't seem markedly different from theirs. He too speaks of Donne and the rest as versifiers rather than poets, ridicules their exclusive concern with shows of learned ingenuity, denies them most of the qualities good writing must have, and attributes to them many quite damningly vicious qualities. The measured manner of his account doesn't conceal his antipathy to writers who err so extravagantly from the way of good sense, and the terms of his judgments are severe and uncompromising. Metaphysical poetry is the reverse of natural, just, common, sublime, pathetic, reasonable; it deals in momentary novelties not general truths; and its effects are fragmented, far-fetched, obscure, ingeniously absurd, grossly expressed, inappropriate, indecorous, unnecessarily scholastic or subtle, apt to confound confusions or swell in enormous and disgusting hyperboles.

It is something that a man who feels this degree of distaste for his subjects can find anything good to say of them at all. But Johnson generously allows that some of them at least had great natural abilities and show originality, and concedes that their writing may yield unexpected truths and genuine wit amid the mass of false conceits. This scarcely amounts to an important revaluation of metaphysical poetry, such as recent commentators detect in Johnson.[11]

Johnson was a very great man and never less than a judicious critic; it is no discredit to him if he could not recognise a genius so uncongenial to his own at all points. But there is no doubt that his *Cowley* essay harmed Donne. He is certainly the most influential of Donne's critics, magisterially formulating charges and attitudes which long remained prescriptive and which every fresh enthusiast for Donne had to resist. For a hundred years most people knew Donne at first only by what Johnson said and quoted in this essay, and the idea they had of him is that he is a frigid conceit-monger.

Johnson had evidently read Donne, or quarried a copy of the 1719 edition for his *Cowley* essay, as for the *Dictionary* earlier. In his *Cowley* he quotes from some fifteen poems over a wide range of Donne's work—four *Songs and Sonnets,* five verse letters, two *Epithalamions,* one *Elegy,* two funeral poems, *The first Anniversary*; though he gives three times as much from Cowley, and some Cleveland too. That he lumps Donne with Cowley and Cleveland and treats all three poets on a par is a telling circumstance in itself which some nineteenth-century commentators sharply pointed out; and his indifferent intermingling of gobbets from all three of them suggests what he evidently believed, that metaphysical poets are to be distinguished only by the degree of their ingenious absurdity. He has nothing to say of Herbert, Vaughan,

Marvell, whom he either didn't know or didn't think of as metaphysical poets.

Much the most memorable thing in Johnson's essay is his account of metaphysical images as 'heterogeneous ideas . . . yoked by violence together'; and this, by its very brilliance, has distracted his readers from the true sense of Donne's vision. Johnson gives them no inkling that a poem by Donne makes sense overall and is to be read as a whole, which is what Coleridge discovered with surprise some thirty years later. But Johnson's signal disservice to Donne is that he reduces Donne's poetry to wit and wit to a random trick of style. No one who reads the *Cowley* essay with Donne's real qualities in mind can think that Johnson's strictures touch them.

The true heroes of eighteenth-century criticism are the few independent spirits who spoke up for Donne in spite of the prevailing detraction and in spite of their own offended ears. John Brown singled him out from an age of pedants for sense and strength of thought. Birch recognized the 'prodigious fund of genius' his poems display. Both Warburton and Hurd praised the *Metempsychosis* highly and found much that is fine and noble in the *Satyres*. Kippis, heralding the coming revival, flatly contradicted the orthodox reviewers who could find no poetry in Donne and referred them to the last four stanzas of the 'Valediction: forbidding Mourning'. Cowper at least showed an eagerness to read Donne's verse and a freedom from the current prejudices against it.

The weight of hostile opinion was considerable to judge by the way some people went back on their first favourable impressions of Donne, and if anything it increased as the century went on. Warburton's great eulogy of *Satyre iii*, 'the noblest work not only of this, but perhaps of any satiric Poet', quite loses its force when it reappears two years later in 1753 altered to 'which treats the noblest subject not only of this, but perhaps of any satiric Poet'. Joseph Warton showed himself still less engagingly suggestible. In 1756 he was savaged for placing Donne in the second class of poets and allowing him even a moderate degree of poetical genius. So the rewritten passage six years later quietly relegated Donne to the third class of poets, mere men of wit and lively fancy in describing familiar life. By 1782 Johnson had pronounced on the metaphysical poets and we find Warton dismissing Donne altogether, in thoroughly orthodox terms, as a corrupter of taste who is full of false thoughts, far-sought sentiments, and unnatural conceits.

IV

These orthodox judgments were countered almost as soon as the century turned. In 1802 *The Edinburgh Review* complained that it detected a smack of 'the quaintness of Quarles and Dr Donne' in the style of the school of poets just then emerging, and hit on an affinity which some of the coming writers undoubtedly felt. For the new road English poets took in the last years of the eighteenth century gave them a very different view of our older writers, showing them a Donne no eighteenth-century critic had as much as glimpsed and so prompting some of the best observations ever made about his poetry. Things have dramatically turned about when Donne is commended for his warmth of soul and read aloud with evident emotion, when his conceits are said to be the outcome not of cold wit but of an excess of erotic warmth and fervour, and his extravagances explained as the overplus of a too-powerful imagination. That Donne should come back in the train of a deliberate reversion to the 'Gothic', in revolt against neoclassical ideals, is not surprising. But the reversal of the eighteenth-century attitudes happened very abruptly.

Coleridge was reading Donne for himself between 1800 and 1803–4, drew on him in *The Friend* in 1809, and made his celebrated notes on Donne's poems in Lamb's copy in 1811. Lamb wrote glowingly of Donne's warmth of passion in 1808, and showed that he was moved by it when he read *Elegie xvi*, 'On his Mistris', aloud in company, as Hazlitt recalled. Both men championed Donne among their friends and around London, and Coleridge's enthusiasm for some of the lengthier and obscurer poems long remained a notorious hazard of salon conversation. From the way Coleridge instances and quotes Donne throughout his writings one plainly sees that the poems came quite naturally to his mind.

This was a genuine rediscovery for it owes nothing to previous ideas of Donne and runs consciously counter to most eighteenth-century opinion. These early nineteenth-century enthusiasts make Donne their own property, as if they had unearthed a new Donne who was hitherto unknown or unnoticed; and we soon begin to hear of Donne the true poet, the superb craftsman, the spiritual agoniser, the man of powerful imagination and the like. No doubt there is a novel sensibility at work here but a changed attitude to the past has as much to do with this powerful reversal of established views. Poets who themselves looked for

INTRODUCTION

metaphysical correspondences in nature found something to admire in
the wit of Shakespeare and Donne, so lately dismissed as mere clever
quibbling. For Coleridge Donne was a member of a 'race of Giants';
and it was to be just such an attitude that took many nineteenth-century
critics and editors to our older writers, especially our seventeenth-
century writers.

A concern with individuality, the *this*-ness of things, began to replace
the implicit appeal to the manners of urbane society. When Phillips
compared Donne with Chaucer and Giotto in 1827 it was because all
three antique artists are themselves and no one else. The taste for whatever is original, spare, strange, extended to mental operations, and both
rhetoric and scholastic metaphysics provoked an interest that disposed
people to countenance Donne. William Godwin, no less, called
Donne 'the most deep-thinking and philosophical of our poets' and said
of him that he is 'full of originality, energy, and vigour. . . . Every
sentence is exclusively his own . . . his thoughts are often in the
noblest sense of the word poetical'. By the 1840s the search for the
Fathers of the English Church drew young priests to study, even revere,
Donne's devotional writings and some of them grew to value his
poetry too. Donne's sentimental history, duly romanticised, disposed a
different class of nineteenth-century reader in his favour; though it also
provoked Campbell's sour comment, endlessly parroted round the
reference works, that 'the life of Donne is more interesting than his
poetry'.

Whatever ordinary readers made of Donne's poetry in the nineteenth century (and there was still no lack of pundits to tell them that it is
not worth reading), many leading writers showed active interest in it.
The sheer quantity of published comment speaks for itself; it is clear
that not only had Donne become respectable reading again but the
people who mattered were enjoying him, judging him afresh, discovering his force for themselves. His illustrious admirers included not
only Coleridge and Lamb but de Quincey, Godwin, Leigh Hunt,
Elizabeth Barrett, Robert Browning, Emerson, Thoreau, G. H. Lewes,
George Eliot, Lowell, Swinburne, Rossetti. Some of these, notably
Browning, Emerson and Lowell, were lifelong devotees. Browning
notoriously felt a sense of special kinship with Donne the obscure.
Even Wordsworth and Tennyson, whose writing has so little in
common with his, held in high regard those of his poems they knew.

Appreciative accounts of Donne, full of proselytising enthusiasm,
began to appear in the major literary magazines from the 1820s and a

little later in the popular journals of self-education. Some of these essays were genuine pieces of independent criticism, as is the article in *The Penny Cyclopaedia* for 1837. But for a long time Donne's critics had first to introduce the poetry they discussed. Such popular reprints as Chalmers's in England and Sanford's in America still had not made his poetry widely available. The poems people knew were just those which now began to turn up often in the anthologies, that is, some secular lyrics and a good deal of moral and religious verse.

The crying need for an authoritative edition of the poems was well recognised by the 1840s, Alford having conspicuously failed to supply it in his *Works of Donne*; and Barron Field tackled the *Songs and Sonnets* for an antiquarian society, without reaching print. But quite early in the century scholars were taking Donne seriously enough to aim at a full canon of his writings and true versions of them. J. P. Collier, in 1820, accurately indicated what an edition of Donne's poems would call for in the way of work on the surviving manuscripts and early printed texts, and the labours of many men furthered the task—which they still, however, thought of more as a matter of gathering in the old documents indiscriminately than of systematically analysing and placing the evidence before them. The names of some who contributed to this work, and still put modern editors in their debt, are worth recording: Waldron, Collier himself, Haslewood, Viscount Kingsborough, Alford, Jessopp, Simeon, Field, W. C. Hazlitt, Dyce, O'Flaherty, Lord Houghton, Phillipps. Many contributions to learned journals in the 1850s and 1860s had an edition in prospect. A new edition actually came out in Boston in 1855 though it was based upon a collation of the early printed texts only. The huge task of collating the manuscripts daunted O'Flaherty, who had set his heart on accomplishing it, and it fell to Grosart to give England its first modern edition of Donne's poems in 1872–3. Scholars gradually came to understand the need for a scientific discrimination of the early versions towards a good text of Donne, and there were three further editions of the poems in the next forty years.

One can't say that Donne's poetry was 'popular' by 1872 or for some time after that. The libraries of nineteenth-century literary men still didn't carry their copies of Donne as a matter of course; among those who had no text of his poems on their shelves, at least when their libraries came to be sold, were Scott, Byron, Peacock, Hazlitt, Rogers, Macaulay, Wilde. Even Beckford had Donne only in Anderson's collection. Barron Field prepared his edition of the *Songs and Sonnets* in the 1840s believing that Donne was not yet generally known; and in

1850 C. D. Cleveland, in America, could still write of Donne that he was 'almost entirely forgotten'. Possibly both men were out of touch with the current English interest for by 1864 a contributor to a London magazine felt able to assume that his readers would know Donne's poetry, which is 'familiar to all who have diligently studied English literature'. But Jessopp's account of the ferment in mid-century Cambridge which drew young men to read Donne is borne out by Allibone's cautious remark in 1859 that Donne had received some attention in recent years after long neglect. It seems to have been in the 1850s and 1860s that Donne's poetry passed from the care of a few leaders of taste to a wider audience of literary students. None the less Donne became an established figure in the literary histories only after Grosart's edition of 1872–3, and both Swinburne and Lowell testify that he was still not generally acknowledged in the 1880s. The Donne whom Swinburne admired may not be generally acknowledged yet, for Swinburne's classic remark probably holds true to this day. He found it odd that thousands of people who knew Gray's *Elegy* have never as much as heard of Donne's *Anniversaries*, which are so far superior to it in all the essential powers of thought, imagination, and expression.

Throughout most of the nineteenth century students of Donne had to struggle against a severe version of Johnson's view of him which at first preponderated and then gradually dwindled into the stock patter of the literary histories. In the first quarter of the century Donne repeatedly took his accustomed drubbing, both in the literary reviews and at the hands of such pundits as Kirke White, Southey, Hazlitt, and Campbell. For these critics he remains a writer of tasteless and unfeeling ingenuity who can't be called a poet because he lacked all ear for verse, and whose decadence corrupted his followers. They aren't always repeating an accepted line. Such committed Victorian entrepreneurs as Palgrave, Ward, and Hales, who must certainly have struggled with Donne's poetry, had no greater taste for it and pitch into it no less harshly; while the historians of culture, led by Hallam and Taine, not only express an uncompromising moral distaste for it but find it simply baneful in its tendencies. Avowed moral repugnance to some poems, a new element in Donne criticism, undoubtedly prompted austere critics to reject the verse altogether as Southey did at first. We hear tiresomely of Donne's gross indelicacy, offensive indecency, prurience, loose morals and the like, which reverend commentators one after another find the more shocking in a prospective Dean of St Paul's. Even so passionate a devotee as the Rev. Grosart had moral scruples to overcome when he set to work to give Donne whole, and he remarked that it 'requires some courage'. Still more people found a literary reason for the affront to their moral sensibilities and condemned his poetry because it isn't natural, simple, sincere, direct, sentimental, smooth, luscious, or whatever qualities they expected of the poets they favoured.

Many nineteenth-century critics of Donne's poetry struggled with such preconceptions but felt its power too strongly to judge it adversely in the end, and admired it in spite of its blemishes. Cattermole and Stebbing took a common line in 1836 when they claimed that behind the conceits and affections lie genuine simplicity and plainness, depth of sentiment, originality of thought, and a demanding rigour which puts off readers accustomed to relishing only voluptuous sweetness of language. Coleridge's famous sally on Donne's manner—'iron pokers into true-love knots'—gave the cue to people who were bowled over by Donne but baffled by the contradictory qualities they found in him, and much-qualified admiration became the standard reaction to his work.

Right through the nineteenth century Donne remains the poet of puzzling self-contradictions, 'mingled beauties and deformities', who can throw off passages of unequalled imaginative grandeur then go back like a hog to his wallow (as Swinburne felicitously put it). He is a great genius flawed by a false system or a corrupted taste, a man almost equally fascinating and repellent in whom deep passions and genuine spiritual agonies disturbingly coexist with trivial affectations, just thoughts with wild extravagances, pure melody with barbaric harshness. These critics show a genuine appreciation of Donne's poetry at times but they can hardly be said to have grasped his poems.

Donne's formal rehabilitators are seldom as effective as they might be, much as one warms to their rebuttal of Theobald or Johnson and their enthusiasm for particular qualities of the verse. They accept too much of their adversaries' case when they think of Donne's style as something added to the thought or sentiment, now embellishing it and now distracting from it. The Retrospective Review essay of 1823 (in which Mrs Tillotson somewhat generously detects the accent of discovery) is a case in point; but even the perceptive studies in The Penny Cyclopaedia for 1837 and Lowe's Edinburgh Magazine for 1846 fall into this error. All three essayists are men who speak as they find and who recognise how grotesquely Donne's qualities are belied by talk of 'a continued Heap of Riddles' or assimilation to the worst of Cowley. Yet each gravely offsets Donne's splendours with his lapses and judges the poems in the end as gatherings of mingled beauties and deformities strung on a sentiment—minor art of the second or third order is *The Retrospective Review* man's estimate. They are connoisseurs rather than students of Donne. Having no grasp of a poem as a whole they don't see how its manner grows out of the vision and is integral to the sense.

Coleridge had seen not only this but more of Donne than most readers before him or since. His comments, as Lowell's later, stand free of their time and occasion and might have resolved some issues which critics continued to dispute. Much follows upon his simple recognition that a reader must grasp the thought of a whole poem before he can place its elements. This means that Donne's versification depends upon his sense, for the sense determines the rhythm and not vice versa: 'in poems where the writer *thinks*, and expects the reader to do so, the sense must be understood in order to ascertain the metre'. It also means for Coleridge that Donne's wit is not wanton ingenuity but a purposeful mental life, and the necessary expression of the thought. He put Donne with Shakespeare for sheer opulence of creative imagination, the quintessential poetic power; and it was Donne's poetry which came to his mind when he wanted a paradigm of true poetic fervour. But then all Coleridge's jottings on Donne speak of a man who has made these poems his own and is ready to live by them. Here is the first reader since the seventeenth century who avowedly draws sustenance and truth from Donne's lines, fastens on them with enthusiasm because they speak to him.

De Quincey writes of Donne's rhetoric only in passing but his achievement was to reassert its poetic value, as a conscious effect of art, against the neo-Johnsonian assumption that all beyond spontaneous nature is perversion. Like Coleridge he is concerned with whole poems; and though he shows more interest in the process of reading than in its outcome there's a convincing inwardness in his account of what it demands to follow such performances as Donne's poems present. He writes as a reader who knows the exhilaration of being caught up in the urgent elaborations of another man's thought and is alert to the mental exertions which 'auditor and performer' share: 'To hang upon one's own thoughts as an object of conscious interest, to play with them, to watch and pursue them through a maze of inversions, evolutions, and harlequin changes . . .'. This is surely part of the pleasure of reading Donne as of listening to Bach, and to find it a legitimate exercise of mind in itself is better than to think of it, with Johnson, as a corruption of taste: 'There cannot be a falser thought than this.' It follows that what matters in Donne is 'the management of the thoughts' rather than 'the ornaments of style'.

As some earlier critics had done, de Quincey singles out the *Metempsychosis*. For him it exemplifies the 'extraordinary compass of powers' one finds in Donne's poems, which uniquely combine 'the last sublimation of dialectical subtlety and address with the most impassioned majesty'. Here is a truth, finely put, which more than vindicates Donne's derided wit and versification. It reminds us of the poet we ourselves don't always honour enough for his distinctive mastery of our language, Browning's 'magisterial Donne' whose sonorous music also overwhelmed Swinburne.

Victorian critics who thought well of Donne felt that they had Johnson to contend with, and following the lead given by *The Retrospective Review* and de Quincey set themselves to rebut him. *The Penny Cyclopaedia* in 1837, Leigh Hunt in 1841, and *Temple Bar* in 1876 all attempt to counter some of the standard Johnsonian charges; the *Temple Bar* critic, for example, makes a very good defence of Donne's versification, using Coleridge's argument that the rhythms depend upon the sense. Many more commentators implicitly denied the orthodox accounts of Donne's qualities by proclaiming their opposite experience of his verse, freely endowing him with the fervour, depth of understanding, and even pure melody, he was notoriously supposed to lack. Like de Quincey they see a somewhat different Donne from us, and scarcely mention at all some of the poems we most discuss such as the major lyrics. They praise the verse letters, or the funeral poems, or the epithalamions; and they value the love poems chiefly for their song-like qualities, though some were curiously struck by 'The Will', and many admire 'A Valediction: forbidding Mourning' for the beauty (rather than the ingenuity) of its closing stanzas.

The magisterial essay in *Lowe's Edinburgh Magazine* for 1846 acknowledges the 'divine *aura*' of a true poet in Donne. But the only love poem this critic thinks anything of at all is 'A Valediction: forbidding Mourning', which he considers to be 'Perhaps, the most perfect thing of its length in Donne's whole volume . . . and indeed the only considerable passage of continuous beauty in the love-poems'. Nor does he have much to say for the *Divine Poems*, whose abundance of 'splendid thoughts and splendid words' still leaves them far inferior to other things by the poet. The poems he most admires are the funeral elegies, the satires, and the St Valentine's Day epithalamion. For him Donne's funeral elegies are Shakespearean in their concentration of wisdom and poetry; while the satires are simply the best in the English language and far superior to Pope's arrogant 'improvements' of them. In the epithalamion he finds something finer still, an 'inexplicable, incommunicable *aura*' of great art, and lines 'perhaps, unsurpassed in descriptive poetry'.

This critic, who measures Donne up to Shakespeare, recalls Coleridge in several other ways. He too understands that Donne's versification serves the sense, and he prefers its demanding ruggedness to the smooth flats of modern song-writers—for him it is they who are corrupt and Donne who is wholesome. But he also recognises what disciplined attention Donne's poems demand, and why they repel most readers, who simply aren't able to follow their 'profundity of thought'. In his view Donne is a devotee's poet, a man for fit audience though few, whose very virtues debar him from popular repute.

Donne had his devotees in New England, where there seems to have been a continuing interest in his poetry from the early nineteenth century. Emerson's circle admired and championed it, and one of them, J. R. Lowell, came to prize it more highly than even Coleridge and Browning had done. Lowell's scattered observations on Donne's poetry must count among the finest things anyone has said of it and seem to spring direct from an excited response to its distinctive combination of great qualities—beauty, subtlety, depth of thought. Here indeed the wheel of Donne's repute all but comes full circle. Lowell thinks him a truly sublime poet—'one of the subtlest and most self-irradiating minds that ever sought an outlet in verse'—who wrote 'more profound verses' than anyone else in English save Shakespeare, and was capable of 'the supreme function of poetry'. This supreme function, of opening 'vistas for the imagination through the blind wall of the senses', is very strikingly attributed to the poet whom readers in our century have deemed quintessentially poetic precisely for his subtle interfusion of thought and sense. Lowell is the first critic to remark the peculiar power of 'A bracelet of bright haire about the bone'. But he is not a mere connoisseur of effects and well describes how the dialectic of Donne's thought works upon the reader. What he didn't do, to our loss, is concentrate his fragmentary impressions in a coherent account of Donne's poetry. As it was, C. E. Norton incorporated them in the notes to the Grolier Club edition of the poems in 1895, but that edition was immediately superseded by the Chambers edition of 1896 and Lowell has never had the recognition he deserves for his appraisal of Donne.

Grosart's Fuller Worthies edition of Donne's poems in 1872, despite its thoroughly botched text, must be counted a major literary event. It is the first version of the poems since the seventeenth century which takes any account of the early manuscripts. Hardly less important, it gave Donne back whole to the general reader in a fine volume and with the strongest possible recommendation to read him. Grosart set out to put Donne among the great English poets and enshrined in his Dedication the homage of the greatest living English poet, then much compared with Donne. His Introduction waxes fulsome in its enthusiasm; he gave Donne what might be fairly described as a rave notice, much as Saintsbury would do when he introduced E. K. Chambers's text some twenty-four years later. But Grosart's account of Donne is to the point none the less, and his claims consistently take account of the standard criticisms of Donne from the eighteenth century to his own day. What he does, albeit tacitly, is to make great virtues of the very features for which metaphysical poetry had been conventionally condemned.

Grosart asks that the poetry should be studied as a whole and not just perfunctorily perused. Against the Johnsonians he claims that Donne is a great poet, an 'absolute and unique genius', who can't be fitly represented by a few extracts and whose language and methods need to be mastered before he is appreciated—one must approach them, he says, 'with all reverence and humility'. In the face of commentators who found evidence of a general debasement of taste in the terms of the funeral elegies for Donne, collected in the 1633 edition of Donne's poems, he wholly endorses those contemporary estimates of him and allows that they were both genuine and just. This charge of corrupting his age, indeed, he quietly turns back upon Donne's eighteenth-century accusers when he finds that it was Pope and his followers who didn't know true poetry from versifying; for they thought Pope's versions of Donne's satires an improvement on Donne and didn't see how they robbed the originals of all their force, nobility and justness. Grosart himself professes to discover Donne's pulsating heart in the satires no less than in the love poetry; but he finds that Donne's satiric passion has 'tragical reality' and the force of a spiritual agony. From the passionate Donne whom Lamb and Coleridge discovered we seem to be moving towards the tormented spirit, the soul in conflict which some modern readers have found in the poems.

Grosart values Donne's creative gifts as highly as his intellect and doesn't hesitate to make 'the supremest claim' for his powers of thought and imagination together. On this view of Donne the properties custom had allowed his poetry are quite transformed. Where Johnson found mere extravagance and fancy Grosart recognises a peculiar force of imaginative thought. He speaks of Donne's 'sudden out-flashing from the common level of the subject in hand', and remarks how his seemingly quaint allusions and images are found to carry in their heart 'some splendid thought altogether out of the beaten track . . . which comes with absolute surprise in the place'. Here is true criticism of Donne, for which Grosart has not had credit. That it is genuine insight he shows in an account of 'A Valediction: forbidding Mourning' which does better justice to the simile of the compasses than any previous commentary, allowing not only the witty truth of its 'out-of-the-wayness' but the imaginative power and daring of it too.

Well within the hundred years Donne had risen from low order among minor versifiers to the standing of a great poet. No one could claim higher place for him than Grosart does. But he was still not generally read and acknowledged; there was still no authoritative edition of his verse; and no more was known of his career as an artist and the circumstances of his writing than Walton intimated. Nor had he yet struck readers as the poet who speaks peculiarly to our times. In the fifty years following Grosart's edition Donne gradually moved centre stage. The work of Gosse, Chambers, Saintsbury, Dowden, Norton, Symons, Grierson, and many others, established him firmly as a major poet; and in their writings, and the discussions they provoked, that modern view of Donne begins to emerge which Eliot formulated in 1921. This is incomparably the richest and most illuminating body of commentary on Donne's poetry. But it doesn't break with earlier attitudes in the way that Coleridge broke with the eighteenth-century critics; on the contrary, anyone who looks at the whole pattern is likely to be struck by the continuous development of ideas about Donne from Coleridge's time to Eliot's. The pattern needs to be seen as a whole.

NOTES

1 Letter 'To my honoured friend G.G., Esquire', written from Paris, 14 April 1612. In E. Gosse, *The Life and Letters of John Donne* (1899), 1959, i, pp. 303–4.

2 'To The Generall Reader', *Poly-Olbion*, 1612. In *The Works of Michael Drayton*, ed. J. W. Hebel, Oxford, 1933, iv, p.v.

3 Letter, *c.* 1600, possibly to Sir Henry Wotton. In *John Donne, Complete Poetry and Selected Prose*, ed. J. Hayward (1929), 1945, pp. 440–1.

4 My account of the manuscript evidence draws heavily on the researches of Mr R. A. Bryan and Mr Alan MacColl. I am indebted to Mr MacColl in particular for permission to summarise the findings of his essay 'The Circulation of Donne's Poems in Manuscript' in *John Donne: Essays in Celebration*, ed. A. J. Smith, 1972, pp. 28–46.

5 Letter to P. C. Hooft, 1630. In H. J. C. Grierson, *The Poems of John Donne*, Oxford, 1912, ii, pp. lxxvii–lxxviii.

6 'The Circulation of Donne's Poems in Manuscript', ed. cit., p. 45.

7 F. P. Wilson, *Elizabethan and Jacobean*, Oxford, 1945, p. 55.

8 W. Milgate, 'The Early References to John Donne', *NQ*, June 1950, p. 247.

9 Art. cit., p. 41.

10 Introductory note to the catalogue of 'An Exhibition to Celebrate the Work and Reputation of John Donne 1572–1631', 1972, p. 2. The exhibition was presented in the Cambridge University Library from 23 October to 23 December 1972.

11 See in particular W. B. C. Watkins, *Johnson and English Poetry Before 1660*, Princeton, 1936, pp. 7, 78–84, 96–9; W. R. Keast, 'Johnson's Criticism of the Metaphysical Poets', *ELH*, xvii, 1950, pp. 59–70; W. J. Bate, *Criticism: The Major Texts*, New York, 1952, pp. 204 and 217–19; D. Perkins, 'Johnson on Wit and Metaphysical Poetry', *ELH*, xx, 1953, pp. 200–17.

Note on the Text

Documents follow the form of the original texts. Extracts are shown as such and excisions noted. Quotations from Donne's poems have been omitted, and line-references supplied, save where a comment depends upon some special feature of the writing such as the reader needs to see. Titles and lines of poems are given as they were quoted, and regularized by the standard modern editions only in the editor's commentary. The editions of Donne used for this purpose are the following:

The Poems of John Donne, ed. H. J. C. Grierson, Oxford, 1912.
John Donne: the Divine Poems, ed. Helen Gardner, Oxford, 1952.
John Donne: the Elegies and The Songs and Sonnets, ed. Helen Gardner, Oxford, 1965.
John Donne: The Satires, Epigrams and Verse Letters, ed. W. Milgate, Oxford, 1967.
John Donne: The Complete English Poems, ed. A. J. Smith, Harmondsworth, 1971.

THE SEVENTEENTH CENTURY

'The highest Poet our Language can boast of'

1. Some quotations, imitations, echoes of Donne's poems

1598–1700

1598

Everard Gilpin opened a satiric poem by paraphrasing Donne's *Satyre i* (*Skialetheia*, 1598. See R. M. Alden, *The Rise of Formal Satire in England*, 1899, p. 153, and R. E. Bennett, 'John Donne and Everard Gilpin', *RES*, xv, 1939, pp. 66–72):

> Let me alone I prethee in thys Cell,
> Entice me not into the Citties hell;
> Tempt me not forth this *Eden* of content,
> To tast of that which I shall soone repent:
> Prethy excuse me, I am not alone
> Accompanied with meditation,
> And calme content, whose tast more pleaseth me
> Then all the Citties lushious vanity.
> I had rather be encoffin'd in this chest
> Amongst these bookes and papers I protest,
> Then free-booting abroad purchase offence,
> And scandale my calme thoughts with discontents. . . .

1602–3

John Manningham referred familiarly to Donne's affairs in an entry he made in his diary (*The Diary of John Manningham*, 1602–3, ed. J. Bruce, 1868, p. 99, entry made between 7 and 12 December 1602):

Dunne is undonne; he was lately secretary to the Lord Keeper, and cast of because he would match him selfe to a gentlewoman against his Lords pleasure.

A few months later Manningham copied into his diary a loose version of lines 71–2 of Donne's verse letter 'The Storme'. He also gave a version of Donne's epigram 'A Lame Begger' with the heading 'Of a beggar that lay on the ground drunk' (p. 156, entry for 31 March 1603).

33

1607

Thomas Dekker, in a description of a storm, quoted part of lines 71–2 of Donne's verse letter 'The Storme' (*A Knights Coniuring. Donne in earnest: Discovered in Iest*, 1607, B2ʳ):

The battaile of *Elements*, bred such another *Chaos*, that (not to bee ashamde to borrow the wordes of so rare an *English Spirit*,)

> *Did not GOD say*
> *Another Fiat, It had n'ere been day.*

Dekker also quoted a version of Donne's epigram 'A Lame Begger'.

1607

Thomas Deloney adapted the conceit of Donne's epigram 'A Lame Beggar' in an epigram of his own (*Strange Histories of Songes and Sonets*, 1607, ed. J. P. Collier, 1841, p. 69).

1609

Joseph Wybarne drew on Donne and Spenser to illustrate an account of Antichrist (*The New Age of Old Names*, 1609, pp. 112–13):

This is their Antichrist, a thing stranger then the Crocodile of Nilus, then all the rare things of Arenoque or Guianoque, rivers in America: But because I cannot in prose express it, you shall heare the tenth Muse her selfe, utter it in her owne language thus,

> *A thing more strange, then on Niles slime.* . . .

[He quotes lines 18–23a of *Satyre iv*, which are glossed in the margin 'Dunne in his Satyres'.]

This Antichrist is most poetically figured also by the famous heire Apparant to *Homer* and *Virgil*, in his *Fairey Queene* under the names of *Archimagus*, *Duessa*, *Argoglio* the Soldane and others, throughout the first and fift Legends. . . .

1609

A character in Act 1, Scene 1 of Ben Jonson's play *The Silent Woman* picks up a phrase from Donne's *Elegie ix*, 'The Autumnall'. Clerimont, a gentleman about town, exclaims against the president of a new college of amorous ladies, Lady Haughty:

A pox of her autumnal face, her pieced beauty. . . .

1609

Alfonso Ferrabosco gave one stanza of 'The Expiration', with a musical setting, in his *Ayres*. This is the first appearance in print of one of the *Songs and Sonnets*, though Donne is not named as the author.

1611

'Upon Mr Thomas Coryats *Crudities*' is given among the panegyrical poems which introduced *Coryats Crudities*. Two other poems in the set are attributed to Donne but one of them is probably not his; the other is the 'In eundem Macaronicon'.

All three poems were reprinted with the rest of the panegyrics in *The Odcombian Banquet*, 1611.

1611

Ben Jonson built an ode for the coming of age of a young nobleman on an argument from Donne's *Satyre iii* ('Ode. To Sir William Sydney, on his Birth-Day', *The Forrest*, xiiii):

> Your vow
> Must now
> Strive all right wayes it can,
> T'out-strip your peeres:
> Since he doth lacke
> Of going backe
> Little, whose will
> Doth urge him to runne wrong, or to stand still. . . .

1611

An Anatomie of the World (*The first Anniversary*) published separately. Donne evidently authorised the publication but is not named as the poet.

1612

Of the Progresse of the Soule (*The second Anniversary*) published with a fresh edition of *The first Anniversary*. Donne had finished the poem while he was in France with the Druries, and evidently sent it back to England for immediate publication.

1612

William Corkine gave one stanza of 'Breake of Day', with a musical setting, in his *The Second Booke of Ayres*.

1612

John Taylor, 'the Water Poet', a contributor to the joke over *Coryats Crudities*, published a series of epigrams in which he comments one at a time on the mock-commendatory poems to Coryate. A long epigram headed *Johannes Donne* takes up Donne's poem 'Upon Mr Thomas Coryats *Crudities*' and embroiders it (*Laugh, and be Fat*, 1612, pp. 17–19).

1612–13

John Webster repeatedly echoed Donne's *Anniversaries* in works written soon after Donne's poems were published.

The Duchess of Malfi (played before 1614 but not published until 1623) has some ten borrowings from the *Anniversaries*, four of them from *The first Anniversary* and six from *The second Anniversary*. Webster's poem *A Monumental Column* (1613), mourning Prince Henry's death, has some three borrowings from the *Anniversaries*, two of them from *The first Anniversary* and one from *The second Anniversary*.

The following examples may indicate how closely Webster imitates Donne at times:

(i)
ANTONIO. . . . Since we must part,
Heaven hath a hand in't: but no otherwise,
Then as some curious Artist takes in sunder
A Clocke, or Watch, when it is out of frame
To bring't in better order.
[*The Duchess of Malfi*, III.5.74–8. Cf. *The first Anniversary*,
A Funerall Elegie, lines 37–46.]

(ii)
ANTONIO. Doe not weepe:
Heaven fashion'd us of nothing: and we strive,
To bring our selves to nothing. . . .
[*The Duchess of Malfi*, III.5.97–8. Cf. *The first Anniversary*,
lines 155–7.]

(iii)

CARDINAL. Now sir, how fares our sister?
I do not thinke but sorrow makes her looke
Like to an oft-di'd garment. . . .
[*The Duchess of Malfi*, V.2.110–12. Cf. *The first Anniversary*,
lines 355–6.]

(iv)

Why should the *Stag* or *Raven* live so long?
And that their age rather should not belong,
Unto a righteous *Prince*?
[*A Monumental Column*, lines 124–6. Cf. *The first
Anniversary*, lines 115–16.]

1613

J. Sylvester gave the 'Elegie upon the untimely death of the incomparable
Prince Henry', with other elegies on Prince Henry's death, in the third
edition of his *Lachrymae Lachrymarum*, 1613. The poem is ascribed to
'Mr Donne'.

1613–14

Many of the funeral tributes to Prince Henry, who died in 1612, show
the impression made by Donne's *Anniversaries*. Some writers simply
take over lines and ideas from those poems as does Prince Henry's
chaplain, Dr Daniel Price, in a series of sermons on the prince's death:

(i)

Oh, why is there not a generall thaw through-out all mankinde? why
in this *debashed Ayre doe not all things expire*, seeing *Time* lookes upon us
with watry eues, *disheveld* lockes, and heavie dismall lookes; now that
the Sunne is gone out of our Firmament, the *ioy*, the beautie, the *glory*
of *Israel* is departed?
[*Lamentations for the death of the late illustrious Prince Henry*. . . . *Two
Sermons*, 1613, second sermon, p. 35. Cf. *The first Anniversary*, lines
43–54, *The second Anniversary*, lines 1–6.]

(ii)

  . . . his body was so *faire* and *strong* that a soule might have been
pleased to live an age in it . . . *vertue* and *valor*, *beauty* and *chastity*,
armes and *arts*, *met* and *kist* in him, and his goodnesse lent so much
mintage to other Princes, that if *Xenophon* were now to describe a

37

Prince, Prince HENRY had beene his *Patterne*. . . . Hee hath gon his *Pass-over* from *death* to *life*, where there is more *grace* and more capacity . . . where earthly *bodies* shalbe more *celestiall*, then man in his *Innocency* or *Angels* in their *glory*, for they could *fall*: Hee is there with those *Patriarchs* that have expected *Christ* in *earth*, longer then they have *enjoyed* him in *heaven*; He is with those holy *Penmen* of the holy *spirit*, they bee now his *paterns*, who were here his *teachers*; . . .

['Meditations of Consolation in our Lamentations', in *Spirituall Odours to the Memory of Prince Henry. In Four of the Last Sermons Preached in St James after his Highnesse Death*, Oxford, 1613, pp. 16–17. Cf. *The second Anniversary*, lines 221–4, 345–6, 361–4, 465–7, 491–4.]

(iii)
He, He is dead, who while he lived, was a *perpetuall Paradise*, every season that he shewd himselfe in a *perpetuall spring, every exercise* wherein he was seene a *special felicity: He, He* is dead before us. . . *Hee, Hee* is dead; that blessed *Model* of heaven his *face* is covered till the *latter day*, those *shining lamps* his eyes in whose *light* there was *life* to the beholders, they bee *ecclipsed* untill the *sunne* give over shining. . . . *He, He* is dead, and now yee see this. . . .

[*Teares Shed over Abner. The Sermon Preached on the Sunday before the Prince his funerall in St James Chappell before the body*, Oxford, 1613, pp. 25–6. Cf. *The first Anniversary*, lines 361–6, *The second Anniversary*, lines 77–80.]

Price also wrote two prose *Anniversaries* on Prince Henry's death, in 1613 and 1614, again drawing freely on Donne's poems:

in HIM, a *glimmering light* of the *Golden* times appeare, all *lines* of expectation met in this *Center*, all *spirits* of vertue, *scattered* into others were *extracted* into him,

[*Prince Henry His First Anniversary*, Oxford, 1613, p. 4. Cf. *The second Anniversary*, lines 69–70, and *The first Anniversary*, lines 148–50.]

Price's borrowings from Donne are discussed in B. K. Lewalski, *Donne's Anniversaries and the Poetry of Praise*, Princeton, 1973, pp. 312–16.

1614

Sir Michael Scott twice quoted from Donne in a compendium of natural philosophy (*The Philosophers Banquet*, 1614, pp. 124–5 and 204). Speaking of the general decline of man's faculties he remarked:

To which purpose he well meditated, that thus pithily wrote to that
effect . . .

and then gave lines 127–44 of *The first Anniversary*. In a section 'Of the
Excellencie, vertue, and nature of stones' he referred again to Donne,
quoting *The first Anniversary*, lines 343–4:

with which our Poet thus accordeth in his comparison. . . .

1614

An epitaph on the tomb of Lady Dorothea Dodderidge, in the Lady
Chapel of Exeter Cathedral, adapts the figure of the clock in Donne's
Obsequies to the Lord Harrington (lines 131–54). Lord Harrington died in
February 1614 and Lady Dorothea died later in the same year. Both
Lady Dorothea's husband and Lord Harrington had been members of
the circle of Prince Henry, Sir John Dodderidge as 'First Sergeant at
Law' to the Prince and Lord Harrington as the Prince's close companion.

> As when a curious clocke is out of frame
> a workman takes in peeces small the same
> and meditatinge what amisse is to be found,
> the same reivyves and makes it trewe and sound
> so god this Ladie into two partes tooke
> too soone her soule her mortal corse forsooke
> But by his might att length her bodie sound
> Shall rise reivyvd unto her soule now crownd
> Till then they rest in earth and heaven sundred
> att which conioynd all such as lived then wondred.[1]

?1615

The following poem appears in a section headed 'Epitaphes' of the
(much enlarged) fifth impression of William Camden's *Remaines Concerning Britaine*, 1636, pp. 417–18. It imitates Donne's 'Song. Goe, and
catche a falling starre':

Impossibilities

> Embrace a Sun-beame, and on it
> The shadow of a man beget.
> Tell me who raignes in the Moone

[1] The stonemason has actually carved 'all such as live we thē wondred', presumably
misreading the manuscript draft of the poem before him.

Set the thunder to a tune,
Cut the Axel-tree that beares
Heaven and earth, or stop the spheares
With thy finger; or divide
Beggery from lust and pride
Tell me what the Syrens sing,
Or the secrets of a King,
Or his power, and where it ends,
And how farre his will extends.
Goe and finde the bolt that last
Brake the clouds, or with like heast
Fly to the East, and tell me why
Aurora blushes: if to lie
By an old man trouble her minde,
Bid *Cephalus* be lesse unkinde.
Canst thou by thine art uncase
The mysteries of a Courtiers face.
Canst thou tell me why the night
Weeps out her eyes? If for the sight
Of the lost Sunne, she put on blacke,
Post to his fall, and turne him backe,
If not for him, then goe and finde
A widdow, or all woman kinde,
Like to their outward shew, and he
More then a Delphian Deity.

1616

William Browne in Part ii of *Britannia's Pastorals* recalled phrases in Donne's poems. *Song iv* speaks of Xerxes and the plane-tree, a 'lank purse' (*Elegie ix*, 'The Autumnall', lines 29–30 and 38), and the Indias of spice and mine ('The Sunne Rising', lines 17–18). *Song v* refers to the sudden height of Teneriffe (*The first Anniversary*, lines 286–8), describes a faithful love in terms of the shadows cast by the sun at various times of day ('A Lecture upon the Shadow'), and juggles with a comparison of lovers to the sun and the moon (*An Epithalamion . . . on the Lady Elizabeth and Count Palatine . . . on St Valentines day*, lines 85–8). (See Jack Lindsay, *The Times Literary Supplement*, 30 April 1931.)

An undated poem by Browne, 'Poor silly fool! thou striv'st in vain to know,/ If I enjoy, or love whom thou lov'st so', appears to be an answer to Donne's 'The Curse' (*The Poems*, ed. G. Goodwin, 1894, ii, p. 197). A manuscript of 1647 in the Bodleian Library, Oxford, gives the poem with the title 'An Answere to Dr Donnes curse Who ever guesses etc—' (MS, Rawlinson, Poet. 147, fol. 83. See A. Alvarez, *The School of Donne*, 1961, p. 196).

1617

William Fennor several times used phrases from Donne's *Satyre iv* in giving an account of his arrest and imprisonment for debt (*The Compters Common-Wealth*, 1617, pp. 3, 14, and 20):

(i)
The one had a face ten times worse than those Jewes that are pictured in Arras-hangings whipping Christ. . . .

(ii)
I got up, and beganne in a solitary and sadde manner to mourne and pitty my selfe, being more amazed then those that dreamed they saw hell, and had felt the tortures thereof. . . .

(iii)
I have read that *Italian Mountebankes*, before they speak in their drug-tongue and Fustian language to the auditory of innocent and ignorant people. . . .

1618

The opening lines of an anonymous poem echo lines 78–82 of Donne's *Satyre iii* (*The Mirrour of Majestie*, 1618, Emblem no. 28, p. 55):

> Th'ascending Path that up to wisedome leades
> Is rough, uneven, steepe: and he that treades
> Therein, must many a tedious *Danger* meet,
> That, or trips up, or clogs his wearied feet. . . .

1619

Patrick Hannay picked up a number of phrases from Donne's *Anniversaries*, as well as ideas, in a funeral poem for Anne of Denmark, 'The First Elegie', in *Two Elegies on the Late Death of Our Soveraigne Queene Anne*, 1619, A4^r–B1^v. He says, for example, that the world will die with Queen Anne for

> this *Queene* was the *soule*,
> Whose faculties worlds frailties did controule;
> Corrected the ill *humors*, and maintain'd
> In *it*, a wholesome *concord*, while *she* raign'd:
> But now (*she* gone) the *world* seems out of frame. . . .
> [Cf. *The second Anniversary*, lines 71–2, and *The first Anni-*
> *versary*, lines 191–2.]

And he finds that Queen Anne was the heavenly power and pattern of all virtues whom the ancient writers divined:

> Twas *she* the Antique *Poets* so admird,
> When with prophetique furie *they* inspired,
> Did faine the heavenly *powers*, they did see,
> (As in a dreame) that *such a one* should be: . . .
> The Morallists did all of *her* devine,
> When they made every vertue foeminine;
> And but *they* knew that *such a one* should be,
> Doubtless with *them vertue* should have ben HE.
> [Cf. *The first Anniversary*, lines 175–9.]

1619

In a meditation upon death, possibly written in 1612 or 1613, William Drummond used several phrases and arguments from Donne's *The first Anniversary* (*A Midnights Trance*, 1619, pp. 33–4. See R. Ellrodt, 'An Earlier Version (1619) of William Drummond's Cypresse Grove', *English*, vii, 1949, pp. 228–31):

. . . the Element of fire is quite put out . . . the Sunne is lost. . . . What is all we know, compared to what we know not.

Drummond expanded this essay into *A Cypresse Grove*, 1623, drawing on more arguments from Donne. See the extract given under 1623.

1621

The first Anniversary and *The second Anniversary* were republished together in a fresh edition. Donne was not named as the author.

1623

In a meditation upon death and the insufficiency of our standing in this life William Drummond picked up the argument and phrases of

Donne's *The first Anniversary* (*A Cypresse Grove*, 1623. In *The Poetical Works of William Drummond of Hawthornden*, ed. L. E. Kastner, 1913, p. 78). Drummond asked if 'the dearest Favourites of the World' can lay claim to knowledge, and continued—

we have not yet attained to a perfect Understanding of the smallest Flower, and why the Grasse should rather be greene than red. The Element of Fire is quite put out, the Aire is but Water rarified, the Earth is found to move, and is no more the Center of the Universe, is turned into a Magnet; Starres are not fixed, but swimme in the etheriall Spaces, Cometes are mounted above the Planetes; Some affirme there is another World of men and sensitive Creatures, with Cities and Palaces in the Moone; the Sunne is lost, for, it is but a Light made of the conjunction of manie shining Bodies together, a Clift in the lower Heavens, through which the Rayes of the highest defuse themselves, is observed to have Spots; Thus, Sciences by the diverse Motiones of this Globe of the Braine of Man, are become Opiniones, nay, Errores, and leave the Imagination in a thousand Labyrinthes. What is all wee knowe compared with what wee knowe not? . . . *cf. death (Dryden)*

1623

Donne's friend Sir Henry Goodyer paraphrased lines 1–2 of Donne's verse letter 'To Mr E.G.' in a poem defending the Prince of Wales's journey into Spain in 1623. He wrote to Secretary Conway on 17 May 1623 asking him to send the poem with some packets for Spain (*Calendar of State Papers, Domestic Series, of the Reign of James I, 1619–23*, ed. M. A. E. Green, 1858, p. 585).

1625

The first Anniversary and *The second Anniversary* were again republished together in a fresh edition. Donne was still not named as the author.

1625

A character in Ben Jonson's play *The Staple of News* (1625) parodies the first line of Donne's 'Elegie upon the untimely death of the incomparable Prince Henry'. Pennyboy Junior, inviting the whole world to admire him as the play opens, says—

> Look to me, wit, and look to my wit, land
>
> [Act 1, Scene 1]

43

c. 1626

A funerall Elegy on Kinge James, signed 'J.B.', in a manuscript in the library of Trinity College, Dublin, repeatedly adapts lines and ideas from Donne's *Anniversaries*. It has a letter of dedication 'To the reverend and learned Doctor Donne, Deane of St Paules', which was evidently meant to be sent to Donne with a copy of the poem and 'with his hand, and hart whoe honors, and admires you'.

The manuscript, press mark F.4.20, contains poems by Sir John Davies, Hoskins, Corbet, and others of Donne's contemporaries, all written out in the same fine hand. It has a group of funeral elegies, two of which are ascribed to 'J.B.' in the title and signed with the same initials at the end, suggesting that their author was in fact the compiler of the manuscript. He may have been James Barry, later Baron Santry and Chief Justice of the King's Bench, who was Recorder of Dublin in the late 1620s.

The *Elegy on Kinge James* is a long poem in heroic couplets. It catches Donne's manner throughout, as well as ingeniously imitating particular features of the *Anniversaries*. Here is an extract from the poem:

> Let his death teach us what a sea of glasse
> This whole worlde is, since he our ioye, whoe was
> The soule of it is fled, and could not be
> Freed from that common fate mortality.
> Could knolledge, vertue, greateness or the rest
> Of those poore thinges wch we doe count the best,
> Had [*sic*] beene preservatives against death, he then,
> Whom we lament, had overlived all men,
> For we do celebrat his funerall
> Whoe was more learned, great, good then all,
> His very name was learninge, and his breast
> As a well furnisht liberary was possest
> Wth Artes, and Languages, soe as who lookes
> Into these ragges in print, wch we call bookes,
> Shall see, that he was the originall,
> And they but coppeys, he inform'd them all,
> And us, beinge ablere to improve a man
> Then Bodeleys booke case, or the Vatican: . . .

1629

A character in Ben Jonson's play *The New Inn* (1629) echoes line 14 of

Donne's verse letter 'The Calme'. Prudence the chambermaid, having presided over a Court of Love, now concludes it—

> The court's dissolv'd, removed, and the play ended . . .
>
> [Act 4, Scene 4, line 248]

1630

'The Broken Heart' and part of the 'Song. Goe, and catche a falling starre' were given in *A Helpe to Memory and Discourse*. The book is a 'Compendium of witty, and usefull Propositions, Problemes, and Sentences, Extracted from the larger Volumes of Physicians, Philosophers, Orators and Poets', and Donne's poems occur in a section called 'Table-Talke as Musicke to a Banquet of Wine'. 'The Broken Heart' appears as 'The Lovers complaint written by a Gentleman of quality'. No more is given of the 'Song. Goe, and catche' than a half of the first stanza and the whole of the second stanza.

Donne's poems may have appeared in earlier editions of the book published in 1620 and 1621 but there is no copy extant which has them.

c. 1630–c. 1640

The love poets of the Court of Charles I frequently echo Donne, taking for granted attitudes which had been his original insights in the *Songs and Sonnets* and *Elegies*. Here are some obvious examples:

> When, cruel fair one, I am slain
>   By thy disdain,
> And, as a trophy of thy scorn
>   To some old tomb am borne, . . .
>
> [Thomas Stanley, 'The Tomb']

> Fie upon hearts that burn with mutual fire!
> I hate two minds that breathe but one desire. . . .
>
> [Suckling, 'Against Fruition']

> I am confirm'd a woman can
> Love this, or that, or any other man. . . .
>
> [Suckling, 'Verses']

> I gave, when last I was about to die. . . .
>
> [Davenant, 'To Endymion Porter'. In *Madagascar*, 1638]

> Let wilder youth, whose soule is sense. . . .
>
> [Habington, 'To Castara . . . the Reward of Innocent Love']

1634

A short poem in Habington's *Castara*, 'Against them who lay Un-chastity to the Sex of Women', pointedly answers Donne's 'Song. Goe, and catche a falling starre' (*Castara*, 1634, second part, pp. 33–4). Here is the first stanza:

> They meet but with unwholesome Springs,
> And summers which infectious are:
> They heare but when the Meremaid sings
> And onely see the falling starre,
>   Who ever dare
> Affirme no woman chaste and faire.

1635

Anthony Stafford, a devotional writer, conflated some phrases from Donne's *A Litanie*, stanza 12, when he invited those who have vowed virginity to kneel down before the Virgin Mary, 'The Grand white Immaculate Abbesse of your snowy Nunneries' (*The Femall Glory: or, The Life, and Death of our Blessed Lady the holy Virgin Mary*, 1635, pp. 148–9).

1635–8

James Howell used ideas and expressions from Donne's 'Goodfriday, 1613. Riding Westward' in a letter in *Epistolae Ho-Elianae* (Letter xxxii, Sect. 6, to Sir *Ed.* B. Knight, dated 25 July 1635. Edition of 1645, p. 50).

1637

A poem in Thomas Jordan's *Poeticall Varieties: or, Varietie of Fancies*, 1637, imitates Donne's *Elegie xix*, 'To his Mistris Going to Bed'. Here it is:

> *To Leda his coy Bride, on the Bridall Night*
> Why art thou coy (my *Leda*) ar't not mine:
> Hath not the holy *Hymeneall* twine
> Power to contract our *Natures*? must I be
> Still interpos'd with needlesse *Modesty*?
> What though my former passions made me vow
> You were an *Angell*; be a *Mortall* now.
> The bride-maides all are vanish'd, and the crew
> Of Virgin *Ladies* that did waite on you,

Have left us to our selves; as loth to be
Injurious to our *loves wish'd privacie*.
    Come then undresse; why blush you, prethee smile;
    Faith ile disrobe ye, nay I will not spoyle
Your *Necklace*, or your *Gorget*; Heres a *Pin*
Pricks you (faire *Leda*) twere a cruell sin
Not to remove it; Oh how many *gates*
Are to *Elizium*? (yet the sweetest *Straits*
That e're made voyage happy) here's a *Lace*
Me thinks should stifle you; it doth embrace
Your body too severely, take a knife,
Tis tedious to undoe it; By my life,
It shall be cut. Let your Carnation gowne
Be pull'd off (too) and next let me pull downe
This *Rosie Peticoe*; That is this cloud
That keepes the day light from us, and's allow'd
More priviledge then I? (Though it be white)
Tis not the white I aime at (by this light)
It shall goe off (too) noe? then let't alone,
Come, let's to bed, why look you so? here's none
See's you, but I; be quicke or (by this hand)
Ile lay you downe my selfe; you make me *stand*
Too long i'th cold; Why doe you lie so farre,
Ile follow you, this distance shall not barre
Your body from me; Oh, tis well, and now
Ile let thy *Virgin innocence* know how
Kings propagate young Princes, marriage beds
Never destroy, but erect *mayden-heads*:
Faire *Virgins*, fairely wedded, but repaire
Declining *beauty* in a prosperous heire.
Come then lets kisse, let us embrace each other,
Till we have found a babe, faire (like the mother.)
Such *face*, *brest's*, *waste*, soft *belly*, such a . . . why
Doe you thrust back my hand so scornefully?
Youle make me strive (I thinke) *Leda*, you know,
I have a *warrant* for what ere I doe,
And can commit no trespasse; therefore come
Make me beleeve theirs no *Elizium*
Sweeter then these embraces. . . . Now ye'are kind,
(My gentle *Leda*) since you have resign'd,

47

Ile leave my talking (too) *lovers* grow mutes
When *Amrous Ladies* grant such pretty sutes.

1638

Several poets writing in the memorial volume for Edward King echo
Donne's *Anniversaries* (*Justa Edouardo King*, Cambridge, 1638). In particular, the elegies by R. Brown and Henry King pick up phrases and
ideas from Donne.

1638

Thomas, Viscount Wentworth (later Earl of Strafford), referred to
Donne's *Elegie ii*, 'The Anagram', in a letter he wrote to Archbishop
Laud from Dublin on 10 April 1638 (*Letters and Dispatches*, ed. W.
Knowler, 1739, ii, p. 158):

The Lady *Astrea*, the Poet tells us, is long since gone to Heaven: but
under Favour I can yet find Reward and Punishment on Earth; indeed
sometimes they are like Doctor *Donn's* Anagram of a good Face, the
ornaments mis-set, a yellow Tooth, a red Eye, a white Lip or so. . . .

c. 1638–9

Catherine Thimelby (?1618–58) quoted a line from Donne's 'The
Legacie' in a passionate letter to the poet Herbert Aston of Tixall whom
she later married (*Tixall Letters*, ed. A. Clifford, 1815, i, p. 147):

How infinite a time will it seme till I se you; for lovers hours are full
eternity. Doctor Dun sayd this, but I think it.

This is the earliest acknowledged quotation from Donne's *Songs and
Sonnets* so far discovered. The correspondence of both Thimelby and
Aston families at this time shows an eager interest in the current writers
and writings.

c. 1640

A poem in a British Museum manuscript, 'A Lovers Testament dying
for Love' is a version in couplets of Donne's 'The Will'. In the same
manuscript the first six lines of Donne's 'Epitaph: on himselfe' are converted into a love-lyric. (BM Add. MS. 10309 f. 50^v and f. 98^v. This
manuscript also gives in full some five other poems by Donne.)

c. 1640

Some characters in Thomas Killigrew's play *The Parsons Wedding* use as received truths phrases from three of Donne's *Songs and Sonnets*—'A Lecture upon the Shadow', 'Breake of Day', and 'Loves Alchymie' (Act 2, Scene 1 and Act 4, Scene 1. In *Comedies and Tragedies*, 1664, pp. 88 and 122. *The Parsons Wedding* has a separate title page dated 1663; but it had been written long before that and was played, in fact, at some time between 1637 and 1642. See W. R. Keast, 'Killigrew's Use of Donne in *The Parsons Wedding*', *MLN*, xlv, 1950, pp. 512–15).

(i) Jolly pretends love to old Lady Love-all so as to get a string of pearls she wears.

> JOLLY. Dear, do not too fast pour in my joys, lest I too soon reach my heaven.
>
> LOVE-ALL. Be gone then, lest we prove (having gain'd that height) this sad truth in Love; The first minute after noon is night.

(ii) Love-all offers to show Jolly her pearls when he returns from a trip to the country.

> JOLLY. Can your love endure delays? or shall business thee from hence remove? these were your own Arguments; come, you shal shew it me.

(iii) Mrs Wanton offers to please both Wild and Jolly in return for a trick they are playing on her husband, Wild by allowing him to lie with her, and Jolly by giving him leave to boast that he lies with her although he doesn't.

> JOLLY. Faith, and my part is some pleasure, else, I have loved, enjoyed, and told, is mistook.
>
> WANTON. I, but never to love, seldom enjoy, and always tell? Faugh, it stinks, and stains worse then *Shoreditch* durt, and women hate and dread men for it.. . . .

1640

An epigram entitled 'A raritie' in Sir J. Mennes's *Witts Recreations, selected from the finest Fancies of Moderne Muses*, 1640, is a version of the second stanza of Donne's 'Song. Goe, and catche a falling starre' (Epigram no. 464, sig. L 2). Epigram no. 161 in this miscellany loosely imitates in couplets the whole of the same poem:

> Goe, catch a star that's falling from the skye,
> Cause an imortall creature for to dye,

> Stop with thy hand the current of the seas,
> Post ore the earth to the Antipodes,
> Cause time return and call back yesterday,
> Cloake January with the month of May;
> Weigh out an ounce of flame, blow back the winde,
> And then find faith within a womans minde.   [Sig. E3]

Witts Recreations also gives Donne's *Elegie ii*. There were nine editions of the miscellany by 1683.

1641

In a set of forty epigrams by the German Court poet Georg Rudolf Weckherlin (1584–1653) some six appear to be translated or adapted from Donne. There are versions of 'Niobe', 'Hero and Leander', 'A Licentious Person', 'Antiquary', 'A Lame Begger', 'Phryne'. (*Gaistliche und Weltlich Gedichte*, 1641, pp. 177–93.)

Weckherlin finally settled in England in 1626 but had long known English writings well then, and it is possible that the imitations of Donne were written up to thirty-five years before he published them.

1641

The poet Henry Oxinden, writing to his confidante Elizabeth Dallison, adapted part of *Elegie xv*, 'The Expostulation', to a situation of his own (*The Oxinden Letters*, 1607–42, ed. D. Gardiner, 1933, pp. 245–6). Oxinden altered pronouns from feminine to masculine and put 'her lying tunge that desyved me' for 'his falser tongue/ That utter'd all'. He later cited another poem by Donne:

I will now acquaint you with a lovers abiure which a friend of mine gave mee; but I desire you to kepe it secret, especially from such women as have a smale opinion of mee.

Goe and catch a falling starre, etc. Don p. 3.

The poem is on page 3 of the 1635 and 1639 editions of Donne's poems.

1641

A broadside poem purporting to have been written by Strafford just before his execution adapts the first line of Donne's 'Song. Goe, and catche a falling starre'. ('Verses Lately written by Thomas Earle of Strafford', 1641, in Thomason Tracts (single sheets), 3 January 1640—

24 March 1641, and in *Humorous, Political, Historical and Miscellaneous Ballads* (broadsheets), British Museum Luttrell Collection, vol. 2.)

1642

Sir Francis Kynaston imitated Donne's *Elegie ii*, 'The Anagram', in a poem 'To Cynthia, On a Mistresse for his Rivals'. He shows his scorn for his rivals in Cynthia's love by devising a gross and loathsome mistress fit for their palates, who is the absolute antithesis of Cynthia. The following extracts are representative (*Leoline and Sydanis . . . Together with Sundry Affectionate Addresses to his Mistresse, Under the Name of Cynthia*, 1642, pp. 124–7, lines 15–24, 27–8, 53–6);

> For I for their sakes will a mistress choose,
> As never had a mayden-head to loose,
> Or if she had, it was so timely gone,
> She never could remember she had one.
> She by antiquity, and her vile face
> Of all whores els, a bawds shall have the place;
> One whose all parts, her nose, eyes, foot, and hand,
> Shall so farre out of all proportion stand,
> As it by Symmetry shall not be guest,
> By any one, the feature of the rest. . . .
> A Bare anatomiz'd unburied coarse
> Shall not more ghastly looke, nor yet stinke worse: . . .
> Her cheeks and buttocks shall so neere agree
> In shape and semblance, they shall seeme to bee
> Twins by their likenesse, nor shall it be eath
> To know, which is which by their fulsome breath: . . .

c. 1643

Charles, second Lord Stanhope, adapted lines 229–30 of Donne's *The first Anniversary* in a comment he made in the margin of Cresacre More's *Life and Death of Sir Thomas More*, 1642 (Ddd2r) which he read about 1643 (see G. P. V. Akrigg, 'The Curious Marginalia of Charles, Second Lord Stanhope', in *Adams Memorial Studies*, Folger Shakespeare Library, 1948, pp. 785–802):

> She guilds ye West Indyes, and perfumes ye east, good silly cheat, Diamond Violett a Citty cheat.

1645

Epitaph no. 88 in Sir J. Mennes's poetical miscellany *Recreation for Ingenious Head-peeces* is a poem *On Doctor Donns death*. It is in fact a version of Dr Corbet's elegy *On Doctor Donne*, first given in *Poems, by J.D.* 1633.

1647

Abraham Cowley's cycle of love poems, *The Mistress*, published in 1647 when the poet was twenty-nine years old, shows a heavy obligation to Donne. Cowley directly imitated Donne's *Songs and Sonnets* and *Elegies* in at least a dozen poems, and followed Donne throughout in the form, openings, titles, and even the subjects of poems. (See John Sparrow, *The Mistress, with Other Select Poems of Abraham Cowley 1618–67*, 1962, p. xvi.)

1647

A celebratory poem by one John Harris 'On the Death and Workes of Mr John Fletcher', prefixed to the first collected edition of the *Comedies and Tragedies* of Beaumont and Fletcher, picked up a phrase from Donne's 'The Exstasie'. Harris referred to Fletcher as 'the intelligence that did move that Spheare'.

1649

John Dryden, in his juvenile poem 'Upon the death of the Lord Hastings', drew heavily upon Donne. He directly echoed the *Anniversaries*, the *Metempsychosis*, and some of the *Epigrams*, but followed Donne in a conceited manner of writing too.

A number of other poems in the memorial volume for Lord Hastings draw upon Donne's *Anniversaries* (*Lachrymae Musarum*, 1649).

1650

The second stanza of 'A Song' in J. Gough's poetical miscellany *The Academy of Complements. The Last Edition*, is a version of the first stanza of Donne's 'Breake of Day'.

c. 1650

A poem in a Bodleian Library manuscript imitates Donne's *Elegie viii*,

'The Comparison', contrasting the several beauties of the poet's mistress with the foul deformities of a rival's mistress. The following are
the first three stanzas (*Seventeenth Century Songs Now First Printed from
a Bodleian Manuscript*, ed. J. P. Cutts and F. Kermode, Reading, 1956,
no. xiii, pp. 25–6):

> Laugh not fond foole, cause I a face
>   admired through a vaile,
> thy Mistris through hir nasty case
>   did wound thee with hir taile,
>
> such diffirence is betweene our flame,
>   as reasons diffrent be,
> for thine must hide her selfe for shame
>   as mine for modesty.
>
> Mine farr outsparkles pretious stones
>   through cleerenes of her blood
> thine's like the light of old fish bones
>   or that of rotten wood. . . .

1651

There are echoes of Donne's verse letter 'The Calme' in William Cartwright's 'On the Great Frost, 1634'. Cartwright's 'No Platonique Love'
reworks the argument of Donne's 'The Exstasie' and 'Loves Alchymie'.
(*W. Cartwright, Comedies, Tragi-Comedies, With other Poems*, 1651, pp.
204–6 and 246–7.)

A poem in a British Museum manuscript, 'On the Hott Summer
following the Great Frost, in imitation of the Verses made upon it by
W.C.', also echoes Donne's 'The Calme' (Harleian MS. 6931, ff. 80–1).

1653

The royalist writer Samuel Sheppard, who had been Ben Jonson's
amanuensis, quoted, adapted and paraphrased lines from a number of
poems by Donne in the preliminary matter of a satirical pamphlet.
Sheppard drew upon *Elegie xvi*, all five *Satyres*, 'Upon Mr Thomas
Coryats Crudities', *Epithalamion made at Lincolnes Inne, The first Anniversary, Obsequies to the Lord Harrington*, 'The Calme', and verse letters
to Sir Henry Wotton, Rowland Woodward, Sir Edward Herbert, the

Countess of Bedford, and the Countess of Salisbury. (*Merlinus Anonymus. An Almanack, And no Almanack. A Kalender, And no Kalendar. An Ephemeris (between jest, and earnest) for the year, 1653*, 1653, A2^r–C3^v.)

1653

Stanzas 1 and 2 of Donne's 'Song. Goe, and catche a falling starre' were reprinted in the second (enlarged) edition of Francis Beaumont's *Poems*, 1653, as Beaumont's, and with the title 'A Song'.

1654

Elegie xviii, 'Loves Progress', and *Elegie xix*, 'To his Mistris Going to Bed', were printed for the first time in an anthology called *The Harmony of the Muses: or, The Gentlemans and Ladies Choisest Recreation*, 1654, pp. 2–3 and 36–7. Both had been refused a licence for the 1633 edition of Donne's poems and excluded from subsequent editions. They appeared again in a miscellany called *Wit and Drollery*, 1661, and finally took their place among Donne's collected poems in the edition of 1669. The texts printed in *The Harmony of the Muses* differ markedly from those in the 1669 edition and evidently have a separate manuscript source.

In *The Harmony of the Muses* both elegies are firmly ascribed to Donne, *Elegie xviii* as *Loves Progress by Dr Don*, and *Elegie xix* as *An Elegie made by J.D.* This anthology also gives four of the *Songs and Sonnets* ('A Valediction: forbidding Mourning', 'Loves Diet', 'The Prohibition', and 'The Will'), and attributes a number of other erotic poems to *Dr Dun* or *J.D.* 'Dr Joh. Donn' heads the list of nine contributors, 'unimitable Masters of learning and Invention', which appears on the title page.

1655

Samuel Sheppard adapted the opening of Donne's *Elegie xv* in a mock-discourse on lovers' etiquette (*The Marrow of Complements*, 1655, B11):

The Lover finding himself abus'd by her who promis'd him Marriage (she deserting him and electing another) may thus vent himselfe. '*Mistresse*

To make the doubt clear that no Woman can be constant, was it my fate to prove it folly in you?'

1655

An anonymous poet in J. Cotgrave's poetical miscellany *Wit's Inter-preter, The English Parnassus*, 1655 (Part 4, pp. 25–6), conflated Donne's 'Breake of Day' with another poem called 'Break of Daye' sometimes attributed to Donne. The poetic conflation has a new title, and Donne is not mentioned:

Two loath to depart

Lye neer my Dear, why do'st thou rise?
The light that shines comes from thy eyes;
'Tis not the day breaks, but my heart,
To think that thou and I must part:
Oh stay! oh stay! or else my joyes must die,
And perish in their infancy.

'Tis true, 'tis day, what if it be?
Wilt thou therefore arise from me?
Did we lie down because 'twas night?
And must we rise because 'tis light?
Oh no! since that in darknesse we came hither,
In spight of light wee'l lye together.

1656

John Aubrey, writing the life of his kinsman Dr William Aubrey, adapted some lines from Donne's 'Loves diet' to his own situation, as he ruefully reckoned where he himself stood in the line of entailment of Dr William Aubrey's Breconshire estates (*Brief Lives*, ed. A. Clark, Oxford, 1898, i, p. 59):

. . . and so I am heire, being the 18th man in remainder, which putts me in mind of Dr Donne,

For what doeth it availe
To be the twentieth man in an entaile?

1657

Joshua Poole listed *Dunns poems* as one of the 'Books principally made use of' in the compiling of a poetical thesaurus. Poole used Donne chiefly in a collection of 'choicest Epithets and Phrases', illustrating from him such terms as 'Amaz'd', 'Brain', 'Elephant', 'Goodly', 'Noahs Ark',

'Strange', and 'Tempest' (*V. Dunnes storm*). (*The English Parnassus: Or, A Helpe to English Poesie*, 1657, pp. 42, 235, 266, 273, 329, 425, 502, 526, and other places.)

1658

Three of Donne's poems were given, with facing translations into Greek, in H. Stubbe, *Deliciae Poetarum Anglicanorum in Graecum versae*, 1658. The poems are 'A Valediction: forbidding Mourning', and the epigrams 'Hero and Leander' and 'A Licentious Person'.

1658

Sir Aston Cokain repeatedly quoted or adapted Donne's *Anniversaries* in a collection of epigrams and short poems, *Small Poems of Divers Sorts, 1658*. These are some examples:

(Of Women)

> In Paradise a Woman caused all
> The ruine of mankind by Adams fall:
> What wonder then if they o'recome us here
> When w'are more weak, and they perhaps as fair?
> [No. 99. The first Book. Cf. *The first Anniversary*, lines 106–10.]

An Epitaph on Elizabeth the Lady Reppington etc.

> She was their Paradise, and her bright soul
> The Deity that did command the whole. . . .
> [No. 4. The third Book. Cf. *The second Anniversary*, lines 77–80.]

For Cokain's praises of Donne in the same volume see No. 42.

1658

Wit Restor'd, 1658, an anthology of witty poetry compiled by Sir J. Mennes and J. Smith, has a number of echoes of Donne, as of other older poets. Thus a poem called 'On a Ribband' opens

> This silken wreath that circles in my arms
> Is but an emblem of your mystick charmes; . . .

(Cf. Donne's 'The Funeral', lines 1–4.)

Another poem, 'On a good Legg and Foot', imitates Donne's *Elegie xviii*, 'Loves Progress'. The following is an extract from this poem (lines 11–14 and 31–4, pp. 90–1):

> . . . The round and slender foot,
> Is a prov'd token of a secret note,
> Of hidden parts, and well this way may lead,
> Unto the closet of a mayden-head. . . .
> Let others view the top, and limbs throughout,
> The deeper knowledge is to know the root.
> In viewing of the face, the weakest know
> What beauty is, the learned look more low: . . .

1659

William Chamberlayne picked up a few words and phrases from Donne's 'The Flea' in his *Pharonnida: a Heroick Poem*, 1659, book ii, canto i, lines 161–4. He describes a treacherous butchery of Spartan knights during festivities at the Court of Princess Pharonnida. The poem was probably drafted in the mid-1640s:

> Sudden and cruel was the Act, yet stands
> Not Treason here, but whilst their purpl'd hands
> Yet wreakt in blood, their guilty Souls to stain,
> With blacker sins (her weak Defenders slain)
> Rush towards the trembling Princess. . . .

1659

The bookseller Humphrey Moseley quoted from Donne's verse letter 'The Storme' in introducing Sir John Suckling's fragmentary tragedy *Mortimer* (*The Last Remains of Sir John Suckling*, 1659, To the Reader, n.p.):

It being true of our *Author*, what Dr *Donne* said of a famous Artist of his time,

> A hand or eye
> By Hilliard drawn, is worth a History
> By a worse Painter made.

1660

Donne's 'The Sunne Rising' is quoted in a letter from 'A most humble Servant in the Country, to a great Noble Lady at Court, written at

New-years-tide' (*A Collection of Letters Made by Sr Tobie Mathews Kt.* ed. John Donne, 1660, p. 203):

. . . Whatsoever was lesse perfect in that health of yours, I wish may passe away with the past-year; and that, whatsoever is most excellent, in the way of glory, and beautie, may still be present with you; not onely in the year which is present, but in those others also, which shall ever come to be so; and that all the raggs of time, as *Dunne* calls them, may prove no worse than fair Embroideries to you. . . .

1660

T. Forde alluded to Donne's verse letter to Sir Henry Wotton, 'Sir, more then kisses, letters mingle Soules', in describing the proper mode of '*Familiar Letters*' (*Faenestra in Pectore. Or, Familiar Letters*, 1660, To the Reader, n.p.):

. . . in *Familiar Letters* . . . friends mingle souls

In an anthology of witty sayings Forde quoted lines 21–2 of '*Donnes Sat.*' (i.e., *Satyre ii*) in writing of authors who dedicate their work in hope of gain (*A Theatre of Wits. Ancient and Modern. Represented in a Collection of Apothegmes*, 1660, To the Reader, Dr).

1661

Elegie xviii, 'Loves Progress', was given in *Wit and Drollery. By Sir J.M., J.S., Sir W.D., J.D., and the most refined Wits of the Age,* 1661.

1662

The Lady Ward, a character in the Duchess of Newcastle's play *The Second Part of the Lady Contemplation*, quotes a version of lines 35–6 of Donne's verse letter 'The Storme' (Act 1, Scene 9. In *Playes written by . . . the Lady Marchioness of Newcastle*, 1662, p. 219):

. . . for I remember a witty Poet, one Doctor Don, saith,

> Sleep is pains easie salve, and doth fulfil
> All Offices, unless it be to kill.

1663

Samuel Butler picked up a phrase from Donne's *Metempsychosis*, line 511, in his mock-heroic poem *Hudibras* (The First Part, canto 1, 1663 edition, p. 49). Petitioning the Muse for poetic aid he cited the 'sullen Writs,/And cross-grain'd Works of modern wits' which she had lately inspired.

1664

In his libertine love poems, in *Poems Lyrique Macaronique Heroique, &c*, 1664, pp. 8, 10, 13, Henry Bold adapted phrases or arguments from a number of Donne's *Songs and Sonnets* and *Elegies*. Thus his 'Song v' picks up attitudes and phrases from *Elegie xvii* ('Variety'), 'Communitie', and 'The Indifferent'; 'Song vii' rewords the opening of 'Womans Constancy'; 'Song x' has such direct echoes as

> Faith use me *kindly*! let me *dye*,
> The *fairest death*!

(Cf. 'The Prohibition', lines 17–19, 'The Dampe', lines 21–2.)

1664

A character in a play by Etherege adapts the first line of Donne's 'Twicknam Garden' in upbraiding one of her lovers who has just fought a duel with a rival for her hand, though she expressly forbade them to fight over her (*The Comical Revenge; or, Love in a Tub*, 1664, Act 4, Scene 5, p. 48):

GRACIANA. Perfidious man, can you expect from me
     An approbation of your Treachery!
     When I, distracted with prophetick fears,
     Blasted with sighs, and almost drown'd in tears,
     Begg'd you to moderate your Rage last night,
     Did you not promise me you wou'd not fight?
     Go now and triumph in your Victory. . . .

1669

John Playford reworked Donne's 'Song. Goe, and catche a falling starre' in a poem entitled 'On Womens Inconstancy' which he gave in a volume of lyrics with musical settings he himself edited. A large number of the poems in the volume bear titles reminiscent of Donne's *Songs and Sonnets*—'The Primrose', 'Reciprocal Love', 'A Protest against Love', 'To his *Chloris* at Parting', 'Lovers Wantonnesse', 'A Resolution not to Love', and so on. 'On Womens Inconstancy' is signed 'John Playford' (*The Treasury of Musick: Containing Ayres and Dialogues To Sing to the Theorbo-Lute or Basse-Viol*, 1669, p. 11):

> Catch me a Star that's falling from the Skie,
> Cause an Immortall creature for to die;
> Stop with thy hand the Current of the Seas.
> Peirce the earths Center to th'Antipodes;
> Cause Time return, and call back Yesterday,
> Cloath *Ja-nu-a-ry* like the moneth of *May*;
> Weigh me an ounce of Flame, Blow back the wind;
> Then hast thou found Faith in a Womans mind.

1670

Samuel Woodforde, 'To his very Worthy and much Honoured Friend Mr Izaak Walton, upon his Excellent Life of Mr George Herbert', lines 60-5 (a poem prefixed to Walton's *The Life of Mr George Herbert*, 1670, pp. 3-5. The poem is subscribed '*Bensted*, Apr. 3 1670'):

> *Herbert*, and *Donne*, again are joyn'd,
> Now here below, as they're above;
> These friends, are in their old embraces twin'd;
> And since by you the Enterview's design'd,
> Too weak, to part them, death does prove;
> For, in his book they meet again: as, in one Heav'n they love.

1679

The minor poet Thomas Shipman adapted lines 19-20 of Donne's *A Litanie* in a poem of his own called 'True Nobility. 1679. Upon the Death of the Right Honourable John Earl of Rutland' (*Carolina: or, Loyal Poems*, 1683, p. 225, lines 15-17 of the poem).

1680

Nathaniel Lee quoted from three poems by Donne, attributing the lines to 'Dr Donn', in a very brief *Epistle Dedicatory to the Dutchess of Richmond* (*Theodosius: Or, The Force of Love*, 1680, A2^r-13^r). The poems are *The first Anniversary*, lines 112-20, *The second Anniversary*, lines 244b-46, and the verse letter 'To the Countesse of Bedford' ('Honour is so sublime perfection'), lines 22-4.

1680

John Aubrey, in his life of Lord Herbert of Cherbury, quoted the first seven lines of Donne's 'The Primrose', ascribing them to Donne and implying that they describe a 'Prim-rose-hill' in the grounds of Montgomery Castle. Donne visited Herbert at Montgomery Castle in the spring of 1613 (*Aubrey's Brief Lives*, ed. O. L. Dick, 1949, p. 134).

c. 1680

Sedley made an urbane version of Donne's 'The Will' which he retitled 'The Lover's Will'. It appeared among his works as his own poem. The following extracts show what he did with Donne (*The Works of the Honourable Sir Charles Sedlay Bar.*, 1722, ii, pp. 1–2):

> Let me not sigh my last e're I bequeath
> Some Legacies (Great Love) I have to leave.
> Mine Eyes to *Argus*, if mine Eyes can see:
> If they be blind, then, Love, I give them thee:
> My tongue to Fame, t'Embassadors mine Ears,
> And unto Women, or the sea, my Tears. . . .

[He follows Donne closely as far as the last stanza]

> Thou, Love, taught'st me, by making me adore ⎫
> That charming Maid, with twenty Servants more, ⎬
> To give to those who had too much before, ⎭
> To those that love where there no Love can be,
> I give and grant my Incapacity.

1681

An anonymous poet adapted lines 15–16 of Donne's 'A Nocturnall upon S. Lucies Day' and lines 97–8 of *The first Anniversary* in a historical poem (*A Paradox Against Life. Written By the Lords in the Tower. An Heroick Poem*, 1681, p. 6, lines 18–19, p. 9, lines 10–11).

1684

A poet who signed himself 'J.C.' reworked many lines and images from Donne's *Anniversaries* in *An Elegie, Upon the Death of the most Incomparable, Mrs Katharine Philips, the Glory of Her Sex*, 1684.

1688

One Jos. Walker attributed to Donne an image he used in the Epistle Dedicatory of an essay on Pascal ('A Discourse Upon Monsieur Pascall's Thoughts', in *Monsieur Pascall's Thoughts, Meditations, and Prayers*, 1688, n.p.—but p. 267 in fact):

I have liv'd a good while in the World, and have concern'd my self but with few Persons, nor Businesses, nor do I much desire it; I desire as Dr *Donn* did, to swim like a Fish, quietly to my Long Home. . . .

Presumably Walker is recollecting Donne's *Metempsychosis* and has conflated stanza 6 of the poem, 'I launch at paradise, and saile toward home', with the fish episode, stanzas 25–36.

1689

The poet Charles Cotton the Younger repeatedly reworked in his own poems phrases, images, and ideas from Donne (*Poems on Several Occasions*, 1689). Many of Cotton's titles follow Donne—'The Expostulation', 'The Picture', 'Day-Break', 'The Storm', 'The Litany', 'The Token', 'A Valediction', 'Her Name'. Here are somee xamples from the poems:

(i)
Stay, *Phoebus*, stay, and cool thy flaming Head
In the Green bosom of thy liquid Bed:
   Betray not, with thine envious Light,
   Th'embraces of an happy Night:
For her fair blushes, if thou dar'st to rise,
Will, by Eclipse, hoodwink thy saucy Eyes. . . .
Why should we rise t'adore the rising *Sun*,
And leave the Rites to greater Lights undone? . . .
           ['Day-Break']

(ii)
Oh! canst thou know, that losing thee,
The *Universe* is dead to me,
And I to it . . .?
        [*Ode: Valedictory*]

(iii)
Quench not those *Stars*, that to my bliss should Guide,
   Oh, spare that precious Tear!

Nor let those drops unto a deluge Tide,
   To drown your Beauty there, . . .
   ['Song. Why, *Dearest* should'st thou weep . . .?']

(iv)
To write your Name upon the Glass,
   Is that the greatest you'l impart
Of your Commands? . . .
And, if you add Faith to my Vows and Tears,
More firm, and more trasparent it appears, . . .
         ['Her Name']

(v)
Spare (*Laura*) spare those Beauties twins
Do not our World of Beauty drown, . . .
      ['Laura *Weeping: Ode*']

1692

The politician and essayist Sir Thomas Pope Blount adapted a phrase from Donne's 'The Will' in speaking of learning in the possession of a fool (*Essays on Several Subjects,* 1692, p. 61). He said that such learning is

then but a Bawble, and like Dr Donne's *Sun-Dial in the Grave, a* trifle, and of no use.

1692

Eleonora, Dryden's commemorative poem on the Countess of Abingdon who had died in the previous year, is plainly modelled on Donne's *Anniversaries*. In his prefatory letter to the Earl of Abingdon, at whose commission the poem was written, Dryden likens his task to Donne's in the *Anniversaries* in that both poets were writing of ladies they had never met (see No. 49 (ii)). In fact Dryden imitates the hyperbolic design of the *Anniversaries*, follows the plan of *The first Anniversary* in particular, repeatedly adapts figures, phrases, and ideas from these and other poems by Donne, and at one point takes two lines verbatim from Donne's *Obsequies to the Lord Harrington* (*Eleonora*, lines 342–3).

1700

Dryden adapted ideas from Donne's *Anniversaries* for a funeral poem,

'The Monument of a Fair Maiden Lady who dy'd at *Bath*, and is there Interr'd', in *Fables Ancient and Modern*, 1700. Here are some examples (lines 15–20 and 24–8):

> Each Thought was visible that rowl'd within:
> As through a Crystal Case, the figur'd Hours are seen.
> And Heav'n did this transparent Veil provide,
> Because she had no guilty Thought to hide.
> All white, a Virgin-Saint, she sought the Skies:. . . .
> For Marriage, tho' it sullies not, it dies. . . .

(Cf. 'A Funerall Elegie', lines 59–76).

> Yet she had learn'd so much of Heav'n below,
> That when arriv'd, she scarce had more to know:
> But only to refresh the former Hint;
> And read her Maker in a fairer Print.

(Cf. *The second Anniversary*, lines 311–14.)

2. Some general references to Donne's poems, or to Donne as a poet

c. 1608–30

---

c. 1608

The poet Francis Davison jotted down a list of 'Manuscripts to gett' which included 'Satyres, Elegies, Epigrams etc. by John Don. qre. some from Eleaz. Hodgson, and Ben: Johnson'. On the other side of the leaf Davison listed some 'Papers lent', which include 'John Duns Satyres.— my br. Christopher'. (*A Poetical Rhapsody*, ed. A. H. Bullen, 1890, i, pp. i–iv.)

Between 1608 and 1612

In a macaronic poem 'Convivium philosophicum', which pokes fun at the poetaster and traveller Thomas Coryate, John Hoskins describes a scene of witty revelry at the Mitre Tavern. The guests at what seems to have been an actual assembly of notable wits are denoted in the poem by quibbling pseudonyms, and Donne appears as 'Johannes *Factus*' among a group of his known associates—Christopher Brooke, Hoskins himself, Richard Martin, Sir Henry Goodyer, Inigo Jones. (L. L. Osborn, *The Life, Letters, and Writings of John Hoskyns, 1566–1638*, Yale, 1937, pp. 196–9. An English version of the poem, attributed to John Reynolds, is given in Andrew Clark's edition of Aubrey's *Brief Lives*, Oxford, 1898, ii, pp. 50–3.)

1612

The opening lines of Joshua Sylvester's funeral elegy for Prince Henry, *Lachrimae Lachrimarum*, seem to refer to Donne and to Donne's own elegy on Prince Henry's death which Sylvester published in the third edition of *Lachrimae Lachrimarum*, 1613:

> How-ever short of Others *Art and Witt*
> I knowe my powers for such a Part unfitt;
> And shall but light my Candle in the *Sunne*,
> To doe a Work shalbe so better Donne:

?1618

The historian and poet Edmund Bolton praised Donne among others in an essay on poets and poetry (*Hypercritica* (?1618), Oxford, 1722, p. 237):

The English Poems of Sir *Walter Raleigh*, of *John Donne*, of *Hugh Holland*, but especially of Sir *Foulk Greville* in his matchless *Mustapha*, are not easily to be mended. . . . But if I should declare mine own Rudeness rudely, I should then confess that I never tasted *English* more to my liking, nor more smart, and put to the height of Use in Poetry, then in that vital, judicious, and most practicable Language of *Benjamin Johnson's* Poems.

1620

John Taylor, 'the Water Poet', in a verse discourse upon paper as a derivative of hemp-seed, mentioned Donne as one of the notable writers who owed their literary being to paper. Taylor lists some old authors, classical and English, then his contemporaries with King James at their head; Donne comes in the first batch after the king (*The Praise of Hemp-Seed*, 1620, p. 27):

> And many there are living at this day
> Which do in paper their true worth display:
> As *Davis*, *Drayton*, and the learned *Dun*,
> *Ionson*, and *Chapman*, *Marston*, *Middleton*,
> With *Rowlye*, *Fletcher*, *Withers*, *Messenger*,
> *Heywood*, and all the rest where e're they are,
> Must say their lines, but for the paper sheete
> Had scarcely ground, whereon to set their feete.

1621, 1624, 1625

John Chamberlain several times mentioned Donne in writing to Sir Dudley Carleton, at that time Ambassador at The Hague, who evidently shared his interest in Donne's writing. In a letter of 17 November 1621 he remarked on some recent appointments—'Dr Donne is to be Dean of St Paul's, so that if Ben Jonson could be Dean of Westminster, St Paul's, Westminster and Christchurch would each have a poetical Dean' (*Calendar of State Papers, Domestic Series, of the Reign of James I, 1619–23*, ed. M. A. E. Green, 1858, p. 310. The Dean of Christchurch was Dr Richard Corbet).

On 21 February 1624 Chamberlain expressed his regret that he had found no messenger to carry to his correspondent a new Irish proclamation against the Jesuits together with Donne's recently published '*Devotions*, in his sickness . . . wherein are many curious and dainty conceits, not for common capacities, but surely full of piety and true feeling' (*Letters*, ed. E. M. Thomson, London, 1966, p. 321).

On 23 April 1625 Chamberlain sent Carleton a copy, presumably one he had made himself, of the 'Verses of the Dean of St Paul's, on the death of the Marquis Hamilton' (*Calendar of State Papers, Domestic Series, of the Reign of Charles I, 1625, 1626*, ed. J. Bruce, 1858, p. 12).

1629–30

Lucius Cary, later Viscount Falkland, mentioned Donne in a long unpublished poem he wrote when he was nineteen or so, on the recent death of his twenty-one-year-old friend Sir Henry Morison. A short address to Cary's future wife, 'To my dearest freind and Sister M^{ris} Lettice Moryson', introduces 'An Elegie on the death of my dearest (and allmost only) freind Syr Henry Moryson', which celebrates Morison's promise, and especially his gifts of poetry and statecraft. Donne is introduced as the most celebrated poet of the day who none the less has to acknowledge Morison's superiority. (See K. B. Murdock, 'An Elegy on Sir Henry Morison, by Lucius Cary, Viscount Falkland', *Harvard Studies and Notes in Philology and Literature*, xx, 1938, pp. 29–42.)

3. Ben Jonson

c. 1610, 1619, ?1630

Jonson (?1573–1637) was a friend and admirer of Donne, and the two men wrote for the same Court circle. Jonson's comments on Donne's poetry thus have peculiar authority.

(i) Possibly in 1610 Ben Jonson addressed several epigrams to Donne, and also sent Donne's *Satyres* to the Countess of Bedford, their common patroness, with an accompanying poem of his own. These poems appeared at the head of the editions of Donne's poems from 1650 to 1669:

(a)

To Iohn Donne.
DONNE, the delight of PHŒBVS, and each *Muse*,
   Who, to thy one, all other braines refuse;
Whose euery worke, of thy most earely wit,
   Came forth example, and remaines so, yet:
5 Longer a knowing, then most wits doe liue.
   And which no' affection praise enough can giue!

To it, thy language, letters, arts, best life,
  Which might with halfe mankind maintayne a strife.
All which I meant to praise, and, yet, I would;
10   But leaue, because I cannot as I should!

(b)

To Iohn Donne.

Who shall doubt, Donne, where I a *Poet* bee,
  When I dare send my *Epigrammes* to thee?
That so alone canst iudge, so'alone dost make:
  And, in thy censures, euenly, dost take
5 As free simplicitie, to dis-auow,
  As thou hast best authoritie, t‹o›'allow.
Reade all I send: and, if I find but one
  Mark'd by thy hand, and with the better stone,
My title's seal'd. Those that for claps doe write,
10   Let pui'nees, porters, players praise delight,
And, till they burst, their backs, like asses load:
  A man should seeke great glorie, and not broad.

(c)

To Lucy, Countesse of Bedford,
with M. Donnes Satyres.

Lucy, you brightnesse of our Spheare, who are
Life of the *Muses* day, their morning Starre!
If works (not th'Authors) their own grace should look
Whose poems would not wish to be your book?
But these, desir'd by you, the makers ends
Crown with their own. Rare Poems ask rare friends.
Yet, *Satyres*, since the most of mankind bee
Their unavoided subject, fewest see:
For none ere took that pleasure in sins sense,
But, when they heard it tax'd, took more offence.
They, then, that living where the matter is bred,
Dare for these Poems, yet, both ask, and read,
And like them too; must needfully, though few,
Be of the best: and 'mongst those best are you;
Lucy, you brightnesse of our Spheare, who are
The *Muses* evening, as their morning-Starre.

(ii) Jonson visited Scotland in 1619 and spent some time conversing with
William Drummond of Hawthornden, a fellow poet. Drummond

68

wrote down Jonson's remarks on poets and poetry, a number of which refer to Donne. We have no means of knowing how faithfully Drummond reports Jonson's views but the comments on Donne are very much in Jonson's manner ('Conversations with William Drummond of Hawthornden', in *Ben Jonson*, ed. C. H. Herford and Percy Simpson, Oxford, 1925, i, pp. 133–47):

(a)

that Dones Anniversarie was profane and full of Blasphemies that he told Mr. Donne, if it had been written of ye Virgin Marie it had been something to which he answered that he described the Idea of a Woman and not as she was. that Done for not keeping of accent deserved hanging.

(b)

to me he read the Preface of his arte of Poesie, upon Horace Arte of poesie, wher he heth ane apologie of a Play of his St Bartholomees faire, by Criticus is understood Done.

(c)

he esteemeth John Done the first poet in the World in some things his verses of the Lost Chaine, he heth by Heart and that passage of the calme, that dust and feathers doe not stirr, all was so quiet. affirmeth Done to have written all his best pieces err he was 25 years old.

(d)

Verses on the Pucelle of the Court Mistris Boulstred, whose Epitaph Done made.

(e)

the Conceit of Done transformation or *Metempsychosis* was that he sought the soule of that Aple which Eva pulled, and thereafter made it the soule of a Bitch, then of a sheewolf and so of a woman. his generall purpose was to have brought in all the bodies of the Hereticks from ye soule of Cain and at last left it in ye body of Calvin. of this he never wrotte but one sheet, and now since he was made Doctor repenteth highlie and seeketh to destroy all his poems.

(f)

Dones Grandfather on the mother side was Heywood the Epigrammatist.

(g)

That Done said to him he wrott that Epitaph on Prince Henry
Look to me Faith
to match Sir Ed: Herbert in obscurenesse.

(h)
that Done himself for not being understood would perish.

(iii) Jonson also alluded to Donne in *Discoveries* (*Ben Jonson*, viii (1947), p. 618):

And as it is fit to reade the best Authors to youth first, so let them be of the openest, and clearest. As *Livy* before *Salust*, *Sydney* before *Donne*. . . .

4. John Davies of Hereford

c. 1611, 1612

The Catholic poet Davies of Hereford (?1565–1618), who tried his hand at whatever kinds of writing were in fashion, seems to have looked to Donne for a model in satiric poetry, and in funeral verses too.

(i) Davies addressed a sonnet to Donne in a collection of satiric poems (*The Scourge of Folly*, ?1611):

> *To the no less ingenious then ingenuous Mr.* John Dun
>
> *Dunne* is the *Mouse* (they say) and thou art *Dunne*:
> But no dunne *Mouse* thou art; yet thou art one
> That (like a *Mouse*) in steepe high-waies dost runne,
> To finde foode for thy *Muse* to prey upon.
> Whose pallat is so dainty in her taste,
> That she distasts the least unsavory Bit:
> But that's unlike a Mouse; for, he will wast,
> All in his way; and oft himself with it,
> Not much unlike some Poets of our Times,
> That spoile good paper with their byting Pen,

> Like this of mine, but yet my doggrell Rimes
> Do byte at none but *Monsters* like to men:
>   *And that (I know) thy Pen hath rightly donne,*
>   *Which doing right, makes bright the Name of* Dunne.

(ii) Davies must have read Donne's *The second Anniversary* as soon as it came out for he alludes to it by its particular title *Of the Progresse of the Soule*, in a funeral elegy published in the same year. Davies's elegy was written on a girl of sixteen, Elizabeth Dutton, who died in 1611 ('A Funerall Elegie, on the death of the most vertuous, and no less lovely, Mris *Elizabeth Dutton*' in *The Muses Sacrifice, or Divine Meditations,* 1612, f.117ᵛ–18ʳ):

> I must confesse a *Priest* of *Phebus*, late,
> Upon like Text so well did meditate,
> That with a sinlesse *Envy* I doe runne
> In his *Soules* Progresse, till it all be DONNE.
> But, he hath got the *start* in setting forth
> Before me, in the Travell of the WORTH:
> And me out-gone in Knowledge ev'ry way
> Of the *Soules* Progresse to her finall *stay.*
> But his sweet *Saint* did usher mine therein;
> (Most blest in that) so, he must needs beginne;
> And read upon the rude Anatomy
> Of this dead World; that, now, doth putrifie.

5. Thomas Fitzherbert

1613

The Catholic controversialist Thomas Fitzherbert (1552–1640), who turned Jesuit in 1613, attacked Donne's *Pseudo-Martyr* in that year (*Supplement to the Discussion of M. D. Barlowe's Answere*, 1613, pp. 80–107).

Fitzherbert denounced Donne for his 'many Lucianicall, impious, blasphemous, and Atheisticall jests against Gods Saints and Servants'. He accused Donne of having now passed '*ultra crepidam*, that is to say, beyond his old occupation of making Satyres (wherein he hath some talent, and may play the foole without controule)'. He said that the 'Canon of the Councell of *Lateran* . . . is not in any way impeached . . . by the quintessence of M. Donne's extravagant conceytes'.

6. Thomas Freeman

1614

The minor versifier Freeman (*fl.* 1614) addressed 'To John Dunne' one of a collection of epigrams (*Runne, and a great Cast*, 1614, Epigram 84).

> The *Storme* describ'd, hath set thy name afloate,
> Thy *Calme*, a gale of famous winde hath got:
> Thy *Satyres* short, too soone we them o'relooke,
> I pre thee *Persius* write a bigger booke.

7. William Drummond of Hawthornden

1613–31

The Scottish poet Drummond of Hawthornden (1585–1649), friend of Ben Jonson, was an early admirer of Donne and a collector of his writings.

(i) Drummond included a manuscript book of 'Jhone Dones lyriques' in a list of books he read in 1613 (MS. 2059, Hawthornden MSS. vol. vii, f. 336^r, National Library of Scotland).

(ii) Drummond sought to place Donne's poetry in giving the 'Character of several Authors', apparently as a reply to Jonson's remarks during their famous conversation in January 1619 ('Heads of a Conversation betwixt the Famous Poet Ben Johnson and William Drummond of Hawthornden', in *Works*, Edinburgh, 1711, p. 226). But the passage occurs in a manuscript which may have been written several years before that conversation (see W. Milgate, *John Donne: The Satires, Epigrams and Verse Letters*, Oxford, 1967, p. 196):

Donne among the Anacreontick Lyricks, is Second to none, and far from all Second; But as *Anacreon* doth not approach *Callimachus*, tho' he excels in his own kind, nor *Horace* to *Virgil*; no more can I be brought to think him to excel either *Alexander*'s or *Sidney*'s Verses: They can hardly be compared together, trading diverse Paths; the one flying swift, but low; the other, like the Eagle, surpassing the Clouds. I think, if he would, he might easily be the best Epigrammatist we have found in *English*; of which I have not yet seen any come near the Ancients.

Compare Song, *Marry and Love*, &c. with *Tasso's Stanzas against Beauty*; one shall hardly know who hath the best.

(iii) In a draft letter to the poet Michael Drayton, probably written in 1619, Drummond picked up the first line of Donne's verse letter 'To Sir Henry Wotton', 'Sir, more then kisses, letters mingle Soules' (given in B. H. Newdigate, *Michael Drayton and his Circle*, Oxford, 1941, p. 183):

I am oft with S^r W [Alexander] and you in my thoughts, and desire no thing more than that by letters wee may ofte meet *with their Ladder* and mingle our Soules.

(iv) In 1627 Drummond presented to the University of Edinburgh a copy of Donne's 'First Sermon preached to King Charles . . . 1625', with manuscript copies of 'A Satyre' and 'An Hymne to the Saints, and Marquis Hamilton' (written in 1625). (*Auctarium Bibliothecae Edinburgenae, sive Catalogus Librorum quos Guilielmus Drummondus ab Hawthornden Bibliothecae D.D.Q.*, Edinburgh, 1627.)

(v) When Michael Drayton died late in December 1631 Drummond made several attempts to draft a letter to their common friend Sir William Alexander (who had become Earl of Stirling in the previous year). The second draft of the letter mentions Donne (it is given in *Archaeologia Scotica: or Transactions of the Society of Antiquaries of Scotland*, Edinburgh, 1792–1890, iv (1857), p. 93):

. . . Of all the good race of Poets who wrot in the tyme of Queen Elizabeth, your L. now alone remaines.

Daniel, Sylvester, King James, Done, and now Drayton. . . .

8. King James VI and I

c. 1620

Archdeacon Thomas Plume (1630–1704) jotted down in his notebook a comment on Donne's poetry which he attributed to the king (see Percy Simpson, letter to *The Times Literary Supplement*, 25 October 1941, p. 531):

King James said Dr Donne's verses were like ye peace of God they passed all understanding.

But Plume was born five years after King James's death and the remark is sometimes said to have really been made of Bacon's *Novum Organum*, published in 1620.

9. John Cave

1620

John Cave (d. 1657), of Lincoln College, Oxford, graduated M.A. in 1619 and became an Anglican divine. On 3 June 1620 he wrote down a poem addressed to Donne at the head of the manuscript of Donne's poems now known as the John Cave MS. (the manuscript is in the George Arents Tobacco Collection, New York Public Library). The same poem opens the Dyce MS. (in the Victoria and Albert Museum) where it is signed, or inscribed, 'Johannes Cave'. The Dyce MS. bears the name of its first owner, or compiler, and a date, 'Johannes Nedlam Collegio Lincolniense Marii 31 die Anno 1625'.

Oh how it joys me that this quick brain'd Age
can nere reach thee (Donn) though it should engage
at once all its whole stock of witt to find
out of thy well plac'd words thy more pure minde.
Noe, wee are bastard Aeglets all; our eyes
could not endure the splendor that would rise
from hence like rays from out a cloud. That Man
who first found out the Perspective which can
make starrs at midday plainly seen, did more
then could the whole Chaos of Arte before
or since; If I might have my wish't shuld bee
That Man might be reviv'd againe to see

75

If hee could such another frame, whereby
the minde might bee made see as farr as th'eye.
Then might we hope to finde thy sense, till then
The Age of Ignorance I'le still condemn.

IO. CA.

June.3. 1620.

10. Roger Tisdale

1622

Nothing is known of Tisdale save that he published several small
volumes in the early 1620s versifying public themes. He addressed
to 'the Learned and Reverend John Donne, D. of Divinitie, Deane
of the Cathedrall *Church* of St. Paule *London*' the 'Epistle Dedi-
catorie' of one of these books, an essay in verse on the profession
of law, and spoke of the pattern of Donne's career (*The Lawyers
Philosophy; or, Law brought to Light. Poetized in a Divine Rhapsodie
or Contemplative Poem*, 1622, A3ʳ–A5ᵛ).

'Tis you, deare Sir, that after a soaring flight of many yeeres, have now
lighted upon a faire Tree. . . . Yet I must ingenuously confesse, as an
ancient observant of your worth, that your yong daies were to me of
much admiration, as these dayes are now of deserved reverence. . . .
I know you doe love pure, and undefiled *Poesie*. . . . And I hope for
the love of the Muses (who in your Youth initiated you their Son, and
now in your Age have elected you a Patron) you will open the im-
braces of favour. . . . And so with my Love and Duty equally twined
together, either into a Lawrell or a Willow Garland (which you please
to account it) I offer it up with a desire it were worthy (I will not say
your best, but) any little acceptance. . . .

11. The Bridgewater manuscript

c. 1625

One of the compilers of the Bridgewater manuscript of Donne's poems starred line 31 in *Elegie xix*, 'To his Mistris Going to Bed', as he was copying it out, and wrote a comment on it sideways down the margin of the page. The manuscript originated in the family of Donne's old employer Lord Chancellor Sir Thomas Egerton, Baron Ellesmere; it is signed 'John Bridgewater' on an initial leaf in the hand of Egerton's only surviving son, whose wife's initials, 'F.B.', are stamped in gilt on the vellum binding. John Egerton (1579–1649) became first Earl of Bridgewater in 1617.

The line is given below as it appears in the manuscript, with the copier's comment (Henry Huntington Library MS. EL 6893, folio 106ᵛ).

To★ entere in theize bonds, is to be free.

★ why may not a man write his owne Epithalamion if he can doe it so modestly

12. Anon., lines written in a copy of Donne's *Devotions*

c. 1627

A copy of the third edition (1627) of Donne's *Devotions Upon Emergent Occasions*, now in the library of the University of Sheffield (press mark 821.33), bears some lines on Donne written in a contemporary hand. The copy has been signed by several former owners but none of these hands corresponds with that in which the lines are written and there is no clue to the author (see G. C. Moore Smith, 'Donniana', *MLQ*, vii, 1901, p. 92).

> On this witty & pious Book.
> Here Wit and Piety together shine;
> That, shows the Poet; This, the sound Divine
> Then why so few, or Good, or Witty, share
> Wit, with the Poett; with the Preacher, prayer
> The Reason's plain: The Good the Preacher quit
> Lest they shd. be corrupted by the Witt
> And Witt's denye to read the Poet's jest(e)
> For fear they be converted by the Priest.

13. Robert Hayman

1628

Hayman (d. 1631?), sometime of Exeter College, Oxford, became governor of Newfoundland about 1625. He published a volume of epigrams in 1628, from Newfoundland, addressing one of the epigrams to Donne as the author of divine poems (*Quodlibets, Lately Come Over from New Britaniola, Old Newfoundland*, 1628).

To the Reverend and divinely witty John Dun, Doctor in Divinity, Deane of Saint Pauls, London

> As my *John Owen* Seneca did praise,
> So might I for you a like piller raise,
> His Epigrams did nothing want but verse;
> You can yours (if you list) that way rehearse:
> His were neat, fine, divine morality;
> But yours, pure, faithfull, true Divinity.

14. Constantine Huygens

1630, *c.* 1687

Huygens (1596–1687), the Dutch diplomat and poet, was one of Donne's most devoted champions and expressed his admiration over more than fifty years. Huygens lived in London for long periods between 1618 and 1624 as a member of the Dutch embassy, and met Donne in 1622–3 when they came together in a circle of musicians, poets, scientists, and diplomats which gathered at the house of Sir Robert Killigrew to hear music.

(i) In 1629 or 1630 Huygens translated some of Donne's poems into Dutch. Nineteen of Donne's poems, translated into Dutch, were published in Huygens's *Koren-Bloemen* in 1658. The poems are 'The Flea', 'The Apparition', 'Witchcraft by a Picture', 'Twicknam Garden', 'Song. Goe, and catche a falling starre', 'The Triple Foole', 'A Valediction: of Weeping', 'The Dreame', *Elegie ii* ('The Anagram'), part of *Elegie vi* ('Oh, let me not serve so'), 'The Exstasie', 'The Blossome', 'Womans Constancy', 'A Valediction: forbidding Mourning', 'The Sunne Rising', 'Breake of Day', 'Loves Deitie', 'The Legacie', 'Goodfriday, 1613. Riding Westward'.

(ii) In 1630 Huygens sent his translations from Donne to a fellow poet in Holland, P. C. Hooft, with a letter in which he spoke of Donne (see H. J. C. Grierson, *The Poems of John Donne*, Oxford, 1912, ii, pp. lxxvii–lxxviii):

I think I have often entertained you with reminiscences of Dr. Donne, now Dean of St. Pauls in London, and on account of this remunerative post (such is the custom of the English) held in high esteem, in still higher for the wealth of his unequalled wit, and yet more incomparable eloquence in the pulpit. Educated at Court in the service of the great; experienced in the ways of the world; sharpened by study; in poetry, he is more famous than anyone. Many rich fruits from the green branches of his wit have lain mellowing among the lovers of art, which now, when nearly rotten with age, they are distributing. Into my hands have fallen, by the help of my special friends among the gentlemen of that nation, some five and twenty of the best sort of medlars. Among our people, I cannot select anyone to whom they ought to be communicated sooner than to you, as this poet's manner of conceit and expression are exactly yours, Sir.

(iii) In an autobiographical poem, *Sermones de Vita Propria*, written in 1687 at the end of his life, Huygens recorded the impression Donne had made upon him over sixty years before (Grierson, op. cit., ii, p. lxxvii):

Suffer me, all-surpassing Donne, virtuous teacher, to name you first and above all; and sing your fame as god-like poet and eloquent preacher. From your golden mouth, whether in the chamber of a friend, or in the pulpit, fell the speech of Gods, whose nectar I drank again and again with heartfelt joy.

15. King Charles I

c. 1629, *c.* 1633

Donne had been Dean of St Paul's over three years when Charles I came to the throne, in 1625, and preached frequently before the king thereafter. The king is sometimes said to have been a devotee of Donne's poetry but there is very little evidence of this.

(i) The Dutch poet Constantine Huygens reported that when Charles I heard of his intention of translating some of Donne's poems into Dutch he 'declared that he did not believe that anyone could acquit himself of that task with credit' (*Koren-Bloemen*, In's Graven-Hage, 1658, pp. 1089–90).

(ii) A copy of the 1633 edition of Donne's poems, now in the British

Museum (press mark G.11415), bears the royal coat of arms stamped on the leather cover, front and back, and is marked 'This Copy appears to have belonged to Charles Iˢᵗ'. The copy has been said to bear marks of the king's interest in particular passages (see H. J. C. Grierson, *The Poems of John Donne*, ii, p. lxxvii). No such marks are now discernible.

16. Anon., manuscript verses on Donne

?1631

A manuscript in the British Museum, MS. Harl. 6918, contains anonymous poems which refer to Donne.

(i)

An Epitaph on Dr Donne

That Epitaph Christ uttered on the Crosse
may be his servants here, in whose great losse
somewhat he seemes to loose for gaine of soules,
for which perswasive power heaven him inrolls;
Christs consummatum was his last best word,
by his worke actuated; what that Lord
purchac'd, this Legate preacht, salvation;
finisht his course, rests in his Christ, tis Donne.

‹f.6ᵛ

(ii) The third stanza of a poem on a dead person makes a reference to lines 19–20 of Donne's *The second Anniversary*:

Elegy

. . . The Lute, saith high sould Donne, thus rings
Even her owne knell with her owne strings;
When suffering too much with the weeping skye
They cracke, the concave groanes an Elegye; . . .

17. Joost van den Vondel

c. 1633

The Dutch poet Vondel (1587–1679) commented in verse on Huygens's translation of Donne's poems into Dutch (see No. 14), indicating that he thought Donne greatly overrated (*Die Werken van Vondel*, ed. J. F. M. Sterck and H. W. E. Moller, Amsterdam, 1929, iii, p. 415). Here is a prose translation of Vondel's lines. 'The Sheriff' is P. C. Hooft, Sheriff of Muiden; Tesselscha was the popular and talented daughter of Roemer-Visscher; and 'Mustard' is Daniel Mostart. All three evidently prized Donne's poetry highly.

On the recondite epigrams of the English poet John Donne, translated by C. Huygens

The English poet Donne, that obscure sun, does not shine for everyone's eyes, Huygens has said, rightly—this language scholar from the Hague, who relishes caviar, snuff and smoking, which clouds the brain of the inexperienced. But this unusual fare is a feast for the Sheriff, and our young friend, sweet Tesselscha. O dear nymph Tesselscha, if you do not understand it, then make a guess at it or get someone to explain it to you: for these are songs more exalted than the Song of Songs of Solomon, which elude the shrewdest minds except the most experienced of learned doctors. But why should my judgement disapprove of what appeals to the taste of my piquant friend, my Mustard, who can never have enough of such salads! Now good people, eat your fill, adding vinegar and peppers; for I do not covet these delicacies at all.

18. The first collected edition of Donne's poems

1633

We do not know who edited *Poems, By J. D. With Elegies on the Authors Death*, 1633. It may have been Donne's friend, the poet Henry King. Whoever it was, he brought together not only Donne's poems but a body of tributes to their author which constitutes far and away the best evidence of what Donne's contemporaries valued in his writings. The items that follow are all given in this edition.

(i) An unsigned address to the reader, presumably by the 'M.F.' who is named on the title page as the printer of the edition for the publisher John Marriot. 'M.F.' was probably Miles Fletcher, a well-known printer of the day:

THE
PRINTER
TO THE
UNDERSTANDERS

For this time I must speake only to you: at another, *Readers* may perchance serve my turne; and I thinke this a way very free from exception, in hope that very few will have a minde to confesse themselves ignorant.

If you looke for an Epistle, as you have before ordinary publications, I am sory that I must deceive you; but you will not lay it to my charge, when you shall consider that this is not ordinary, for if I should say it were the best in this kinde, that ever this Kingdome hath yet seene; he that would doubt of it must goe out of the Kingdome to enforme himself, for the best judgments, within it, take it for granted.

You may imagine (if it please you) that I could endeare it unto you by saying, that importunity drew it on; that had it not beene presented here, it would have come to us from beyond the Seas; (which perhaps is true enough,) That my charge and paines in procuring of it hath beene such, and such. I could adde hereto, a promise of more correctness, or enlargement in the next Edition, if you shall in the meane time content you with this. But these things are so common, as that I should profane this Peece by applying them to it; A Peece which who so takes not as he findes it, in what manner soever, he is unworthy of it, sith a scattered limbe of this Author, hath more amiablenesse in it, in the eye of a discerner, then a whole body of some other; Or, (to expresse him best by himselfe)

> —*A hand, or eye,*
> By Hilyard *drawne, is worth a history*
> By a worse Painter *made;—*

⟨In the Storme⟩

If any man (thinking I speake this to enflame him for the vent of the Impression) be of another opinion, I shall as willingly spare his money as his judgement. I cannot lose so much by him as hee will by himselfe. For I shall satisfie my selfe with the conscience of well doing, in making so much good common.

Howsoever it may appeare to you, it shall suffice mee to enforme you, that it hath the best warrant that can bee, publique authority, and private friends.

There is one thing more wherein I will make you of my counsell, and that is, That whereas it hath pleased some, who had studyed and did admire him, to offer to the memory of the Author, not long after his decease, I have thought I should do you service in presenting them unto you now; onely whereas, had I placed them in the beginning, they might have serv'd for so many Encomiums of the Author (as is usuall in other workes, where perhaps there is need of it, to prepare men to digest such stuffe as follows after,) you shall here finde them in the end, for whosoever reades the rest so farre, shall perceive that there is no occasion to use them to that purpose; yet there they are, as an attestation for their sakes that knew not so much before, to let them see how much honour was attributed to this worthy man, by those that are capable to give it. *Farewell.*

(ii) A preliminary commendation by John Marston (?1575–1634), the satiric poet and playwright who became an Anglican priest. Marston's work owes much to Donne:

Hexastichon Bibliopolae.

I see in his last preach'd, and printed Booke,
His Picture in a sheet; in *Pauls* I looke,
And see his Statue in a sheete of stone,
And sure his body in the grave hath one:
Those sheetes present him dead, these if you buy,
You have him living to Eternity.

JO. MAR.

(iii) An anonymous commendation:

Hexastichon ad Bibliopolam.
Incerti.

In thy Impression of *Donnes* Poems rare,
For his Eternitie thou hast ta'ne care:
'Twas well, and pious; And for ever may
He live: Yet shew I thee a better way;
Print but his Sermons, and if those we buy,
He, We, and Thou shall live t' Eternity.

(iv) The collection of funeral elegies on Donne which concludes the
1633 edition contains some notable criticism of his writings as well as
direct evidence of his reputation among other writers in his own day.
The first elegy is by Henry King (1592–1669), later Bishop of Chichester,
a considerable poet of small output who had been an intimate friend in
Donne's last years. This elegy, with that by Edward Hyde (No. 18 (iv)
(c)), was originally published unsigned in 1632 as an appendix to
Donne's sermon *Deaths Duell*:

(a)
ELEGIES UPON THE AUTHOR

TO THE MEMORIE OF
MY EVER DESIRED FRIEND
D. DONNE.

To have liv'd eminent, in a degree
Beyond our lofty'st flights, that is, like Thee,
Or t' have had too much merit, is not safe;
For, such excesses finde no Epitaph.

At common graves we have Poetique eyes
Can melt themselves in easie Elegies,
Each quill can drop his tributary verse,
And pin it, like the Hatchments, to the Hearse:
But at Thine, Poeme, or Inscription
(Rich soule of wit, and language) we have none.
Indeed a silence does that tombe befit,
Where is no Herald left to blazon it.
Widow'd invention justly doth forbeare
To come abroad, knowing Thou art not here,
Late her great Patron; Whose Prerogative
Maintain'd, and cloth'd her so, as none alive
Must now presume, to keepe her at thy rate,
Though he the Indies for her dowre estate.
Or else that awfull fire, which once did burne
In thy cleare Braine, now falne into thy Urne
Lives there, to fright rude Empiricks from thence,
Which might prophane thee by their Ignorance.
Who ever writes of Thee, and in a stile
Unworthy such a Theme, does but revile
Thy precious Dust, and wake a learned Spirit
Which may revenge his Rapes upon thy Merit.
For, all a low pitch't phansie can devise,
Will prove, at best, but Hallow'd Injuries.
    Thou, like the dying Swanne, didst lately sing
Thy Mournfull Dirge, in audience of the King;
When pale lookes, and faint accents of thy breath,
Presented so, to life, that peece of death,
That it was fear'd, and prophesi'd by all,
Thou thither cam'st to preach thy Funerall.
O! had'st Thou in an Elegiacke Knell
Rung out unto the world thine owne farewell,
And in thy High Victorious Numbers beate
The solemne measure of thy griev'd Retreat;
Thou might'st the Poets Service now have mist
As well, as then thou did'st prevent the Priest;
And never to the world beholding bee
So much, as for an Epitaph for thee.
    I doe not like the office. Nor is 't fit
Thou, who did'st lend our Age such summes of wit,

Should'st now re-borrow from her bankrupt Mine,
That Ore to Bury Thee, which once was Thine,
Rather still leave us in thy debt; And know
(Exalted Soule) more glory 't is to owe
Unto thy Hearse, what we can never pay,
Then, with embased Coine those Rites defray.
   Commit we then Thee to Thy selfe: Nor blame
Our drooping loves, which thus to thy owne Fame
Leave Thee Executour. Since, but thine owne,
No pen could doe Thee Justice, nor Bayes Crowne
Thy vast desert; Save that, wee nothing can
Depute, to be thy Ashes Guardian.
   So Jewellers no Art, or Metall trust
    To forme the Diamond, but the Diamonds dust.
                    H.K.

(b) Probably by Sir Thomas Browne (1605–82), the physician and writer; though Browne was at this time a young medical student who had published nothing of note, and was unknighted. These lines do not appear in subsequent editions of Donne's poems:

To the deceased Author,

Upon the *Promiscuous* printing of his Poems, the
Looser sort, with the *Religious.*

When thy *Loose* raptures, *Donne*, shall meet with Those
      That doe confine
    Tuning, unto the Duller line,
  And sing not, but in *Sanctified Prose*;
    How will they, with sharper eyes,
  The *Fore-skinne* of thy phansie circumcise?
And feare, thy *wantonnesse* should now, begin
Example, that hath ceased to be *Sin*?
And that *Feare* fannes their *Heat*; whilst knowing eyes
      Will not admire
    At this *Strange Fire*,
  That here is *mingled with thy Sacrifice*:
    But dare reade even thy *Wanton Story*,
  As thy *Confession*, not thy *Glory*.

And will so envie *Both* to future times,
That they would buy thy *Goodnesse*, with thy *Crimes*.

                                              Tho: Browne.

(c) Probably by Edward Hyde (1607–59), Anglican divine and theologian; though the future Earl of Clarendon (1609–74) has been suggested:

On the death of Dr DONNE.

I cannot blame those men, that knew thee well,
Yet dare not helpe the world, to ring thy knell
In tunefull *Elegies*; there's not language knowne
Fit for thy mention, but 'twas first thy owne;
The *Epitaphs* thou writst, have so bereft
Our tongue of wit, there is not phansie left
Enough to weepe thee; what henceforth we see
Of Art or Nature, must result from thee.
There may perchance some busie gathering friend
Steale from thy owne workes, and that, varied, lend,
Which thou bestow'st on others, to thy Hearse,
And so thou shalt live still in thine owne verse;
Hee that shall venture farther, may commit
A pitied errour, shew his zeale, not wit.
Fate hath done mankinde wrong; vertue may aime
Reward of conscience, never can, of fame,
Since her great trumpet's broke, could onely give
Faith to the world, command it to beleeve;
  Hee then must write, that would define thy parts:
  Here lyes the best Divinitie, All the Arts.

                                              Edw. Hyde.

(d) By Dr Richard Corbet (1582–1635), Bishop of Oxford and Norwich. Corbet wrote verses and is the author of the well-known poem 'Farewell, rewards and fairies':

On Doctor Donne,
By Dr C. B. of O.

He that would write an Epitaph for thee,
And do it well, must first beginne to be
Such as thou wert; for, none can truly know

Thy worth, thy life, but he that hath liv'd so;
He must have wit to spare and to hurle downe:
Enough, to keepe the gallants of the towne.
He must have learning plenty; both the Lawes,
Civill, and Common, to judge any cause;
Divinity great store, above the rest;
Not of the last Edition, but the best.
He must have language, travaile, all the Arts;
Judgement to use; or else he wants thy parts.
He must have friends the highest, able to do;
Such as *Mecœnas*, and *Augustus* too.
He must have such a sicknesse, such a death;
Or else his vaine descriptions come beneath;
    Who then shall write an Epitaph for thee,
    He must be dead first, let'it alone for mee.

(e) By Henry Valentine (*fl.* 1600–50), Rector of Deptford and later D.D. of the University of Oxford. These are extracts from his long elegy on Donne:

An Elegie upon the incomparable
D[r] DONNE.

All is not well when such a one as I
Dare peepe abroad, and write an *Elegie*;
When smaller *Starres* appeare, and give their light,
Phœbus is gone to bed: Were it not night,
And the world witlesse now that DONNE is dead,
You sooner should have broke, then seene my head.
Dead did I say? Forgive this *Injury*
I doe him, and his worthes *Infinity*,
To say he is but dead; I dare averre
It better may be term'd a *Massacre*,
Then *Sleepe* or *Death*; See how the *Muses* mourne
Upon their oaten *Reeds*, and from his *Vrne*
Threaten the World with this *Calamity*,
    They shall have *Ballads*, but no *Poetry*.

Language lyes speechlesse; and *Divinity*,
Lost such a *Trump* as even to *Extasie*
Could charme the Soule, and had an *Influence*
To teach best *judgements*, and please dullest *Sense*,

The *Court*, the *Church*, the *Vniversitie*,
Lost *Chaplaine, Deane,* and *Doctor*, All these, Three.
  It was his *Merit*, that his *Funerall*
  Could cause a losse so *great* and *generall*. . . .

Me thinkes, *Corruption, Wormes*, what else is foule
Should spare the *Temple* of so faire a *Soule*.
I could beleeve they doe; but that I know
What inconvenience might hereafter grow:
  Succeeding ages would *Idolatrize*,
  And as his *Numbers*, so his *Reliques* prize.

If that Philosopher, which did avow
The world to be but Motes, was living now:
He would affirme that th'*Atomes* of his mould
Were they in severall bodies blended, would
Produce new worlds of *Travellers, Divines,*
Of *Linguists, Poets*: sith these severall *lines*
In him concentred were, and flowing thence
Might fill againe the worlds *Circumference*. . . .

Let this suffice thee, that his *Soule* which flew
A pitch of all admir'd, known but of few,
(Save those of purer mould) is now translated
From Earth to Heaven, and there *Constellated*.
  For, if each *Priest* of God shine as a *Starre*,
  His *Glory* is as his *Gifts*, 'bove others farre.
                                    HEN. VALENTINE.

(f) By Izaac Walton (1593–1683), Donne's friend and biographer, who
later wrote *The Compleat Angler* and the lives of some celebrated contemporary poets and writers. Walton revised his elegy many times and
in 1658 transferred it to his *Life of Donne* where he continued to revise
it in the successive republications of that work (see No. 27 (i)). Thus in
all the seventeenth-century editions of Donne's poems after 1633 the
elegy closes with four additional lines which refer to Donne's 'match-
lesse worth'. In the 1658 edition of the *Life of Donne*, and subsequently,
the poem opens with these lines:

    Our Donne is dead: and we may sighing say,
    We had that man where language chose to stay
    And shew her utmost power. I would not praise
    That, and his great Wit, which in our vaine dayes

JOHN DONNE

Makes others proud; but as these serv'd to unlocke
That Cabinet, his mind, where such a stock
Of knowledge was repos'd, that I lament
Our just and generall cause of discontent.

Most interesting of all, the reference in the 1633 version to Donne's
youth scattering poetry 'wherein/ Was All Philosophie' becomes in the
final form of the poem 'wherein/ Lay Loves Philosophy'. The following
are extracts from the version of the elegy given in 1633:

An Elegie upon Dr Donne.

Is *Donne*, great *Donne* deceas'd? then England say
Thou 'hast lost a man where language chose to stay
And shew it's gracefull power. I would not praise
That and his vast wit (which in these vaine dayes
Make many proud) but as they serv'd to unlock
That Cabinet, his minde: where such a stock
Of knowledge was repos'd, as all lament
(Or should) this generall cause of discontent. . . .

    Dull age, Oh I would spare thee, but th'art worse,
Thou art not onely dull, but hast a curse
Of black ingratitude; if not, couldst thou
Part with *miraculous Donne*, and make no vow
For thee and thine, successively to pay
A sad remembrance to his dying day?
    Did his youth scatter *Poetrie*, wherein
Was all Philosophie? Was every sinne,
Character'd in his *Satyres*? made so foule
That some have fear'd their shapes, and kept their soule
Freer by reading verse? Did he give *dayes*
Past marble monuments, to those, whose praise
He would perpetuate? Did hee (I feare
The dull will doubt:) these at his twentieth yeare?
    But, more matur'd: Did his full soule conceive,
And in harmonious-holy-numbers weave
A *Crowne of sacred sonets*, fit to adorne   *La Corona.*
A dying Martyrs brow: or, to be worne
On that blest head of *Mary Magdalen*:
After she wip'd Christs feet, but not till then? . . .

Did hee (fit for such penitents as shee
And hee to use) leave us a *Litany*?
Which all devout men love, and sure, it shall,
As times grow better, grow more classicall.
Did he write *Hymnes*, for piety and wit
Equall to those great grave *Prudentius* writ?
Spake he all *Languages*? knew he all *Lawes*?
The grounds and use of *Physicke*; but because
'Twas mercenary wav'd it? Went to see
That blessed place of *Christs nativity*?
Did he returne and preach him? preach him so
As none but hee did, or could do? They know
(Such as were blest to heare him know) 'tis truth.
Did he confirme thy age? convert thy youth?
Did he these wonders? And is this deare losse
Mourn'd by so few? (few for so great a crosse.)

(g) By Thomas Carew (?1598–?1639), the poet and courtier, who was at
this time sewer-in-ordinary to King Charles. Carew's elegy contains
some of the most memorable things ever said about Donne's poetry:

An Elegie upon the death of the
Deane of Pauls, D^r. Iohn Donne:
By M^r. Tho: Carie.

Can we not force from widdowed Poetry,
Now thou art dead (Great DONNE) one Elegie
To crowne thy Hearse? Why yet dare we not trust
Though with unkneaded dowe-bak't prose thy dust,
Such as the uncisor'd Churchman from the flower
Of fading Rhetorique, short liv'd as his houre,
Dry as the sand that measures it, should lay
Upon thy Ashes, on the funerall day?
Have we no voice, no tune? Did'st thou dispense
Through all our language, both the words and sense?
'Tis a sad truth; The Pulpit may her plaine,
And sober Christian precepts still retaine,
Doctrines it may, and wholesome Uses frame,
Grave Homilies, and Lectures, But the flame
Of thy brave Soule, that shot such heat and light,
As burnt our earth, and made our darknesse bright,
Committed holy Rapes upon our Will,

Did through the eye the melting heart distill;
And the deepe knowledge of darke truths so teach,
As sense might judge, what phansie could not reach;
Must be desir'd for ever. So the fire,
That fills with spirit and heat the Delphique quire,
Which kindled first by thy Promethean breath,
Glow'd here a while, lies quench't now in thy death;
The Muses garden with Pedantique weedes
O'rspred, was purg'd by thee; The lazie seeds
Of servile imitation throwne away;
And fresh invention planted, Thou didst pay
The debts of our penurious bankrupt age;
Licentious thefts, that make poëtique rage
A Mimique fury, when our soules must bee
Possest, or with Anacreons Extasie,
Or Pindars, not their owne; The subtle cheat
Of slie Exchanges, and the jugling feat
Of two-edg'd words, or whatsoever wrong
By ours was done the Greeke, or Latine tongue,
Thou hast redeem'd, and open'd Us a Mine
Of rich and pregnant phansie, drawne a line
Of masculine expression, which had good
Old Orpheus seene, Or all the ancient Brood
Our superstitious fooles admire, and hold
Their lead more precious, then thy burnish't Gold,
Thou hadst beene their Exchequer, and no more
They each in others dust, had rak'd for Ore.
Thou shalt yield no precedence, but of time,
And the blinde fate of language, whose tun'd chime
More charmes the outward sense; Yet thou maist claime
From so great disadvantage greater fame,
Since to the awe of thy imperious wit
Our stubborne language bends, made only fit
With her tough-thick-rib'd hoopes to gird about
Thy Giant phansie, which had prov'd too stout
For their soft melting Phrases. As in time
They had the start, so did they cull the prime
Buds of invention many a hundred yeare,
And left the rifled fields, besides the feare
To touch their Harvest, yet from those bare lands

Of what is purely thine, thy only hands
(And that thy smallest worke) have gleaned more
Then all those times, and tongues could reape before;
But thou art gone, and thy strict lawes will be
Too hard for Libertines in Poetrie.
They will repeale the goodly exil'd traine
Of gods and goddesses, which in thy just raigne
Were banish'd nobler Poems, now, with these
The silenc'd tales o'th'Metamorphoses
Shall stuffe their lines, and swell the windy Page,
Till Verse refin'd by thee, in this last Age,
Turne ballad rime, Or those old Idolls bee
Ador'd againe, with new apostasie;
Oh, pardon mee, that breake with untun'd verse
The reverend silence that attends thy herse,
Whose awfull solemne murmures were to thee
More then these faint lines, A loud Elegie,
That did proclaime in a dumbe eloquence
The death of all the Arts, whose influence
Growne feeble, in these panting numbers lies
Gasping short winded Accents, and so dies:
So doth the swiftly turning wheele not stand
In th'instant we withdraw the moving hand,
But some small time maintaine a faint weake course
By vertue of the first impulsive force:
And so whil'st I cast on thy funerall pile
Thy crowne of Bayes, Oh, let it crack a while,
And spit disdaine, till the devouring flashes
Suck all the moysture up, then turne to ashes.
I will not draw the envy to engrosse
All thy perfections, or weepe all our losse;
Those are too numerous for an Elegie,
And this too great, to be express'd by mee.
Though every pen should share a distinct part,
Yet art thou Theme enough to tyre all Art;
Let others carve the rest, it shall, suffice
I on thy Tombe this Epitaph incise.

  Here lies a King, that rul'd as hee thought fit
  The universall Monarchy of wit;

> Here lie two Flamens, and both those, the best,
> Apollo's first, at last, the true Gods Priest.

(h) By Sir Lucius Cary (1610–43), poet and courtier, who became Viscount Falkland in 1633. The following are extracts from Cary's elegy:

An Elegie on Dʳ DONNE: By Sir Lucius Carie.

Poets attend, the Elegie I sing
Both of a double-named Priest, and King:
In stead of Coates, and Pennons, bring your Verse,
For you must bee chiefe mourners at his Hearse,
A Tombe your Muse must to his Fame supply,
No other Monuments can never die;
And as he was a two-fold Priest; in youth,
Apollo's; afterwards, the voice of Truth,
Gods Conduit-pipe for grace, who chose him for
His extraordinary Embassador,
So let his Liegiers with the Poets joyne,
Both having shares, both must in griefe combine:
Whil'st Johnson forceth with his Elegie
Teares from a griefe-unknowing Scythians eye,
(Like Moses at whose stroke the waters gusht
From forth the Rock, and like a Torrent rusht.)
Let Lawd his funerall Sermon preach, and shew
Those vertures, dull eyes were not apt to know, . . .

Nor only in the Pulpit dwelt his store,
His words work'd much, but his example more,
That preach't on worky dayes, His Poetrie
It selfe was oftentimes divinity,
Those Anthemes (almost second Psalmes) he writ
To make us know the Crosse, and value it,
(Although we owe that reverence to that name
Wee should not need warmth from an under flame.)
Creates a fire in us, so neare extreme
That we would die, for, and upon this theme.
Next, his so pious Litany, which none can
But count Divine, except a Puritan,
And that but for the name, nor this, nor those
Want any thing of Sermons, but the prose. . . .

Now to conclude, I must my reason bring,
Wherefore I call'd him in his title King,
That Kingdome the Philosophers beleev'd
To excell Alexanders, nor were griev'd
By feare of losse (that being such a Prey
No stronger then ones selfe can force away)
The Kingdome of ones selfe, this he enjoy'd,
And his authoritie so well employ'd,
That never any could before become
So Great a Monarch, in so small a roome;
He conquer'd rebell passions, rul'd them so,
As under-spheares by the first Mover goe,
Banish't so farre their working, that we can
But know he had some, for we knew him man.
Then let his last excuse his first extremes,
His age saw visions, though his youth dream'd dreames.

(i) By Jasper Mayne (1604–72), poet and dramatist, who later abandoned
poetry and became an Anglican divine:

On Dr DONNES *death:*
By M^r. Mayne *of Christ-Church in Oxford.*

Who shall presume to mourn thee, *Donne*, unlesse
He could his teares in thy expressions dresse,
And teach his griefe that reverence of thy Hearse,
To weepe lines, learned, as thy Anniverse,
A Poëme of that worth, whose every teare
Deserves the title of a severall yeare.
Indeed so farre above its Reader, good,
That wee are thought wits, when 'tis understood,
There that blest maid to die, who now should grieve?
After thy sorrow, 'twere her losse to live;
And her faire vertues in anothers line,
Would faintly dawn, which are made Saints in thine.
Hadst thou beene shallower, and not writ so high,
Or left some new way for our pennes, or eye,
To shed a funerall teare, perchance thy Tombe
Had not beene speechlesse, or our Muses dumbe;
But now wee dare not write, but must conceale
Thy Epitaph, lest we be thought to steale,

For, who hath read thee, and discernes thy worth,
That will not say, thy carelesse houres brought forth
Fancies beyond our studies, and thy play
Was happier, then our serious time of day?
So learned was thy chance; thy haste had wit,
And matter from thy pen flow'd rashly fit,
What was thy recreation turnes our braine,
Our rack and palenesse, is thy weakest straine.
And when we most come neere thee, 'tis our blisse
To imitate thee, where thou dost amisse.
Here light your muse, you that do onely thinke,
And write, and are just Poëts, as you drinke,
In whose weake fancies wit doth ebbe and flow,
Just as your recknings rise, that wee may know
In your whole carriage of your worke, that here
This flash you wrote in Wine, and this in Beere,
This is to tap your Muse, which running long
Writes flat, and takes our eare not halfe so strong;
Poore Suburbe wits, who, if you want your cup,
Or if a Lord recover, are blowne up.
Could you but reach this height, you should not need
To make, each meale, a project ere you feed,
Nor walke in reliques, clothes so old and bare,
As if left off to you from *Ennius* were,
Nor should your love, in verse, call Mistresse, those,
Who are mine hostesse, or your whores in prose;
From this Muse learne to Court, whose power could move
A Cloystred coldnesse, or a Vestall love,
And would convey such errands to their eare,
That Ladies knew no oddes to grant and heare;
But I do wrong thee, *Donne*, and this low praise
Is written onely for thy yonger dayes.
I am not growne up, for thy riper parts,
Then should I praise thee, through the Tongues, and Arts,
And have that deepe Divinity, to know,
What mysteries did from thy preaching flow,
Who with thy words could charme thy audience,
That at thy sermons, eare was all our sense;
Yet have I seene thee in the pulpit stand,
Where wee might take notes, from thy looke, and hand;

And from thy speaking action beare away
More Sermon, then some teachers use to say.
Such was thy carriage, and thy gesture such,
As could divide the heart, and conscience touch.
Thy motion did confute, and wee might see
An errour vanquish'd by delivery.
Not like our Sonnes of Zeale, who to reforme
Their hearers, fiercely at the Pulpit storme,
And beate the cushion into worse estate,
Then if they did conclude it reprobate,
Who can out pray the glasse, then lay about
Till all Predestination be runne out.
And from the point such tedious uses draw
Their repetitions would make Gospell Law.
No, In such temper would thy Sermons flow,
So well did Doctrine, and thy language-show,
And had that holy feare, as, hearing thee,
The Court would mend, and a good Christian bee.
And Ladies though unhansome, out of grace,
Would heare thee, in their unbought lookes, and face.
More I could write, but let this crowne thine Urne,
Wee cannot hope the like, till thou returne.

(j) By Arthur Wilson (1595–1652), dramatist, historian, and civil servant:

Upon Mr J. Donne, and his Poems.

Who dares say thou art dead, when he doth see
  (Unburied yet) this living part of thee?
This part that to thy beeing gives fresh flame,
  And though th'art *Donne,* yet will preserve thy name.
Thy flesh (whose channels left their crimsen hew,
  And whey-like ranne at last in a pale blew)
May shew thee mortall, a dead palsie may
  Seise on't, and quickly turne it into clay;
Which like the Indian earth, shall rise refin'd:
  But this great Spirit thou hast left behinde,
This Soule of Verse (in it's first pure estate)
  Shall live, for all the World to imitate,
But not come neer, for in thy Fancies flight
  Thou dost not stoope unto the vulgar sight,

99

But, hovering highly in the aire of Wit,
    Hold'st such a pitch, that few can follow it;
Admire they may. Each object that the Spring
    (Or a more piercing influence) doth bring
T'adorne Earths face, thou sweetly did'st contrive
    To beauties elements, and thence derive
Unspotted Lillies white; which thou did'st set
    Hand in hand, with the veine-like Violet,
Making them soft, and warme, and by thy power,
    Could'st give both life, and sense, unto a flower.
The Cheries thou hast made to speake, will bee
    Sweeter unto the taste, then from the tree.
And (spight of winter stormes) amidst the snow
    Thou oft hast made the blushing Rose to grow.
The Sea-nimphs, that the watry cavernes keepe,
    Have sent their Pearles and Rubies from the deepe
To deck thy love, and plac'd by thee, they drew
    More lustre to them, then where first they grew.
All minerals (that Earths full wombe doth hold
    Promiscuously) thou couldst convert to gold,
And with thy flaming raptures so refine,
    That it was much more pure then in the Mine.
The lights that guild the night, if thou did'st say,
    They looke like eyes, those did out-shine the day;
For there would be more vertue in such spells,
    Then in Meridians, or crosse Parallels:
What ever was of worth in this great Frame,
    That Art could comprehend, or Wit could name,
It was thy theme for Beauty; thou didst see,
    Woman, was this faire Worlds Epitomie.
Thy nimble *Satyres* too, and every straine
    (With nervy strength) that issued from thy brain,
Will lose the glory of their owne cleare bayes,
    If they admit of any others praise.
But thy diviner Poëms (whose cleare fire
    Purges all drosse away) shall by a Quire
Of Cherubims, with heavenly Notes be set
    (Where flesh and blood could ne'r attaine to yet)
There purest Spirits sing such sacred Layes,
    In Panegyrique Alleluiaes.   *Arth. Wilson.*

(k) Possibly by Richard Braithwaite (?1588–1673), a poet and voluminous writer. But Ralph Brideoake (1613–78), a minor versifier who much later became Bishop of Chichester, has also been suggested, as has Richard Brome (d. ?1652), the dramatist, friend of Ben Jonson. The following are some extracts from the elegy:

In memory of Doctor Donne:
*By M*r R. B.

. . . Mee thinkes some Comet bright should have foretold
The death of such a man, for though of old
'Tis held, that Comets Princes death foretell,
Why should not his, have needed one as well?
Who was the Prince of wits, 'mongst whom he reign'd,
High as a Prince, and as great State maintain'd?
Yet wants he not his signe, for wee have seene
A dearth, the like to which hath never beene,
Treading on harvests heeles, which doth presage
The death of wit and learning, which this age
Shall finde, now he is gone; for though there bee
Much graine in shew, none brought it forth as he,
Or men are misers; or if true want raises
The dearth, then more than dearth *Donnes* plenty praises.
Of learning, languages, of eloquence,
And Poësie, (past ravishing of sense,)
He had a magazine, wherein such store
Was laid up, as might hundreds serve of poore.

But he is gone, O how will his desire
Torture all those that warm'd them by his fire?
Mee thinkes I see him in the pulpit standing,
Not eares, or eyes, but all mens hearts commanding,
Where wee that heard him, to our selves did faine
Golden Chrysostome was alive againe;
And never were we weari'd, till we saw
His houre (and but an houre) to end did draw.
How did he shame the doctrine-men, and use,
With helps to boot, for men to beare th'abuse
Of their tir'd patience, and endure th'expence
Of time, O spent in hearkning to non-sense,
With markes also, enough whereby to know,
The speaker is a zealous dunce, or so.

'Tis true, they quitted him, to their poore power,
They humm'd against him; And with face most sowre
Call'd him a strong lin'd man, a Macaroon,
And no way fit to speak to clouted shoone,
As fine words ‹truly› as you would desire,
But ‹verily,› but a bad edifier.
Thus did these beetles slight in him that good,
They could not see, and much lesse understood.
But we may say, when we compare the stuffe
Both brought; He was a candle, they the snuffe. . . .

    But what doe I? A diminution 'tis
To speake of him in verse, so short of his,
Whereof he was the master; All indeed
Compar'd with him, pip'd on an Oaten reed.
O that you had but one 'mongst all your brothers
Could write for him, as he hath done for others:
(Poets I speake to) When I see't, I'll say,
My eye-sight betters, as my yeares decay,
Meane time a quarrell I shall ever have
Against these doughty keepers from the grave,
Who use, it seemes their old Authoritie,
When (Verses men immortall make) they cry:
Which had it been a Recipe true tri'd,
Probatum esset, DONNE had never dy'd.

    For mee, if e'r I had least sparke at all
Of that which they Poetique fire doe call,
Here I confesse it fetched from his hearth,
Which is gone out, now he is gone to earth.
This only a poore flash, a lightning is
Before my Muses death, as after his.
Farewell (faire soule) and deigne receive from mee
This Type of that devotion I owe thee,
From whom (while living) as by voice and penne
I learned more, then from a thousand men:
So by thy death, am of one doubt releas'd,
And now beleeve that miracles are ceas'd.

(l) By Endymion Porter (1587–1649), ambassador, courtier, and patron of poets. Porter was one of Charles I's chief advisers on paintings and helped build the royal collection. The following is an extract from his elegy:

Epitaph upon Dr. DONNE,
By *Endy: Porter.*

. . . Now from the Pulpit to the peoples eares,
Whose speech shall send repentant sighes, and teares?
Or tell mee, if a purer Virgin die,
Who shall hereafter write her Elegie?
Poets be silent, let your numbers sleepe,
For he is gone that did all phansie keepe;
Time hath no Soule, but his exalted verse;
Which with amazements, we may now reherse.

19. Lord Herbert of Cherbury

c. 1633

The poet Edward Herbert (1583–1648), who became Baron
Herbert of Cherbury in 1629, was the brother of George Herbert
and the son of Donne's intimate friend and patroness Mrs
Magdalen Herbert. Donne visited Sir Edward Herbert (as he was
then) at the family home, Montgomery Castle, in the spring of
1613 and several of his poems are connected with that journey
and sojourn. Edward Herbert's poems were not published until
long after his death but the elegy for Donne, from which the
following is a short extract, was evidently written very little
later than the elegies given in *1633*.

Elegy for Doctor Dunn
. . . Having delivered now what praises are,
It rests that I should to the world declare
Thy praises, DUNN, whom I so lov'd alive
That with my witty Carew I should strive

To celebrate the dead, did I not need
A language by itself, which should exceed
All those which are in use: For while I take
Those common words, which men may even rake
From Dunghill-wits, I find them so defiled,
Slubber'd and false, as if they had exiled
Truth and propriety, such as do tell
So little other things, they hardly spell
Their proper meaning, and therefore unfit
To blazon forth thy merits, or thy wit.

Nor will it serve that thou didst so refine
Matter with words that both did seem divine
When thy breath utter'd them, for thou being gone
They streight did follow thee. Let therefore none
Hope to find out an Idiom and Sense
Equal to thee and to thy Eminence, . . .

20. 'J.V.'

c. 1633

A copy of the 1633 edition of Donne's poems now in the library of Christ Church, Oxford, carries some lines written in commendation of the book and of Donne. They are signed with the initials 'J.V.', but a Latin line scribbled below them gives the name 'Vaughani'. They may well have been written by John Vaughan (1603–74), a Christ Church man who had a distinguished career in law and was knighted in 1668.

An early offer of him to your sight
Was the best way to doe the Author right
My thoughts could fall on; which his soule which knew
The weight of a just Prayse will think't true.
Our commendation is suspected, when
Wee Elegyes compose on sleeping men,
The Manners of the Age prevayling so
That not our conscience wee, but witts doe show.
And 'tis an often gladnes, that men dye
Of unmatch'd names to write more easyly.
Such my religion is of him; I hold
It injury to have his merrit tould;
Who (like the Sunn) is righted best when wee
Doe not dispute but shew his quality.
Since all the speech of light is less than it.
An eye to that is still the best of witt.
And nothing can express, for truth or haste
So happily, a sweetnes as our taste.
Which thought at once instructed me in this
Safe way to prayse him, and your hands to kisse.
                    Affectionately yours
                         J.V.

21. Thomas Carew

c. 1633

Carew (?1595–?1639) and Aurelian Townsend (*fl.* 1601–43) were fellow-members of the circle of wits and poets at the Court of Charles I, and both of them wrote masques and poems which were highly regarded at Court. Carew's intelligent admiration of Donne's poetry is plain in the elegy he wrote for Donne's death, which was given in the 1633 edition of the poems (see No. 18 (g)). In the following extract Carew protests that he is incapable of writing a worthy poem on the death of the King of Sweden. King Gustavus Adolfus, the hope of Protestant Europe, had been killed in battle in 1632.

In answer of an Elegaicall Letter upon the death of the King of Sweden *from* Aurelian Townsend, *inviting me to write on that subject*

> . . . Alas! how may
> My Lyrique feet, that of the smooth soft way
> Of Love, and Beautie, onely know the tread,
> In dancing paces celebrate the dead
> Victorious King, or his Majesticke Hearse
> Prophane with th'humble touch of their low verse?
> *Virgil*, nor *Lucan*, no, nor *Tasso*, more
> Then both, not *Donne*, worth all that went before,
> With the united labour of their wit,
> Could a just Poem to this subject fit,
> His actions were too mighty to be rais'd
> Higher by verse: let him in prose be prays'd,
> In modest faithful story, which his deedes
> Shall turn to Poëms. . . .

22. Thomas Pestell

c. 1633–52

Pestell (1585–1667) was a divine, who served as chaplain to the Earl of Essex in the Civil War, and a copious minor poet. All items here save the last are given from *The Poems of Thomas Pestell*, ed. H. Buchan, Oxford, 1940.

(i) An extract from 'Elegie on the noble Eliz: Countess of Hunt'. Elizabeth Hastings, Countess of Huntingdon, to whom Donne addressed several laudatory verse letters, died in 1633.

> Call Godlike Sydney from Elizian shade
> (So might a noble Epitaph be made)
> Then let the gentle Beaumont rise, and he
> Of whom all poëts hold in Capite
> Black prince of witts, ye most illustrious Dunn
> To make new Seas of praise that upwards run.

(ii) From 'Elegie on the truly noble Katherine Countesse of Chesterfield, 1636':

> Come glorious Drury Donns eternall mayd . . .
> Not such a mistresse, but herself to grace
> Donns wittsick muse chose an Autumnall face; . . .

(iii) An epigram dated 1640 refers to the verse letter 'Since ev'ry Tree beginns to blossome now' written in alternate stanzas by Donne and Sir Henry Goodyer:

> Here two rich ravisht spirrits kisse and twyne;
> Advanc'd, and weddLockt in each others Lyne.
> Gooderes rare match with only him was blest,
> Who haes out donne, and quite undonne the rest.

(iv) In 'On Dr T. Goad and Dr H. King two rare Divines and poëts', *c.* 1650:

. . . and hee: (D. Don)
  The late Copernicus in Poëtrie,
  That rappt the whole Earth round, and gave it sence,
  Of Love, to move by his Intelligence. . . .

(v) An extract from a commendatory poem 'For the Author, Truly Heroick, by Bloud, Virtue, Learning' in *Preface to Benlowe's Theophila*, 1652:

  . . . But, Sir, as though HEAV'NS Straits discover'd were,
  By Science of your Card, UNKNOWNS appear:
  Sail then with *Prince* of *Wits*, illustrious *Dunne*,
  Who rapt Earth round with *Love*, and was its *Sun*.

23. George Garrard

1634

Garrard was one of Donne's closest friends and most frequent correspondents from the time they shared lodgings between 1607 and 1611; Donne treated him as his literary confidant. He was the second son of Sir William Garrard and came of wealthy merchant stock on both sides. In late life he entered the service of the Percy family, with whom Donne too had close connections, and then became Master of the Charterhouse, of which Donne had been a governor.

He mentioned Donne's poems in a letter to Viscount Wentworth (later Earl of Strafford) written 1 November 1634, several years after Donne's death (*The Earl of Strafford's Letters and Dispatches*, ed. W. Knowler, 1739, i, p. 338).

I send your Lordship Verses made in the Progress. I that never had Patience in all my life to transcribe Poems, except they were very transcendent, such as Dean *Donn* writ in his younger Days, did these with some Pain.

24. The second collected edition of Donne's poems

1635

The 1635 edition of Donne's poems was again 'Printed by M.F. for John Marriot' and edited anonymously. This unknown editor didn't just follow his predecessor but added about a dozen poems by Donne (as well as a number of spurious ones), and gave three fresh elegies on the author. It is in this edition that the poems first appear in their familiar groups under such headings as *Songs and Sonets, Epicedes and Obsequies, Divine Poems*. Here, too, some poems are given the titles by which we know them.

Poems added in *1635* include 'Farewell to Love', 'A Lecture upon the Shadow' (called 'Song'), four of the *Elegies* which had been excluded from *1633*, several funeral elegies, and several *Divine Poems*, among them the 'Hymn to God my God, in my Sicknesse'.

25. John Chudleigh and Sidney Godolphin

1635

Funeral elegies on Donne by 'I. Chudleigh' and Sidney Godolphin were added to the body of *Elegies upon the Author* in the 1635 edition of Donne's poems and given in the subsequent seventeenth-century editions of the poems. John Chudleigh (?1606–?1634) is known for a few poems in manuscript collections. Godolphin (1610–43), M.P. for Helston, was a poet of note among the Court wits of the 1630s and friend of the great men of the day; he fought on the royalist side in the Civil War and fell in a skirmish at Chagford.

(i) Extracts from Chudleigh's elegy:

> On Dr John Donne, *late Deane of S*. Paules, *London*.
> Long since this taske of teares from you was due,
> Long since, ô Poëts, he did die to you,
> Or left you dead, when wit and he tooke flight
> On divine wings, and soard out of your sight.
> Preachers, 'tis you must weep; The wit he taught
> You doe enjoy; the Rebels which he brought
> From ancient discord, Giants faculties,
> And now no more religions enemies;
> Honest to knowing, unto vertuous sweet,
> Witty to good, and learned to discreet,
> He reconcil'd, and bid the Vsurper goe;
> Dulnesse to vice, religion ought to flow;
> He kept his loves, but not his objects; wit
> Hee did not banish, but transplanted it,
> Taught it his place and use, and brought it home
> To Pietie, which it doth best become;
> He shew'd us how for sinnes we ought to sigh,

And how to sing Christs Epithalamy:
The Altars had his fires, and there hee spoke
Incense of loves, and fansies holy smoake:
Religion thus enrich'd, the people train'd,
And God from dull vice had the fashion gain'd.
The first effects sprung in the giddy minde
Of flashy youth, and thirst of woman-kinde,
By colours lead, and drawne to a pursuit,
Now once againe by beautie of the fruit,
As if their longings too must set us free,
And tempt us now to the commanded tree.
Tell me, had ever pleasure such a dresse,
Have you knowne crimes so shap'd? or lovelinesse
Such as his lips did cloth religion in?
Had not reproofe a beauty passing sinne?
Corrupted nature sorrow'd when she stood
So neare the danger of becomming good,
And wish'd our so inconstant eares exempt
From piety that had such power to tempt:
Did not his sacred flattery beguile
Man to amendment? The law, taught to smile,
Pension'd our vanitie, and man grew well
Through the same frailtie by which he fell. . . .

Who treats with us must our affections move
To th' good we flie by those sweets which we love,
Must seeke our palats, and with their delight
To gaine our deeds, must bribe our appetite.
These traines he knew, and laying nets to save,
Temptingly sugred all the health hee gave.
But, where is now that chime? that harmony
Hath left the world, now the loud organ may
Appeare, the better voyce is fled to have
A thousand times the sweetnesse which it gave.

(ii) Godolphin's elegy:

Elegie on D. D.

Now, by one yeare, time and our frailtie have
Lessened our first confusion, since the Grave
Clos'd thy deare Ashes, and the teares which flow

In these, have no springs, but of solid woe:
Or they are drops, which cold amazement froze
At thy decease, and will not thaw in Prose:
All streames of Verse which shall lament that day,
Doe truly to the Ocean tribute pay;
But they have lost their saltnesse, which the eye
In recompence of wit, strives to supply:
Passions excesse for thee wee need not feare,
Since first by thee our passions hallowed were;
Thou mad'st our sorrowes, which before had bin
Onely for the Successe, sorrowes for sinne,
We owe thee all those teares, now thou art dead,
Which we shed not, which for our selves we shed.
Nor didst thou onely consecrate our teares,
Give a religious tincture to our feares;
But even our joyes had learn'd an innocence,
Thou didst from gladness separate offence:
All mindes at once suckt grace from thee, as where
(The curse revok'd) the Nations had one eare.
Pious dissector: thy one houre did treate
The thousand mazes of the hearts deceipt;
Thou didst pursue our lov'd and subtill sinne,
Through all the foldings wee had wrapt it in,
And in thine owne large minde finding the way
By which our selves we from our selves convey,
Didst in us, narrow models, know the same
Angles, though darker, in our meaner frame.
How short of praise is this? My Muse, alas,
Climbes weakly to that truth which none can passe,
Hee that writes best, may onely hope to leave
A Character of all he could conceive
But none of thee, and with mee must confesse,
That fansie findes some checke, from an excesse
Of merit most, of nothing, it hath spun,
And truth, as reasons task and theame, doth shunne.
She makes a fairer flight in emptinesse,
Than when a bodied truth doth her oppresse.
Reason againe denies her scales, because
Hers are but scales, shee judges by the lawes
Of weake comparison, thy vertue sleights

Her feeble Beame, and her unequall Weights.
What prodigie of wit and pietie
Hath she else knowne, by which to measure thee?
Great soule: we can no more the worthinesse
Of what you were, then what you are, expresse.

Sidney Godolphin.

26. Anon., *Wit's Triumvirate*

1635

An anonymous comedy called *Wit's Triumvirate, or The Philo-sopher*, which was presented at Court in 1635 (but never published), has several allusions to the literary fashions then current. (British Museum Add. MS. 45865. See S. Schoenbaum, 'Wit's Triumvirate: A Caroline Comedy Recovered', *SEL*, 1, IV, winter 1964, pp. 227–37.)

(i) In Act 1, Scene 4, one Clyster remarks to Sir Cupid Phantsy, a rhyming lover, that verse which hobbles and is rough 'is the fashion now'. Sir Phantsy replies, 'I S^r, for those that can make no better.'

(ii) Later in the same scene Phantsy bursts out against orthodox love poets:

> In whineing Poetry to weepe, sigh, groane;
> And say thy Hart's hard Flint, or Marblestone,
> A frozen Statue of cold Ice, or snowe;
> I hate these equally, I'll not say soe.
> Prythee as I then scorne these wittless Things,
> Wee'l fly a higher pitch, wth unimp't wings;
> And see what Stuff doth make the bright hott Sun.
> And in our Similies damne Doctor Dunne.

The name 'Dunne' has been scored through in the manuscript.

27. Izaac Walton

1635–75

Walton (1593–1683), author of *The Compleat Angler*, was also the first biographer of Donne and Herbert among others. He was Donne's parishioner in the 1620s and, he claimed, his convert; certainly he was one of the privileged visitors at Donne's death-bed. The brilliant *Life and Death of Dr Donne*, first published with Donne's *LXXX Sermons* in 1640, has peculiar value as the unique testimony of a friend though it cannot be taken for an accurate record of facts. Walton is chiefly concerned with the pattern of Donne's life and priesthood, but his admiration of Donne's poetry breaks out in occasional quotations and in the comments which are given below.

The *Life of Donne* was reissued separately in 1658, and then given as the first of the *Lives* from 1670 on. Walton revised it for each new issue and the revisions that bear upon Donne's poetry are noted.

(i) As well as the funeral elegy on Donne first printed in the 1633 edition of Donne's poems (see No. 18(iv)(f)), Walton wrote an epigram which was printed underneath the engraved portrait of Donne, to which it refers, in the second edition of the poems, 1635:

> This was for youth, Strength, Mirth, and wit that Time
> Most count their golden Age; but t'was not thine.
> Thine was thy later yeares, so much refind
> From youths Drosse, Mirth, and wit; as thy pure mind
> Thought (like the Angels) nothing but the Praise
> Of thy Creator, in those last, best Dayes.
> Witnes this Booke, (thy Embleme) which begins
> With Love; but endes, with Sighes, and Teares for sins.
>
> IZ: WA:

(ii) Walton made some 'Notes for the Life of Dr Donne' before the *Life* was first published in 1640 (they are given in *The Compleat Walton*, ed. G. Keynes, 1928, p. 579). He refers to Donne's prose letters, the 'letter to Tilman', 'Sir Philip Sidney's Salms', and the elegies on Donne, especially those by Chudleigh and Godolphin. There are also several attempts at formulating one of the best known critical sentiments in the *Life*:

on this book folyo 28, of himns and psalms wch was his holy recreation the latter part of his life and is now his imployment in heven where he makes new ditties in his praise of that god in 3 persons to whome be glorie.

And his better part is now doing that in heaven which was most of his imployment on earth magnifying the mercies and making himns and singing them, to that god to whome be glory and honor.

in heaven wher his imployment is to sing such himns as he made on erth in prase of that god to whome be glory and honor.

(iii) From the 1640 version of *The Life and Death of Dr Donne*, speaking here of Donne's ordination in January 1615 (*LXXX Sermons*, 1640, B2):

Now all his studies (which were occasionally diffused) were concentrated in Divinity; Now he had a new calling, new thoughts, new imployment for his wit and eloquence. Now all his earthly affections were changed into divine love, and all the faculties of his soule were ingaged in the conversion of others, in preaching glad tidings, remission to repenting sinners, and peace to each troubled soule: To this he applyed himselfe with all care and diligence; and such a change was wrought in him, that he was *gladder to be a doore-keeper in the house of God, then to enjoy any temporall employment.*

(iv) The following passage, a comment on Donne's poetic career, evidently gave Walton concern over the years for he continued to modify it down to 1670. The text below is that of the 1640 *Life* with the later variants and additions given in square brackets (*1640* B4^r–^{v}; *1658*, pp. 75–86; *1670*, pp. 54–61; *1675*, pp. 52–9):

The recreations of his youth were Poetry, in which he was so happy, as if nature with all her varieties had been made to exercise his great wit [sharp wit, *1658–75*], and high fancy. And in those pieces which were carelessly scattered in his younger daies [were facetiously Composed and carelessly scattered, *1658–75*] (most of them being written before the twentieth yeare of his age) it may appeare by his choice Metaphors, that all the Arts joynd to assist him with their utmost skill.

It is a truth, that in his penitentiall yeares, viewing some of those pieces loosely scattered [that had been loosely (God knows too loosely) scattered, *1670–75*] in his youth, he wisht they had been abortive, or so short-liv'd, that he had witnessed their funeralls: But though he was no friend to them, he was not so falne out with heavenly Poetry, as to forsake it, no not in his declining age, witnessed then by many divine Sonnets, and other high, holy, and harmonious composures; yea even on his former sick bed, he wrote this heavenly Hymne, expressing the great joy he then had in the assurance of Gods mercy to him

A Hymne to God the Father
[he gives it entire]

[I have the rather mentioned this *Hymne*, for that he caus'd it to be set to a most grave and solemn tune, and to be often sung to the *Organ* by the *Choristers* of that *Church* in his own hearing, especially at the Evening Service; and at his return from his Customary Devotions in that place, did occasionally say to a friend, *The words of this* Hymne *have restored to me the same thoughts of joy that possest my soule in my sicknesse when I composed it. And, Oh the power of Church musick! that Harmony added to it has raised the affections of my heart, and quickned my graces of zeal and gratitude*; and I observe, *that I alwaies return from paying this publick duty of* Prayer *and* Praise *to God, with an unexpressible tranquillity of mind*, and a willingness *to leave the world.* . . .

. . . he did also shorten and beguile many sad hours by composing other sacred Ditties; and he writ an Hymn on his death-bed, which beares this title, *An Hymn to God my God in my sicknesse, March 23, 1630. 1658–75*]

And on this (which was his Death-bed) writ another Hymne which bears this Title,

A Hymne to God my God in my sicknesse.

If these fall under the censure of a soule whose too much mixture with earth makes it unfit to judge of these high illuminations, let him know, that many devout and learned men have thought the soule of holy *Prudentius* was most refined, when not many dayes before his death, he charged it to present his God each morning with a new and spirituall Song; . . .

[He cites King David and King Hezekias as people who didn't disdain to write sacred songs]

(v) From the 1640 version of the *Life* (C^r):

His fancie was un-imitable high, equalled by his great wit, both being made usefull by a commanding judgement.

(vi) The following passage was added in the 1675 version of the *Life*, immediately after the story of Donne's vision of his wife when he was in France in 1611–12. It is not foreshadowed by anything Walton had written before and presumably represents his latest view of Donne more than forty years after the poet's death. In admitting one of Donne's love poems to the *Life* for the first time, with such high praise, he was careful to indicate that it was written for Mrs Donne, and he thus gave the poem and that supposed circumstance a fame which persisted down into the nineteenth century among commentators who sometimes seem to have read nothing else of Donne for themselves (*Life*, 1675, pp. 32–4):

I forbear the Readers farther trouble, as to the relation and what concerns it; and will conclude mine, with commending to his view a Copy of Verses given by Mr *Donne* to his wife at the time that he then parted from her. And I beg leave to tell, that I have heard some Criticks, learned, both in Languages and Poetry, say, that none of the Greek or Latine Poets did ever equal them.

[He quotes the whole of 'A Valediction, forbidding to Mourn', as he entitles it.]

(vii) In the *Life of Sir Henry Wotton*, published in 1651, Walton alluded to the lifelong friendship between Wotton and Donne which began when they were at Oxford together (*Reliquiae Wottonianae*, 2nd ed., 1654, pp. 22–3 and 36–8):

I must not omit the mention of a love that was there begun betwixt him and Doctour *Donne* . . . a man of whose abilities I shall forbear to say anything, because he of this Nation, that pretends to Learning or ingenuity, and is ignorant of Doctour Donne, deserves not to know him. The friendship of these two, I must not omit to mention, being such a friendship, as was generously elemented; And as it was begun in their youth, and in an University, and there maintained by correspondent Inclinations and Studies, so it lasted till Age and Death forced a Separation.

[Walton later gives Donne's verse letter 'To Sir Henry Wotton, at his going Ambassador to Venice' ('After those *reverend Papers*').]

(viii) In *The Compleat Angler*, 1653, pp. 66–8 and 184–6, Walton has a milkmaid sing Marlowe's 'Passionate Shepherd to his Love' and her mother sing Raleigh's reply; later on Viator speaks Donne's poem 'The Baite', introducing it as

a Copie of Verses that were made by Doctor *Donne*, and made to shew the world that hee could make soft and smooth Verses, when he thought fit and worth his labour; and I love them the better, because they allude to Rivers, and fish, and fishing.

Piscator replies to the reading

Well remembered, honest Scholer. I thank you for those choice Verses, which I have heard formerly, but had quite forgot, till they were recovered by your happie memorie.

28. Nathaniel Whiting

1637

We know little more of Whiting than that he was a Queens' College, Cambridge, man who became a Puritan minister and flourished 1629–63. His *Il Insonio Insonnadado*, 1637, one of two long narratives he wrote in verse, is a vindication of poetry by way of a dream-fiction. The poet is taken before Jove, and an actor speaks a panegyric of poetry and poets which includes a praise of Donne (lines 429–32).

Dun was a Poet, and a grave Divine,
Highly esteemed for the sacred Nine,
That aftertimes shall say whilest there's a Sun,
This Verse, this Sermon was compos'd by *Dun*.

29. Some general references to Donne's poems, or to Donne as a poet

1630s and 1640s

1638

An elegy by Ralph Brideoake in a mourning garland for Ben Jonson mentions Donne in praising Jonson as the loftiest writer of his time. Brideoake (1613–78) was an occasional versifier in Latin and English who became Bishop of Chichester late in his life. (*Jonsonius Virbius*, 1638. Given in *The Works of Ben Jonson*, ed. W. Gifford, 1816, ix, p. 402.)

> . . . Were all the choice of wit and language shown
> In one brave epitaph upon thy stone,
> Had learned Donne, Beaumont, and Randolph, all
> Surviv'd thy fate, and sung thy funeral,
> Their notes had been too low: take this from me,
> None but thyself could write a verse for thee.

1639

A minor poet Thomas Bancroft (*fl.* 1633–58) addressed an epigram to Donne in a collection of short poems celebrating men of letters of the time (*Two Bookes of Epigrammes, and Epitaphs, 1639*):

To Doctor *Donne*

> Thy Muses gallantry doth farre exceed
> All ours; to whom thou art a *Don* indeed.

1640

A prefatory poem by one W. Ling commending John Tatham's *The Fancies Theater*, 1640, praises Donne with other writers:

To his Friend the Author

> Had I *Chapmans* Line or Learning, *Johnsons* Art,
> *Fletchers* more accurate Fancie, or that part

Of *Beaumont* that's divine, *Dun's* profound skill,
Making good Verses live, and damning ill:
I then would prayse thy Verses, which sho'd last,
Whilst *Time* ha's sands to run, or Fame a blast. . . .

1640

One R. Gostelow referred to Donne in an elegiac poem 'On the death of Mr Randolph', published in Thomas Randolph's *Poems, with the Muses Looking-Glass and Amyntas*, Oxford, 1640:

When *Donne*, and *Beaumont* dyed, an Epitaph
Some men (I well remember) thought unsafe;
And said they did *presume to write, unlesse*
They could their teares in their expressions dresse.

c. 1640

An anonymous manuscript poem found among the Tixall papers is addressed 'To Mr Edward Thimelby, dissuading him from translating Dr Donne into Italian' (*Tixall Poetry*, ed. A. Clifford, Edinburgh, 1813, p. xxvi). Edward Thimelby was the brother of Catherine Thimelby, who quoted from the *Songs and Sonnets* in a letter written *c.* 1638.

c. 1640

Sir Lucius Cary (?1610–43) quoted a version of some lines from Donne's *Satyre ii*. He later referred to Donne as 'one of the most wittie, and most eloquent of our modern Divines'. (*Sir Lucius Cary. . . . His Discourse of Infallibility*, 1651, pp. 107 and 288.)

1641

Thomas Beedome (d. ?1641) addressed a poem 'To the Memory of his honoured friend Master *John Donne*, an Anniversary', in his *Poems: Divine and Humane*, 1641. The poem itself does not bear upon Donne's reputation.

1641

A character called Dogrel in Abraham Cowley's comedy *The Guardian*, 1650 (first performed in 1641), alludes to Donne in Act 3, Scene 1:

Go thy ways girl. . . . I see thou'lt never turn Semstress, nor teach girls; thou'dst be a rare wife for me, I should beget on thee *Donnes*, and *Johnsons*: but thou art too witty.

1644

Anon. in *Vindex Anglicus; or the Perfections of the English Language defended and asserted*, Oxford, 1644 (quoted in G. Keynes, *A Bibliography of Dr John Donne*, Cambridge, 1958, p. 260):

There is no sort of verse either ancient, or modern, which we are not able to equal by imitation: we have our English Virgil, Ovid, Seneca, Lucan, Juvenal, Martial, and Catullus: in the Earl of Surry, Daniel, Johnson, Spencer, Don, Shakespeare, and the glory of the rest, Sandys and Sydney.

1645

William Cavendish (1592–1676), Duke of Newcastle, mentioned Donne in a poem called 'The Unexpressible love', given in *The Phanseys addressed to Margaret Lucas*, 1645:

> Love, forty years agoe, serv'd Doctor Dunn. . . .

1646

Martin Llewellyn made what seems to have been a common joke in a poem 'To my Ingenious Freind Captain Ll.', given in *Men Miracles with other Poemes*, 1646. After a discussion of what happens if rhyming and versifying aren't done well and in accordance with sense, he concludes

> *Thus we climbe* downwards, *and advance as much*
> *As He that turn'd* Donn's Poems *into Dutch*.

Llewellyn (1616–81) was a Christ Church man. He was ejected from his living in 1648, became Principal of St Mary Hall at the Restoration, and served as physician to the king.

30. George Daniel

c. 1640

George Daniel of Beswick (1616–57), a cavalier poet, praised Donne in a work in verse entitled *A Vindication of Poesie*, written about 1640. The poem is given in *The Poems of George Daniel, Esq.*, ed. A. B. Grosart, 1878, i, p. 29.

The reverent Donne, whose quill God purely fil'd
Lives to his Character; & though he claime
A greater glory, may not be exil'd
This commōwealth; ye entrance of his fame
  Thus as ye Sun, to either Hemisphere
  Still ye same Light Hee movèd w^h vs here.

But as a Poet; all ye softnesses
The Shadow, Light, ye Ayre, & Life, of Love;
The Sharpnes of all Witt; ev'n bitternes
Makes Satire Sweet; all wit did God emprove
  'Twas flamed in him, 'Twas but warm vpon
  His Embers; He was more; & y^t is Donne.

31. Sir John Suckling

c. 1640

Suckling (1609–42) was one of the leading wits of the Court of Charles I, a playwright and poet whose verse remained in favour down to the end of the seventeenth century. He exchanged verse-missives with other members of the Court coterie, notably Carew. His poems were not printed until after his death.

TO MY FRIEND WILL D'AVENANT, ON HIS OTHER
POEMS
Thou hast redeem'd us, Will, and future times
Shall not account unto the age's crimes
Dearth of pure wit. Since the great lord of it,
Donne, parted hence, no man has ever writ
So near him, in 's own way: I would commend
Particulars; but then, how should I end
Without a volume? Ev'ry line of thine
Would ask (to praise it right) twenty of mine.

32. Henry Glapthorne

1642

Glapthorne (*fl.* 1639) was a well-known Court dramatist and poet. In a poem written after the outbreak of the Civil War and dedicated to Richard Lovelace he recalled the glories of the preceding era, now lost (*White-Hall. A Poem* (composed in 1642), 1643, B2ᵛ).

The Muses then did florish, and upon
My pleasant mounts planted their Helicon.
Then that great wonder of the knowing age,
Whose very name merits the amplest page
In Fames faire book, admired *Johnson* stood
Up to the chin in the Pierian flood,
Quaffing crownd bowles of Nectar, . . .
Beaumont and *Fletcher* gloriously did sit
Ruling the Theater . . .
And noble *Donne* (borne to more sacred use)
Exprest his heavenly raptures: As the juice
Of the Hyblean roses did distill
Through the Alembick of his nectard quill.

33. Sir Richard Baker

1643

Baker (1568–1645) was a religious and historical writer who had shared rooms with Wotton at Hart Hall, Oxford, Donne's college, and then studied law as Donne did. In the course of a survey of English kings Baker recalled the 'Men of note' during 'The Raigne of King James' (*A Chronicle of the Kings of England From the Times of the Romans Government unto the Death of King James*, 1643, p. 156).

Of Men of note in his time. . . . And here I desire the Reader leave to remember two of my old acquaintance, the one was Mr *John Dunne*, who leaving *Oxford*, lived at the *Innes of Court*, not dissolute, but very neat; a great visiter of Ladies, a great frequenter of Playes, a great writer of conceited Verses; until such time as King *James* taking notice of the pregnancy of his Wit, was a meanes that he betooke him to the study of Divinity; and thereupon proceeding Doctour, was made Deane of *Paules*; and become so rare a Preacher, that he was not only commended, but even admired by all that heard him. The other was Sir *Henry Wootton* (mine old acquaintance also, as having been fellow pupils, and chamber fellows in *Oxford* divers yeares together).

34. 'G.O.'

c. 1648

A certain 'G.O.', possibly the royalist divine and poet Giles Oldis-worth (1619–78), annotated a copy of the 1639 edition of Donne's poems. John Sampson, who found the copy, reported 'G.O.'s' markings as evidence of the attention contemporary readers gave to the poems. The following summarises Sampson's account of them in his essay 'A Contemporary Light Upon John Donne', in *Essays and Studies by Members of the English Association*, vii, 1921, pp. 82–107.[1]

The book demonstrates its owner's close concern with particular read-ings of Donne's lines. 'G.O.' had collated his 1639 text with the first edition of 1633, correcting words, weighing the versions, and at times suggesting emendations of his own. He gives poems titles to bring out the situation, identifies some of the personages of the occasional pieces, puts pointing marks to show the metrical movement of a line. Thus he scans the tricky first line of 'Twicknam Garden' as a clear iambic pentameter:

> Blast*ed with* sighs, and surround*ed with* teares

'G.O.'s' marginal notes frequently show him turning Donne's lines to some interest of his own. He adds a date, *1646, Oct. 6th*, to point a line quite arbitrarily to a black moment in royalist fortunes. He writes *Court Ladyes* against the reference to naked savages in the verse letter to the Countess of Huntingdon, *Church of England* against the lines from 'Twicknam Garden'

> And that this place may thoroughly be thought
> True Paradise, I have the serpent brought

Bishops against some lines from *Satire ii*

---

[1] Quotations from Sampson's essay appear by courtesy of the English Association.

> As in some Organ, Puppits dance above
> And bellows pant below, which them do move.

He glosses profane poems with scriptural references, sometimes giving them a spiritual sense. Thus he refers 'Tell me, where all past yeares are' to Eccles. 4:16; glosses a line from an apocryphal *Elegie*, 'The Sunne would shine, though all the world were blind', with 2 Tim. 2:13 to make it figure God's living fidelity towards us; redirects to *Xts Love* the lines in 'The Good-morrow' 'If ever any beauty I did see,/ Which I desir'd, and got, t'was but a dreame of thee'; transfers to God Donne's praise of the Countess of Bedford

> So'intire are all your deeds, and you, that you
> Must do the same thinge still; you cannot two

and makes Sappho's lesbian love for Philaenis an emblem of Christ's relationship to Christianity.

Other comments are pertinent to our own reading of Donne. He identifies 'His highnesse sitting in a golden Chaire' ('Farewell to Love') as *A fayreing*, and 'holy *Ianus*' and the 'soveraigne boate' (*Metempsychosis*) as *Noah* and the *Arke*; moreover he approves Donne's version of metempsychosis which locates the soul in the apple before man was created. He amends the title of 'The Exstasie' so that it reads *Excellent is The Extasie*, and adds at the end of the poem *This drives ye Reader to an Extasye*. In 'The Flea' he curiously reinforces the poet's plea to his mistress to spare the life of the flea which has bitten them both

> Though use make you apt to kill mee,
> Let not to that, selfe murder added bee,
> And sacrilege, three sinnes in killing three.

'G.O.' adds a line of his own here

> Doing despight to ye blessed Trinitye

and he brings authority from Acts and Hebrews against the triple sin.

Throughout the copy 'G.O.' scrawled comments in verse. He put a couplet before *The Progresse of the Soule*

> Knowledg of evil, proness to controll
> All good this is the progress of Eves Soul

and carried on the sense of the prose Epistle

> The sum of *this booke* you shall find to bee

More sin, then Soule keeping some qualitye
Of every vile beast, full of Treacherye
Rapine, Deceipt, and Lust, and ills enough
To be a Woman, Mother of mischeife, Eve

Above all, he prefixed each section of the edition with an observation
in verse:

The *Songs and Sonets*
How vile, and, yet how good are Great Witts, whan
They write not what they shou'd but what they can.

The *Elegies*
How sharpe, and yet how sweete, are Poets, who
Describe not what is meete, but, what is new.

The *Epithalamions*
Learned yet stupid, all those Poetts are
Which undresse Cupid, and paint Venus bare.

The *Satires*
Both bolde and rare needes must those writers bee
Who can and dare write all they heare and see!

The *Verse Letters*
What verse? what prose? what volumnes can bee better
Then his, who showes such witt in every letter?

The First Anniversary
Stark naught, because so good's that Elegye
Which equalls flesh and Blood to th' Deity.

The prose letters
Loe here a Treasure! there ye Poet showes
Witt without measure, where he writes in prose.

The Second Anniversary
A heavenly Progresse makes that Soule whose flight
Soares here, on earth, above ye sharpest sight.

The *Holy Sonnets*
Marke his Soules Progresse! hee which sang of fleas
At first, at last sings Halleluiahs!

35. Donne's son on his father's poems

1650

The fifth edition of Donne's poems appeared under the supervision of Donne's son, John Donne D.C.L. (1604–62), who had been petitioning since 1637 to prevent the unauthorised publication of his father's poems. The younger Donne wrote a dedication to Lord Craven in which he spoke of the poems.

My Lord,
Many of these Poems have, for severall impressions, wandred up and down trusting (as well they might) upon the Authors reputation; neither do they nôw complain of any injury but what may proceed either from the kindnesse of the Printer, or the curtesie of the Reader; the one by adding something too much, lest any spark of this sacred fire might perish undiscerned, the other by putting such an estimation upon the wit & fancy they find here, that they are content to use it as their own: as if a man should dig out the stones of a royall Amphitheatre to build a stage for a countrey show. . . .

. . . In this sad condition these learned sisters are fled over to beg your *L^{ps}*. protection, who have been so certain a patron both to arts and armes, and who in this generall confusion have so intirely preserved your Honour, that in your Lordship we may still read a most perfect character of what *England* was in all her pompe and greatnesse, so that although these poems were formerly written upon severall occasions, and to severall persons, they now unite themselves, and are become one pyramid to set your Lordships statue upon, where you may stand like Armed *Apollo* the defendor of the Muses, encouraging the Poets now alive to celebrate your great Acts by affording your countenance to his poems that wanted onely so noble a subject.

My Lord,
Your most humble servant
JOHN DONNE.

36. Some general references to Donne's poems, or to Donne as a poet

1650s

---

c. 1650

Charles, second Lord Stanhope (1595–1660), scribbled notes in the margins of a copy of Jonson's *Works*, 1640, and several other books. He frequently mentions Donne as an eminent poet and wit—'John Selden and Doctour alias Dean Dunne were two great witts'—and applies to him Ben Jonson's reference in the 'Epistle to Elizabeth Countess of Rutland' to 'a better Verser' who had supplanted Jonson in the favour of Lucy, Countess of Bedford (see G.P.V. Akrigg, 'The Curious Marginalia of Charles, Second Lord Stanhope', in *Adams Memorial Studies*, Folger Shakespeare Library, 1948, pp. 785–802, and J. M. Osborn, 'Ben Jonson and the Eccentric Lord Stanhope', *The Times Literary Supplement*, 4 January 1957, p. 16).

1651

A commendatory poem by W. Bell prefixed to William Cartwright's *Comedies, Tragi-Comedies, with other Poems*, 1651, compares Cartwright with Donne and Jonson. Bell speaks of

> Don's rich Gold, and Johnson's silver Mine.

1654

Edmund Gayton (1608–66), a former 'son' of Ben Jonson, recalled Donne's lines on Hilliard in the verse letter 'The Storme' (lines 3–5) when he commented on the decline of portrait painting in his own day (*Pleasant Notes upon Don Quixot*, 1654, p. 35):

. . . Especially since the loss of that famous Hyliard, made more famous by the Incomparable expression of the dead Author, [He quotes the lines].

1654

The title of a poetical miscellany edited by 'R.C.' and published in 1654 runs:

The Harmony of the Muses, or the Gentlemans and Ladies Choicest Recreations; Full of various pure and transcendent Wit, containing severall excellent Poems, Some Fancies of Love, some of Disdain, &c. written by those unimitable Masters of Learning and Invention, Dr. Joh. Donn, Dr. H. King. . . .

1656

John Phillips (1631–1706), Milton's nephew, essayed a stock joke when he addressed the reader in a poetical miscellany he edited (*Sportive Wit: The Muses Merriment*, 1656, Address to the Reader, n.p.):

. . . we shall see Ballads inserted shortly, to as much dishonour of our English Wit, as if Don's Poems were turned into Dutch.

1656

In another poetical miscellany John Phillips gave Donne's *Elegie xviii*, 'Loves Progress', among wittily erotic pieces by several leading wits of the age such as Suckling. Donne is one of the authors listed by his initials in the commendatory title of the book, and he appears again in the address to the 'Courteous Reader' (*Wit and Drollery, Jovial Poems. Never before Printed. By Sir J.M. Ja.S. Sir W.D. J.D. And other admirable Wits*, 1656, A3^v and pp. 157–60):

What hath not been extent [sic] of Sir J.M. of Ja.S. of Sir W.D. of J.D. and other miraculous Muses of the Times, are here at thy Service. . . .

1656

Abraham Wright (1611–90) gave Donne's *Elegie ii*, 'The Anagram', and *Elegie ix*, 'The Autumnall', in a poetical miscellany with the titles 'On the praise of an ill-favoured Gentlewoman', and 'On an aged Gentlewoman'. In the prefatory address 'To the Ingenuous Reader' Wright praises *Elegie ix* as a mirror which will 'teach you how to raise a beauty out of wrinkles fourscore years old, and to fall in love even with deformity and uglinesse'; but he does not name Donne as the author (*Parnassus Biceps*, 1656, A3^v, pp. 86–8 and 118–19).

1656

The royalist writer John Collop (*fl.* 1660), editing a miscellany of verses directed against the sectaries, defended poetry by reference to the gravity of some of its practitioners in an 'Epistle Dedicatory to the Marquis of Dorchester' (*Poesis Rediviva: or, Poesie Reviv'd*, 1656, A3^r):

Nor is Poesie unworthy of your Patronage, which a *Sir Philip Sidney* hath prais'd, our Seraphick *Donne* us'd, the learned *Scaliger*, and he who makes all praises modest, the excellent *Hugo Grotius* labour'd in.

1657

H. Belasye, a commender of England, denied the familiar theory that the heavy English atmosphere produces sluggish intelligences, pointing to some of our famous wits in proof of his contention (*An English Traveler's First Curiosity, or The Knowledge of his owne Countrey*, 1657, Historical Manuscripts Commission's *Report on MSS in Various Collections*, ii, p. 193. Given in J. F. Bradley and J. Q. Adams, *The Jonson Allusion-Book*, New Haven, 1922, p. 313):

Good witts in England. Some think that this thicknesse of the ayre must needs breed in them thick witts, but it is not soe, England being like Athens in that, of whome it is sayd. *Athenis pingue coelum, sed tenua ingenia; id est* a thick ayre but thin witts, for what nation can shew more refined witts then those of our Ben, our Shakespeare, our Beaumont, our Fletcher, our Dunn, our Randol, our Crashaw, our Cleveland, our Sidney, our Bacon, &c. . . .

1657

The bibliographer William London (*fl.* 1658) listed various writings by Donne in *A Catalogue of the most vendible Books in England*, 1657, M2^r, V2^v, Ee3^v, Gg^r. Donne merited entries in four categories, the entry under *Romances, Poems, and Playes* being 'Dr Donne, Poems. 8°'.

1658

In a commendatory poem prefixed to Thomas Flatman's *Naps upon Parnassus*, 1658, A. Samuel lists some great English poets who don't remotely measure up to Flatman, among them Donne:

> To thee compar'd, our English Poets all stop,
> And vail their Bonnets, even *Shakespear's Falstop*,

Chaucer the first of all wasn't worth a farthing. . . .
Beaumont, and Fletcher; Donne, Jeremy Candish,
Herbert, and Cleeveland, and all the trin noble
Are *Saints-bells* unto *thee*, and *thou* great *Bow-bell*,
Ben Johnson. . . .

37. Clement Barksdale

1651

Barksdale (1609–87) was an Anglican divine who published
religious writings and a little verse. In a collection of his poems
he announced his opposition to the mode still current (*Nympha
Libethris or the Cotswold Muse*, 1651).

To the Readers. Conclusion
My verse, because they are not *hard and rare*,
As some of *Dav'nants, Don's* and *Cleveland's* are,
You censure. Pray Sir, must all men write *so*?
Or can *wee all* unto fair *Corinth* go?
But, Truth is, I'd not write so, if I cou'd:
I *write*, just as *I speak*, to be *understood*.
Whose sense will not without much *study* come,
Let him, for me, be altogether *dumb*.
  No *Persius* be my Reader; but such may,
  As *He*, who once threw *Persius* away.

38. Humphrey Moseley

1651

The publisher Humphrey Moseley (d. 1661) addressed himself *To the Reader* in commendation of Cartwright's writings (in *Comedies, Tragi-Comedies, with other Poems* (by William Cartwright), 1651, n.p.).

The highest Poet our Language can boast of (the late Dean of St Paul's) you'l grant was afterwards an excellent Preacher. . . .

39. Richard Whitlock

1654

In an anatomy of English manners in his time Whitlock (*c.* 1616–*c.* 1672) several times cited Donne or quoted from him, with appreciative comments (*Zootomia, or Observations on the Present Manners of the English: Briefly Anatomizing the Living by the Dead*, 1654, pp. 218, 322, 339, 350).

Whitlock uses Donne in an argument for intellectual conservatism:

Stand in the old wayes, or enquire for them, before we enlarge our Discoveries of new. And that inimitable Poets Rule [*Dr Donne*— marginal gloss] is true in al mending of our Intellectuals,

He quotes *Satyre iii*, lines 77–9, 'doubt wisely; . . . To sleepe, or runne wrong, is'.

Later, he defends women with arguments and phrases from Donne's *The second Anniversary*, acknowledging his debt without needing to name Donne:

. . . for the *same Pen* in his learned *Anniversary* confineth vertue not only to that *Sex* (and so gives it away from himself and *party*) but to that *particular Mrs.* of his *Fancy*, which (though writ not so much as an *Historian*, as *Poet* . . .) may serve for *Pattern*, or *Rule* to try the reall *worth* of *Feminine worthies* by . . ..

Arguing from women's physical beauty to their moral excellence, Whitlock praises Donne's skill in depicting a woman in both aspects by applying to him some lines Donne himself had written of the painter Hilliard in 'The Storme'. He calls Donne

that rare *Beauties* (*I*, or *Vertues*) *Hilliard*, and *masterly Painter*, in his Anniversary; . . .

And he quotes from *The second Anniversary* the six lines beginning 'She, of whose soule, if wee may say, 'twas Gold' (lines 241–6), which include the image of 'her pure, and eloquent blood' speaking in her cheeks so that 'one might almost say, her body thought'. Again 'Dr *Donne*' is acknowledged in the margin. Finally he cites the Virgin Mary, once more finding an apt quotation from *The second Anniversary*—

. . . that it is true what our best of Poets [Dr *Donnes Poems*—marginal gloss] said,

> Where thou shalt see the blessed Mother-maid
> Joy in not being that, which men have said.

40. Philip King

1656

Dr Philip King (d. 1666/7) was the nephew of Bishop Henry King, Donne's friend and literary executor. He mentions Donne in the course of some observations on books and reading cast in the form of a letter signed 'P.K.'; but it is not clear from the context whether he has Donne's poetry in mind as well as his preaching (*The Surfeit. To A.B.C.*, 1656. Given in *Reliquiae Hernianae*, ed. P. Bliss, Oxford, 1857, ii, pp. 930–1).

For bishop *Andrews* and Dr *Donne*, I could never conceive better of them, then as a voluntarie before a lesson to the lute, which is absolutely the best pleasing to the eare; but after finished absolutely forgotten, nothing to be remembred or repeated.

41. Francis Osborn

1656

Osborn (1593–1659) twice instanced Donne in prudently advising young men not to follow fashion indiscriminately, not to seem more brilliant than their superiors, and so on (*Advice to a Son* (1656), 1673, To the Reader, and p. 68). Osborn's *Advice to a Son* was one of the most highly esteemed and popular works of its time.

(i)
This breeds matter of wonder, why so many should hazard their Fame, by running and yelping after those prodigious Wits of this last Age, B [Buckingham], D [Donne], H [Hudibras, i.e. Butler].

(ii)
This made the Lord Chancellor Egerton the willinger to exchange incomparable Doctor D for the less sufficient, though in this more modest, Mr T.B.

42. Sir Aston Cokain

1658

Cokain (1608–84), a landowner in the Midlands, was a poet and translator of some note in his day. As well as imitating and echoing Donne in his verses (see No. 1, 1658) he several times paid explicit tribute to him (*Small Poems of Diverse Sorts*, 1658, p. 113, and Epigram 99, The second Book).

(i)
To my learned friend Mr Thomas Bancroft *upon his Book of* Satyres

> . . . (But all in one t' include) So our prime wit
> (In the too few short *Satyres* he hath writ)
> Renowned *Don* hath so rebuk'd his times,
> That he hath jear'd vice-lovers from their crimes.

(ii) In an epigram, Cokain gives Donne pride of place among his illustrious contemporaries, and claims to have known him:

> *To my honoured Cousin* Mr Charles Cotton *Junior*
>
> . . . *Donne, Suckling, Randolph, Drayton, Massinger,*
> *Habbington, Sandy's, May, My Acquaintance were:* . . .
> *Johnson, Chapman,* and *Holland* I have seen,
> And with them too should have acquainted been. . . .

43. Some general references to Donne's poems, or to Donne as a Poet

1660–1700

1667–8

Donne's name occurs in a list of the leading English poets which an Italian traveller through England, one Lorenzo Magalotti, noted in his journal of the excursion (Magalotti's account was published in Florence in 1936 as *Un'inedita relazione di un viaggio in Inghilterra nel 1667–8*).

c. 1668

An anonymous poet wrote an 'Elegy on Sir William Davenant' on the flyleaves of a copy of Denham's *Poems*, 1668. Stanza 7 of the elegy refers to Donne (*Inedited Poetical Miscellanies 1584–1700*, ed. W. C. Hazlitt, 1870, S2b):

> He out of breath himself did run,
> When with high rapture he begun,
> By emulating Doctor Dunne—
> I mean the father, not the son.

1674

The bookseller Samuel Speed (d. 1681) alluded to Donne in 'The Legend of Duke Humphrey', part of his doggerel poem *Fragmenta Carceris: or, The Kings-Bench Scuffle: with the Humours of the Common-Side*, 1674:

> . . . I never yet knew one
> Could quench his thirst, with reading Doctor Donne.

1679

The German poet and diplomat Hofmann von Hofmannswaldau (1617–79), a devotee of Marino, mentioned Donne for his religious poems in a list of the English poets whose work shows learning, art and elegance (*Deutsche Übersetzungen und Gedichte*, 1679. Quoted in G. Waterhouse, *The Literary Relations of England and Germany in the Seventeenth Century*, Cambridge 1914, p. 119):

The English have at all times shown themselves to be lovers of poetry, though not always with equal felicity, for the poems of merit are mostly by modern writers. In Chaucer, the English Homer, as his countrymen call him, and Robert of Gloucester we do not meet with the same learning, art and elegance as in Edmond Spencer's faerie Queene and Michael Draiton's Poly-Olbion, Johnson's comedies and tragedies, and the religious poems of Quarles and Don.

1681

H. White in *Diarium Biographicum*, Danzig, 1688, Ddla-b, gives a brief account of Donne and mentions some of his writings.

1683

In an academic dissertation on poetry Olaus Borrichius listed the recommended English poets and included Donne (*Dissertationes Academicae de Poetis*, Frankfurt, 1683, p. 161).

1684

The publisher's advertisement to *Poems and Translations by John Oldham*, 1684 (given in *The Works of Mr John Oldham, Together with his Remains*, 1686, n.p.), cites Donne and Cowley as examples of poets whose sacred and profane poems have been printed together in miscellanies:

Nor is the Printing of such Miscellanies altogether so unpresidented, but that it may be seen in the Editions of Dr *Donne*, and Mr *Cowley's* Works, whether done by their own appointment, or the sole direction of the Stationers, I am not able to determine.

1689

John Evelyn, writing to Pepys on the 12 August 1689, described a project of the Earl of Clarendon's father 'to furnish all the rooms of state and other apartments with the pictures of the most illustrious of our nation, especially of his Lordships time and acquaintance, and of divers before it'. Evelyn listed these pictures by groups, according to professions and times. Donne appears among the ecclesiastics—

Dr Sanderson, Brownrigg, Dr Donne, Chillingworth, and several of the Cleargie and others of the former and present age.

He is not mentioned among the poets—'old Chaucer, Shakespeare, Beaumont and Fletcher, who were both in one piece, Spencer, Mr Waller, Cowley, Hudibras. . . .' (*The Diary and Correspondence of John Evelyn F.R.S.*, ed. W. Bray, 1852, iii, pp. 294–311).

c. 1690

A long poem entitled *The Immortality of Poesie*, in a manuscript collection begun by the Hon. Herbert Aston, praises the celebrated English poets—Chaucer, Spenser, Jonson, Shakespeare, Cowley, Milton, Dryden, Wycherley, Lee, Otway, Sedley, Etherege. But there is no mention of Donne. (*Tixall Poetry*, ed. A. Clifford, Edinburgh, 1813, pp. 250–3.)

1690

Sir William Temple (1628–99) in his *Miscellanea. The Second Part*, 1690, p. 127, remarked of Lucy, Countess of Bedford, that she was

esteemed among the greatest Wits of Her time, and celebrated by Doctor *Donne*.

1691

Gerald Langbaine the younger cited Donne's poetic praises of Jonson's *Volpone*, and Beaumont's, as sufficient testimony to the value of that play (*An Account of the English Dramatick Poets*, Oxford, 1691, p. 298).

1692–3

Donne appears well down a list of nineteen English poets who are recommended in 'an essay on Poetry' addressed to young students ([John Dunton], *The Young-Students-Library Containing Extracts and Abridgements of the Most Valuable Books Printed in England, and in the Forreign Journals, From The Year Sixty Five, to This Time. By the Athenian Society*, 1692, p. xiiib). Dunton (1659–1733), bookseller, traveller, and journalist, treated literary matters as topics of polite conversation in his journal *The Athenian Mercury*. The issue for Tuesday, 24 October 1693 (vol. 12, no. 1), gives Donne in a somewhat different list of poets to be read by the young:

Question 4. *What Books of Poetry wou'd you Advise one that's Young, and extreamly delights in it, to read, both Divine and other?* Answ. . . . *Spencer's* Fairy Queen, &c. *Tasso's* Godfrey of Bulloign, *Shakespear, Beaumont* and *Fletcher, Ben Johnson, Randal, Cleaveland,* Dr *Donne, Gondibert, Waller,* all DRYDEN, *Tate, Oldham, Flatman, The Plain Dealer.* . . .

44. William Winstanley

1660

Winstanley (?1628–98), a literary compiler, included a 'Life of Doctour Donne' extracted from Walton in a volume of lives of notable Englishmen (*England's Worthies*, 1660, pp. 298–308). Most of the lives in Winstanley are of statesmen, though he has accounts of the eminent poets of the sixteenth and early seventeenth centuries—Shakespeare, Jonson, Drayton, Daniel, Raleigh, Spenser, Sidney, Surrey. Winstanley included a revised version of the 'Life of Doctour Donne' in his *The Lives of the most Famous English Poets,* 1687.

In the Preface to *England's Worthies*, arguing that great poets set the pace for the rest in the trouble they take to get their verses artistically right, Winstanley instances Virgil and Ben Jonson then quotes Jonson himself on Donne and Cleveland (a2ᵛ).

. . . like *Ben. Jonson*, who to one that told him of his oyl and his lamp, the pains he took before his *Births*, those happy abstracts of the humours and manners of men; gave this answer, *That his were Works, the other printed things for the Stage were but Playes*, Dons and Cleavelands *Poems, how have they whipt and pedantized the other Locusts of Poetry*? thus a true Diamond is to be esteemed above heaps of *Bristol*-Stones.

45. Samuel Butler

c. 1660

Butler (1612–80), the author of *Hudibras*, was neglected in later years and some of his pieces remained in manuscript until the 1750s. In some 'Thoughts Upon Various Subjects', published long after his death, he alludes to Donne (*The Genuine Remains in Verse and Prose*, ed. R. Thyer, 1759, ii, p. 498).

Dr *Donne's* writings are like Voluntary or Prelude, in which a Man is not tyd to any particular Design of Air, but may change his Key of Mood at Pleasure; So his Compositions seem to have been written without any particular Scope.

46. John Hacket

c. 1660

John Hacket (1592–1670), Bishop of Coventry and Lichfield in
the 1660s, had been Chaplain to Lord Keeper Williams and, after
the Restoration, was Canon Residentiary at St Paul's. In his
*Scrinia Reserata: A Memorial Offer'd to the Great Deservings of John
Williams, D.D.*, 1693, Part i, p. 63, Hacket described how Lord
Keeper Williams helped bring about the advancement in the
Church of two divines who had served a former Lord Keeper.

The Bishopric of *Exon* being also then void, it came into the Lord-
Keeper's head to gratifie a brace of worthy Divines, if he could attain it,
his old Friends, who had been both bred in the House of Wisdom, with
the Lord-Chancellor *Egerton*. Dr *Carew* who had been his Chaplain, a
man of great Reason and polish'd Eloquence, and Dr *Dunn* who had
been his Secretary, a Laureat Wit; neither was it possible that a vulgar
Soul should dwell in such promising Features. The Success was quickly
decided, for these two prevailed by the Lord-Keeper's Commendation
against all Pretenders; the Bishopric of *Exeter* was conferred upon Dr
Carew, and Dr *Dunn* succeeded him in his Deanery of St *Paul's*.

47. Robert Sidney, second Earl of Leicester

1661

In a letter to Algernon, Earl of Northumberland, written at Penshurst on 17 February 1661, Leicester refers to the death at Leicester House four days previously of Elizabeth, Queen of Bohemia. This was the Elizabeth, eldest daughter of James I, for whose wedding on St Valentine's Day, 1613, Donne had written his epithalamion beginning 'Haile Bishop Valentine' (*Letters and Memorials of State, in the Reigns of Queen Mary, Queen Elizabeth, King James, King Charles the First, Part of the Reign of King Charles the Second, and Oliver's Usurpation*, ed. A. Collins, 1746, ii, p. 723).

I heare, that as your Lordship foretold in your Letter, my Royal Tenant is departed. It seems the Fates did not think it fit that I should have the Honor, which indeed I never much desyred, to be the Landlord of a Queene. It is pitty that she lived not a few Houres more to dye upon her Weddingday, and that there is not as good a Poet to make her Epitaph, as Doctor *Donne*, who wrote her *Epithalamium* upon that Day unto St *Valentine*.

48. Thomas Shipman

1667, 1677

Shipman (1633–80), a minor poet, was a friend of Cowley and Flatman. He praised Donne incidentally in a poem celebrating Cowley, dated 1667. In a poem written ten years later, addressed to Sir Edward Rich, Shipman cited Donne as a leading example of a poet-priest (*Carolina, or, Loyal Poems*, 1683).

(i)

GRATITUDE. 1667
Some grateful Acknowledgments to that most
excellent Poet, Mr *A.C.*

. . . Hail *God of Wit*! *England's Apollo*, hail!
Thou art no Off-spring of an *idle Tale*,
Like *Homer's Deity*. But since that fame ⎫
All Ages gave him, is thy proper claim;   ⎬
Accept the Veneration and the *Name*.   ⎭
Fulfill'd in thee is what the *Ancients* feign,
And *Pallas* is the *issue* of thy *Brain*,
As th' *Muses* of thy *Wit*: when safely laid,
Of thy *first-sheets* their *swathing Cloaths* were made.
Others there are would thy fair *Off-spring* claim;
Theirs (by their want of heed) o're-laid or lame.
But when it comes to Tryal they resign;
Justice decrees the *Living Child* for thine.

The *Muses Empire* bears so great a Name,
Thou hast two *Rivals* in thy *Lady-Fame*;
Waller and *Donne*. You are the only three
Who justly can pretend that *Monarchy*.
Donne's Judgment, Fancy, Humour, and his Wit,
Strong, searching, happy, and before ne're hit,
Gives him a fair pretence to climb the Throne;

But *Waller* rather stops than plucks him down.
Rich he appears; his courtly Vesture grac'd
With golden *Similes* all over lac'd.
But *Cowley* (like the *Infant* of the *Sun*)
Out-glitters *Waller*, and ev'n dazzles *Donne*.
Both of 'em, to *Augustus,* leave the Field;
Like *Lepidus* and *Anthony*, they yield.
He triumphs! their triumv'racy of Rays
Unite in *Cowley* and compound his blaze.

(ii)

Wit and Nature. 1677. *A Pindaric Ode* to Sr. Edw. Rich

. . . *Nature*—I cannot yet define;
More fit for some *seraphical Divine*:
Tho they but *Graces* three, and we have *Muses* nine. . . .

Priests we are both alike, and both alike are fir'd
With sacred heat: *Poets* have been inspir'd,
Shar'd in their gifts of *Prophecy*,
As they in ours of *Poetry*,
   And both have *Lawrels* won;
They have their *Doctor Sprat,* and had their *Doctor Donne*. . . .

49. John Dryden

As a youth of eighteen Dryden imitated Donne in his poem 'Upon the death of the Lord Hastings' (see No. 1, 1649). In his later writings he tended to cite both Donne and Shakespeare as poets who had the highest inventive gifts but didn't write smoothly or decorously enough ('If I would compare him [Ben Jonson] with *Shakespeare*, I must acknowledge him the more correct Poet, but *Shakespeare* the greater wit.' *An Essay of Dramatick Poesie* (1668), in *The Works of John Dryden*, California, 1971, xvii (ed. S. H. Monk), p. 58). One can see this opinion hardening over the years into the celebrated dicta of the 1690s.

Nevertheless Dryden was still taking ideas, and sometimes phrases, from Donne at the very end of his career (see No. 1, 1700).

(i) In *An Essay of Dramatick Poesie* (1668), ed. cit., pp. 29–30, Dryden reprobates writers who are 'infinitely too bold in . . . Metaphors and coyning words', and cites Horace as a poet who was properly 'cautious to obtrude a new word on his Readers, and makes custom and common use the best measure of receiving it into our writings'. He continues—

The not observing this Rule is that which the world has blam'd in our Satyrist *Cleveland*; to express a thing hard and unnaturally, is his new way of Elocution: 'Tis true, no Poet but may sometimes use a *Catachresis*. . . . But to do this alwayes, and never be able to write a line without it, though it may be admir'd by some few Pedants, will not pass upon those who know that wit is best convey'd to us in the most easie language; and is most to be admir'd when a great thought comes drest in words so commonly receiv'd that it is understood by the meanest apprehensions, as the best meat is the most easily digested: but we cannot read a verse of *Cleveland*'s without making a face at it, as if every word were a Pill to swallow: he gives us many times a hard Nut to break our Teeth, without a Kernel for our pains. So that there is this difference betwixt his Satyres and Doctor *Donns*, That the one gives us deep thoughts in common language, though rough cadence; the other gives us common thoughts in abstruse words: . . .

(ii) In 1692 Dryden was commissioned by the Earl of Abingdon to write a poem in commemoration of the Countess of Abingdon who had died in the previous year. His *Eleonora: A Panegyrical Poem Dedicated to the Memory of the Late Countess of Abingdon* is modelled on Donne's *Anniversaries* (see No. 1, 1692), and he acknowledged a debt to Donne in the prefatory letter he addressed 'To the Right Honourable The Earl of Abingdon, &c.' (ed. cit., iii, ed. Earl Miner, p. 233):

Doctor *Donn* the greatest Wit, though not the best Poet of our Nation, acknowledges, that he had never seen Mrs. *Drury*, whom he has made immortal in his admirable *Anniversaries*; I have had the same fortune; though I have not succeeded to the same Genius. However, I have follow'd his footsteps in the Design of his Panegyrick, which was to raise an Emulation in the living, to Copy out the Example of the dead. And therefore it was, that I once intended to have call'd this Poem, the Pattern: And though on a second consideration, I chang'd the Title into the Name of that Illustrious Person, yet the Design continues, and *Eleonora* is still the Pattern of Charity, Devotion, and Humility; of the best Wife, the best Mother, and the best of Friends.

(iii) In 1693 Dryden issued his verse translation of the satires of Juvenal and Persius on which he had worked for some years. He prefixed to the poems a long disquisition on satiric poetry which he dedicated to Charles, Earl of Dorset, the Eugenius of the *Essay of Dramatick Poesie*. Dorset himself wrote satiric verses, and the first part of Dryden's essay is a fulsome eulogy of these (*A Discourse Concerning the Original and Progress of Satire*, 1693, in *The Poems of John Dryden*, ed. James Kinsley, Oxford, 1958, ii, pp. 603–4 and 661):

I will not attempt in this place, to say any thing particular of your *Lyrick Poems*, though they are the Delight and Wonder of this Age, and will be the Envy of the next. The Subject of this Book confines me to Satire; And in that, an Author of your own Quality, (whose Ashes I will not disturb,) has given you all the Commendation, which his self sufficiency cou'd afford to any Man: *The best Good Man, with the worst Natur'd Muse.* In that Character, methinks I am reading *Johnson's* Verses to the Memory of *Shakespeare*: An Insolent, Sparing, and Invidious

Panegyrick: Where good Nature, the most God-like Commendation of a Man, is only attributed to your Person, and deny'd to your Writings: for they are every where so full of Candour, that like *Horace*, you only expose the Follies of Men, without Arraigning their Vices; and in this excel him, That You add that pointedness of Thought, which is visibly wanting in our Great *Roman*. There is more of Salt in all your Verses, than I have seen in any of the Moderns, or even of the Ancients: But you have been sparing of the Gaul; by which means you have pleas'd all Readers, and offended none. *Donn* alone, of all our Countrymen, had your Talent; but was not happy enough to arrive at your Versification. And were he Translated into Numbers, and *English*, he wou'd yet be wanting in the Dignity of Expression. That which is the prime Vertue, and chief Ornament of *Virgil*, which distinguishes him from the rest of Writers, is so conspicuous in your Verses, that it casts a shadow on all your Contemporaries; we cannot be seen, or but obscurely, while you are present. You equal *Donn*, in the Variety, Multiplicity, and Choice of Thoughts; you excel him in the Manner, and the Words. I Read you both, with the same Admiration, but not with the same Delight. He affects the Metaphysicks, not only in his Satires, but in his Amorous Verses, where Nature only shou'd reign; and perplexes the Minds of the Fair Sex with nice Speculations of Philosophy, when he shou'd ingage their hearts, and entertain them with the softnesses of Love. In this (if I may be pardon'd for so bold a truth) Mr *Cowley* has Copy'd him to a fault; so great a one, in my Opinion, that it throws his *Mistress* infinitely below his Pindariques, and his latter Compositions; which are undoubtedly the best of his Poems, and the most Correct. For my own part, I must avow it freely to the World, that I never attempted any thing in Satire, wherein I have not study'd your Writings as the most perfect Model. . . .

Much later in his essay Dryden argues that modern poets should not be bound by primitive precedent:

Has not *Virgil* chang'd the Manners of *Homer's* Hero's in his *Aeneis*? certainly he has, and for the better. For *Virgil's* Age was more Civiliz'd, and better Bred; and he writ according to the Politeness of *Rome*, under the Reign of *Augustus Caesar*; not to the Rudeness of *Agamemnon's* Age, or the Times of *Homer*. Why shou'd we offer to confine free Spirits to one Form, when we cannot so much as confine our Bodies to one Fashion of Apparel? Wou'd not *Donn's* Satires, which abound with so much Wit, appear more Charming, if he had taken care of his Words, and of his Numbers? But he follow'd *Horace* so very close, that of necessity he must fall with him: And I may safely say it of this present Age, That if we are not so great Wits as *Donn*, yet, certainly, we are better Poets.

50. Mrs John Evelyn

1668

Mary Evelyn (*c.* 1635–1709), wife of the diarist, kept up a correspondence with the sometime tutor to her children, Ralph Bohun of New College, Oxford. She showed herself an acute critic of current plays and books. She commented on Donne in a letter to Bohun dated 21 May 1668 (*Evelyn's Diary and Correspondence,* ed. H. B. Wheatley, 1906, iv, p. 55).

There is a lucky hit in reputation, which some obtain by the defect in their judges, rather than from the greatness of their merit; the contrary may be instanced in Doctor Donne, who had he not been a really learned man, a libertine in wit and a courtier, might have been allowed to write well. . . .

51. The seventh collected edition of Donne's poems

1669

This last seventeenth-century edition of Donne's poems is the only one that names him in full as the author: *Poems, &c. By John Donne late Dean of St Pauls*, 1669. It was published by Herringman whereas the first five editions, up to 1650, had been published by Marriot.

Several pieces are added. The full version of *Elegie xii*, 'His parting from her', appears for the first time, and *Elegies xviii*, 'Loves Progress', and *xix*, 'Going to Bed', are given for the first time in an edition of Donne's poems.

52. Andrew Marvell

1673

In a long reply to the various published attacks on his *The Re-hearsall Transpros'd* (1672), Marvell claimed that they all came from the same hand, or at least had the same sponsor. He called in Donne's *Metempsychosis* to illustrate his description of this assailant's successive transformations, but then slipped into a five-page account of the poem itself, part summary and part quotation, numbering the stanzas in the margin as he came to them. He claims that Donne's fiction quite closely applies to his present case, but doesn't show how (*The Rehearsall Transpros'd: The Second Part*, 1673, pp. 62–7).

So that upon perusal of all those books that have appear'd in so many several shapes against me, first *Rosemary and Bayes,* then the *Common Places,* next the *Transproser Rehears'd,* fourthly *S'too him Bays,* afterwards the *Reproof,* and in fine, *Gregory Gray-beard*; I find plainly that 'tis but the same Ghost that hath haunted me in those differing dresses and Vehicles. Insomuch that upon consideration of so various an identity, methinks after so many years I begin to understand Doctor *Donn's* Progress of the Soul, which pass'd through no fewer revolutions, and had hitherto puzzled all its Readers.

For—[he quotes stanza 7 of the poem then launches into his account of the whole]

This was the sum of that witty fable of Doctor *Donne's* which if it do not perfectly suit with all the transmigrations of mine Answerer, the *Author of the Ecclesiastical Politie,* nor equal the Progress of so great a Prince, yet whoever will be so curious as himself to read that Poem, may follow the parallel much further than I have done, lest I should be tedious to the Reader by too long and exact a similitude. But if it do not quadrate here, the resemblance will perhaps be more visible upon the examination of what remains to be consider'd. . . .

53. John Wilmot, Earl of Rochester

c. 1675

Suckling in his 'A Session of the Poets', 1637, represented Jonson, Carew, Davenant and others as contending for Apollo's laurel crown. A satiric poem with the same title giving a post-Restoration version of the contest appeared in *Poems on Several Occasions: by the Right Honourable The E. of R.*, Antwerp, 1680. It shows Apollo's attempts to 'Establish a Government, *Leader*, and *Laws*' amid a chaos of literary factions and pretenders. '*J*—— *D*——' is the first of the poets who answers Apollo's general summons.

In the *Head* of the *Gang J*—— *D*—— appear'd,
That Ancient grave *Wit*, so long lov'd and fear'd;
But *Apollo* had heard a Story i'th' *Town*,
Of his quitting the *Muses*, to wear a Black *Gown*;
And so gave him leave, now his *Poetry's* done,
To let him turn *Priest*, now R—— is turn'd *Nun*.
This Reverend *Author* was no sooner set by,
But *Apollo* had got gentle *George* in his Eye, . . .

54. Edward Phillips

1675, 1679

Edward Phillips (1630–?1696), Milton's nephew, had an undistinguished career as a tutor, hack writer, and compiler. He gave a potted survey of Donne's career in a collection of material on the poets, neatly adapting Walton to the manners of a different age (*Theatrum Poetarum*, 1675, pp. 106–7). Phillips praised Donne more forthrightly in a Latin account of him published a few years later ('Compendiosa Enumeratio Poetarum', in J. Buchler, *Sacrarum Profanarumque Phrasium Poeticarum Thesaurus*, 17th ed., 1679, p. 398).

(i)
John Donne, a Student in his younger years in *Lincoln's Inne*, whither he betook himself from the University of *Oxford*; but instead of pouring upon teadious Reports, Judgments and Statute Books, he accomplisht himself with the politer kind of Learning, moderately enjoy'd the pleasures of the Town, and frequented good Company, to which the sharpness of his Wit, and gayety of Fancy, render'd him not a little grateful; in which state of life he compos'd his more brisk and Youthful Poems, which are rather commended for the height of Fancy and acuteness of conceit, then for the smoothness of the Verse. At last by King *James* his command, or rather earnest persuasion, setting himself to the study of Theology, and entring into Holy Orders, he was first made Preacher of *Lincoln's Inne*, afterwards advanc't to be Dean of *Pauls*: and as of an Eminent Poet he became a much more Eminent Preacher, so he rather improved then reliquisht his Poetical Fancy; only converting it from human and worldly to Divine and Heavenly subjects.

(ii)
John Donne, who in his youth first of all produced love poems and then satires and verse letters, at length when his old age was approaching

turned to sacred and holy songs; in all of which he displayed a surpassing keenness of wit. In his last years he entered the priesthood, gaining the Deanship of St Paul's, and became a most celebrated preacher.

55. Anon., Preface to Rochester's *Valentinian*

1685

In a Preface to the Earl of Rochester's play *Valentinian*, published
posthumously, an anonymous friend of the author spoke of wit
as 'a true and lively expression of Nature' and approved of Dryden's definition 'a Propriety of Thoughts and Words—*or*
Thoughts and Words elegantly adapted to the Subject'. He went
on to give advice to the would-be witty poet, adjuring him
among other things not to write verses like Donne's (*Valentinian:
A Tragedy. As 'tis Alter'd by the late Earl of Rochester . . .*, 1685,
The Preface, b3ᵛ).

. . . let him remember hereafter, that Verses have Feet given 'em,
either to walk, graceful and smooth, and sometimes with Majesty and
State, like Virgil's, or to run, light and easie, like Ovid's, not to stand
stock-still like Dr Donne's, or to hobble like indigested Prose. . . .

56. Francis Atterbury

1690

The writer of an unsigned Preface to *The Second Part of Mr Waller's Poems*, 1690, singled Waller out as the reformer of English verse after the harshness of such as Donne (A3ᵛ–A6ʳ). The editor of the volume was Francis Atterbury (1662–1732) later Bishop of Rochester, a controversialist of considerable power in religious matters. It was probably he who essayed this definitive formulation of the new poetic creed.

The Tongue came into his hands, like a rough Diamond; he polish'd it first, and to that degree that all Artists since him have admired the Workmanship, without pretending to mend it. *Sucklyn* and *Carew*, I must confess, wrote some few things smoothly enough, but as all they did in this kind was not very considerable, so 'twas a little later than the earliest pieces of Mr. *Waller*. He undoubtedly stands first in the List of Refiners, and for ought I know, last too; for I question whether in *Charles* the Second's Reign, *English* did not come to its full perfection; and whether it has not had its *Augustean Age,* as well as the *Latin*. . . .

. . . For though *English* be mouldring Stone, as he tells us there, yet he has certainly pick'd the best out of a bad Quarry.

We are no less beholding to him for the new turn of Verse, which he brought in, and the improvement he made in our Numbers. Before his time, men Rhym'd indeed, and that was all: as for the harmony of measure, and that dance of words, which good ears are so much pleased with, they knew nothing of it. Their *Poetry* then was made up almost entirely of monosyllables; which, when they come together in any cluster, are certainly the most harsh untunable things in the World. If any man doubts of this, let him read ten lines in *Donne*, and he'll be quickly convinc'd. Besides, their Verses ran all into one another, and hung together, throughout a whole Copy, like the *hook't Attoms,* that compose a Body in *Des Cartes*. There was no distinction of parts, no regular stops, nothing for the Ear to rest upon—But as soon as the Copy began, down it went, like a Larum, incessantly; and the Reader was sure to be out of Breath, before he got to the end of it. So that really Verse in those days was but down-right Prose, tagg'd with Rhymes. Mr. *Waller* remov'd all these faults, brought in more Polysyllables, and smoother measures; bound up his thoughts better, and in a cadence more agreeable to the nature of the Verse he wrote in: So that where-ever the natural stops of that were, he contriv'd the little breakings of his sense so as to fall in with 'em. And for that reason, since the stress of our Verse lyes commonly upon the last Syllable, you'll hardly ever find him using a word of no force there. I would say if I were not afraid the Reader would think me too nice, that he commonly closes with Verbs, in which we know the Life of Language consists.

57. Anthony Wood

1691–2

Wood (1632–95) gave a brief account of Donne in his biographical dictionary of Oxford writers and bishops, *Athenae Oxonienses*. He drew it from Walton's *Life* but took a very cool view of Donne's achievements and stature (*Athenae Oxonienses*, 1691–2, i, cols 474–5).

Wood opens with Donne's general standing:

JOHN DONNE, a person somewhat noted for his divinity, knowledge in several languages, and other learning. . . .

He describes Donne's stay at Lincoln's Inn:

After he had continued there two years in exercising his poetical faculty, he began to survey the body of divinity. . . .

He sums Donne up, drawing on Walton's panegyric:

He was a person of great wit, virtue and abilities, learned in several faculties, and religious and exemplary in his life and conversation. In all which being eminent, he was therefore celebrated, and his memory had in great veneration by the wits and virtuosi of his time. [He lists them putting 'Ben Johnson' at the head.]

Wood then gives a list of Donne's writings, chiefly the prose works but with some poems included:

An Anatomy of the World, 1625. . . . *Divine Poems, with Epistles to Sir H. Goodere; Poems, Songs, Sonnets* [he lists some of them] 1633. . . .

Finally Wood refers the reader to Walton's *Life*, which 'is in the hands of every reader, and supersedes the necessity of extending the present article'. He quotes 'Loves Deitie' in full from the edition of 1669. And he closes with a reference to the portraits of Donne, which he ascribes to Marshall, Droeshout, and M. Merian.

58. John Locke

c. 1692

Locke listed a copy of the 1654 edition of Donne's poems among the books in his library. (See J. Harrison and P. Laslett, *The Library of John Locke*, Oxford, 1971, p. 126.)

59. William Walsh

1693

Walsh (1663–1708) was a critic and poet, though he is best remembered as the friend and mentor of the young Alexander Pope whom he advised to be a 'correct' writer. In the Preface to a collection of his letters and poems he argued that the English love poets who preceded him had preferred other qualities, such as wit and learning, to sincerity of passion (*Letters and Poems, Amorous and Gallant*, 1692, A4–5).

There are no Modern Writers perhaps who have succeeded better in Love Verses than the English. . . . Never was there a more copious Fancy or greater reach of Wit, than what appears in Dr. Donne; nothing can be more gallant or *gentile* than the Poems of Mr. Waller; nothing more gay or sprightly than those of Sir John Suckling; and nothing fuller of Variety and Learning than Mr. Cowley's. However it may be observ'd, that among all these, that Softness, Tenderness, and Violence of Passion which the Ancients thought most proper for Love Verses is wanting; and at the same time that we must allow Dr. Donne to have been a very great Wit; Mr. Waller a very gallant Writer; Sir John Suckling a very gay one and Mr. Cowley a great Genius; yet methinks I can hardly fancy any one of them to have been a very great Lover. And it grieves me that the Ancients, who could never have handsomer Women than we have, should nevertheless be so much more in Love than we are.

[He goes on to give reasons for this—the cruelty of our ladies, and the like.]

60. Sir Thomas Pope Blount

1694

Blount (1649–97), a politician, published essays on literary matters and on natural history. He gave a brief account of Donne in a section entitled 'Characters and Censures' of an essay on poetry, *De re poetica,* 1694, pp. 67–9. It repeats word for word that given by Edward Phillips in *Theatrum Poetarum,* 1675, save that Blount tells how Donne set himself 'to the Study of Divinity' whereas Phillips wrote 'to the study of Theology'. Blount does however add some critical opinions of Donne's poetry—by Walton, by 'the *Publisher* of Mr *Waller's* 2d Part of his *Poems,* in the *Preface',* and by Dryden. They are all given elsewhere in the present volume (see Nos. 27, 49, 56).

61. Christian Wernicke

1697

Wernicke (1661–1725) was a German poet who served in Paris as Danish envoy. A devotion to French literature prompted him to attack the poetic style of the school represented by von Hofmannswaldau and to oppose the ideals of that school. The extract given below specifically contradicts von Hofmannswaldau's account of the most noted English poets (see No. 43, 1679). (*Auf die Schlesische Poeten*, 1697. Given in G. Waterhouse, *The Literary Relations of England and Germany in the Seventeenth Century*, Cambridge, 1914, p. 119).

Of the English writers he mentions with admiration Donn and Quarles, whom no Englishman ever reads, and has not a word for Milton, Cowley, Denham and Waller, whom they justly regard as their best poets.

THE EIGHTEENTH CENTURY

'Donne is a dull ass'

62. References to Donne's poetry, or to Donne as a poet, and quotations from Donne's poems

1700–99

Undated

An anonymous eighteenth-century comment in the margin of a copy of the 1633 edition of Donne's poems (reported by Geoffrey Keynes, 'The Donne Revival' in *A City Tribute to John Donne*, the programme of the events held in the City of London to celebrate the 400th anniversary of Donne's birth, 1–8 October 1972):

Donne is a dull ass.

c. 1700

On the flyleaf of a copy of Martial's epigrams (Leyden, 1661), now in the library of the University of London, someone has written 'Dr Donn sen. on Raderus' and accurately copied out Donne's epigram 'Raderus'. If the writer was the 'Ja: Astry' who owned and signed the copy then he would have been either Sir James Astry, 1653–1709, or his son James, 1675–1716. (See J. H. P. Pafford, 'An Early Donne Reference', *NQ*, ccxi, October 1966, p. 377.)

1702

An editor of Bacon's letters mentioned Donne in a footnote (*The Letters of Sir Francis Bacon, Baron of Verulam*, ed. R.S., 1702, p. 168, fn. (a) to Letter lxxviii addressed to Sir George Villiers):

Having occasionally mention'd two or three *Ladies*, eminent for their Wit and Beauty; I could not in good Manners pass over in Silence my *Lady* of *Bedford*; so much celebrated for both, by that rare Wit of his Time Doctor *Donne*; . . .

1707

Paradox xciv of a collection of versified paradoxes couples Donne and Cowley as poets who have written vast quantities of verse on trivial subjects. The paradox is entitled 'In Praise of a Shock-Bitch', the poet preferring to praise his dog than his mistress. Stanzas 9 and 10 are given below. A footnote to stanza 10 refers to Quevedo's *Busion* in which the poet makes several hundred thousand stanzas on a pin dropped from his mistress's sleeve ('Philaret' [John Dunton?], *Athenian Sport: or, Two Thousand Paradoxes Merrily Argued, to Amuse and Divert the Age*, By a Member of the Athenian Society, 1707, pp. 408–10):

> Let the entranced *loving Ass*
> A Picture woo, and buss the Glass,
> Covering his Mistresses surpas—
> > sing Beauty!

> Then steal from *Cowley*, or from *Done*
> (Since none will miss 'em when they're gone)
> Two hundred thousand Stanza's on
> > Her Shoo-ty!

1711

Steele used some lines from Donne to bear out a moral distinction in *The Spectator*, no. 41, 17 April 1711 (ed. D. F. Bond, 1965, i, p. 176). He contrasts the character of women who paint their faces (whom he calls Picts) with the outward and inward artlessness of such natural unpainted British ladies as Lindamira and Statira. He adds of Statira

How like is this Lady, and how unlike is a *Pict*, to that Description Dr *Donne* gives of his Mistress?

And he quotes lines 244b–46 of *The second Anniversary*.

1714

Daniel George Morhof gave a brief account of Donne in a section 'De Oratoribus atque Sacris' of his *Polyhistor Literarius Philosophicus et Practicus*, Lubeck, 1714, i, p. 994. He mentioned the first published edition of Donne's poems, 1633, said that Donne had written them at the age of eighteen, and described them as 'most ingenious' and 'full of the wittiest conceit'.

1729

J. P. Niceron gave a lengthy account of Donne's life and a list of the writings in his *Memoires Pour Servir A L'Histoire Des Hommes Illustres Dans La Republique Des Lettres. Avec Un Catalogue Raisonné de leurs Ouvrages*, Paris, 1729, viii, pp. 138–53. The life is abridged from Walton but a quite disproportionate amount of space is given to Donne's marriage. The list of writings mentions the editions of 1633 and 1635 but describes them very oddly: *1633*, for example, is said to consist of '*Poemes sacrez, & Lettres au Sieur Henri Goodere (en Anglois)* . . .'. The one critical comment on these editions is that 'Les Lettres sont ingénieuses'.

?c. 1730

In *The Works of the Late Aaron Hill Esq.*, 1753, iv, pp. 58–9, appears the following imitation of Donne's 'The Baite' (see P. A. Tasch, *NQ*, ccxvi, 1971, p. 464):

> *To a Lady, who lov'd* Angling, *from a Hint, out of Dr* DONNE
>
> i
> Some, by the bending *reed's* slow aid,
> May *boast* th'unwary *fish* betray'd:
> Others may *finny shoals* beset,
> And *sweep* 'em, with the treach'rous *net*.
>
> ii
> But, why shou'd SYLVIA use *deceit*,
> Who is, *herself*, her own *best bait*?
> Step but, *undress'd*, within the *brook*,
> And smile at every *needless* hook.
>
> iii
> Each *willing fish* will, round thee, *swim*,
> *Gladder* to catch thee, than thou *him*.
> Or, if *one* fish, *uncaught*, goes by
> *That* fish, is *wiser, far*, than *I*!

1733–4

Over some six months in 1733–4 *The Universal Spectator and Weekly Journal*, edited by Henry Stonecastle, published five poems imitated in part or whole from Donne:

No. cclviii, 15 September 1733: '*To Sir* Gimcrack Noddy'. From Donne's epigram 'Antiquary'.

No. cclx, 29 September 1733: '*The Man* of Business *no* Lover. *A Morning Dialogue*, varied from Dr *Donne*'. From 'Breake of Day'.

No. cclxxviii, 2 February 1734: 'The Oxonian's Trip to the Drawing Room'. Draws on Donne's *Satyre iv*.

No. cclxxx, 16 February 1734: 'The General Lover'. From 'The Indifferent'. 'The Lover's Curse'. From 'The Curse'.

The last two poems were also printed in *The Gentleman's Magazine*, iv, February 1734, p. 102. (See Brijraj Singh, *NQ*, xviii, 1971, p. 50. Singh wrongly says that these poems appeared in 1736.)

The opening lines of 'The General Lover' show what the adapter did with Donne:

> Let my *Fair One* only be
> *Female Sex, and she's for me:*
> I can love her, Fair or *Brown*,
> Of the *Country* or the *Town*: . . .

Here is the typically neat adaptation of 'Breake of Day':

Damon.	*Silvia* 'tis *Day* (*Sylvia*) what if it be?
	Damon, what's that to you or me?
	Went we to *Bed* because 'twas *Night*?
	Then should we *rise* because 'tis *Light*?
Dam.	*Love* hither *Sylvia*, was our Guide;
Sylv.	Here let us still with Love abide:
Dam.	But should the *Sun* our Love reveal,
	And to the World for Envy tell,—
Sylv.	Let him, the *Worst* that he can say
	Is, I'd not let my *Heart* away;
	And that I lov'd my *Honour* so,
	I'd not let *him* that *had it* go.
Dam.	But *Business*, Child—(*Sylv.*) does *Business* call?
	Ah! that's the worst Excuse of all;
Dam.	My *Levee* waits,—the *Chair's* at th' *Door*:
Sylv.	Adieu—but never see me more—
	Venus, propitious to the Fair,
	Venus in Pity hear my pray'r:
	Gallants when *Men* of *Business*, far remove,
	Give *them* whose *only* Business is to *Love*.

1734

A brief biographical account of Donne in a German lexicon treats him entirely as a theologian and divine. A list of his writings mentions no poems save 'the anatomy of the World ib.1625 in 8' and the spurious Latin epigrams. (J. H. Zedler, *Grosses vollständiges universal Lexicon*, Halle and Leipzig, 1734, vii, p. 1279b.)

1738

John Wesley quoted Donne in his journal on Tuesday, 24 January 1738, during a moment of peril on the return journey from his Georgia mission (*An Extract of The Rev. Mr John Wesley's Journal From his Embarking for Georgia To his Return to London*, Bristol, undated (but 1739), pp. 71–2. See also M. W. England and John Sparrow, *Hymns Unbidden: Donne, Herbert, Blake, Emily Dickinson and the Hymnographers*, New York, 1966, p. 3):

I went to *America*, to convert the *Indians*: But oh! Who shall convert me! Who, what is He that will deliver me from this evil Heart of Unbelief? I have a fair Summer-Religion. I can talk well; nay, and believe myself, while no Danger is near: But let Death look me in the Face, and my Spirit is troubled. Nor can I say, *To die is Gain*!

> I have a Sin of Fear, that when I've spun
> My last Thread, I shall perish on the Shore!

1741

Sir John Hawkins and Mr Foster Webb, in friendly rivalry, tried their hand at imitating Donne's 'The Canonization'. They sent the two imitations, unsigned, to Moses Browne and asked him to judge between them. He replied in a letter dated 23 November 1741:

S^r. I have considerately read over the enclosed Peices and compared them with Dr Donne's Cannonization from whence they appear to be imitated. In my Opinion they have both their Merit and are each of them Improvements of the D^{rs}. . . .

He then expressed his preference for the piece by Hawkins. Both poems survive in a manuscript in the Bodleian Library (MS. Eng. poet C.9), the one headed 'Sonnet imitated from Dr Donne by Mr J. Hawkins, 1741', and the other headed 'Paraphrased from Dr Donne by Mr

Foster Webb 1741'. (See P. A. Scholes, *The Life and Activities of Sir John Hawkins*, 1953, pp. 258–67.)

Here is the first stanza of Hawkins's attempt:

> I Prithee cease to chide my harmless Love,
>   Nor tire my Patience with thy loath'd Advice;
> The Sordid Pleasures which thoud'st have me prove,
>   May suit the aged Sons of Avarice
> But the mean Wisdom of acquiring Gold
>   As Ill becomes the Young as Love the Old.

The compiler of the manuscript notes that Hawkins later improved upon lines 3–5 as follows:

> Canst thou expect a soul like mine to move
>   Or tempt my Youth to sordid Avarice
> In vain! The selfish Act of heaping Gold
>   As ill, etc. . . .

1741

A poem entitled 'A SONG. Blow, blow, thou Winter Wind' in *The London Magazine: And Monthly Chronologer*, June 1741, p. 301b, is an adaptation of Donne's 'Song. Goe, and catche a falling starre'. Here are the opening lines:

> Go, catch a falling star,
>   Tell me where past years are,
> Make me hear mermaids sing:
> Tell me at court what wind
> Promotes an honest mind,
>   Or keeps off envy's sting. . . .

1741

'Tim. Vinegar', in a letter to Captain Vinegar, Saturday, 24 November 1739; part of the imaginary transactions of the Vinegar family related in Henry Fielding's *The Champion*, 1741, p. 29:

I shall conclude, Sir, with observing, for the Honour of this august Metropolis, that however singular it may seem to see the Man of Business, and the Poet center in the same Person, no one City in the Universe has produc'd so many Ornaments of polite Learning as this; and when I mention the great Names of *Chaucer, Spencer, Donne,*

Milton, and *Cowley*, with those of Mr. *Pope*, and Mr. *Glover*, all Natives of *London*; no Body will presume to treat the Word *Citizen*, as a Term of Reproach any more. . . .

1749

In *The History of Tom Jones, A Foundling*, 1749, ii, p. 11, Henry Fielding applied to Sophia Western Donne's description of Elizabeth Drury:

Her Complexion had rather more of the Lilly than of the Rose; but when Exercise, or Modesty, encreased her natural Colour, no Vermilion could equal it. Then one might indeed cry out with the celebrated Dr *Donne*. . . .

He quotes *The second Anniversary*, lines 244b–46.

c. 1750

The poet and dramatist George Jeffreys (1678–1755) defended the use of monosyllabic lines in poetry by endorsing the opinion of Donne's versification expressed in the anonymous Preface to Rochester's *Valentinian*, 1685 ('On the Use of Monosyllables in Poetry', one of the 'Letters by several eminent Persons deceased' in *The Critical Review*, xxxiv, 1772, p. 455):

As far, therefore, as the constant practice of our most celebrated poets can be of weight, monosyllable verses are justified; and, to prove that they deserve to be so, instead of being only excused, as slips and defects incident to the best writers, I shall admit what a certain author says, that 'verses ought to run like Ovid's, or walk like Virgil's, and not to stand stock still like doctor Donne's'.

1754

The official hymnbook of the Moravian Brethren, published in 1754, contains two hymns adapted from poems by Donne. Hymn no. 383 is patched together out of four of the *Holy Sonnets*—nos *i, ii, xi*, and *xii*. Hymn no. 384 is an adaptation of the first three stanzas of *A Litanie* (see M. W. England and John Sparrow, *Hymns Unbidden*, ed. cit., pp. 19–20).

1755

In a letter 'To Mr Fitz-Adam' in *The World*, cxxxvi, Thursday, 14 August 1755, p. 825, one 'A.C.' argues that most things of value in the dead languages are quite as good when translated into the living languages. He instances 'the paraphrases and translations of Donne, Dryden, Garth, Congreve and Hammond' as rendering without loss the various qualities of Horace, Ovid, Juvenal, and Tibullus.

1758

In his *Catalogue of Royal and Noble Authors* (1758), 1806, p. 194, Horace Walpole mentioned Donne's verses on the translation of the psalms by Sir Philip Sidney and his sister, and quoted part of the title.

1759

In a manuscript *Book of Memoranda*, pp. 26, 35, 66, 107, Walpole made several jottings concerning Donne. He mentioned 'A poem called Twickenham-gardens in Donne's, p. 22' ('Twicknam Garden' occurs on p. 22 of the 1650 and 1654 editions of Donne's poems); conjectured that 'some of Dr Donne's' poems were written to Christiana, Countess of Devonshire; and noted the accounts of Donne in Winstanley's *England's Worthies* and in Baker's *Chronicle of the Kings of England*. (Sir Geoffrey Keynes, *A Bibliography of Dr John Donne*, 4th ed., Oxford, 1973, p. 307b. The manuscript is in a private collection in America.)

1762

Sterne picked up an idea from Donne's 'The Will' in chapter XII of *The Life and Opinions of Tristram Shandy*, 1762, v, pp. 62–3:

In short, my father . . . advanced so very slow with his work . . . that . . . I verily believe, I had put by my father, and left him drawing a sun-dial, for no better purpose than to be buried under ground.

1772

In a footnote to 'A short Account of the several sorts of ORGANS used for CHURCH Service' one 'W.L.' of Leicester quoted lines from Donne to support his description of a curious feature of an old organ (*The Gentleman's Magazine, and Historical Chronicle*. For the year 1772, xlii, p. 565b):

The old organ at Lynn had on it a figure of King David playing on the harp cut in solid wood, larger than the life: likewise several moving figures which fear time, &c. This is an old practice, and alluded to by Dr Donne:

He quotes lines 15–16 of *Satyre ii*.

1774

Horace Walpole quoted a line from Pope's version of Donne's *Satyre iv* (line 75 in Donne, line 102 in Pope's version) in a letter to the Hon. Henry Seymour Conway, Arlington Street, 26 December 1774 (*The Letters of Horace Walpole, Fourth Earl of Oxford*, ed. Mrs Paget Toynbee, Oxford, 1904, ix, p. 111):

I am delighted with all the honours you receive, and with all the amusements they procure you, which is the best part of honours. For the glorious part, I am always like the man in Pope's Donne,

> Then happy he who shows the tombs, said I.
> That is, they are least troublesome there. . . .

1780

In an admiring footnote to a poem by Carew, J. Nichols bore out Wood's remark that Carew was 'adored by the poets of his time' with a list of 'the first men of the age' who were Carew's admirers, notably Donne, Davenant, May and Suckling. (*A Select Collection of Poems: with Notes, Biographical and Historical*, 1780, p. 282.)

1790

George Ellis (1753–1815), antiquarian and historian, gave Donne's 'Song. Goe, and catche a falling starre', and the first nine lines of 'Negative Love', in his *Specimens of the Early English Poets*, 1790, pp. 140–1. For the second and third editions, 1801 and 1803, Ellis added a one-paragraph outline of Donne's life, quoting Dryden on the *Satyres* and commending Pope's version of *Satyres ii* and *iv* (1803, ii, p. 383).

1793

Donne's 'The Baite' is given in Joseph Ritson's *The English Anthology*, 1793, i, pp. 20–1, and ascribed to him as Dean of St Paul's. A footnote points out that 'This song is in imitation of a still more beautiful one by Christopher Marlowe, beginning with the same line'. This first volume of the anthology gives two poems each by Spenser, Drayton, Shakespeare, Wotton, Jonson, three poems each by Corbet, Carew, King, Waller, four poems by Milton, and so on.

?c. 1795

William Blake used part of lines 35–6 of Donne's *Metempsychosis* as the legend for a sketch in his notebook. The sketch shows a patriarchal figure squatting with legs crossed under him and his wrists manacled; very faintly underneath, and picked out by a border from a mass of surrounding commentary, is written

> Whose changeless brow
> Neer smiles nor frowns
> Donne.

Donne's lines refer to 'Great Destiny the commissary of God', which is presumably what the sketched figure represents. (*The Note-Book of William Blake Called the Rossetti Manuscript*, ed. G. Keynes, 1935, p. 85.)

63. Jeremy Collier

1701

The nonjuring clergyman Collier (1650–1726), scourge of the English stage, gave an account of Donne's life and character which mentions only casually that Donne wrote poetry (*The Great Historical, Geographical, Genealogical and Poetical Dictionary*, 1701, entry under 'Donne').

[Donne] had a good Genius for Poetry, Extraordinary Parts, and Considerable Learning; as appears by his Works; which are his *Pseudo-Martyr, Biathanatos, A Volume of Sermons in Folio* &c. As to his Character in point of Morality and Religion, he was, after his going into *Orders*, remarkably Regular and Pious, and very Charitable.

64. Anon., *A Comparison Between the Two Stages*

1702

In an anonymous dialogue on dramatic poetry 'Critick' argues that good writing doesn't call for good sense, and that wit is a matter of fashion. (*A Comparison Between the Two Stages*, 1702, pp. 77–8. Modern edition by S. B. Wells, Princeton Studies in English, xxvi, Princeton, 1942, pp. 43–4.)

Ramble. Your Comparisons are remote Mr *Critick*.

Critick. Not so remote as some successful Authors are from good sense: Wit and Sense are no more the same than Wit and Humour; nay there is even in Wit an uncertain Mode, a variable Fashion, that is as unstable as the Fashion of our Cloaths: This may be prov'd by their Works who writ a hundred Years ago, compar'd with some of the modern; Sir *Philip Sidney, Don, Overbury*, nay *Ben* himself took singular delight in playing with their Words: Sir *Philip* is every where in his *Arcadia* jingling, which certainly by the example of so great a Man, proves that sort of Wit then in Fashion; now that kind of Wit is call'd Punning and Quibbling, and is become too low for the Stage, nay even for ordinary Converse; so that when we find a Man who still loves that old fashion'd Custom, we make him remarkable, as who is more remarkable, than *Capt. Swan*.

65. Alexander Pope

1706–36

Pope's interest in Donne extended over most of his poetic life, but it was Donne the satirist who chiefly concerned him. In general he took Dryden's line, praising Donne's wit at the expense of his versification.

(i) As a young man Pope was befriended by the elderly dramatist Wycherley, some of whose verses he undertook to polish. He wrote to Wycherley about the task on 10 April 1706 (*The Correspondence of Alexander Pope*, ed. G. Sherburn, Oxford, 1956, i, p. 16):

Donne (like one of his Successors) had infinitely more Wit than he wanted Versification: for the great dealers in Wit, like those in Trade, take least Pains to set off their Goods; while the Haberdashers of small Wit, spare for no Decorations or Ornaments. You have commission'd me to paint your Shop, and I have done my best to brush you up like your Neighbours. But I can no more pretend to the Merit of the Production, than a Midwife to the Virtues and good Qualities of the Child she helps unto the Light,

(ii) Pope acknowledged a borrowing from Donne's *Satyre iv* (lines 94–6) in a verse letter, 'An Epistle to Henry Cromwell, Esq.', written in 1707 (lines 11–20):

> I know you dread all those who write,
> And both with Mouth and Hand recite;
> Who slow, and leisurely rehearse,
> As loath t'enrich you with their Verse;
> Just as a Still, with Simples in it,
> Betwixt each Drop stays half a Minute.
> (That Simile is not my own,
> But lawfully belongs to *Donne*)

(You see how well I can contrive a
Interpolatio Furtiva). . . .

(iii) Pope rewrote, or 'versified' as he called it, two of Donne's *Satyres*
as an adjunct to his *Imitations of Horace*. He essayed a version of *Satyre ii*
in 1713, probably revised it in 1733, and published it in 1735 as *The
Second Satire of Dr John Donne, Dean of St Paul's Versifyed*. In 1733 he
published a version of *Satyre iv*, which may also be a revision of a much
earlier attempt, as *The Fourth Satire of Dr John Donne, Dean of St Paul's,
Versifyed*; this version bears a subtitle which links Donne's poem with
Horace, *Satires*, l. ix, 'The Impertinent, or a Visit to the Court'.

When Pope published both versions together in the 1735 volume of
his *Works* he gave Donne's original text alongside his own, inviting
direct comparison. Here, as a sample of what Pope did with Donne, are
lines 175–91 of Donne's *Satyre iv* alongside Pope's version of them in
lines 212–35 of *The Fourth Satire of Dr John Donne . . . Versifyed*:

Donne

'Tis ten a clock and past; All whom the Mues,
Baloune, Tennis, Dyet, or the stewes,
Had all the morning held, now the second
Time made ready, that day, in flocks, are found
In the Presence, and I, (God pardon mee.)
As fresh, and sweet their Apparrels be, as bee
The fields they sold to buy them; 'For a King
Those hose are,' cry the flatterers; And bring
Them next weeke to the Theatre to sell;
Wants reach all states; Me seems they doe as well
At stage, as court; All are players; who e'r lookes
(For themselves dare not goe) o'er Cheapside books,
Shall finde their wardrops Inventory. Now,
The Ladies come; As Pirates, which doe know
That there came weak ships fraught with Cutchannel,
The men board them; and praise, as they thinke, well,
Their beauties; they the mens wits; Both are bought.

Pope

See! where the *British* Youth, engag'd no more
At *Fig's* at *White's*, with *Felons,* or a *Whore,*
Pay their last Duty to the *Court,* and come

All fresh and fragrant, to the *Drawing-Room*:
In Hues as gay, and Odours as divine,
As the fair Fields they sold to look so fine.
'That's *Velvet* for a *King*!' the Flattr'er swears;
Tis true, for ten days hence 'twill be *King Lear's*.
Our Court may justly to our Stage give Rules,
That helps it both to *Fool's-Coats* and to *Fools*,
And why not Players strut in Courtiers Cloaths?
For these are Actors too, as well as those:
Wants reach all States; they beg but better drest,
And all is *splendid Poverty* at best.
    Painted for sight, and essenc'd for the smell,
Like Frigates fraught with Spice and Cochine'l,
Sail in the *Ladies*: How each Pyrate eyes
So weak a Vessel, and so rich a Prize!
Top-gallant he, and she in all her Trim,
He boarding her, she striking sail to him.
'*Dear Countess*! you have Charms all Hearts to hit!'
And '*sweet Sir Fopling*! you have so much wit!'
Such Wits and Beauties are not prais'd for nought,
For both the Beauty and the Wit are *bought*.

(iv) Pope's friend Joseph Spence (1699–1768), sometime Professor of Poetry and Regius Professor of Modern History at Oxford, took notes of the conversation of Pope and his circle. The notes, probably made between 1730 and 1736, were widely known in the eighteenth century but they did not appear in print until 1820. Spence recorded Pope's particular commendation of Donne's epistles, *Metempsychosis*, and *Satyres* as his best poetry, and noted a number of other comments on Donne (*Spence's Anecdotes*, ed. J. M. Osborn, Oxford, 1966, i, pp. 187–9):

Donne had no imagination, but as much wit I think as any writer can possibly have.

Herbert is lower than Crashaw, Sir John Beaumont higher, and Donne a good deal so.

Donne is superior to Randolph, and Sir William Davenant a better poet than Donne.

Cowley is a fine poet, in spite of all his faults. He, as well as Davenant, borrowed his metaphysical turn from Donne.

Sir William Davenant's *Gondibert* is not a good poem, if you take it in the whole, but there are a great many good things in it. He is a scholar of Donne's, and took his sententiousness and metaphysics from him.

(v) Pope's biographer Owen Ruffhead (1723–69) reported that Pope thought 'to pen a discourse on the rise and progress of English poetry', and classed the English poets by schools as a first step. Ruffhead gives Pope's list, which has a large 'School of Donne' but makes no mention of Herbert, Vaughan, or Marvell. Here is the relevant part of it (*The Life of Alexander Pope Esq.*, 1769, pp. 424–5):

1. School of Provence	Chaucer's Visions, Romaunt of the Rose. Pierce Plowman, Tales from Boccace. Gower.
2. School of Chaucer	Lydgate, T. Occleve, Walt. de Mapes, Skelton.
3. School of Petrarch	E. of Surrey, Sir Thomas Wyat, Sir Philip Sydney, G. Gascoyn, Translator of Ariosto's Com.
4. School of Dante	Mirror of Magistrates, Lord Buckhurst's Induction, Gorboduck, — Original of good Tragedy, — Seneca [his Model]

ÆRA II.

SPENCER, Col. Clout, from the School of Ariosto and Petrarch, translated from Tasso.

5. School of Spencer, and From Italian Sonnets	W. Brown's Pastorals, Ph. Fletcher's Purple Island, Alabaster, Piscatory Ec. S. Daniel, Sir Walter Raleigh, Milton's Juvenilia. Heath. Habinton.
Translators from Italian	Golding, Edm. Fairfax, Harrington.

6. School of Donne
{
Cowley, Davenant,
Michael Drayton,
Sir Thomas Overbury,
Randolph,
Sir John Davis,
Sir John Beaumont,
Cartwright,
Cleveland,
Crashaw,
Bishop Corbet,
Lord Falkland.
}

Carew,
T. Carey,
} in Matter

G. Sandys,
in his Par.
of Job
} in Versification

Fairfax,

Models to Waller.

Sir John Mennis,
Tho. Baynal,
} Originals of Hudibras.

(vi) In the advertisement to *The First Satire of the Second Book of Horace Imitated*, 1733, Pope defended his imitations of Horace by the example of 'Dr Donne':

The Occasion of publishing these *Imitations* was the Clamour raised on some of my *Epistles*. An Answer from *Horace* was both more full, and of more Dignity, than any I cou'd have made in my own person; and the Example of much greater Freedom in so eminent a Divine as Dr. *Donne*, seem'd a proof with what Indignation and Contempt a Christian may treat Vice or Folly, in ever so low, or ever so high, a Station. Both these Authors were acceptable to the Princes and Ministers under whom they lived: The Satires of Dr. *Donne* I versify'd at the Desire of the Earl of *Oxford* while he was Lord Treasurer, and of the Duke of *Shrewsbury* who had been Secretary of State; neither of whom look'd upon a Satire on Vicious Courts as any Reflection on those they serv'd in. And indeed there is not in the world a greater Error, than that which Fools are so apt to fall into, and Knaves with good reason to incourage, the mistaking a *Satyrist* for a *Libeller*; whereas to a *true Satyrist* nothing is so odious as a *Libeller*, for the same reason as to a man *truly Virtuous* nothing is so hateful as a *Hypocrite*.

66. William Balam

c. 1707

The Dobell manuscript of Donne's poems, now in the Houghton Library of Harvard University (MS. Eng. 966/4), was copiously scribbled over by one of its early possessors. He has been identified as William Balam of Ely (1652–1726), who studied at St John's College, Cambridge, and Lincoln's Inn and became an ecclesiastical lawyer. Balam used the manuscript as a general commonplace book in fact; but he also shows particular interest in the poems themselves and discloses that he owned at least one other manuscript copy of them. He went over the texts of the poems in the manuscript and made them good from the printed editions, writing in the established titles, supplying deficiencies, and amending errors. He also underscored passages which appealed to him, paraphrased or explained lines (he paraphrased in prose the whole of *Satyre iv*), and compared thoughts in Donne with places in other poets. His one critical remark is that 'Loves Growth' 'raises you to the utmost extent of pleasure of which Human nature is capable'. (See Mabel Potter, 'A Note on Donne', *NQ* n.s. 13, 10, October 1966, pp. 376–7, and 'A Seventeenth-Century Literary Critic of John Donne: The Dobell Manuscript Re-Examined', *Harvard Library Bulletin*, xxiii, i, January 1975, pp. 63–89.)

67. Jonathan Swift

c. 1710

A pencilled note on a preliminary page of the O'Flaherty manu-script of Donne's poems indicates that Swift wanted to see the poems properly edited and thought there would be an audience for them. The eighteenth-century possessor of the manuscript who wrote and signed the note evidently knew something of Parnell's affairs, but we do not know how close to Swift's circle he stood. Parnell had 'versified' Donne's *Satyre iii* (see No. 69). The O'Flaherty manuscript is now in the Houghton Library of Harvard University, MS. Eng. 966/5.

Parnels good friend Swift, advised him to publish the following poems, with Notes, and a life of the author, by subscription, which his great indolence, and too constant attendance to what was his ruin prevented.

Thos Burton

68. *The Guardian*

1713

Richard Steele edited and partly wrote *The Guardian* in 1713, and Addison and Parnell were contributors. In no. xvi, dated Monday, 30 March 1713, there is an essay on the art of writing songs (i.e., lyric poems) in the form of a letter to Mrs Annabella Lizard, accompanying two songs. The writer first praises Latin and French songs, then turns to English writers.

Our writers generally crowd into one Song Materials enough for several; and so they starve every Thought, by endeavouring to purse up more than one at a time. They give you a string of imperfect Sonnets, instead of one finished Piece, which is a fault Mr. Waller (whose Beauties cannot be too much admired) sometimes falls into. But, of all our Countrymen, none are more defective in their Songs, through a Redundancy of Wit, than Dr. *Donne* and Mr. *Cowley*. In them one Point of Wit flashes so fast upon another, that the Reader's Attention is dazzled by the continual sparkling of their Imagination; you find a new Design started in almost every Line, and you come to the end, without the Satisfaction of seeing any one of them executed.

69. Thomas Parnell

c. 1714

The Irish poet and clergyman Parnell (1679–1718), a friend of Swift and Pope, attempted to emulate Pope by 'versifying' Donne's *Satyre iii*, Parnell renders Donne in smoothly anonymous couplets with none of the individual character that Pope gave to his own versions. This is what he makes of lines 1–16 and 79–89 of Donne's poem:

DR DONNE'S THIRD SATIRE VERSIFIED

Compassion checks my spleen, yet scorn denies
The tears a passage through my swelling eyes:
To laugh or weep at sins, might idly show
Unheedful passion, or unfruitful woe.
Satire! arise, and try thy sharper ways,
If ever satire cur'd an old disease.
Is not Religion (Heaven-descended dame)
As worthy all our soul's devoutest flame,
As moral Virtue in her early sway,
When the best Heathens saw by doubtful day?
Are not the joys, the promis'd joys above,
As great and strong to vanquish earthly love,
As earthly glory, fame, respect, and show,
As all rewards their virtue found below?
Alas! Religion proper means prepares,
These means are ours, and must its end be theirs?
And shall thy father's spirit meet the sight
Of heathen sages cloth'd in heavenly light,
Whose merit of strict life, severely suited
To reason's dictates, may be faith imputed,
Whilst thou, to whom he taught the nearer road,
Art ever banish'd from the blest abode?

Oh! if thy temper such a fear can find,
This fear were valour of the noblest kind. . . .

On a large mountain, at the basis wide,
Steep to the top, and craggy at the side,
Sits sacred Truth enthron'd; and he who means
To reach the summit, mounts with weary pains,
Winds round and round, and every turn essays,
Where sudden breaks resist the shorter ways.
Yet labour so, that ere faint age arrive,
Thy searching soul possess her rest alive:
To work by twilight were to work too late,
And age is twilight to the night of fate.
To will alone, is but to mean delay,
To work at present is the use of day.
For man's employ much thought and deed remain,
High thoughts the soul, hard deeds the body strain,
And mysteries ask believing, which to view,
Like the fair Sun, are plain, but dazzling too.

70. Matthew Prior

1718

From Prior's Preface to his 'Solomon on the Vanity of the World. A Poem in Three Books' (*Poems on Several Occasions*, 1718, p. 389).

I would say one Word of the Measure, in which This and most Poems of the Age are written. Heroic with continued Rhime, as DONNE and his Contemporaries used it, carrying the Sense of one Verse most commonly into another, was found too dissolute and wild and came very often too near Prose. As DAVENANT and WALLER corrected, and DRYDEN perfected it: It is too Confined: It cuts off the Sense at the end of every first Line, which must always rhime to the next following; and the Sound, and brings every Couplet to the Point of an Epigram. . . .

71. Jacob Tonson

1719

The edition of Donne's poems published by Tonson in 1719 gave some preliminary matter which was reprinted in subsequent editions down to 1855. The dedication Donne's son wrote for the 1650 edition is given without explanation, as though it is by the poet himself. Then there is an account of Donne's life, and a few critical observations, both drawn from Walton but reworded in eighteenth-century terms. (*Poems on Several Occasions Written by the Reverend John Donne, D.D. late Dean of St Paul's*, 1719, A7ᵛ.)

The Reader will find the same Spirit of Religion I have been speaking of in several of the following Pieces; especially his *Hymn to God the Father,* and that which he wrote on his Deathbed, bearing this Title, *An Hymn to God my God in my Sickness.* . .

As to the more airy Part of his Poetical Compositions, they were only the innocent Amusement and Diversion of his Youth, being most of them writ before his twentieth Year; so happy at this Age was he in the Sprightliness of his Wit, and the Delicacy of his Fancy. His Poem called *the Autumnal* he wrote at *Oxford* upon the lady *Herbert*. . . .

72. Giles Jacob

1720

The compiler Giles Jacob (1686–1744) gave a brief life of 'John Donne, D.D.' in a set of biographies of the chief English poets. It is a résumé of Walton's *Life of Donne*, even the few general remarks on Donne's qualities being blatant rewordings of Walton (*An Historical Account of the Lives and Writings of our most Considerable English Poets*, 1720, pp. 46–8).

. . . This learned Divine, admired for his Great Wit. . . .

He soon enjoyed the best Conversation in Town, to whom the acuteness of his Wit, and the natural gaiety of his Temper, soon rendered him highly acceptable: In which state of Life, he composed most of his *Love-Poems*. . . .

. . . thus from an Eminent Poet he became a much more eminent Divine. . . .

73. John Oldmixon

1728

Oldmixon (1673-1742), historian, pamphleteer, and poet, expressed what soon became the orthodox eighteenth-century attitude to Donne and anticipated Johnson's account of 'metaphysical' poetry (*The Arts of Logick and Rhetorick*, 1728, index, vi–viii, pp. 309, 332–3).

(i) From the Index:

> Donne, *Dr his metaphysical Gallantry*, 309.
> *His other Errors*, 332.

(ii) From the Dedication:

How many great Genius's have miscarry'd, by not thinking rightly on Subjects they were otherwise well able to handle and adorn, and for Want of considering that Truth, in all the Productions of the Mind, is what only renders them agreeable and useful, and that the false Brillant of Thoughts is like the Glare of Lightning, which dazles and hurts the Sight, as that does the Understanding!

Thus it was that Bishop *Andrews*, and the most eminent Divine sat the Beginning of the last Century, reduc'd Preaching to Punning, and the Eloquence of the Chair to the Buffoonry of the Stage. Thus it was that Dr. *Donne*, and Mr. *Cowley*, confounded Metaphysicks and Love, and turn'd Wit into Point.

It was thus that *Dryden* also confounded Epick Poetry and Elegy, Tragedy and Farce, and taught his Contemporary Poets, by his Example, to make their Heroes and Heroines, in the Agonies of Despair and Death, sigh out their great Souls in Simile and Rhime. This Vice in Thought is the most obvious, and yet the most common, in *English* Poetry occasion'd either by the Poets Ignorance of it, or their Dependance on the Ignorance of their Hearers and Readers, tho' they have been taught better, as by the last Duke of *Bucks*.

> Figures of Speech, which Poets think so fine,
> Are all but Paint upon a beauteous Face,
> And in Description only claim a Place;
> But to make Rage declaim, and Grief discourse,
> From Lover in Despair fine Things to force,
> Must needs succeed; for who can choose but pity
> A dying Hero miserably witty?

And again,

> Or else the Bells eternally they chime,
> They sigh in Simile, and die in Rhime.

I shou'd not have presum'd to have touch'd the Chair, which is sacred even its Faults, but that I found the Lord *Lansdown* had been more free with it on the like Occasion, where he speaks of Truth in Thought, or Right-thinking; without which the Poet's and Orator's Brain is always delirious,

> But let the bold Adventurer be sure
> That every Line the Test of Truth endure.
> On this Foundation may the Fabrick rise,
> Firm and unshaken, till it touch the Skies.
> From *Pulpits* banish'd, from the Court and Love,
> Abandon'd Truth seeks Shelter in the Grove.
> Cherish, *ye Muses*, the forsaken Fair,
> And take into your Train the beauteous Wanderer.

The noble Critick plainly alludes to the punning Sermons in the Reign of King *James* I. and the Metaphysical Love-Verses by which *Donne* and *Cowley* acquir'd so much Fame.

(iii)
I expect to be censur'd by many Lovers of Poetry, for being so free with the Character of the great *Cowley*, who, as a Wit, deserves that Title; but as a Poet he seems to have lost almost all his Merit in our Time. *Dryden* tells us, in his Preface to *Juvenal*, that *Cowley* copy'd Dr. *Donne* to a Fault in his *Metaphysicks*, which his Love Verses abound with. . . .

(iv)
But those Wits that subtilize, need only follow their Genius to take Flight, and lose themselves in their own Thoughts. Dr. *Donne* and Mr. *Cowley* are sufficient Instances of this Vice in our Language: The Latter, as has been hinted, copy'd the Former in his Faults; and it seems strange

to me, that after *Suckling* and *Waller* had written, whose Genius's were so fine and just, Mr. *Cowley* should imitate Dr. *Donne*; in whom there's hardly any Thing that's agreeable, or one Stroke which has any Likeness to Nature: Two or three Examples will serve to shew his Manner; as this of his falling in Love.

[He quotes lines 14–24 of 'The Broken Heart', running the stanzas together.]

But what follows is still more extraordinary. 'Tis on Love too, the most natural Subject which can be thought of.

[He quotes lines 21–36 of 'A Valediction: forbidding Mourning', running the stanzas together.]

What Woman's Heart in the World could stand out against such an Attack as this, after she once understood how to handle a Pair of Compasses? Both *Donne* and *Cowley* were Men of Learning, and must consequently have read the Antients over and over. They could never learn this from them, but owe all the Extravagance in it to their own Genius's.

74. Elijah Fenton

1729, 1731

Fenton (1683–1730), schoolmaster, poet, and assistant to Pope, alluded to Donne in a commentary on Waller's 'Song: Stay, Phoebus, stay!' (*The Works of Edmund Waller* (1729), 1730, p. lxi). Fenton had in his library a copy of the 1633 edition of Donne's poems, a copy of the 1650 edition of the poems, and a copy of the 1670 edition of Walton's *Lives*. The library came up for sale on 17 February 1731 and the three volumes are listed in the catalogue. (See *Sale Catalogues of Libraries of Eminent Persons*, v, ed. S. Parks, 1972, pp. 54, 63, 66.)

The latter Stanza of these verses (which are certainly of Mr. *Waller's* earliest production) alludes to the *Copernican* system, in which the earth is suppos'd to be a planet, and to move on its own axis round the sun, the centre of the universe. *Dr. Donne* and Mr *Cowley* industriously affected to entertain the fair sex with such philosophical allocutions; which in his riper age Mr. *Waller* as industriously avoided.

75. Walter Harte

1730

Harte (1709–74), a friend of Pope, was successively travelling tutor, Oxford don, and Canon of Windsor. He wrote on historical and moral topics, and his later verse was chiefly religious. He compared Donne unfavourably with Pope as a mock-heroic poet in a long poem in couplets published when he was twenty-one, *An Essay on Satire, Particularly on the Dunciad*, 1730, lines 63–70. Presumably he had Donne's *Metempsychosis* in mind.

As thinking makes the Soul, low things exprest
In high-raised terms, define a *Dunciad* best.
Books and the Man demands as much, or more,
Than *He* who *wander'd to the Latian shore:*
For here (eternal Grief to *Dun's* soul,
And *B—'s* thin Ghost!) the *Part* contains the *Whole:*
Since in Mock-Epic none succeeds, but he
Who tastes the Whole of Epic Poesy.

76. Joseph Spence

?1732-3

Spence (1699–1768), friend of Pope, wrote in French for a pupil at some time in the early 1730s a historical account of English poetry. His remarks on the seventeenth-century poets clearly demonstrate Augustan standards of judgment. Donne stands as a corrupter of taste and an inept versifier. Spence singles out Suckling as by far the best poet of his age—'The only genius of them all; who by his purity didn't let himself be infected by the general contagion'; and he also praises Waller as 'The sweetest of our lyric poets'. These are the poets who anticipate 'our Augustan Age' which began with the Restoration of Charles II. Taking Milton for an Augustan in that sense Spence hails him as 'the Prince of all us poets'. But he reprehends Cowley for being always 'too full of an affectation of brilliance'. (*Quelques Remarques Hist: sur les Poëts Anglois*, ?1732–3. Given in J. M. Oxborn, 'The First History of English Poetry', in *Pope and his Contemporaries*, ed. J. L. Clifford and L. A. Landa, Oxford, 1949, p. 247.)

There was no copy of Donne's poems in Spence's library when it was sold the year after his death, though this magnificent collection was rich in the works of the English poets from Wyatt and Surrey on and there were many sets of some of the major ones (*Sale Catalogues of Libraries of Eminent Persons*, v, ed. S. Parks, 1972, pp. 87–256).

The other branches of poetry were not so well cultivated. The lyric for example, which was the most frequently practised, was also the most corrupt. The greater part of poets then, as in the previous century, imitated Italian models; but the Italians themselves were beginning to decline, and our lyric poets chiefly followed what was most corrupt in Italy. They affected much ornament and detested the simplicity of nature. A very bad taste prevailed in their work. All was full of plays on words, of glittering thoughts, of strange comparisons and of out-landish metaphors.

Donne was universally declared the Prince of Wit [*Esprit*] in this interregnum of good sense. To be truthful, one can find plenty of judicious sentiments in his Satires, and in several of his epistles; but these sentiments are always encumbered by a puerile affectation of seeking to say something fine. This is the reason that the majority of his pieces are nothing but a tissue of epigrams. His versification, like that of other poets of his time, is very bad.

77. Lewis Theobald

1733

Theobald (1688–1744), hero of the earlier *Dunciad*, was a poet, translator, and editor. He edited Shakespeare's works in seven volumes in 1733. The items given below are an extract from Theobald's Preface to this edition, and his note on Polonius's speech beginning 'My liege, and madam, to expostulate / What majesty should be, what duty is', in *Hamlet,* Act 2, Scene 2 (*The Works of Shakespeare*, 1733, i, pp. xlvi–xlvii, and vii, p. 267).

(i)

Besides, *Wit* lying mostly in the Assemblage of *Ideas*, and in the putting Those together with Quickness and Variety, wherein can be found any Resemblance, or Congruity, to make up pleasant Pictures, and agreeable Visions in the Fancy; the Writer, who aims at Wit, must of course range far and wide for Materials. Now, the Age, in which *Shakespeare* liv'd, having, above all others, a wonderful Affection to appear Learned, They declined vulgar Images, such as are immediately fetch'd from Nature, and rang'd thro' the Circle of the Sciences to fetch their Ideas from thence. But as the Resemblances of such Ideas to the Subject must necessarily lie very much out of the common Way, and every piece of Wit appear a Riddle to the Vulgar; This, that should have taught them the forced, quaint, unnatural Tract they were in, (and induce them to follow a more natural One,) was the very Thing that kept them attach'd to it. The ostentatious Affectation of abstruse Learning, peculiar to that Time, the Love that Men naturally have to every Thing that looks like Mystery, fixed them down to this Habit of Obscurity. Thus became the Poetry of DONNE (tho' the wittiest Man of that Age,) nothing but a continued Heap of Riddles. And our *Shakespeare*, with all his easy Nature about him, for want of the Knowledge of the true Rules of Art, falls frequently into this vicious Manner.

(ii)
Then as to the *Jingles*, and *Play* on Words, let us but look into the Sermons of Dr *Donne* (the wittiest Man of that Age,) and we shall find them full of this Vein; only, there they are to be admired, here to be laugh'd at.

78. Anon., 'On Reading Dr. Donne's poems'

1733

The following poem appears in *The Barbados Gazette* for Wednesday, 18 July 1733. It is said to have been 'composed by a young lady', who presumably intended it as an imitation of Donne. R. C. Fox reprinted it in the *History of Ideas Newsletter*, v. 1960, pp. 77–80, attributing to its unknown author a Romantic view of Donne as a poet of natural expression, tenderness, and passion, quite contrary to the standard eighteenth-century accounts of him. But the poem itself hardly sustains that interpretation:

ON READING DR. DONNE'S POEMS

In vain I to the Dead return,
To read how Lovers us'd to burn;
From *Cowley's* melting Thoughts I rove,
To gentle *Waller*, fam'd for Love;

From them to *Lansdown*, I retire,
To *Congreve*, *Addison*, and *Prior*.
Their Art and Numbers I admire;
 Their different Beauties I confess;
 But oh! they wanted Tenderness.

Wit and Art their Numbers speak,
Fame they sought, but Love I seek:
Waller has a Softness too,
Something that I feel for you;
But my Heart cou'd teach his Lays
How to love; tho' not to praise:
Waller shou'd my Fondness bless,
 And, with weeping Eyes, confess
 My superior Tenderness.

Were my Passion to appear,
What Description would it bear?
All Conceits my Flame would wrong,
If it wou'd adorn my Song.
Be it the Business of my Thought,
To move my Heart by Nature taught;
Art I scorn, forgive the Fault,
 And, with my fond Pen, confess
 Undissembled Tenderness.

Thy Eyes I will forbear to blame;
From Heaven itself my Passion came,
In every Atom of my Frame;
My Hands, my Feet, my Soul agree,
And every Nerve in loving thee.
My trembling Fingers write the Lines,
Which the Neighbouring Soul divines;
 My Heart, with Beatings too, confess
 With the rest, its Tenderness.

Didst thou not the Fondling hear,
Courting tenderly thy Ear;
As you lean'd upon my Breast,
It my very Soul express'd.
As my Eyes were ranging o'er

All the Beauties I adore,
With a Joy unknown before;
   Did not Silence self confess,
   Then, a World of Tenderness?

Say, has any Bosom shown
Half my Love?—Oh! not thy own.
Show my Eyes, or faithful Heart,
Such a Passion, free from Art:
Let my Soul be open laid,
In Absence all my Thoughts survey'd.
Every Wish that it has made;
   Then with Love itself confess
   My unbounded Tenderness.

79. Bayle's Dictionary

1736

In an augmented translation of Bayle's Dictionary some six folio pages are devoted to Donne, with extensive notes (*A General Dictionary, Historical and Critical. . . .*, 1736, entry under *Donne*).

DONNE (JOHN), an excellent Poet and Divine of the Seventeenth Century. . . .

His writings shew him to be a man of incomparable wit and learning; and he was highly celebrated by all the great men of that age. [There follow some praises of Donne by Falkland, Walsh, and Dryden. See Nos. 18 (iv) (h), 49, 59.]

Mr. Pope has given us two of his Satires in a very beautiful dress.

80. Mrs Elizabeth Cooper

1737

Mrs Cooper (*fl.* 1736–7), the widow of an auctioneer, was an anthologist and playwright. She edited a selection of extracts from the British poets and introduced it with a sketch of the history of poetry in English. Donne is mentioned only in passing. (*The Muses Library: or a Series of English Poetry from the Saxons to the Reign of King Charles II*, 1737, pp. xii and 332.)

Donne, and Corbet added Wit to Satire, and restor'd the almost forgotten Way of making Reproof it self entertaining: Carew and Waller taught Panegyrick to be delicate, Passion to be courtly, and rode the Pegasus of Wit, with the Curb of good Manners. . . .

[Introducing extracts from the poetry of Sir John Davies, she gives a list of] more valuable Witnesses of his Merit, than all the titles that Heraldry can invent, or Monarch bestow: The joint Applauses of *Cambden*, Sir *John Harington, Ben Johnson, Selden, Donn, Corbet*, &c. These are great, and unquestionable Authorities in Favour of this Author. . . .

81. William Mason

1747, *c*. 1755, 1796

Mason (1724–97), a clergyman-poet, was sometime Fellow of Pembroke College, Cambridge, and a close friend of Gray, whose biographer he became. He served as chaplain to the king in 1757, and then as a Canon of York. Mason greatly admired Pope, and it was probably Pope's satires which led him to Donne; but his interest in Donne's poetry seems to have been limited, and brief. (See D. A. Low, 'An Eighteenth-Century Imitation of Donne's First Satire', *RES*, n.s., xvi, 1965, pp. 291–8.)

(i) In his *Musaeus: A Monody To the Memory of Mr Pope, in Imitation of Milton's Lycidas*, 1747, p. 18, Mason mentions Donne as one of the fathers of satiric poetry. The lines are spoken by Musaeus (Pope himself), who here replies to the praises lavished on him by Chaucer, Spenser, and Milton:

> Come then that honest fame; whose sober ray
> Or gilds the satire, or the moral lay;
> Which dawns, tho' thou, rough DONNE! hew out the line,
> But beams, sage HORACE! from each strain of thine.

(ii) In 1753 Mason borrowed Donne's poems from his college library. Some time later he wrote an imitation of Donne's *Satyre i* in the manner of Pope's versions of Donne, retaining much of the sense and spirit of the original as well as some of the words, but smoothing out the verse and directing all the references at his own contemporaries. Here is the opening of Mason's version:

> Away, fond Fop! mad motley thing begone.
> Fatigued alike with thee and this vile town
> I quit ye both, and henceforth swear to dwell

Here close immur'd in this small studious cell;
Here rest composd, till Lifes vain vision ends,
These shelves my world, these few choice books my friends. . . .

(iii) Some forty years later, in a note to his *Religio Clerici*, Mason spoke of Dryden's youthful poem on the death of Lord Hastings:

I find it of that species of poetry, which Doctor Johnson calls Metaphysical, but which I should rather term Pseudo-physical (if I had as great a licence to coin words as the Doctor); for the Poets in vogue at that time thought it a test of excellence to combine true and natural images in a forced, a false, and unnatural manner. In this style Dr Donne appears to have been Dryden's archetype. With respect to the poem in question, he appears to aim at rivalling him not only in false wit and false thoughts, but in prosaic phrase, and unmetrical or ill-accented verses. In the former he even outstrips his master, as a young hound, got upon a wrong scent is said by huntsmen to throw himself more out of chace than an old one.

82. John Brown

1748

Brown (1715–66), Vicar of Newcastle-upon-Tyne, was a poet, playwright, and moralist. He wrote in verse 'An Essay on Satire, occasioned by the Death of Mr POPE', which was published in one of Dodsley's miscellanies (*A Collection of Poems by Several Hands*, 1748, iii, p. 333), and is said to have earned him the friendship of Warburton. Brown represents Donne as a true though primitive satirist, the scourge of a corrupt age.

'Twas then plain DONNE in honest vengeance rose,
His wit refulgent, tho' his rhyme was prose:
He 'midst an age of puns and pedants wrote
With genuine sense, and *Roman* strength of thought.

83. James Thomson

1749

Thomson had in his library a copy of the 1669 edition of Donne's poems. It was listed in the catalogue of the sale of the library, 15 May 1749. (See *Sale Catalogues of Libraries of Eminent Persons*, i, ed. A. N. L. Munby, 1971, p. 56.)

84. Moses Browne

1750

Browne (1704–87), Vicar of Olney from 1753, wrote a set of poems called *Piscatory Eclogues* and contributed verses to *The Gentleman's Magazine*. In the Preface to an edition of Izaac Walton's *Compleat Angler* Browne quotes a poem in praise of Walton which mentions Walton's *Lives* of Donne and Wotton. Browne adds a comment on Donne, supporting it with what appears to be a rewording of Dryden (*The Compleat Angler*, 1750, p. vi).

Dr *Donne* here named, whose Writings are at this Day very justly admired, and who, a celebrated Critick of the last Age says 'had more Wit than is to be found in all our other Poets put together', was remarkable for being the very Person who was the instrument of Mr *Walton's* Conversion. . . .

85. William Warburton

1751, 1766

Warburton (1698–1779) became Bishop of Gloucester in 1759. He was a controversialist in theology and literature, the editor of Shakespeare (1747), and the friend and executor of Pope. He brought out an edition of Pope's works in 1751, revising it for fresh publication in 1753 and reissuing the revised version in 1766 and 1770.

Warburton spoke of Donne when he introduced and annotated Pope's version of Donne's *Satyre ii* and *Satyre iv*, which he printed alongside the original poems as Pope himself had done in the 1735 volume of his *Works*. But he took the opportunity to praise the *Metempsychosis* and *Satyre iii*, giving Parnell's version of *Satyre iii* to show the superiority of the original and of Pope's rewriting of Donne.

The extracts given below are taken from the 1751 edition of Pope's works. Important alterations or additions made in the 1753 edition are given in square brackets or separately noted. (*The Works of Alexander Pope Esq.*, 1751, iv, pp. 247, 253, 256, 258, 264, 275, 282–3; 1753, iv, p. 243; 1766, iv, p. 272; 1770, iv, pp. 239–40.)

(i)

The *manly Wit* of Donne, which was the Character of his genius, suited best with *Satire*; and in this he excelled, tho' he wrote but little; six short poems being all we find amongst his writings of this sort. Mr Pope has embellished two of them with his wit and harmony. He called it *versifying* them, because indeed the lines have nothing more of numbers than their being composed of a certain quantity of syllables. This is the more to be admired, because, as appears by his other poems, and especially from that fine fragment, called the *Progress of the Soul*, his Verse did not want harmony. But, I suppose, he took the *sermoni propiora*[1] of Horace too seriously; or rather, he was content with the character his master gives of Lucilius,

Emunctae naris durus componere versus.[2]

Having spoken of his *Progress of the Soul*, let me add, that Poetry scarce ever [never] lost more than by his not pursuing and finishing that noble Design; of which he has only given us the Introduction. With regard to his Satires, it is almost as much to be lamented that Mr Pope did not give us a Paraphrase, in his manner, of the Third, the noblest work [which treats the noblest subject *1766*] not only of this, but perhaps of any satiric Poet. To supply this loss, though in some [a very] small degree, I have here inserted it, in the versification of Dr Parnell. It will at least serve to shew the force of Dr Donne's genius, and of Mr Pope's; by removing all that was rustic and shocking in the one, and by not being able to reach one [a] single grace of the other.

[Here Warburton gives Parnell's version of *Satyre iii*, and comments upon it.]

This noble similitude, with which the Satire concludes, Dr Parnell did not seem to understand and so [;or] was not able to express it in its original force. Dr Donne says,

[He quotes lines 103–9a of *Satyre iii*]

Dr Donne expressly compares *Power* or Authority to Streams: *Souls* to Flowers; but not being so explicit in the latter, Dr Parnell overlooked that part of the Simile, and [*power* to streams:but the comparison of souls to flowers being only implied, Dr Parnell overlooked that part; and] so has hurt the whole thought, by making the Flowers *passive*; whereas the Original says, *they leave their roots, and give themselves to the stream*: that is, wilfully prefer human Authority to divine; and this makes them the object of his Satire; which they would not have been, were they irresistibly carried away, as the Imitation supposes.

(ii) Warburton commented on Pope's version of Donne's *Satyre ii*, comparing various lines in it with the original:

[Donne, line 33b]

VER. 38. *Irishmen out-swear.*] The Original says,

outswear the Letanie,

---

[1] '[lines] more like prose [than verse]'. Horace, *Satires*, I. iv. 42.
[2] 'Keen-nosed, but harsh in his versification'. Horace, *Satires*, I. iv. 8.

improved by the Imitator into a just stroke of Satire. Dr Donne's is a low allusion to a licentious quibble used, at that time, by the enemies of the English Liturgy, who disliking the frequent invocations in the *Letanie*, called them the *taking God's Name in vain*, which is the Scripture periphrasis for *swearing*.

[Donne, line 38]

VER. 44. *In what Commandment's large contents they dwell*.]
The Original is more humorous;

> *In what Commandment's large* receit *they dwell*

[Donne, lines 93–6]

VER. 104. *So Luther, etc*.] Our Poet, by judiciously transposing this fine similitude, has given new lustre to his Author's thought.

(iii) In the 1766 edition of *The Works of Pope* Warburton added a comment on Donne's *Pseudo-Martyr* to his notes on *Satyre ii* (iv, p. 260):

In the 191st page, and elsewhere, he maintains that the office of the civil Sovereign extends to the care of Souls. For this absurd and blasphemous trash. James I made him Dean of St Paul's; all the wit and sublimity of his genius having never enabled him to get bread throughout the *better* part of his life.

(iv) Warburton threw out some remarks on Donne's *Satyre iv*, in annotating Pope's version of it:

[Donne, line 1]

VER. 1. *Well, if it be, etc*.] Donne says,

> *Well; I may now* receive *and die*.

which is very indecent language on so ludicrous an occasion.

[Donne, lines 58–61]

VER. 78. *Yet these were all poor Gentlemen!*] Our Poet has here added to the humour of his original. Donne makes his thread-bare Traveller content himself under his poverty, with the reflection, that [even] Panurge himself, the great Traveller and Linguist in Rabelais, went a begging. [There is infinite wit in this passage of Donne, yet very licentious, in coupling the Apostles and Panurge, in this buffoon manner.]

[Donne, lines 107–8]

VER. 151. *What Lady's face, etc.*] The Original is here very humorous. This torrent of scandal concludes thus,

> And wiser than all us,
> He knows what Lady—

the reader expects it will conclude,—*what Lady is painted*. No, just the contrary,

> what Lady is not painted;

satirically insinuating, that this is a better Proof of the goodness of his intelligence than the other. The Reader sees there is greater force in the use of these plain words, than in those which the Imitator employs. And the reason is, because the satire does not turn upon the *odiousness* of painting; in which case, the terms of a *painted wall* had given force to the expression; but upon the *frequency* of it, which required only the simple mention of the thing.

(v) In the 1770 edition of *The Works of Pope* Warburton added a brief prefatory note to Pope's 'Satires of Dr John Donne . . . versified':

The wit, the vigour, and the honesty of Mr Pope's Satiric Writings had raised a great clamour against him, as if the *Supplement*, as he calls it, *to the Public Laws*, was a violation of morality and society. In answer to this charge he had it in his purpose to shew, that two of the most respectable characters in the modest and virtuous age of Elizabeth, Dr Donne and Bishop Hall, had arraigned Vice publicly, and shewn it in stronger colours, than he had done, whether they found it, 'On the Pillory, or near the Throne'.

In pursuance of this purpose, our Poet hath admirably *versified*, as he expresses it, two or three Satires of Dr Donne. He intended to have given two or three of Bishop Hall's likewise, whose force and classical elegance he much admired; but as Hall was a better versifier, and as a mere Academic had not his vein vitiated like Donne's, by the fantastic language of Courts, Mr Pope's purpose was only to correct a little, and smooth the versification. . . .

86. Thomas Gray

c. 1752, 1770

Gray (1716–71) drafted a scheme of English versification in which he cited Donne's *Satyres* as an example of a free decasyllabic movement. He commented that Spenser affords 'an instance of the decasyllabic measure with an unusual liberty in its feet' in the opening of the August Eclogue of *The Shepheards Calendar*, but that Donne goes reprehensibly further (*Gray's Essays and Criticisms*, ed. C. S. Northup, 1904, pp. 37 and 48). Gray referred to Donne's *Satyres* again in a letter to Thomas Warton, when he compared them with Hall's *Virgidemiarum* (ibid., p. 175).

In the year before his death Gray sent Warton a sketch 'of a design, I once had to give a history of English poetry'. Donne and his followers appear in it as 'A *third Italian* School', presumably derived from such poets as Guarini and Marino (*The Correspondence of Thomas Gray*, ed. P. Toynbee and L. Whibley, Oxford, 1935, iii, pp. 1122–4).

(i)
And after him [Spenser] Dr Donne (in his Satires) observes no regularity in the pause, or in the feet of his verse, only the number of syllables is equal throughout. I suppose he thought this rough uncouth measure suited the plain familiar style of satirical poetry.

(ii)
Have you seen Bishop Hall's Satires, called Virgidemiae, republished lately, they are full of spirit and poetry; as much of the first, as Dr Donne, and far more of the latter. . . .

(iii)
INTRODUCTION
On the poetry of the *Galic* (or Celtic) nations, as far back as it can be traced.

On that of the Goths; its introduction into these islands by the Saxons & Danes, & its duration. on the origin of rhyme among the Franks, the Saxons, & Provençaux. some account of the Latin rhyming poetry from its early origin down to the 15th Century.

P: 1

On the School of Provence, wch rose about the year 1100, & was soon followed by the French & Italians. their heroic poetry, or romances in verse, Allegories, fabliaux, syrvientes, comedies, farces, canzoni, sonnets, balades, madrigals, sestines, &c:

Of their imitators the *French*, & of the first *Italian* School (commonly call'd the Sicilian) about the year 1200 brought to perfection by Dante, Petrarch, Boccace, & others.

State of Poetry in England from the Conquest (1066) or rather from Henry 2d's time (1154) to the reign of Edward the 3d (1327).

P: 2

On *Chaucer* who first introduced the manner of the Provençaux improved by the Italians into our country. his character & merits at large; the different kinds in wch he excell'd. Gower, Occleve, Lydgate, Hawes, G: Douglas, Lindsay, Bellenden, Dunbar, &c:

P: 3

Second Italian School (of Ariosto, Tasso, &c:) an improvement on the first, occasion'd by the revival of letters [at] the end of the 15th century. The lyric poetry of this & the former age introduced from Italy by Ld Surrey, Sr T. Wyat, Bryan, Ld Vaux, &c: in the beginning of the 16th century.

Spenser, his character. Subject of his poem allegoric & romantic, of Provençal invention: but his manner of [treating] it borrow'd from the Second Italian School. Drayton, Fairfax, Phin: Fletcher, Golding, Phaer, &c: this school ends in Milton.

A *third Italian* School, full of conceit, begun in Q: Elizabeths reign, continued under James, & Charles the first by *Donne*, Crawshaw, Cleveland; carried to its height by Cowley, & ending perhaps in *Sprat*.

P: 4

School of France, introduced after the Restoration. Waller, Dryden, Addison, Prior, & Pope, wch has continued down to our own times.

87. Dr Thomas Birch

1752

Birch (1705–66) was successively rector of a number of churches in England and Wales. He was a historian and biographer, and a Fellow of the Royal Society, serving as secretary of the society for some thirteen years. He mentioned Donne in a Life of Archbishop Tillotson, when he described Tillotson's election to 'the place of preacher of *Lincoln's-Inn*' (*The Life of the Most Reverend Dr John Tillotson* (1752), 1753, pp. 26–7).

His predecessors in this post had been generally men of the greatest eminence for learning; and among these were . . . Dr. JOHN DONNE, Dean of *St. Paul*'s . . . whose poetical works shew a prodigious fund of genius under the disguise of an affected and obscure style and a most inharmonious versification. . . .

88. Theophilus Cibber/Robert Shiels

1753

Cibber (1703–58), actor and playwright, was the son of Colley Cibber. He was known as a writer, but the work from which the following extract is taken, though it bears his name on the title page, was mainly compiled by Robert Shiels (d. 1753). It is a collection of biographies of the British poets, which includes a life of Donne culled from Walton and a list of Donne's writings. Donne's 'A Hymne to God the Father' is given entire in the course of the life and introduced with a critical comment, the only such recognition of Donne's claim to be considered as a poet (*The Lives of the Poets of Great Britain and Ireland*, 1753, i, p. 211).

The piece from whence I shall take the following quotation, is called a Hymn to God the Father, was composed in the time of his sickness, which breathes a spirit of fervent piety, though no great force of poetry is discoverable in it [*sic*].

89. David Hume

1754–62

Hume (1711–76), philosopher, historian, and diplomat, appended
to his history of England in the reigns of James I and Charles I
an account of the state of literature in the seventeenth century.
He argued that Renaissance writers reproduced the decadent
elements of ancient culture in its decline and that the writers of the
age of James I exemplify the prevailing bad taste. He essayed an
analytical account of the history of literary taste, drawing on
ancient and modern examples (*The History of England* (1754–62),
1813, vi, pp. 171–5).

Though the age was by no means destitute of eminent writers, a very
bad taste in general prevailed during that period; and the monarch
himself was not a little infected with it.

On the origin of letters among the Greeks, the genius of poets and
orators, as might naturally be expected, was distinguished by an
amiable simplicity, which, whatever rudeness may sometimes attend
it, is so fitted to express the genuine movements of nature and passion,
that the compositions possessed of it must ever appear valuable to the
discerning part of mankind. The glaring figures of discourse, the pointed
antithesis, the unnatural conceit, the jingle of words; such false ornaments were not employed by early writers; not because they were
rejected, but because they scarcely ever occurred to them. An easy
unforced strain of sentiment runs through their compositions; though
at the same time we may observe, that amidst the most elegant simplicity of thought and expression, one is sometimes surprised to meet
with a poor conceit, which had presented itself unsought for, and which
the author had not acquired critical observation enough to condemn.
A bad taste seizes with avidity these frivolous beauties, and even perhaps
a good taste, ere surfeited by them: They multiply every day more and
more in the fashionable compositions: Nature and good sense are
neglected: Laboured ornaments studied and admired: And a total
degeneracy of style and language prepares the way for barbarism and

ignorance. Hence the Asiatic manner was found to depart so much from the simple purity of Athens. Hence that tinsel eloquence which is observable in many of the Roman writers, from which Cicero himself is not wholly exempted, and which so much prevails in Ovid, Seneca, Lucan, Martial, and the Plinys.

On the revival of letters, when the judgment of the public is yet raw and uninformed, this false glitter catches the eye, and leaves no room, either in eloquence or poetry, for the durable beauties of solid sense and lively passion. The reigning genius is then diametrically opposite to that which prevails on the first origin of arts. The Italian writers, it is evident, even the most celebrated, have not reached the proper simplicity of thought and composition; and in Petrarch, Tasso Guarini, frivolous witticisms and forced conceits are but too predominant. The period during which letters were cultivated in Italy, was so short as scarcely to allow leisure for correcting this adulterated relish.

The more early French writers are liable to the same reproach. Voiture, Balzac, even Corneille, have too much affected those ambitious ornaments, of which the Italians in general, and the least pure of the ancients, supplied them with so many models. And it was not till late, that observation and reflection gave rise to a more natural turn of thought and composition among that elegant people.

A like character may be extended to the first English writers; such as flourished during the reigns of Elizabeth and James, and even till long afterwards. Learning, on its revival in this island, was attired in the same unnatural garb which it wore at the time of its decay among the Greeks and Romans. And, what may be regarded as a misfortune, the English writers were possessed of great genius before they were endowed with any degree of taste, and by that means gave a kind of sanction to those forced turns and sentiments which they so much affected. Their distorted conceptions and expressions are attended with such vigour of mind, that we admire the imagination which produced them, as much as we blame the want of judgment which gave them admittance.

In Donne's satires, when carefully inspected, there appear some flashes of wit and ingenuity; but these totally suffocated and buried by the hardest and most uncouth expression that is any where to be met with.

If the poetry of the English was so rude and imperfect during that age, we may reasonably expect that their prose would be liable still to greater objections.

90. Samuel Johnson

1755–c. 1785

Johnson's account of Donne and the 'metaphysical' poets, in the *Life of Cowley*, was long taken as a definitive dismissal and his analysis of the 'metaphysical' style is still sometimes offered for received truth. Recent commentators have argued that far from lacking sympathy with Donne's poetry and dismissing it, Johnson knew it intimately, admired it, and was trying to establish new criteria for its appraisal. (See W. B. C. Watkins, *Johnson and English Poetry before 1660*, Princeton, 1936, pp. 7, 78–84, 96–9; W. R. Keast, 'Johnson's Criticism of the Metaphysical Poets', *ELH*, xvii, 1950, pp. 59–70; A. D. Atkinson, 'Donne Quotations in Johnson's Dictionary', *NQ*, September 1951, pp. 387–8; W. J. Bate, *Criticism: The Major Texts*, New York, 1952, pp. 204 and 217–19; D. Perkins, 'Johnson on Wit and Metaphysical Poetry', *ELH*, xx, 1953, pp. 200–17.)

The evidence is set out below.

(i) In his *Dictionary of the English Language*, 1755, Johnson sometimes illustrates words with a quotation from Donne's poetry. W. B. C. Watkins has counted ninety-seven such quotations from Donne's poems under the letters Q, R, S; he says that Johnson quotes from eleven of the *Songs and Sonnets*, three *Elegies*, two *Epithalamions*, two *Satyres*, seven verse letters, and six funeral poems. But he points out that the catalogue of Johnson's library lists no copy of Donne's poems. A. D. Atkinson notes 384 quotations ascribed to Donne in the whole of the *Dictionary*, 375 of them from Donne's poems. He gives the following table of frequency:

Songs and Sonnets	89	quotations
Elegies	56	,,
Epithalamions	16	,,
Satyres	51	,,

Verse letters	88	,,
The first Anniversary	36	,,
The second Anniversary	21	,,
Epicedes and Obsequies	17	,,
Divine Poems	1 quotation	
Metempsychosis	nil	

Johnson quotes some passages several times, for various words in them—lines 220-2 of *The first Anniversary* occur five times, as do lines 31-5 of *Elegie xi*; lines 25-30 of 'A Valediction; of my Name in the Window' occur four times; lines 14-15 of 'A Nocturnall upon S. Lucies Day' occur three times. But Johnson himself never notes the poem from which he quotes, merely ascribing the lines to Donne.

These figures need to be placed in perspective, and in the frame of reference that Johnson himself is careful to provide. They argue no more than that Johnson had used a copy of Donne's poems as a word-quarry. In the Preface to the *Dictionary* Johnson expressly warns against the kind of inference that Watkins and Atkinson make. He advises us
(a) that he has been obliged to take words where he could find them, and at times 'from writers who were never mentioned as masters of elegance or models of style'
(b) that he was soon forced to abandon his scheme of including what was 'pleasing or useful in *English* literature' and to reduce his transcripts 'very often to clusters of words, in which scarcely any meaning is retained'. Many of his quotations 'serve no other purpose, than that of proving the bare existence of words'
(c) that he has deliberately eschewed all living and recent writings and confined his choice of illustrations to the period of English writing from Sidney to the Restoration—a matter of some eighty years.

But Johnson does not, in fact, quote frequently from Donne. In the first ten pages of the *Dictionary*—from A to ACE—the relative frequency of quotation is as follows:

Shakespeare	79 quotations	
Dryden	60	,,
Milton	41	,,
Sidney	15	,,
Spenser	15	,,
Donne	3	,,

In the following forty pages of the *Dictionary* there are a further five quotations from Donne, still leaving him with just over half of what

Sidney scored in the first ten pages alone; though no one has yet argued Johnson's intimate grasp of Sidney's poetry. And in all the 'A's—about 140 folio pages—there are some twenty-one quotations from Donne, two from Herbert, three from Crashaw, and three from Cowley; whereas Shakespeare scores twenty-one quotations in the first three pages alone.

Finally, the quotations themselves tend to bear out what Johnson says about the way that such a mode of illustration can rob words of their meaning in a particular context. For they show that his responsibility was to the common uses of a word and not to Donne's lines. Thus he defines *Alchemy* as 'The more sublime and occult part of chymistry', illustrating this definition with line 24 of 'The Sunne Rising' —'All honours mimick, all wealth *alchymy*'. Donne's sense simply contradicts the definition.

(ii) Johnson mentioned Donne in his edition of *The Plays of William Shakespeare*, 1765, ii, p. 55, when he annotated *As You Like It*, Act 3, Scene 2, lines 186–8, 'I was never so berhymed since Pythagoras' time, that I was an Irish rat':

The power of killing rats with rhymes *Donne* mentions in his satires, and *Temple* in his treatises. . . .

(iii) Johnson alluded to Donne in conversations recorded by Boswell as having taken place in 1773, 1775 and 1776 (*The Life of Samuel Johnson, LL.D.* (1791), ed. G. B. Hill, revised L. F. Powell, Oxford, 1950, ii, pp. 363, 445, and 530; v, p. 346). Johnson praised Walton's *Life of Donne*, spoke of Walton's tale of the vision Donne had of his wife when he was in Paris in 1612, and remarked that Donne and King Charles I both used the word 'quotidian' in their writings. There is no mention of Donne's poetry.

(iv) References to Donne in Johnson's *Lives of the English Poets*, 1779–81, ed. G. Birkbeck Hill, Oxford, 1905:

(a) From the *Life of Dryden* (i, p. 426):

Dryden very early formed his versification: there are in this early production [the *Heroic Stanzas* for Cromwell's funeral, 1659] no traces of Donne's or Jonson's ruggedness; but he did not so soon free his mind from the ambition of forced conceits. . . .

(b) From the *Life of Pope* (iii, p. 177):

[Pope] published likewise a revival in smoother numbers of Dr. Donne's

Satires, which was recommended to him by the Duke of Shrewsbury and the Earl of Oxford. They made no great impression on the publick. Pope seems to have known their imbecillity, and therefore suppressed them while he was yet contending to rise in reputation, but ventured them when he thought their deficiencies more likely to be imputed to Donne than to himself.

(c) From the *Life of Cowley* (i, pp. 18–35):

Cowley, like other poets who have written with narrow views and, instead of tracing intellectual pleasure to its natural sources in the mind of man, paid their court to temporary prejudices, has been at one time too much praised and too much neglected at another.

Wit, like all other things subject by their nature to the choice of man, has its changes and fashions, and at different times takes different forms. About the beginning of the seventeenth century appeared a race of writers that may be termed the metaphysical poets, of whom in a criticism on the works of Cowley it is not improper to give some account.

The metaphysical poets were men of learning, and to shew their learning was their whole endeavour; but, unluckily resolving to shew it in rhyme, instead of writing poetry they only wrote verses, and very often such verses as stood the trial of the finger better than of the ear; for the modulation was so imperfect that they were only found to be verses by counting the syllables.

If the father of criticism has rightly denominated poetry $\tau\acute{\epsilon}\chi\nu\eta$ $\mu\iota\mu\eta\tau\iota\kappa\acute{\eta}$, *an imitative art*,[1] these writers will without great wrong lose their right to the name of poets, for they cannot be said to have imitated any thing: they neither copied nature nor life; neither painted the forms of matter nor represented the operations of intellect.

Those however who deny them to be poets allow them to be wits. Dryden confesses of himself and his contemporaries that they fall below Donne in wit, but maintains that they surpass him in poetry.

If Wit be well described by Pope as being 'that which has been often thought, but was never before so well expressed,' they certainly never attained nor ever sought it, for they endeavoured to be singular in their thoughts, and were careless of their diction. But Pope's account of wit is undoubtedly erroneous; he depresses it below its natural dignity, and reduces it from strength of thought to happiness of language.

If by a more noble and more adequate conception that be considered

[1] Aristotle, *Poetics*, I.

as Wit which is at once natural and new, that which though not obvious is, upon its first production, acknowledged to be just; if it be that, which he that never found it, wonders how he missed; to wit of this kind the metaphysical poets have seldom risen. Their thoughts are often new, but seldom natural; they are not obvious, but neither are they just; and the reader, far from wondering that he missed them, wonders more frequently by what perverseness of industry they were ever found.

But Wit, abstracted from its effects upon the hearer, may be more rigorously and philosophically considered as a kind of *discordia concors*; a combination of dissimilar images, or discovery of occult resemblances in things apparently unlike. Of wit, thus defined, they have more than enough. The most heterogeneous ideas are yoked by violence together; nature and art are ransacked for illustrations, comparisons, and allusions; their learning instructs, and their subtilty surprises; but the reader commonly thinks his improvement dearly bought, and, though he sometimes admires, is seldom pleased.

From this account of their compositions it will be readily inferred that they were not successful in representing or moving the affections. As they were wholly employed on something unexpected and surprising they had no regard to that uniformity of sentiment, which enables us to conceive and to excite the pains and the pleasure of other minds: they never enquired what on any occasion they should have said or done, but wrote rather as beholders than partakers of human nature; as beings looking upon good and evil, impassive and at leisure; as Epicurean deities making remarks on the actions of men and the vicissitudes of life, without interest and without emotion. Their courtship was void of fondness and their lamentation of sorrow. Their wish was only to say what they hoped had been never said before.

Nor was the sublime more within their reach than the pathetick; for they never attempted that comprehension and expanse of thought which at once fills the whole mind, and of which the first effect is sudden astonishment, and the second rational admiration. Sublimity is produced by aggregation, and littleness by dispersion. Great thoughts are always general, and consist in positions not limited by exceptions, and in descriptions not descending to minuteness. It is with great propriety that subtlety, which in its original import means exility of particles, is taken in its metaphorical meaning for nicety of distinction. Those writers who lay on the watch for novelty could have little hope of greatness; for great things cannot have escaped former observation.

Their attempts were always analytick: they broke every image into fragments, and could no more represent by their slender conceits and laboured particularities the prospects of nature or the scenes of life, than he who dissects a sun-beam with a prism can exhibit the wide effulgence of a summer noon.

What they wanted however of the sublime they endeavoured to supply by hyperbole; their amplification had no limits: they left not only reason but fancy behind them, and produced combinations of confused magnificence that not only could not be credited, but could not be imagined.

Yet great labour directed by great abilities is never wholly lost: if they frequently threw away their wit upon false conceits, they likewise sometimes struck out unexpected truth: if their conceits were far-fetched, they were often worth the carriage. To write on their plan it was at least necessary to read and think. No man could be born a metaphysical poet, nor assume the dignity of a writer by descriptions copied from descriptions, by imitations borrowed from imitations, by traditional imagery and hereditary similes, by readiness of rhyme and volubility of syllables.

In perusing the works of this race of authors the mind is exercised either by recollection of inquiry; either something already learned is to be retrieved, or something new is to be examined. If their greatness seldom elevates their acuteness often surprises; if the imagination is not always gratified, at least the powers of reflection and comparison are employed; and in the mass of materials, which ingenious absurdity has thrown together, genuine wit and useful knowledge may be sometimes found, buried perhaps in grossness of expression, but useful to those who know their value, and such as, when they are expanded to perspicuity and polished to elegance, may give lustre to works which have more propriety though less copiousness of sentiment.

This kind of writing, which was, I believe, borrowed from Marino and his followers, had been recommended by the example of Donne, a man of very extensive and various knowledge, and by Jonson, whose manner resembled that of Donne more in the ruggedness of his lines than in the cast of his sentiments.

When their reputation was high they had undoubtedly more imitators than time has left behind. Their immediate successors, of whom any remembrance can be said to remain, were Suckling, Waller, Denham, Cowley, Cleiveland, and Milton. Denham and Waller sought another way to fame, by improving the harmony of our numbers. Milton tried the metaphysick style only in his lines upon Hobson the Carrier. Cowley adopted it, and excelled his predecessors; having as much sentiment and more musick. Suckling neither improved versification nor abounded in conceits. The fashionable style remained chiefly with Cowley: Suckling could not reach it, and Milton disdained it.

CRITICAL REMARKS are not easily understood without examples, and I have therefore collected instances of the modes of writing by which this species of poets, for poets they were called by themselves and their admirers, was eminently distinguished.

As the authors of this race were perhaps more desirous of being admired than understood they sometimes drew their conceits from recesses of learning not very much frequented by common readers of poetry. Thus Cowley on *Knowledge*:

> The sacred tree midst the fair orchard grew;
>> The phoenix Truth did on it rest,
>> And built his perfum'd nest,
> That right Porphyrian tree which did true logick shew.
>> Each leaf did learned notions give,
>> And th' apples were demonstrative:
>> So clear their colour and divine,
> The very shade they cast did other lights outshine.

On Anacreon continuing a lover in his old age:

> Love was with thy life entwin'd,
> Close as heat with fire is join'd;
> A powerful brand prescrib'd the date
> Of thine, like Meleager's fate.
> Th' antiperistasis of age
> More enflam'd thy amorous rage.

In the following verses we have an allusion to a Rabbinical opinion concerning Manna:

> Variety I ask not: give me one
> To live perpetually upon.
> The person Love does to us fit,
> Like manna, has the taste of all in it.

Thus *Donne* shews his medicinal knowledge in some encomiastick verses:

> In every thing there naturally grows
> A balsamum to keep it fresh and new,
>> If 'twere not injur'd by extrinsique blows;
> Your youth [birth] and beauty are this balm in you.

But you, of learning and religion,
And virtue and such ingredients, have made
A mithridate, whose operation
Keeps off or cures what can be done or said.

Though the following lines of Donne, on the last night of the year, have something in them too scholastick, they are not inelegant:

This twilight of two years, not past nor next,
   Some emblem is of me, or I of this,
Who, meteor-like, of stuff and form perplext,
   Whose what and where in disputation is,
   If I should call me any thing, should miss.

I sum the years and me, and find me not
   Debtor to th' old nor creditor to th' new;
That cannot say my thanks I have forgot,
   Nor trust I this with hopes; and yet scarce true
   This bravery is, since these times shew'd me you.

DONNE.

Yet more abstruse and profound is *Donne's* reflection upon Man as a Microcosm:

If men be worlds, there is in every one
Something to answer in some proportion
All the world's riches: and in good men this
Virtue, our form's form, and our soul's soul is.

Of thoughts so far-fetched as to be not only unexpected but unnatural, all their books are full.

To a lady, who wrote [made] poesies for rings:

They, who above do various circles find,
Say, like a ring th' æquator heaven does bind.
When heaven shall be adorn'd by thee
(Which then more heaven than 'tis, will be),
'Tis thou must write the poesy there,
For it wanteth one as yet,
Though the sun pass through 't twice a year,
The sun, which [who] is esteem'd the god of wit.

COWLEY.

The difficulties which have been raised about identity in philosophy are by Cowley with still more perplexity applied to Love:

Five years ago (says story) I lov'd you,
For which you call me most inconstant now;
Pardon me, madam, you mistake the man;
For I am not the same that I was then;
No flesh is now the same 'twas then in me,
And that my mind is chang'd yourself may see.
The same thoughts to retain still, and intents,
Were more inconstant far; for accidents
Must of all things most strangely inconstant prove,
If from one subject they t'another move:
My members then, the father members were
From whence these take their birth, which now are here.
If then this body love what th' other did,
'Twere incest, which by nature is forbid.

The love of different women is, in geographical poetry, compared to travels through different countries:

Hast thou not found, each woman's breast
  (The land [lands] where thou hast travelled)
Either by savages possest,
  Or wild, and uninhabited?
What joy could'st take, or what repose,
In countries so uncivilis'd as those?

Lust, the scorching dog star, here
  Rages with immoderate heat;
Whilst Pride, the rugged Northern Bear,
  In others makes the cold too great.
And where these are temperate known,
The soil's all barren sand, or rocky stone.

COWLEY.

A lover burnt up by his affection is compared to Egypt:

The fate of Egypt I sustain,
  And never feel the dew of rain,
From clouds which in the head appear;
  But all my too much moisture owe
  To overflowings of the heart below.—COWLEY.

The lover supposes his lady acquainted with the ancient laws of augury and rites of sacrifice:

And yet this death of mine, I fear,
Will ominous to her appear:

When found in every other part,
Her sacrifice is found without an heart,
For the last tempest of my death
Shall sigh out that too, with my breath.

That the chaos was harmonised has been recited of old; but whence
the different sounds arose remained for a modern to discover:

Th' ungovern'd parts no correspondent knew,
An artless war from thwarting motions grew;
Till they to number and fixt rules were brought
[By the Eternal Mind's poetick thought].
Water and air he for the tenor chose,
Earth made the base, the treble flame arose.

COWLEY.

The tears of lovers are always of great poetical account, but Donne
has extended them into worlds. If the lines are not easily understood
they may be read again.

On a round ball
A workman, that hath copies by, can lay
An Europe, Afric, and an Asia,
And quickly make that, which was nothing, all.
So doth each tear,
Which thee doth wear,
A globe, yea world, by that impression grow,
Till thy tears mixt with mine do overflow
This world, by waters sent from thee my [by] heaven dissolved so.

On reading the following lines the reader may perhaps cry out, 'Confusion worse confounded.'

Here lies a she sun, and a he moon here,
She gives the best light to his sphere,
Or each is both, and all, and so
They unto one another nothing owe.

DONNE.

Who but Donne would have thought that a good man is a telescope?

Though God be our true glass, through which we see
All, since the being of all things is he,
Yet are the trunks, which do to us derive
Things in proportion fit by perspective,
Deeds of good men; for by their living [being] here,
Virtues, indeed remote, seem to be near.

223

Who would imagine it possible that in a very few lines so many remote ideas could be brought together?

> Since 'tis my doom, Love's undershrieve,
>   Why this reprieve?
> Why doth my She Advowson fly
>   Incumbency?
> To sell thyself dost thou intend
>   By candle's end,
> And hold the contrast [contract] thus in doubt,
>   Life's taper out?
> Think but how soon the market fails,
> Your sex lives faster than the males;
> As if to measure age's span,
> The sober Julian were th' account of man,
> Whilst you live by the fleet Gregorian.
>
> CLEIVELAND.

Of enormous and disgusting hyperboles these may be examples:

> By every wind, that comes this way,
> Send me at least a sigh or two,
> Such and so many I'll repay
> As shall themselves make winds to get to you.
>
> COWLEY.

> In tears I'll waste these eyes,
>   By Love so vainly fed;
> So lust of old the Deluge punished.—COWLEY.

> All arm'd in brass the richest dress of war
> (A dismal glorious sight) he shone afar.
> The sun himself started with sudden fright,
> To see his beams return so dismal bright.
>
> COWLEY.

An universal consternation:

> His bloody eyes he hurls round, his sharp paws
> Tear up the ground; then runs he wild about,
> Lashing his angry tail and roaring out.
> Beasts creep into their dens, and tremble there;
> Trees, though no wind is stirring, shake with fear;
> Silence and horror fill the place around:
> Echo itself dares scarce repeat the sound.—COWLEY.

Their fictions were often violent and unnatural.

Of his Mistress bathing:
The fish around her crouded, as they do
To the false light that treacherous fishers shew,
And all with as much ease might taken be,
   As she at first took me:
   For ne'er did light so clear
   Among the waves appear,
Though every night the sun himself set there.

COWLEY.

The poetical effect of a Lover's name upon glass:

My name engrav'd herein
Doth contribute my firmness to this glass;
   Which, ever since that charm, hath been
As hard as that which grav'd it was.—DONNE.

Their conceits were sometimes slight and trifling.

On an inconstant woman:
He enjoys thy calmy sunshine now,
   And no breath stirring hears;
In the clear heaven of thy brow,
   No smallest cloud appears.
He sees thee gentle, fair and gay,
And trusts the faithless April of thy May.

COWLEY.

Upon a paper written with the juice of lemon, and read by the fire:

Nothing [So nothing] yet in thee is seen;
But when a genial heat warms thee within,
A new-born wood of various lines there grows;
   Here buds an L [A], and there a B,
   Here sprouts a V, and there a T,
And all the flourishing letters stand in rows.

COWLEY.

As they sought only for novelty they did not much enquire whether their allusions were to things high or low, elegant or gross; whether they compared the little to the great, or the great to the little.

Physick and Chirurgery for a Lover:

Gently, ah gently, madam, touch
   The wound, which you yourself have made;
That pain must needs be very much,

Which makes me of your hand afraid.
Cordials of pity give me now,
For I too weak for purgings grow.—COWLEY.

The World and a Clock:

Mahol th' inferior world's fantastic face
Through all the turns of matter's maze did trace;
Great Nature's well-set clock in pieces took;
On all the springs and smallest wheels did look
Of life and motion; and with equal art
Made up again the whole of every part.—COWLEY.

A coal-pit has not often found its poet; but, that it may not want its due honour Cleiveland has paralleled it with the Sun:

The moderate value of our guiltless ore
Makes no man atheist, and no woman whore;
Yet why should hallow'd vestal's sacred shrine
Deserve more honour than a flaming mine?
These pregnant wombs of heat would fitter be
Than a few embers, for a deity.
  Had he our pits, the Persian would admire
No sun, but warm's devotion at our fire:
He'd leave the trotting whipster, and prefer
Our profound Vulcan 'bove that waggoner.
For wants he heat, or light? or would have store
Of both? 'tis here: and what can suns give more?
Nay, what's the sun but, in a different name,
A coal-pit rampant, or a mine on flame!
Then let this truth reciprocally run,
The sun's heaven's coalery, and coals our sun.

Death, a Voyage:

No family
Ere rigg'd a soul for heaven's discovery,
With whom more venturers might boldly dare
Venture their stakes, with him in joy to share.

DONNE.

Their thoughts and expressions were sometimes grossly absurd, and such as no figures or licence can reconcile to the understanding.

A Lover neither dead nor alive:

Then down I laid my head,
Down on cold earth; and for a while was dead,

226

And my freed soul to a strange somewhere fled:
    Ah, sottish soul, said I,
    When back to its cage again I saw it fly:
    Fool to resume her broken chain,
    And row her galley here again!
    Fool, to that body to return
Where it condemn'd and destin'd is to burn!
    Once dead, how can it be,
Death should a thing so pleasant seem to thee,
That thou should'st come to live it o'er again in me?
                          COWLEY.

    A Lover's heart, a hand grenado:

Wo to her stubborn heart, if once mine come
    Into the self-same room,
    'Twill tear and blow up all within,
Like a grenado shot into a magazin.
Then shall Love keep the ashes and torn parts
Of both our broken hearts:
    Shall out of both one new one make;
From her's th' allay, fro mine the metal, take.—COWLEY.

    The poetical Propagation of Light:

The Prince's favour is diffus'd o'er all,
From which all fortunes, names, and natures fall;
Then from those wombs of stars, the Bride's bright eyes,
At every glance a constellation flies,
And sows the court with stars, and doth prevent,
In light and power, the all-ey'd firmament:
First her eye kindles [eyes kindle] other ladies' eyes,
Then from their beams their jewels' lustres rise;
And from their jewels torches do take fire,
And all is warmth, and light, and good desire.—DONNE.

They were in very little care to clothe their notions with elegance of dress, and therefore miss the notice and the praise which are often gained by those who think less, but are more diligent to adorn their thoughts.

That a mistress beloved is fairer in idea than in reality is by Cowley thus expressed:

    Thou in my fancy dost much higher stand,
    Than women can be plac'd by Nature's hand;
    And I must needs, I'm sure, a loser be,
    To change thee, as thou'rt there, for very thee.

JOHN DONNE

That prayer and labour should co-operate are thus taught by Donne:

> In none but us, are such mixt engines found,
> As hands of double office: for the ground
> We till with them; and them to heaven we raise;
> Who prayerless labours, or without this prays,
> Doth but one half, that's none.

By the same author a common topick, the danger of procrastination, is thus illustrated:

> —That which I should have begun
> In my youth's morning, now late must be done;
> And I, as giddy travellers must do,
> Which stray or sleep all day, and having lost
> Light and strength, dark and tir'd must then ride post.

All that Man has to do is to live and die; the sum of humanity is comprehended by Donne in the following lines:

> Think in how poor a prison thou didst lie
> After, enabled but to suck and cry.
> Think, when 'twas grown to most, 'twas a poor inn,
> A province pack'd up in two yards of skin,
> And that usurp'd, or threaten'd with a [the] rage
> Of sicknesses, or their true mother, age.
> But think that death hath now enfranchis'd thee;
> Thou hast thy expansion now, and liberty;
> Think, that a rusty piece discharg'd is flown
> In pieces, and the bullet is his own,
> And freely flies: this to thy soul allow,
> Think thy shell broke, think thy soul hatch'd but now.

They were sometimes indelicate and disgusting. Cowley thus apostrophises beauty:

> —Thou tyrant, which leav'st no man free!
> Thou subtle thief, from whom nought safe can be!
> Thou murtherer, which hast kill'd, and devil, which would'st damn me!

Thus he addresses his Mistress:

> Thou who, in many a propriety,
> So truly art the sun to me,
> Add one more likeness, which I'm sure you can,
> And let me and my sun beget a man.

Thus he represents the meditations of a Lover:

> Though in thy thoughts scarce any tracts have been
> So much as of original sin,
> Such charms thy beauty wears as might
> Desires in dying confest saints excite.
> Thou with strange adultery
> Dost in each breast a brothel keep;
> Awake, all men do lust for thee,
> And some enjoy thee when they sleep.

The true taste of Tears:

> Hither with crystal vials, lovers, come,
> And take my tears, which are Love's wine,
> And try your mistress' tears at home;
> For all are false that taste not just like mine.—DONNE.

This is yet more indelicate:

> As the sweet sweat of roses in a still,
> As that which from chaf'd musk-cat's pores doth trill,
> As the almighty balm of th' early East,
> Such are the sweet drops of [on] my mistress' breast.
> And on her neck her skin such lustre sets,
> They seem no sweat-drops, but pearl coronets [carkanets]:
> Rank sweaty froth thy mistress' brow defiles.—DONNE.

Their expressions sometimes raise horror, when they intend perhaps to be pathetick:

> As men in hell are from diseases free,
> So from all other ills am I,
> Free from their known formality:
> But all pains eminently lie in thee.—COWLEY.

They were not always strictly curious whether the opinions from which they drew their illustrations were true; it was enough that they were popular. Bacon remarks that some falsehoods are continued by tradition, because they supply commodious allusions.

> It gave a piteous groan, and so it broke;
> In vain it something would have spoke:
> The love within too strong for 't was,
> Like poison put into a Venice-glass.—COWLEY.

In forming descriptions they looked out not for images, but for conceits. Night has been a common subject, which poets have contended to adorn. Dryden's *Night* is well known; Donne's is as follows:

> Thou seest me here at midnight; now all rest,
> Time's dead low-water; when all minds divest
> To-morrow's business; when the labourers have
> Such rest in bed, that their last church-yard grave,
> Subject to change, will scarce be a type of this.
> Now when the client, whose last hearing is
> To-morrow, sleeps; when the condemned man—
> Who when he opes his eyes must shut them then
> Again by death—although sad watch he keep,
> Doth practise dying by a little sleep;
> Thou at this midnight seest me.

It must be however confessed of these writers that if they are upon common subjects often unnecessarily and unpoetically subtle, yet where scholastick speculation can be properly admitted, their copiousness and acuteness may justly be admired. What Cowley has written upon Hope shews an unequalled fertility of invention:

> Hope, whose weak being ruin'd is,
>   Alike if it succeed, and if it miss;
> Whom good or ill does equally confound,
> And both the horns of Fate's dilemma wound;
>   Vain shadow, which dost vanish quite,
>   Both at full noon and perfect night!
> The stars have not a possibility
>   Of blessing thee;
> If things then from their end we happy call,
> 'Tis Hope is the most hopeless thing of all.
>
>   Hope, thou bold taster of delight,
> Who, whilst thou should'st but taste, devour'st it quite!
> Thou bring'st us an estate, yet leav'st us poor,
> By clogging it with legacies before!
>   The joys which we entire should wed,
>   Come deflower'd virgins to our bed;
> Good fortunes without gain imported be,
>   Such mighty custom's paid to thee:
> For joy, like wine, kept close does better taste:
> If it take air before, its spirits waste.

To the following comparison of a man that travels and his wife that stays at home with a pair of compasses, it may be doubted whether absurdity or ingenuity has the better claim:

Our two souls therefore, which are one,
  Though I must go, endure not yet
A breach, but an expansion,
  Like gold to airy thinness beat.

If they be two, they are two so
  As stiff twin-compasses are two:
Thy soul, the fixt foot, makes no show
  To move, but doth, if th' other do.

And though it in the centre sit,
  Yet when the other far doth roam,
It leans, and hearkens after it,
  And grows erect, as that comes home

Such wilt thou be to me, who must,
  Like th' other foot, obliquely run;
Thy firmness makes my circle just,
  And makes me end where I begun.—DONNE.

In all these examples it is apparent that whatever is improper or vicious is produced by a voluntary deviation from nature in pursuit of something new and strange, and that the writers fail to give delight by their desire of exciting admiration.

(v) An unascribed anecdote, c. 1785, not included in Boswell's *Life of Johnson* (*Johnsonian Miscellanies*, ed. G. Birkbeck Hill, Oxford, 1897, ii, p. 404):

The late Mr. Crauford, of Hyde Park Corner, being engaged to dinner, where Dr. Johnson was to be, resolved to pay his court to him; and, having heard that he preferred Donne's Satires to Pope's version of them, said, 'Do you know, Dr. Johnson, that I like Dr. Donne's original Satires better than Pope's.' Johnson said, 'Well, Sir, I can't help that.'

91. Joseph Warton

1756, 1762, 1782

Warton (1722–1800) was a critic, poet, clergyman, and sometime headmaster of Winchester. He and his brother Thomas are sometimes said to initiate that turning away from the ideas of the 'correct' school of writing, which led to the revival of interest in 'Gothic' poetry. In the Dedication of his critical essay on Pope's writings, 1756, Warton set out a critical classification of the English poets; but it appeared drastically revised in the new edition of 1762, perhaps in response to hostile reviews of the earlier version (see No. 93). The long-promised second volume of the essay appeared in 1782 and has a section on Pope's version of Donne's *Satyre ii* and *Satyre iv*; by then, Warton seems to have hardened in an adverse opinion of Donne's poetry. The extracts given here are identified by the date of their first appearance in the essay on Pope in the form as quoted (*An Essay on the Writings and Genius of Pope*, 1756, i, pp. iv and xi–xii; 1762, i, pp. iv and xi–xii; 1782, ii, pp. 353–4. In the volume published separately in 1782 as the second part of the 1772 edition the fourth extract appears on ii, pp. 421–3).

In Warton's edition of Pope's writings many of the notes to Pope's version of Donne's *Satyres ii* and *iv* compare Pope's lines with Donne's. Some of these notes simply reproduce Warburton's comments (see No. 85) or repeat opinions Warton had already expressed in *An Essay on the Writings and Genius of Pope*. But there are some observations on lines in *Satyre iv* and I give the chief examples in the fifth extract (*The Works of Alexander Pope, Esq.*, 1797, iv, pp. 266, 274, 282, 286, 290, 293).

(i) From the Dedication to the 1756 edition:

We do not, it should seem, sufficiently attend to the difference there is, betwixt a MAN OF WIT, a MAN OF SENSE, and a TRUE POET. Donne and Swift, were undoubtedly men of wit, and men of sense: but what traces have they left of PURE POETRY? [It is remarkable that Dryden says of Donne; He was the greatest wit, tho' not the greatest poet of this nation. . . . *Added in 1762.*]

(ii) From the Dedication to the 1756 edition:

Our English poets may, I think, be disposed in four different classes and degrees. In the first class, I would place, first, our only three sublime and pathetic poets; SPENSER, SHAKESPEARE, MILTON; and then, at proper intervals, OTWAY and LEE. In the second class should be placed, such as possessed the true poetical genius, in a more moderate degree, but had noble talents for moral and ethical poesy. At the head of these are DRYDEN, DONNE, DENHAM, COWLEY, CONGREVE. In the third class may be placed, men of wit, of elegant taste, and some fancy in describing familiar life. Here may be numbered, PRIOR, WALLER, PARNELL, SWIFT, FENTON. In the fourth class, the mere versifiers, however smooth and mellifluous some of them may be thought, should be ranked. Such as PITT, SANDYS, FAIRFAX, BROOME, BUCKINGHAM, LANSDOWN. In which of these classes POPE deserves to be placed, the following work is intended to determine.

(iii) From the Dedication to the 1762 edition (a tacit revision of the passage just given):

Our English poets may, I think, be disposed in four different classes and degrees. In the first class, I would place, our only three sublime and pathetic poets; SPENSER, SHAKESPEARE, MILTON. In the second class should be ranked, such as possessed the true poetical genius, in a more moderate degree, but had noble talents for moral, ethical, and panegyrical poesy. At the head of these are DRYDEN, PRIOR, ADDISON, COWLEY, WALLER, GARTH, FENTON, GAY, DENHAM, PARNELL. In the third class may be placed, men of wit, of elegant taste, and lively fancy in describing familiar life, tho' not the higher scenes of poetry. Here may be numbered, BUTLER, SWIFT, ROCHESTER, DONNE, DORSET, OLDHAM. In the fourth class, the mere versifiers, however smooth and mellifluous some of them may be thought, should be disposed. Such as PITT, SANDYS, FAIRFAX, BROOME, BUCKINGHAM, LANSDOWN. . . .

(iv) From the account of Pope's version of *Satyre ii* and *Satyre iv*, given in the second volume of Warton's *Essay on Pope*, 1782:

Two noblemen of taste and learning, the Duke of Shrewsbury and the Earl of Oxford, desired P o p e to melt down and cast anew the weighty bullion of Dr. Donne's satires; who had degraded and deformed a vast fund of sterling wit and strong sense, by the most harsh and uncouth diction. P o p e succeeded in giving harmony to a writer, more rough and rugged than even any of his age, and who profited so little by the example *Spencer* had set, of a most musical and mellifluous versification; far beyond the versification of *Fairfax*, who is so frequently mentioned as the greatest improver of the harmony of our language. The satires of *Hall*, written in very smooth and pleasing numbers, preceded those of *Donne* many years; for his *Virgidemiarum* were published, in six books, in the year 1597; in which he calls himself the very first English satirist. This, however, was not true in fact; for Sir Thomas Wyatt, of Allington Castle in Kent, the friend and favourite of *Henry VIII.* and, as was suggested, of *Ann Boleyn*, was our first writer of satire worth notice. But it was not in his numbers only that Donne was reprehensible. He abounds in false thoughts, in far-sought sentiments, in forced unnatural conceits. He was the corrupter of *Cowley. Dryden* was the first who called him a *metaphysical* poet. He had a considerable share of learning; and, though he entered late into orders, yet was esteemed a good divine.

Warton goes on to give some of Ben Jonson's comments on Donne from the 'Conversations with Drummond'. He adds in a footnote that Donne 'was one of our poets who wrote elegantly in Latin; as did *Ben Johnson . . . Cowley, Milton, Addison,* and *Gray. . . .*'

(v) From 'Notes on the *Satires of Dr John Donne, Dean of St Paul's, Versified*' in Warton's edition of Pope's *Works*, 1797. Warton is commenting on Pope's version of Donne's *Satyre iv* and his references are to that version. Line references to Donne's poem are given in square brackets after each note:

Ver. 7. *The Poet's hell,*] He has here with great prudence corrected the licentious expression of his Original. [3–4]

Ver. 104. *from King to King*] Much superior to the Original, where is a vile conceit,

The way to it is King's-street   [79–80]

Ver. 184. *Bear me,*] These four lines are wonderfully sublime. . . . The next twenty-two lines are not only far superior to the Original, but, perhaps, equal to any Pope ever wrote, or to any in our language in rhyme. [155 on]

Ver. 218. *That's Velvet*] Much superior to the Original in brevity and elegance. . . .   [181–2]

Ver. 273. *As men from Jails*] A line so smooth that our Author thought proper to adopt it from the Original. There are many *such*, as I have before observed, which shew, that if Donne had taken equal pains, he need not have left his numbers so *much more rugged* and *disgusting*, than many of his cotemporaries, especially one so exquisitely melodious as Drummond of Hawthornden; who, in truth, more than Fairfax, Waller, or Denham, deserves to be called the first polisher of English Versification. . . .   [230]

Ver. 286. *My Wit*] The private character of Donne was very amiable and interesting; particularly so, on account of his secret marriage with the daughter of Sir George More; of the difficulties he underwent on this marriage; of his constant affection to his wife, his affliction at her death, and the sensibility he displayed towards all his friends and relations.
                                                                                        [241–3]

92. Peter Whalley

1756

Whalley (1722–91), a clergyman and sometime schoolmaster, edited Ben Jonson and wrote on Shakespeare. In a 'Life of Benjamin Jonson' prefixed to his edition of Jonson's *Works* he brought in Pope, without naming him, to confirm Jonson's praises of Donne's poetry (*The Works of Ben Jonson*, 1756, i, p. xlviii).

It is to the honour of Jonson's judgement, that the greatest poet of our nation had the same opinion of Donne's genius and wit; and hath preserved part of him from perishing, by putting his thoughts and satire into modern verse.

235

93. *The Monthly Review*

1756

An anonymous reviewer of the first edition of Joseph Warton's *Essay on the Writings and Genius of Pope* (see No. 91) took Warton severely to task for placing Donne in the second category of poets (*The Monthly Review*, xiv, January–June 1756, p. 535).

In the second class after Dryden, the Critic places Donne, as possessing the *true poetical genius, with noble talents for moral poesy*. And yet, but two pages before, he characterizes this author, as a man of wit, and a man of sense, but asks what traces he had left of pure poetry? We readily agree that he has left none; for as an elegant genius of the north has expressed it,* we shall never be induced to regard that as poetry, which Homer and Virgil, if alive, would not have understood. Did any man with a poetical ear, ever yet read ten lines of Donne without disgust? or are there ten lines of poetry in all his works? No. How then comes this Adjuster of literary rank to post him before Denham, Waller, Cowley &c. In truth, Daniel, Drayton, Randolph, or almost any other of his contemporary poets, the translator of Du Bartas not excepted, deserve the place better than he.

After Donne marches Denham.

Indeed Denham is more intitled to his station than the former. . . .

* Drummond of Hawthornden.

236

94. *The Literary Magazine*

1758

The Literary Magazine for January 1758 published 'A Poetical Scale' awarding points out of eighty to the chief English poets, with copious notes on the placings. The twenty-nine authors in the list include Drayton, Lee, Aaron Hill, Rowe, Garth, Southern, and Hughes; but Donne is omitted, and a note explains why. The following are some items from the scale, with the comment on Donne. (Given in J. W. M. Gibbs, *The Works of Oliver Goldsmith*, 1885, iv, pp. 417–28. Gibbs attributes the piece to Goldsmith.)

(i)

	Genius	Judgment	Learning	Versification
Chaucer	16	12	10	14
Spencer	18	12	14	18
Shakespear	19	14	14	19
Milton	18	16	17	18
Pope	18	18	15	19

(ii)

Dr Donne was a man of wit, but he seems to have been at pains not to pass for a poet.

95. Anon., *The Critical Review*

1767

An anonymous reviewer of W. L. Lewis's translation of the *Thebaid* of Statius noted Lewis's unfortunate inclination to discard ideas of correctness and return to the manner of older writers (*The Critical Review*, xxiii, 1767, p. 364).

The versification is mostly smooth and frequently harmonious; circumstances from which the translator may justly claim some praise, considering the great inclination the present age discovers towards the uncultivated measure of Donne and Johnson.

96. James Granger

1769

Granger (1723–76), Vicar of Shiplake, was a biographer and print collector. He gave an account of Donne in *A Biographical History of England, from Egbert the Great to the Revolution*, 1769, i, pp. 186–7, 246, 288. There are separate entries for Donne as poet and as divine, and the Lothian portrait is described in a further entry.

(i)
John Donne, styled by Mr Dryden 'the greatest wit, though not the greatest poet, of our nation,' wrote on various subjects; but his greatest excellency was satire. He had a prodigious richness of fancy; but his thoughts were much debased by his versification. . . . [He says Drummond told Ben Jonson that Donne wrote his best pieces before he was twenty-five; and he quotes John Brown's *Essay on Satire*—"'Twas then plain DONNE in honest vengeance rose', etc. (see No. 82).]

(ii)
[Speaking of Donne as a divine] We hear much of him as a poet, but very little as a divine, though in the latter character he had great merit. . . .

97. Richard Hurd

1776

Hurd (1720–1808) was Bishop of Lichfield and Coventry 1774–8 and Bishop of Worcester 1781–1808. He edited classical texts, engaged in theological controversy, and wrote on moral and literary matters; his *Letters on Chivalry and Romance*, 1762, contributed powerfully to the revival of interest in 'Gothic' writings. He illustrated his commentary upon Horace from the English poets, several times referring to Donne (*Horatius Flaccus*, 1776, pp. 42–3, 97–8, 191–2). He spoke of Donne again in his *Select Works of Mr A. Cowley*, 1772, ii, p. 117.

(i) From the 'Notes on the Art of Poetry':

25—28. BREVIS ESSE LABORO, OBSCURUS FIO: SECTANTEM LENIA NERVI DEFICIUNT ANIMIQUE: PROFESSUS GRANDIA TURGET: SERPIT HUMI TUTUS NIMIUM TIMIDUSQUE PROCELLAE.]¹ If these characters were to be exemplified in our own poets, of reputation, the *first*, I suppose, might be justly applied to Donne; the *second*, to Parnell; the *third*, to Thomson; and the *fourth*, to Addison.

(ii) From 'A Discourse on Poetical Imitation':

The *mutual habitudes and relations* (at least what the mind is capable of regarding as *such*), subsisting between those innumerable objects of thought and sense, which make up the entire natural and intellectual world, are indeed infinite; and if the poet be allowed to associate and bring together all those ideas, wherein the ingenuity of the mind can perceive any remote sign or glimpse of *resemblance*, it were truly wonderful, that, in any number of images and allusions, there should be found a close conformity of them with those of any other writer.

---

1 'Striving to be brief I become obscure; aiming to be smooth I lack sinew and life. The poet who professes grandeur is turgid; and the man who is too fearful of the storm creeps safe along the ground.' Horace, *Ars Poetica*, lines 25–8.

But this is far from being the case. For . . . the more august poetry dis-
claims, as unsuited to its state and dignity, that inquisitive and anxious
diligence, which pries into Nature's retirements, and searches through
all her secret and hidden haunts, to detect a forbidden commerce, and
expose to light some strange unexpected conjunction of ideas. This
quaint combination of remote, unallied imagery, constitutes a species of
entertainment, which, for its *novelty*, may amuse and divert the mind
in other compositions; but is wholly inconsistent with the reserve and
solemnity of the *graver* forms. There is too much curiosity of art, too
sollicitous an affectation of *pleasing*, in these ingenious exercises of the
fancy, to suit with the simple majesty of the *epos* or *drama*; which dis-
claims to cast about for forced and tortured allusions, and aims only to
expose, in the fairest light, such as are most obvious and natural. And
here, by the way, it may be worth observing, in honour of a great
Poet of the last century, I mean Dr. DONNE, that though agreeably to
the turn of his genius, and taste of his age, he was fonder, than ever poet
was, of these *secret and hidden ways* in his lesser poetry; yet when he had
projected his great work '*On the progress of the Soul*' (of which we have
only the beginning), his good sense brought him out into the freer
spaces of nature and open day-light.

(iii) From 'On the Marks of Imitation':

You see with what a suspicious eye, we, who aspire to the name of
critics, examine your writings. But every poet will not endure to be
scrutinized so narrowly.

1. B. Jonson, in his Prologue to the *Sad Shepherd*, is opening the
subject of that poem. The *sadness* of his shepherd is

> For his lost Love, who in the TRENT is said
> To have miscarried! '*las! what knows the head*
> *Of a calm river, whom the feet have drown'd!*

The reflexion in this place is unnecessary and even impertinent.
Who besides ever heard of the *feet* of a river? Of *arms* we have. And so
it stood in Jonson's original.

> Greatest and fairest Empress, know you this?
> Alas! no more than Thames' calm head doth know
> Whose meads his arms drown, or whose corn o'erflow.
>   Dr. DONNE.

The poet is speaking of the corruption of the courts of justice, and the
allusion is perfectly fine and natural. Jonson was tempted to bring it

into his prologue by the mere beauty of the sentiment. He had a river at his disposal, and would not let slip the opportunity. But his unnatural use of it detects his 'imitation.'

(iv) Hurd's editorial note on Cowley's 'Ode upon Liberty', line 122:

Or to the sweetness of the sound, or greatness of the sense] Intimating, that these two things cannot, or should not, be united in poetry. It is certain, that Donne and Jonson (Cowley's great models) seemed to think so, who, when they had a better thing than ordinary to say, were sure to say it in the roughest and harshest metre.

98. William Dodd

1777

Dodd (1729–77), clergyman, writer, forger, had in his library '1 vol. Donne's Poems (Duodecimo)', listed so without further specification in the catalogue of the sale of the library, 13–16 March 1777. (See *Sale Catalogues of Libraries of Eminent Persons*, v, ed. S. Parks, 1972, p. 377.)

99. Anon., *The Encyclopaedia Britannica*

1779

Donne gets an entry in the second edition of *The Encyclopaedia Britannica; Or, A Dictionary of Arts, Sciences, &c*, 1779, iv, pp. 2515b–16a. The writer shows no acquaintance with Donne's work and takes part of his account straight from Granger's *Biographical History* (see No. 96).

DONNE (Dr John), an excellent poet and divine of the seventeenth century. [There follows a brief life, with a list of writings.] . . . His writings shew him to be a man of incomparable wit and learning; but his greatest excellence was satire. He had a prodigious richness of fancy, but his thoughts were much debased by his versification. He was, however, highly celebrated by all the great men of that age.

100. John Bell

The publisher John Bell (1745–1831) brought out at Edinburgh an edition of *The Poetical Works of Dr John Donne* in three small volumes as nos 23–5 of a collection of *Poets of Great Britain*. Before the poems Bell printed Walton's *Life of Donne* (abridged but not, as in the 1719 edition, rewritten), the younger John Donne's address to Lord Craven, Ben Jonson's epigrams to Donne, and all the funeral elegies on Donne.

The text of the poems is that of the 1719 edition, but the several groups of poems are given in a new and quite arbitrary order.

101. Anon., *The Monthly Review*

1779

An anonymous reviewer of Johnson's *The Works of the English Poets* (the Prefaces to which were in fact the *Lives of the English Poets*) quoted the first seven lines of Donne's *Elegie viii*, 'The Comparison', to confirm Johnson's account of 'metaphysical' poetry in the *Life of Cowley* (*The Monthly Review,* lxi, July–December 1779, p. 4). The reviewer remarks: 'It is a most curious specimen of metaphysical gallantry.' He goes on to endorse Johnson's comment that whatever is improper or vicious in such examples is produced by a voluntary deviation from nature in pursuit of something new and strange.

102. Thomas Warton

1781

Warton (1728–90), younger brother of Joseph Warton, became Professor of Poetry and later Professor of Ancient History at Oxford. He was a poet and a historian of poetry. In his history of English poetry to the end of the Elizabethan age he gave no account of Donne, but he referred inaccurately to Donne's *Satyres* and to some of the early commendations of Donne's poetry (*The History of English Poetry*, 1774–81, iii, p. 278; iii (additional section xlvi), p. 50; iii (additional section xlviii), p. 85).

Warton quoted Edmund Bolton's appraisal of Donne and others in the *Hypercritica* (see No. 2, ?1618), without himself commenting on Donne. Later, he briefly praised Hall's *Satires* at the expense of Donne's:

They [Hall's *Satires*] were, however, admired and imitated by Oldham. And Pope, who modernised Donne, is said to have wished he had seen Hall's satires sooner. But had Pope undertaken to modernise Hall, he must have adopted, because he could not have improved, many of his lines. Hall is too finished and smooth for such an operation. Donne, though he lived so many years later, was susceptible of modern refinement, and his asperities were such as wanted and would bear the chisel.

Later still Warton mentions Donne's *Satyres* again:

Donne's SATIRES were written early in the reign of James the first though they were not published till after his death, in the year 1633. Jonson sends one of his Epigrams to Lucy Countess of Bedford, with MR DONNES SATYRES. It is conjectured by Wood, that a lively satirical piece, on the literature of the times . . . with Donne's initials, and connected with another poem of the same cast, is one of Donne's juvenile performances. I had supposed John Davies.

245

The 'lively satirical piece' is in fact by John Davies of Hereford. In a footnote to this passage Warton quotes Freeman's epigram 'To John Dunne' from *Runne, and a great Cast* (see No. 6). He had earlier mentioned Donne as one of the writers who befriended and encouraged Freeman.

103. Vicesimus Knox

1782

Knox (1752–1821) was a clergyman and headmaster who wrote miscellaneous essays. He added an essay on satire to the third edition of a collection of essays first published in 1778, and briefly compared Donne with Juvenal in the course of it. In another essay in the volume he discussed Cowley, moving from him to a general censure of the taste of the age and a consignment of Cowley, Donne, and Jonson to a speedy oblivion (*Essays, Moral and Literary* (1782), 1787, iii, pp. 167–8 and 439–40).

(i)

The Roman is remarkably harmonious. But Donne, his imitator, seems to have thought roughness of verse, as well as of sentiment, a real grace. It is scarcely possible, that a writer who did not studiously avoid a smooth versification, could have written so many lines without stumbling on a good one. Pope has revived his fame by attuning his harsh numbers; a work whose very excellence makes us regret that a *genius* so servile as was the bard's of Twickenham, should have wasted its vigour in paraphrases and translations. . . .

(ii)

Time, the great arbiter of reputation, has already begun to strip the poet of his borrowed honours. A critic, whose genius and judgment keep pace with each other, and who illuminates every subject on which he treats, has allotted Cowley his just species of praise, and has given the world, in a judicious selection of his works, all that they possessed of real value.

Of these the prose forms a principal part. It is written in a style sufficiently flowing to prove that Cowley was not destitute of a musical ear; a circumstance which countenances the opinion of those who maintain that he affected a rugged style. Was it a compliance with the taste of the age, that induced him to affect deformity? unforunate compliance with a deplorable taste! He as well as they whom he imitated, Donne and Johnson, were unquestionably possessed of great learning and ingenuity; but they all neglected the graces of composition, and will therefore soon be numbered among those once celebrated writers, whose utility now consists in filling a vacancy on the upper shelf of some dusty and deserted library.

104. Joseph Ritson

1783

The antiquary and bibliographer Ritson (1752–1803) found little place for Donne in his *A Select Collection of English Songs,* 1783, an anthology of older poetry which was intended to rival or supplant Percy's *Reliques*. In 'A Historical Essay on the Origin and Progress of National Song', prefixed to the collection, Ritson gave Donne's poetry no more than a passing mention (i, p. lix). But he did print a prettified version of 'The Message', untitled and without author's name, in a section of 'Songs Omitted' appended to volume i (i, pp. 257–8). This version, which is given below, seems to have become popular for it appears in several subsequent anthologies of lyric verse.

(i)
Among the songsters of James the Firsts time, one is pleased to meet the name of that elegant writer and accomplished gentleman Sir Henry Wotton. Dr Donnes imitation of Marlow, and other pieces, intitle him to a place in the list. . . .

(ii)

> Send back my long stray'd eyes to me,
> Which oh! too long have dwelt on thee:
> But if from you they've learn'd such ill,
>   To sweetly smile,
>   And then beguile,
> Keep the deceivers, keep them still.
>
> Send home my harmless heart again,
> Which no unworthy thought could stain:
> But if it has been taught by thine,
>   To forfeit both
>   Its word and oath,
> Keep it, for then 'tis none of mine.

Yet send me back my heart and eyes,
For I'll know all thy falsities;
That I one day may laugh, when thou
    Shalt grieve and mourn,
    For one will scorn
And prove as false as thou art now.

105. Anon., *A New and General Biographical Dictionary*

1784

There is a long account of Donne in *A New and General Biographical Dictionary*, new edition, 1784, iv, pp. 469–78. The entry is headed 'DONNE (John), an English poet and divine', and is largely biographical, drawing on Walton and Wood. The poems are mentioned briefly among Donne's extant works, though the only edition cited is that of 1719. Some of Dryden's judgments are quoted, and there is a reference to Pope's versions of *Satyres ii* and *iv* – 'He has shewed the world, that when translated into numbers and English, as Dryden expresses it, they are not inferior to any thing in that kind of poetry. . . .'

106. Henry Headley

1787

Headley (1765–88) was a young poet and critic. The year after graduating at Oxford he published a selection of the beauties of English poetry between 1558 and 1660. He included nothing by Donne and gave no account of him though he offered biographical sketches of many minor poets of the period. But he also omitted the beauties of Sidney, Spenser, and Milton, whose names he repeatedly invoked with Donne's as major writers of that age.

In his introductory scale of poets Headley classified Donne solely as a satirical writer, omitting him from the category of 'Philosophical and Metaphysical' poets and the category of 'Amatory, and Miscellaneous' poets (*Select Beauties of Ancient English Poetry*, 1787, p. xv).

ELIZABETH began to reign in 1558.

Epic Poets.	Philosophical & Metaphysical	Dramatic.	Historical.
Spencer,		G. Gascoyne,	Niccols,
Milton,	Sir J. Davis,	Shakespeare,	Sackville,
Davenant.	Phin. Fletcher,	Massinger,	Daniel,
	Giles Fletcher,	Jonson,	Drayton,
	H. More.	Beaumont &	May,
		Fletcher,	J. Beaumont.
		Shirley.	

Satyrical.	Pastoral.	Amatory, & Miscellaneous.	Translators.
Hall,	Warner,		Fairfax,
Marston,	Drayton,	Raleigh,	Sandys,
Rowlands,	Browne,	Drummond,	Crashawe.
Donne.	Fairfax.	Marlowe,	
		Cowley,	
		Carew,	
		Corbet,	
		King,	
		Habington,	
		Cartwright,	
		Randolph,	
		Suckling.	

107. Anon., *Nouveau Dictionnaire Historique*

1789

There is a wildly inaccurate account of Donne in the seventh edition of the *Nouveau Dictionnaire Historique: ou Histoire Abrégée*, Caen and Lyon, 1789, pp. 331–2. Donne is said to have been born in 1574, son of a rich merchant, and to be the subject of a life by 'Jean Watton', 1658. There is a mention of *Pseudo-Martyr* and a summary of the argument of *Biathanatos*. Otherwise all that is said of his writings is that 'he gained the esteem of his countrymen by productions full of spirit and grace', and that he made in turn poems of gallantry and what his age took for satires. He is declared to have gained prosperity and honours in recompense of his talents.

108. William Cowper

Cowper was related to the family of Donne and had dealings with the poet's descendants. He several times alluded to Donne as a kinsman and fellow-poet. All the following references are addressed to relatives with whom he evidently shared an interest in their common forebear. The first occurs in a letter to Mrs Bodham written from Weston, 27 February 1790. Mrs Bodham's maiden name was Anne Donne; she was Cowper's cousin, daughter of his mother's brother, the Rev. Roger Donne, and had seemingly sent him a picture of his mother (*The Correspondence of William Cowper*, ed. T. Wright, 1904, iii, pp. 434–5). The second item is from a letter to John Johnson dated 31 July 1790, inviting him to visit (*Correspondence*, iii, p. 478). Cowper's sonnet 'Kinsman belov'd', from which the third extract is taken, was also addressed to Johnson; it expresses gratitude for the gift of a bust of Homer, which had none the less caused the poet grief as well as joy.

(i)
There is in me, I believe, more of the Donne than of the Cowper; and though I love all of both names, and have a thousand reasons to love those of my own name, yet I feel the bond of nature draw me vehemently to your side. [He gives various Donne traits in his own character.] . . . Add to all this, I deal much in poetry, as did our venerable ancestor, the Dean of St Paul's, and I think I shall have proved myself a Donne at all points. The truth is that whatever I am, I love you all. . . .

(ii)
If you have Donne's poems bring them with you, for I have not seen them many years, and should like to look them over.

(iii)

> The grief is this, that sunk in Homer's mine
> I lose my precious years, now soon to fall,

Handling his gold, which, howsoe'er it shine,
Proves dross, when balanc'd in the Christian scale.
Be wiser thou—like our fore-father DONNE,
Seek heav'nly wealth, and work for God alone.

109. Andrew Kippis

1793

The Nonconformist divine and biographer Andrew Kippis (1725–95) gave an account of Donne's life and writings in the second edition of the *Biographia Britannica*, a biographical dictionary of British worthies. The main entry is a summary of Walton's *Life of Donne*. But in an extended footnote Kippis listed Donne's writings, gave a very good conspectus of critical views of them from Ben Jonson to Joseph Warton, and made a few comments of his own (*Biographia Britannica*, 1778–93, v. pp. 334–8).

After quoting Dryden's several criticisms of Donne, Kippis takes up a remark in the *Discourse Concerning Satire* (No. 49 (iii)): 'Would not Donne's satires, which abound with so much wit, appear more charming if he had taken care of his words, and of his numbers?' Kippis comments:

Whether our late excellent poet (Mr Pope. See his Satires of Dr J. Donne) took the hint from this question, or not, is uncertain; but he has shewn the world, that Dr Donne's *Satires*, when *translated into numbers and English* (as Mr Dryden above expresses it) are not inferior to any thing in that kind of poetry, even his own admirable writings.

Kippis moralises upon 'the high devotional spirit of the times' as it was exemplified in Donne's hesitation before he took orders, and caps his homily with some lines from Donne:

This sentiment, that prayer and labour should co-operate, is expressed by Donne himself, in one of these poems, though with no elegance of language. . . .

[He quotes 'To the Countesse of Bedford', 'T'have written then', lines 43–7, giving his source as Johnson's *Life of Cowley*.]

Kippis quotes Donne freely in this footnote but always from Johnson or Walton. He refers to the 1719 edition of Donne's poems as the only collection of all the verse but doesn't himself seem to have used even that; evidently he knew Donne as a poet only through other people's quotation of him.

None the less he thought more highly of what little he knew than some of his authorities, and disputed their judgments of Donne:

The name of Dr. Donne is now more generally known as a poet than in any other capacity, though none of his poetical works are read at present, excepting his Satires, which, being modernized by Mr. Pope, are printed on the opposite page. His versification is allowed to be intolerably harsh and unmusical; but different accounts have been given of his genius as a poet. Dr. Birch observes, that his poetical works shew a prodigious fund of genius, under the disguise of an affected and obscure stile, and a most inharmonious versification.[1] A far superior arbiter in subjects of taste (Dr. Warton) has asserted, that Dr. Donne possessed the true poetical genius, with noble talents for moral poesy. The same writer having before characterized him as a man of wit, and a man of sense, but asked what traces he had left of pure poetry, hath been thought by a periodical critic to be guilty of an inconsistency. This, however, we do not perceive to be the case; for Dr. Donne might have noble talents for moral poesy, and yet they might be perverted from being properly displayed, by his want of taste and neglect of harmony. The critic referred to farther says, 'Did any man, with a poetical ear, ever yet read ten lines of Donne without disgust? or are there ten lines of poetry in all his works? No'.[2] We as confidently answer, 'Yes;' and, for the truth of our answer, we shall only appeal to the four stanzas inserted in note K, where there are sixteen lines which, notwithstanding their quaintness, may be read without disgust, and have in them a true spirit of poetry. Dr. Warton, in the second volume of his Essay on the Writings and Genius of Pope, has some additional observations concerning Donne, the greater part of which we shall transcribe.

[1] *Life of Tillotson*, p. 27.   [2] *Monthly Review*, Vol. XIV, p. 535.

The 'sixteen lines' Kippis praises here are the last four stanzas of 'A Valediction: forbidding Mourning', which he quotes from Walton's *Life of Donne*. He reports at length Joseph Warton's criticism of Donne's *Satyres* (see No. 91). Then he gives some of Ben Jonson's remarks from the 'Conversations with Drummond' (No. 3 (ii),) and rounds off the account of Donne's verse with extracts from Johnson's *Life of Cowley*, which includes three quotations from Donne.

Kippis adds a coda which shows his personal attraction to Donne still struggling to define itself:

There is something in the private character of Dr. Donne which attaches the mind, and renders the contemplation of it pleasing and interesting even at the present day. This arises from the story of his marriage, the difficulties in which that event involved him, and the amiable sensibilities which he appears to have displayed in all the relations and circumstances of Life.

110. Robert Anderson

1793

Anderson (1750–1830) abandoned medicine for literature, and became the editor and biographer of British poets. He edited *The Edinburgh Magazine* for a time. He reprinted Donne's poems as the fourth volume of his collection of British poets, prefacing them with a 'Life of Donne' drawn from Walton but offering some independent comment too (*Complete Edition of the Poets of Great Britain*, Edinburgh, 1793, iv, pp. 3–5).

He seems, however, to have divided his studies between law and poetry; for, about this time, he composed most of his love poems, and other levities and pieces of humour, which sufficiently established his poetical reputation, and procured him the acquaintance of all those of his own age, who were most distinguished for acuteness of wit, and gaiety of temper. . . .

Donne is better known as a poet, than as a divine; though in the latter character he had great merit. His prose writings, which are chiefly theological, are enumerated by Walton, who has written his life, with a just admiration of his talents and virtues, but with unnecessary prolixity and amplification, and in a strain of vulgar credulity and enthusiasm, peculiar to the productions of the last century.

His 'Pseudo Martyr', in which he has effectually confuted the doctrine of the papal supremacy is the most valuable of his prose writings. His Sermons abound too much with the pedantry of the times in which they were written, to be at all esteemed in the present age.

His Poems, consisting of 'Songs and Sonnets, Epigrams, Elegies, Epithalamions, Satires, Letters, Funeral Elegies, Holy Sonnets,' &c. published at different times, were printed together in one volume 12 mo. by Tonson, 1719, and reprinted by Bell, in 3 vols. 12mo. 1781, with the addition of Elelegies on his Death, by Jonson, Carew, King, Corbet, and other contemporary wits, a specimen of which is given in the present edition.

All his contemporaries are lavish in his praise. Prejudiced, perhaps, by the style of writing which was then fashionable, they seem to have rated his performances beyond their just value. To the praise of wit and subtility his title is unquestionable. In all his pieces he displays prodigious richness of fancy, and an elaborate minuteness of description; but his thoughts are seldom natural, obvious, or just, and much debased by the carelessness of his versification.

Dryden has very justly given him the character of 'the greatest wit, though not the greatest poet of our nation.'

[A short extract from Dryden's *A Discourse Concerning . . . Satire*— see No. 49 (iii).]

Pope, probably taking the hint from this passage, has shewn that Donne's satires, which abound with so much wit, assume more dignity, and appear more charming, when 'translated into numbers and English.'

Dr. Johnson, in his 'Life of Cowley,' has displayed his prodigious genius and extensive learning, to great advantage, in characterising the metaphysical poetry of Donne, and his imitators.

111. Nathan Drake

1798, 1817

Drake (1766–1836) was a doctor and literary essayist, whose extreme views on literature have gained him some notoriety. He first expressed his disrelish for Donne in a comment on satire, and developed his attack into a general dismissal, on Johnsonian lines, nearly twenty years later (*Literary Hours, or Sketches Critical and Narrative* (1798), 1800, ii, p. 170; *Shakespeare and his Times*, 1817, i, p. 615).

(i)

As to Donne, if it be true, that the purport of poetry should be to please, no author has written with such utter neglect of the rule. It is scarce possible for a human ear to endure the dissonance and discord of his couplets, and even when his thoughts are clothed in the melody of Pope, they appear to me hardly worth the decoration.

(ii)

DONNE, JOHN, D.D. The greater part of the poetry of this prelate, though not published, was written, according to Ben Jonson, before he was twenty-five years of age; and as he was born in London in 1573, he must consequently be ranked as a bard of the sixteenth century. His poems consist of elegies, satires, letters, epigrams, divine poems, and miscellaneous pieces, and procured for him, among his contemporaries, through private circulation and with the public when printed, during the greater part of the seventeenth century, an extraordinary share of reputation. A more refined age, however, and a more chastised taste, have very justly consigned his poetical labours to the shelf of the philologer. A total want of harmony in versification, and a total want of simplicity both in thought and expression, are the vital defects of Donne. Wit he has in abundance, and even erudition, but they are miserably misplaced; and even his amatory pieces exhibit little else than cold conceits and metaphysical subtleties. He may be considered as one of the principal establishers of a school of poetry founded on the worst Italian model, commencing towards the close of Elizabeth's reign, continued to the decease of Charles the Second, and including among its most brilliant cultivators the once popular names of Crashaw, Cleveland, Cowley, and Sprat.

Dr. Donne died in March 1631, and the first edition of his poems was published by his son two years after that event.

THE NINETEENTH CENTURY

'an absolute and unique genius'

112. Samuel Taylor Coleridge

1795–1833

Coleridge and Lamb set out to rediscover the old authors who had fallen out of favour in the eighteenth century, and to reinstate the principles by which they wrote, Coleridge seems to have found Donne's writings peculiarly congenial and he took Donne's stature for granted when he championed him, to the alarm of some hearers. His close comments on Donne's poems, had they been widely known, must have stimulated people to read Donne himself rather than Johnson's account of him; but they were not printed until the 1850s when the general revival of interest in Donne was already well under way, and they are still insufficiently reckoned with.

Some of Coleridge's marginal comments on Donne's letters and sermons are given because they illustrate an attitude to Donne which one finds in the account of the poetry.

(i) Entries Coleridge made in his Notebooks between 1795 and 1804 show that he was reading Donne's poetry, probably in volume iv of Anderson's *The Poets of Great Britain* which came out in 1793. In the winter of 1803–4 Coleridge seems to have got bits of Donne by heart for he familiarly adapts lines from the funeral poems and verse letters. (*The Notebooks of Samuel Taylor Coleridge*, 1794–1804, ed. K. Coburn, 1957. The extracts given below are denoted by the number of their entry in this edition.)

Entry no. 171 (1795–6):

> Satires in the manner of Donne—
> 1. Horace Walpole
> 2. Monthly Reviewers &c . . . Bowles.

No. 698 (February–March 1800):

'The all-ey'd Firmament' Donne—

[*Eclogue, 1613. December 26*, line 28]

Nos 1786–9 (December 1803–January 1804):

Mismotion/to unapparel.

[Both words occur in the *Obsequies to the Lord Harrington*, lines 12 and 132.]

'Bedded and bath'd in all his Ordures'

Donne.

[*The second Anniversary*, line 171]

In heaven/
God help me, Girl! I would not miss you there,
For all the bliss that you can give me here.

['To the Countesse of Bedford' ('Reason is our Soules left hand'), lines 37–8]

For Folly's Lion is but Wisdom's ape—

['To Mr T. W.' ('All haile sweet Poet')]

(ii) About 1796 Coleridge drew up some 'Memoranda for a History of English Poetry, biographical, bibliographical, critical and philosophical, in distinct Essay'. He sketched the topics of eight essays, covering English poetry from the 'English Romances' to 'Modern Poetry'. Donne was to be treated in the seventh essay. (Given in K. Coburn, *Inquiring Spirit,* 1957, pp. 152–3.)

7. Dryden and the History of the witty Logicians, *Butler* (ought he not to have a distinct tho' short Essay?)—B. Johnson, Donne, Cowley——Pope.—

(iii) Coleridge twice quoted lines from Donne in *The Friend*. As the motto for Essay xv (30 November 1809) he adapted lines 5–17 of the verse letter 'To Sir Henry Goodyere' ('Who makes the Past, a paterne for next yeare,'). In Essay xvi (7 December 1809) he used lines 48–52 of the *Eclogue, 1613. December 26*, considerably adapted, to illustrate his argument that 'the previous condition of all insight into truth, is to dare commune with our very and permanent self' (*The Friend*, ed. B. E. Rooke, London, 1969, i, p. 115).

Coleridge adapted Donne's lines seemingly on the principle he set out in his Notebook no. 43, many years later (see (xii) below, p. 276, entry for 1830). Thus he amends what Donne wrote in the verse letter to Goodyer—

> So had your body'her morning, hath her noone,
>   And shall not better; her next change is night:

to

> Our bodies had their morning, have their noon,
>   And shall not better—the next change is night;

And he partly rewrites the extract from the epithalamion, altering Donne's lines—

> So, reclus'd hermits often times do know
> More of heavens glory, then a worldling can

to

> The recluse Hermit oft' times more doth know
> Of the world's inmost wheels, than worldlings can.

(iv) On 2 May 1811 Coleridge scribbled notes in the margin of Charles Lamb's copy of Donne's poems and added a message excusing himself to Lamb—'I shall die soon, my dear Charles Lamb, and then you will not be vexed that I had bescribbled your book'. The notes were printed in *Notes Theological, Political, and Miscellaneous*, 1853, pp, 255–61, and in an American journal, *The Literary World*, New York, 1853, xii, pp. 349–50 (30 April), 393 (14 May), and 433 (28 May). *The Literary World* offered them with a great flourish, plainly not just because they were Coleridge's but because this was Coleridge on Donne:

To read Dryden, Pope, &c., you need only count syllables; but to read Donne you must measure *time*, and discover the time of each word by the sense of passion. I would ask no surer test of a Scotchman's *sub-stratum* (for the turf-cover of pretension they all have) than to make him read Donne's satires aloud. If he made manly metre of them and yet strict metre, then,—why, then he wasn't a Scotchman, or his soul was geographically slandered by his body's first appearing there.

Doubtless, all the copies I have ever seen of Donne's poems are grievously misprinted. Wonderful that they are not more so, considering that not one in a thousand of his readers has any notion how his lines are to be read—to the many, five out of six appear anti-metrical. How greatly this aided the compositor's negligence or ignorance, and prevented the corrector's remedy, any man may ascertain by examining the earliest editions of blank verse plays, Massinger, Beaumont and

Fletcher, &c. Now, Donne's rhythm was as inexplicable to the many as blank verse, spite of his rhymes—*ergo*, as blank verse, misprinted. I am convinced that where no mode of rational declamation by pause, hurrying of voice, or apt and sometimes double emphasis, can at once make the verse metrical and bring out the sense of passion more prominently, that there we are entitled to alter the text, when it can be done by simple omission or addition of *that*, *which*, *and*, and such 'small deer'; or by mere new placing of the same words—I would venture nothing beyond.

[On 'The Triple Fool']

And by delighting many, frees again
Grief which Verse did restrain.

A good instance how Donne read his own verses. We should write, 'The Grief, verse did restrain;' but Donne roughly emphasized the two main words, Grief and Verse, and, therefore, made each the first syllable of a trochee or dactyl:—

Grief, which / verse did re / strain.

Song

And we join to't our strength,
And we teach it art and length.

The anapest judiciously used, in the eagerness and haste to confirm and aggravate. This beautiful and perfect poem proves, by its title 'Song,' that *all* Donne's poems are equally *metrical* (misprints allowed for) though smoothness (*i.e.*, the metre necessitating the proper reading) be deemed appropriate to *songs*; but in poems where the writer *thinks*, and expects the reader to do so, the sense must be understood in order to ascertain the metre.

[On *Satyre iii*]

If you would teach a scholar in the highest form how to *read*, take Donne, and of Donne this satire. When he has learnt to read Donne, with all the force and meaning which are involved in the words, then send him to Milton, and he will stalk on like a master, *enjoying* his walk.

[On 'The Flea']

Be proud as Spaniards. Leap for pride, ye Fleas!
In Nature's *minim* realm ye're now grandees.

Skip-jacks no more, nor civiller skip-johns;
Thrice-honored Fleas! I greet you all as *Dons*.
In Phoebus's archives registered are ye,
And this your patent of nobility.

[On 'The Good-morrow']

What ever dies is not mixt equally;
If our two loves be one, both thou and I
Love just alike in all; none of these loves can die.

Too good for mere wit. It contains a deep practical truth, this triplet.

[On 'Womans Constancy']

After all, there is but one Donne! and now tell me yet, wherein, in
his own kind, he differs from the similar power in Shakespeare? Shakespeare was all men, potentially, except Milton; and they differ from
him by negation, or privation, or both. This power of dissolving orient
pearls, worth a kingdom, in a health to a whore!—this absolute right of
dominion over all thoughts, that dukes are bid to clean his shoes, and
are yet honored by it! But, I say, in this lordliness of opulence, in which
the positive of Donne agrees with *a* positive of Shakespeare, what is it
that makes them *homoi*ousian, indeed: yet not homoousian?

[He quotes the first stanza of 'The Sunne Rising', and four lines of the
second stanza, then comments]

Fine, vigorous exultation, both soul and body in full puissance.

[He quotes the first stanza of 'The Indifferent'.]

How legitimate a child was not Cowley of Donne; but Cowley had
a soul-*mother* as well as a soul-*father*, and who was she? What was that?
Perhaps, sickly court-loyalty, conscientious per accident—a discursive
intellect, *naturally* less vigorous and daring, and then *cowed* by king-
worship. The populousness, the activity, is as great in C. as in D.; but
the *vigor*, the insufficiency to the poet of active fancy without a sub-
strate of profound, tho' mislocate thinking,—the will-worship, in
squandering golden hecatombs on a fetisch, on the first stick or straw
met with at rising—this pride of doing what he likes with his own, fear-
less of an immense surplus to pay all lawful debts to self-subsisting
themes, that rule, while they cannot create, the moral will—this is
Donne! He was an orthodox Christian only because he could have been

an infidel *more* easily; and, therefore willed to be a Christian: and he was a Protestant, because it enabled him to lash about to the right and the left, and without a *motive*, to say better things for the Papists than they could say for themselves. It was the impulse of a purse-proud opulence of innate power! In the sluggish pond the waves roll this or that way; for such is the wind's direction: but in the brisk spring or lake, boiling at bottom, wind this way, that way, all ways, most irregular in the calm, yet inexplicable by the most violent *ab extra* tempest.

[On 'The Canonization']

One of my favourite poems. As late as ten years ago, I used to seek and find out grand lines and fine stanzas; but my delight has been far greater since it has consisted more in tracing the leading thought thro'-out the whole. The former is too much like coveting your neighbour's goods; in the latter you merge yourself in the author, you *become He*.

[On 'A Feaver']

Yet I had rather owner be
Of thee one hour, than all else ever.

Just and affecting, as *dramatic*; *i.e.*, the outburst of a transient feeling, itself the symbol of a deeper feeling, that would have made *one* hour, *known* to be *only* one hour (or even one year), a perfect hell! All the preceding verses are detestable. Shakespeare has nothing of this. He is never *positively* bad, even in his Sonnets. He may be sometimes worthless (N.B., I don't say he *is*), but nowhere is he *unworthy*.

[On 'A Valediction: forbidding Mourning']

An admirable poem which none but Donne could have written. Nothing was ever more admirably made out than the figure of the Compass.

[He quotes the last four stanzas of the poem.]

[On 'The Exstasie']

I should never find fault with metaphysical poems, were they all like this, or but half as excellent.

[On 'The Primrose']

I am tired of expressing my admiration; else I could not have passed by *The Will, The Blossom,* and *The Primrose,* with *The Relique.*

Coleridge also scribbled comments against the material which supported Donne's poems in editions from 1633 on. He had the following to say of Henry King's funeral elegy *To the Memorie of my Ever Desired Friend Dr Donne,* 'To have liv'd eminent, in a degree':

We cannot better illustrate the weight and condensation of metal in the old English Parnassian Guinea, or the immense volume of French writing which it would cover and ornament, if beat into gold leaf, than by recurrence to the funeral poems of our elder writers, from Henry VIII. to Charles II. These on Donne are more than usually excellent, their chief, and, indeed, almost only fault, being want of smoothness, flow, and perspicuity, from too great compression of thought—too many thoughts, and, often, too much thought in each.

There are occasions, in which a regret expresses itself, not only in the most manly but likewise in the most natural way, by intellectual effort and activity, in proof of intellectual admiration. This is one; and with this feeling should these poems be read. This fine poem has suggested to me many thoughts for 'An Apology for Conceits,' as a sequel to an Essay I have written called 'An Apology for Puns.'

A selection of Donne's letters was given with all the early editions of the poems. Some of Coleridge's comments on the letters bear upon Donne's poetry too:

(a) A noble letter. . . . Nothing can be tenderer than the sentence I have lined. [On the letter 'To Sir H.G.', Gosse i, 227–9.]

(b) A truly elegant letter, and a happy specimen of that dignified courtesy to sex and rank, of that white flattery in which the wit unrealizes the falsehood, and the sportive exaggeration of the thoughts, blending with a delicate tenderness, faithfully conveys the truth as to the feelings. [On the letter 'To the Countess of Bedford', Gosse i, 217–18.]

(c) On Donne's letter 'To my honoured friend, G.G. Esq.', Gosse i, 301–3, countering 'the imputation of having said too much' of Elizabeth Drury in his *Anniversaries*:

This excuse reminds me of Sallust's (the Greek Platonic Philosopher's) apology for the Pagan mythology, viz. that the fables are so excessively

JOHN DONNE

silly and absurd, that they are incapable of imposing on any man in his
senses, and therefore to be acquitted of falsehood. To be sure, these
Anniversaries were the strangest caprices of genius upon record. I con-
jecture that Donne had been requested to write something on this girl,
whom he had never seen, and having no other subject in contemplation,
and Miss Drewry herself supplying materials, he threaded upon her
name all his thoughts as they crowded into his mind, careless how extravagant they became, when applied to the best woman on earth. The
idea of degradation and frivolity which Donne himself attached to the
character of a professed poet, and which was only not universal in the
reigns of Elizabeth and James, which yet exhibited the brightest constellation of poets ever known, gives a *settling* answer to the fashionable
outcry about patronage—nothing but patronage wanting to Midasize
their Herr Füssly into Michael Angelo Buonarotti, Mister Shee to a
Raphael, and Rat Northcote into a Titian.

Barron Field independently transcribed the jottings in Lamb's copy of
Donne, intending to publish Coleridge's comments on the *Songs and
Sonnets* as notes to his own edition of those poems (see No. 172).
Field's manuscript records a few comments not printed with the ver-
sions published in 1853 (they are given in R. F. Brinkley, *Coleridge on the
Seventeenth Century*, Duke, 1955, pp. 521–4):

[On the *Songs and Sonnets*]

Not one of these poems is a Legitimate sonnet; but such was the popular
phraseology of those times—'Songs and Sonnets'.

[On the 'Song. Goe, and catche a falling starre']

Life from crown to sole.

[On 'The Undertaking']

A grand poem; and yet the tone, the *riddle* character, is painfully below
the dignity of the main thought. Addressed to those who understand
and feel it, it finds sympathy and admiration, no wonderment. To the
rest, it is a lie; and it was meant therefore to turn the discourse to them.

[On 'Aire and Angels']

The first stanza is able, and reminds one of Wordsworth's apparition-
poem; the second I do not understand.

[On 'Loves Deitie']

But for the last stanza, I would use this poem as my Love-creed.

(v) From a marginal note Coleridge wrote in a copy of Stockdale's edition of the plays of Jonson, and Beaumont and Fletcher, 1811, which he bought in 1815. He was commenting on some lines in Harris's commendatory poem on Fletcher (given in T. M. Raysor, *Coleridge's Miscellaneous Criticism*, 1936, p. 67):

Since Dryden, the metre of our poets leads to the sense: in our elder and more genuine bards, the sense, including the passion, leads to the metre. Read even Donne's satires as he meant them to be read, and as the sense and passion demand, and you will find in the lines a manly harmony.

(vi) In the first chapter of his *Biographia Literaria*, 1817, Coleridge offers some tests of the merit of poems, one of which is that no word of a true poem can be altered without alteration of the meaning. He reflects upon the causes of a vicious diction such as ensues, for example, when a poet puts novelty of expression before originality of thought (ed. J. Shawcross, Oxford, 1907, i, pp. 14–15):

our genuine admiration of a great poet is a continuous *under-current* of feeling; it is everywhere present, but seldom anywhere as a separate excitement. I was wont boldly to affirm, that it would be scarcely more difficult to push a stone out from the pyramids with the bare hand, than to alter a word, or the position of a word, in Milton or Shakespeare, (in their most important works at least,) without making the author say something else, or something worse, than he does say. One great distinction, I appeared to myself to see plainly, between, even the characteristic faults of our elder poets, and the false beauty of the moderns. In the former, from DONNE to COWLEY, we find the most fantastic out-of-the-way thoughts, but in the most pure and genuine mother English; in the latter, the most obvious thoughts, in language the most fantastic and arbitrary. Our faulty elder poets sacrificed the passion and passionate flow of poetry, to the subtleties of intellect, and to the starts of wit; the moderns to the glare and glitter of a perpetual, yet broken and heterogeneous imagery, or rather to an amphibious something, made up, half of image, and half of abstract* meaning. The one sacrificed the heart to the head; the other both heart and head to point and drapery.

---

* I remember a ludicrous instance in the poem of a young tradesman:
'No more will I endure love's pleasing pain,
Or round my *heart's leg* tie his galling chain.'

In chapter XVIII of the *Biographia Literaria* Coleridge considers how metre and impassioned utterance affect diction (ii, pp. 56 and 64–6):

as every passion has its proper pulse, so will it likewise have its character-istic modes of expression. But where there exists that degree of genius and talent which entitles a writer to aim at the honors of a poet, the very *act* of poetic composition *itself* is, and is *allowed* to imply and to produce, an unusual state of excitement, which of course justifies and demands a correspondent difference of language, as truly, though not perhaps in as marked a degree, as the excitement of love, fear, rage, or jealousy. The vividness of the descriptions or declamations in DONNE or DRYDEN is as much and as often derived from the force and fervor of the describer, as from the reflections, forms or incidents, which con-stitute their subject and materials. The wheels take fire from the mere rapidity of their motion.

[He speaks of 'the power of imagination proceeding upon the *all in each* of human nature'.]

Through the same process and by the same creative agency will the poet distinguish the degree and kind of the excitement produced by the very act of poetic composition. As intuitively will he know, what differ-ences of style it at once inspires and justifies; what intermixture of con-scious volition is natural to that state; and in what instances such figures and colors of speech degenerate into mere creatures of an arbitrary purpose, cold technical artifices of ornament or connection. For, even as truth is its own light and evidence, discovering at once itself and falsehood, so is it the prerogative of poetic genius to distinguish by parental instinct its proper offspring from the changelings, which the gnomes of vanity or the fairies of fashion may have laid in its cradle or called by its names. Could a rule be given from *without*, poetry would cease to be poetry, and sink into a mechanical art. It would be μόρφωσις, not ποίησις. The *rules* of the IMAGINATION are themselves the very powers of growth and production. The *words*, to which they are reducible, present only the outlines and external appearance of the fruit. A deceptive counterfeit of the superficial form and colors may be ela-borated; but the marble peach feels cold and heavy, and *children* only put it to their mouths. We find no difficulty in admitting as excellent, and the legitimate language of poetic fervor self-impassioned, DONNE's apostrophe to the Sun in the second stanza of his 'Progress of the Soul:'

[He quotes the first four lines of stanza 2 of the *Metempsychosis*.]

Or the next stanza but one:

[He quotes seven lines of stanza 4 of the poem.]

As little difficulty do we find in excluding from the honors of un-affected warmth and elevation the madness prepense of pseudo-poesy, or the startling *hysteric* of weakness over-exerting itself, which bursts on the unprepared reader in sundry odes and apostrophes to abstract terms. Such are the Odes to Jealousy, to Hope, to Oblivion, and the like in Dodsley's collection and the magazines of that day, which seldom fail to remind me of an Oxford copy of verses on the two SUTTONS, commencing with

'INOCULATION, heavenly maid! descend!'

(vii) Coleridge planned a lecture 'Of Donne, Dante, and Milton' as the tenth of a series of fourteen public lectures he was giving on two even-ings a week in the early months of 1818. But the part of the lecture dealing with Donne has not survived; or Coleridge omitted it in the end. (H. N. Coleridge, *Literary Remains*, 1836–8, i, p. 148. See T. M. Raysor, op. cit., p. 131.)

(viii) Coleridge scribbled notes in a copy of Milton's *Poems on Several Occasions*, ed. Thomas Warton, 1791, which was presented to him in October 1823. They were first published by J. Drinkwater in *The London Mercury*, xiv, September 1926, pp. 491–505. The extract which follows is given from R. F. Brinkley, op. cit., pp. 568–9:

['On the Morning of Christ's Nativity', lines 229–31

> So when the Sun in bed
> Curtain'd with cloudy red
>   Pillows his chin upon an Orient wave, . . .

Warton's note: The words *pillows* and *chin*, throw an air of burlesque and familiarity over a comparison most exquisitely conceived and adapted.]

I have tried in vain to imagine, in what other way the Image could be given. I rather think, that it is one of the Hardinesses permitted to a great Poet. Dante would have written it: tho' it is most in the Spirit of Donne.

(ix) Coleridge wrote a note in the margin of his copy of Theobald's edition of Shakespeare questioning Theobald's comment on Polonius's speech to the king and queen in *Hamlet*, Act 2, Scene 2, 'My Leige, and Madam, to expostulate/ What Majesty should be, what duty is. . . '. Theobald adverts to Polonius's '*Jingles*, and *Play* on Words', and adds that if we 'but look into the sermons of Dr *Donne* (the wittiest Man of that Age) . . . we shall find them full of this Vein: only, there they are to be admired, here to be laugh'd at' (*The Works of Shakespeare* (1733), 1773, viii, p. 145, n. 28. Coleridge's copy is in the British Museum, press mark C. 45. a. 21). Coleridge retorts:

I have (and that most carefully) read Dr Donne's Sermons, and find none of these Jingles. The great art of an orator, to make whatever he talks of appear of importance, this indeed Donne has effected with consummate skill.

(x) W. P. Wood noted in his journal a visit to Coleridge on 29 January 1829 when Coleridge read Donne's poetry aloud to the company (*A Memoir of the Right Hon. William Page Wood, Baron Hatherley*, ed. W. R. W. Stephens, 1883, i, p. 175):

In the evening with B. Montagu to Coleridge's. He had been seized with a fit of enthusiasm for Donne's poetry, which I think somewhat unaccountable. There was great strength, however, in some passages which he read. One stanza or rather division of his poem, on the 'Progress of the Soul,' struck me very much; it was, I think, the fourth, in which he addresses Destiny as the 'Knot of Causes.' The rest of the poem seemed the effusion of a man very drunk or very mad.

(xi) In 1829 Coleridge scribbled notes on poems by Donne in a volume of Chalmers's *The Works of the English Poets* belonging to J. Gillman. Coleridge's nephew and literary executor H. N. Coleridge printed these and some verses on Donne among his uncle's literary remains. He says that the verses 'were added in pencil to the collection of commendatory lines' given with Donne's poems. 'No. i is Mr C.'s; the publication of No. ii I trust the all-accomplished author will, under the circumstances, pardon' (*Literary Remains*, ed. H. N. Coleridge, 1836–8, i, pp. 148–50).

    No one has doubted that S. T. Coleridge is the author of the first quatrain. We do not know who wrote the second set of verses.

I

With Donne, whose muse on dromedary trots,
Wreathe iron pokers into true-love knots;

Rhyme's sturdy cripple, fancy's maze and clue,
Wit's forge and fire-blast, meaning's press and screw.

II

See lewdness and theology combin'd,—
A cynic and a sycophantic mind;
A fancy shar'd party per pale between
Death's heads and skeletons and Aretine!—
Not his peculiar defect or crime,
But the true current mintage of the time.
Such were the establish'd signs and tokens given
To mark a loyal churchman, sound and even,
Free from papistic and fanatic leaven.

The wit of Donne, the wit of Butler, the wit of Pope, the wit of
Congreve, the wit of Sheridan—how many disparate things are here
expressed by one and the same word, Wit!—Wonder-exciting vigour,
intenseness and peculiarity of thought, using at will the almost boundless stores of a capacious memory, and exercised on subjects, where we
have no right to expect it—this is the wit of Donne! The four others I
am just in the mood to describe and inter-distinguish;—what a pity that
the marginal space will not let me!

My face in thine eye, thine in mine appears,
And true plain hearts do in the faces rest;
Where can we find two fitter hemispheres
Without sharp north, without declining west?
                                      Good-Morrow, v. 15, &c.

The sense is;—Our mutual loves may in many respects be fitly
compared to corresponding hemispheres; but as no simile squares (*nihil
simile est idem*), so here the simile fails, for there is nothing in our loves
that corresponds to the cold north, or the declining west, which in two
hemispheres must necessarily be supposed. But an ellipse of such length
will scarcely rescue the line from the charge of nonsense or a bull.
January, 1829.
                    Woman's constancy.
A misnomer. The title ought to be—
                    Mutual Inconstancy.

Whether both th' Indias of spice and *mine*, &c.
                                      Sun Rising, v. 17.
And see at night thy western land of *mine*, &c.
                                      Progress of the Soul, I Song, 2 st.

This use of the word *mine* specifically for mines of gold, silver, or precious stones, is, I believe, peculiar to Donne.

(xii) In his Notebook no. 43, compiled from March to May 1830, Coleridge used some of Donne's *Songs and Sonnets* in a peculiar exercise of his own devising. The Notebook is filled with dated entries which run on, or sometimes run backwards, to within a few pages of the end. But at some point Coleridge turned the book upside down and started again from the back, filling the last three leaves with the sketch of a fresh idea (BM Add. MS 47, 538, folios 80–78; not previously printed as it stands, though R. F. Brinkley, op. cit., pp. 527–8, gives the references to Donne's poems):

THE FILTER

By successive Chipping the rude Block becomes an Apollo or a Venus. By leaving behind I transmute a turbid Drench into a crystalline Draught, the Nectar of the Muses. The parts are another's: the Whole is mine. To eject is as much a living Power, as to assimilate: to excrete as to absorb. Give therefore honor due to the Filter-poet, *ΕΣΤΗΣΕ*.

Donne

The 3rd—perhaps the 2nd—the 4th, and the 7th—are wholes and need not the Filter. The sixteenth supplies the Stuff for

A Song
Break of Day

[He quotes the apocryphal poem which begins 'Stay, O sweet, and do not rise'.]

20th [He quotes lines 28–9 of 'A Valediction: of the Booke'.]
22nd—influence of Spring on Love [He quotes lines 19–20 of 'Loves Growth'.]
23rd Extravaganza truly *Donnesque* [He quotes lines 29–33 of 'Loves Exchange'.]

On Parting

requires an introductory stanza, easily supplied—then

2
Our souls are two indeed but so
As stiff twin compasses are two

Coleridge's cryptic numbering in these notes must refer to the order of the poems in an edition he was using, for the poems he names do occur at precisely those places in the conventional sequence first established by the edition of 1635. The unnamed poems he refers to as 'wholes' which 'need not the Filter' are thus the 'Song. Goe, and catche a falling starre', 'The Good-morrow', 'Womans Constancy', and 'The Indifferent'. 'The sixteenth' poem must be Donne's 'Breake of Day', which 'supplies the Stuff' for the apocryphal version Coleridge quotes.

(xiii) Extracts from notes written in two separate copies of Donne's *LXXX Sermons*, 1640, some of them dated by Coleridge himself October 1831. The notes Coleridge made in one of these copies were published by H. N. Coleridge, with some omissions and alterations, in volume iii of *Literary Remains*, 1836–8. The notes in the other copy were first published by Derwent Coleridge in *Notes on the English Divines*, 1853, i, pp. 115–19. Coleridge's notes in both copies are given in full in R. F. Brinkley, op. cit., pp. 163–204:

(a) It is affecting to observe, how this great man's mind sways and oscillates between his Reason, . . . and the habitual awe for the *letter*. . . . Yea, it is most affecting to see the struggles of so great a mind to preserve its inborn fealty to the Reason under the servitude to an accepted article of *Belief*. . . .

(b) A truly excellent and beautiful paragraph. . . .

(c) The taste for these forced and fantastic analogies Donne with the greater number of the learned prelatic Divines from James I to the Restoration acquired from that too great partiality for the *Fathers*, from Iranaeus to Bernard, by which they sought to distinguish themselves from the Puritans.

[The passage compares the 'miserable revolutions and changes . . . downfalls, . . . breaknecks, and precipitations' we are ordained to in this life, with the way we come into the world head-first from the womb—which prefigures 'that headlong falling into calamities' that we must suffer after. See *The First Anniversary* lines 95–8.]

(d) A beautiful paragraph, well worth extracting aye, and re-preaching.

(e) Beautifully imagined, and happily applied.

(f) Admirable. . . .

(g) A noble passage on death bed Repentance. . . .

(h) A noble instance of giving importance to the single words of a text, each word by itself a pregnant text. Here, too, lies the excellence, the imitable, but alas! unimitated, excellence of the Divines from Elizabeth to William iiird.

(i) A just sentiment, beautifully expressed. . . .

(j) [Donne plays on 'the names of this day', Purification and Candlemas, to arrive at an image of purification in light]:

The illustration of the day, would be censured as quaint by our modern Critics! Would to heaven! we had but even a few Preachers capable of such quaintnesses.

(k) Donne was a truly great man; but he did not possess that full, steady, deep yet comprehensive Insight into the Nature of Faith and Works, which was vouchsafed to Martin Luther. . . .

(l) Dr. Donne was an eminently witty man in a very witty age; but to the honour of his judgement let it be said, that though his great wit is evinced in numberless passages, in a few only is it *shewn off*. . . .

(m) Donne was a poor Metaphysician; i.e. he never closely questioned himself as to the absolute meaning of his words.—What did he mean by the '*Soul*'? what by the '*Body*'?

[Donne's passage argues that although Christ's godhead never left his body after his death on the cross, yet he was no man then for his human soul had departed from it. Coleridge repeatedly objects to Donne's assumption 'that Body + Soul = Man', on the ground that 'man is the unity, the Prothesis, and Body and soul are the two Poles, the — and +, the Thesis and Antithesis of the Man.']

(n) Worthy almost of Shakespeare!

(o) What a beautiful sentence. . . .

(p) A lively instance how much excellent good sense a wise man like Donne, can bring forth on a passage, which he does not understand. . . .

(q) An excellent Paragraph grounded on a mere Pun. Such was the taste of the Age; and it is an awful joy to observe, that not great Learning, great Wit, great Talent, or even (as far as without great virtue that *can* be) no, not even great Genius, were effectual to preserve the man from the contagion, but only the deep and wise enthusiasm of moral Feeling. . . .

(xiv) Coleridge visited Cambridge 'upon occasion of the Scientific Meeting there, in June, 1833'. R. A. Willmott, then an undergraduate at Trinity, immediately afterwards wrote down as much as he could recall of Coleridge's conversation. Here is a snatch of it (R. A. Willmott, *Conversations at Trinity*, 1836, pp. 15–16):

I think you will find the original of Langhorne's celebrated line—

> The child of misery baptised in tears,

in Donne's Sermon on the First Epistle to the Thessalonians. The prose works of this admirable Divine, are Armouries for the Christian Soldier. Such a depth of intellect, such a nervousness of style, such a variety of illustration, such a power of argument, are to be looked for only in the writings of that race of Giants. Donne's poetry must be sought in his prose; yet some of his verses breathe an uncommon fervency of spirit, and when he looked in his heart and wrote, his manner is delightful. The following poem, for sweetness and tenderness of expression, chastened by a religous thoughtfulness and faith, is, I think, almost perfect. It is, you see, the address of a lover, or friend, to one whom he leaves behind;—mark the exquisite allusion in the conclusion of the second and fourth stanzas:

[He quotes, entire, the 'Song. Sweetest love, I do not goe'.]

113. Henry Francis Cary

1800

The Rev. H. F. Cary (1772–1844) was the translator of Dante and Aristophanes. In 1800 he became Vicar of Kingsbury, Warwickshire, having been Vicar of Abbot's Bromley in Staffordshire for the previous four years. His literary journal for March 1800 lists a prodigious programme of reading performed, in several languages (H. Cary, *Memoir of the Rev. Henry Francis Cary . . .*, 1847, p. 159).

March 9. Read Donne's Satires, &c, and Ben Jonson's translation of Horace *Ad Pisones*.

114. The first publication of *Elegie xx* 'Loves Warre'

Francis Godolphin Waldron (1744–1818), a minor actor and writer, published Donne's *Elegie xx*, 'Loves Warre', in *A Collection of Miscellaneous Poetry*, 1802, pp. 1–2. An accompanying elegy (pp. 3–5), 'Is death so great a gamester', also given as Donne's, has not been accepted for his by any subsequent editor.

'Loves Warre' was one of five elegies which were excluded from the first collected edition of Donne's poems, 1633, because the censor refused a licence. But the other four were all in print by 1669. Waldron printed the two poems from the Dyce MS, which is now in the Victoria and Albert Muesum.

115. Anon., *The Edinburgh Review*

1802

A reviewer (possibly Francis Jeffrey) of Southey's *Thalaba, the Destroyer* censured the false taste of the school of English poets then emerging. He characterised the school as deriving ideas from bad continental models—Rousseau, Kotzebue, Schiller, and the like—and as looking back with admiration to the crudities of older poets (*The Edinburgh Review*, i, 1802, p. 64).

[In the new school of poets we find] the homeliness and harshness of Cowper's language and versification, interchanged occasionally with the *innocence* of Ambrose Philips, or the quaintness of Quarles and Dr Donne.

116. Henry Kirke White

c. 1805

Kirke White (1785–1806) was a young poet, son of a Nottingham butcher, who became a protégé of Southey after publishing some juvenile poems. He went up to St John's College, Cambridge, and died, it was said, of overwork. Southey published his papers posthumously ('Melancholy Hours' in *Remains*, ed. R. Southey, 1806, ii, p. 286).

Donne had not music enough to render his broken rhyming couplets sufferable, and neither his wit, nor his pointed satire, were sufficient to rescue him from that neglect which his uncouth and rugged versification speedily superinduced.

117. Robert Southey

1807, 1831, 1835–7

Southey's early hostility to Donne shows him markedly at odds in his standards of taste with some of his fellows of the Lake school of writers. But he abated the severity of his judgment as he grew older, and even admitted some of Donne's poems to an anthology he edited.

(i) From an account of English poetry which prefaces a selection of verse (*Specimens of the Later English Poets*, 1807, pp. xxiv–xxv):

From the time of Shakespeare to that of Milton, our taste was rather retrograde than progressive. The metaphysical poetry, as it has not very happily been termed, gained ground, and seduced many men whose quick and shaping fancy might else have produced works worthy of immortality. Nothing indeed could have made Donne a poet, unless as great a change had been worked in the internal structure of his ears, as was wrought in elongating those of Midas. The power of versifying is a distinct talent, and a metrical ear has little more connexion with intellect than a musical one. Of this, Donne is a sufficient example. In Cowley this style arrived at perfection, and with him it may be said to have ended. Butler is to be classed with these poets, and he has the single merit of having applied happily and appropriately a style so monstrous.

(ii) Many years later Southey allotted some eighteen double-column pages to Donne's poems in a selection from the British poets up to Jonson (*Select Works of the British Poets from Chaucer to Jonson*, 1831, pp. 714–31). He gave thirty-six poems by Donne as against about 150 by Habington. There are five of the *Songs and Sonnets* ('The Anniversarie', 'The Will', 'The Funerall', 'The Baite', 'The Relique'), *Elegie xi*, 'The Bracelet', six verse letters, the whole of *The first Anniversary*, six funeral elegies, and some *Divine Poems*, including all sixteen of the *Holy Sonnets* then known, and 'A Hymne to Christ, at the Authors last going into

Germany'. Southey introduced Donne with a brief biographical note and one sour critical comment:

Two years after his death, his poems were published by his son. He would have shown himself more worthy of such a father, if he had destroyed a considerable part of them.

(iii) In the 'Life of Cowper' which forms the first part of his edition of *The Works of William Cowper*, 1835–7, Southey alluded to Donne in several places (1853 edition, i, pp. 3, 303–5, 308). Early on, he pointed out that the poet Cowper was proud of his family connection with the Donnes and several times refers to John Donne as his poet-ancestor. Southey implied his own opinion of Donne's writings:

Donne, whose name and deserts, if his own works were forgotten, would be preserved by Izaak Walton, was of the same family. . . .

Chapter XII of Southey's *Life of Cowper* consists of 'Sketches of the Progress of English Poetry from Chaucer to Cowper', and has the following account of metaphysical poetry:

'There are three ways,' Dr. Johnson said, 'in which writing may be un-natural; by being *bombastic*, and above nature; *affected*, and beside it, fringing events with ornaments which nature did not afford; or *weak*, and below nature. Neither of the first could please long. The third might, indeed, please a good while, or at least please many, because imbecility, and consequently a love of imbecility, might be found in many.' The bombastic immediately invites ridicule, and soon yields to it: the last personage upon the stage who spake in the vein of King Cambyses and Tamberlain was Ancient Pistol. The affected style lasts longer; and for the same reason as the feeble. That style of poetry belongs to it which Johnson has called the metaphysical; the designation is not fortunate, but so much respect is due to Johnson, that it would be unbecoming to substitute, even if it were easy to propose, one which might be unexceptionable.

   Whether this style spread like a contagion from Italy to Spain and England, or whether it originated in the intellectual temperature of the age, and thus became endemic in the three countries, may be ques-tioned.* It was most out of place when applied to devotional poetry, upon which every species of false taste seems, at different times, to have

* Donne passed some years in Italy and in Spain; he therefore may be supposed to have contracted the fashion in those countries, having 'returned into England perfect in their languages'.—*Izaak Walton*.

fastened. Amatory poems were on the whole improved by it, because it required something more than the common places which were the stock in trade of all mere versifiers. Cowley squandered upon this fashion powers which might have won for him the lasting fame to which he aspired. Butler alone perceived its proper application, and he, in consequence, produced a poem which, in spite of the subject, can never become obsolete while wit and wisdom are understood. With the true tact of genius he adapted his verse to his materials, and creating thus a manner of his own, derived an advantage from one of the causes which had concurred to deteriorate our versification.

Many persons possess a musical ear who have no voice for singing, but a good voice is seldom found where there is not also an ear which is capable of directing it. The case is different in poetry; the poetical feeling sometimes exists, and in a high degree, without the talent for versifying; but the talent very commonly, without a spark of the feeling. Both Donne and Ben Jonson, the two authors by whom the metaphysical poetry was brought into vogue, were rugged versifyers. It was not, however, altogether owing to the influence of their example that the poems of this class were very generally characterised by a rough and careless versification. Their authority, indeed, afforded a sanction, of which inferior writers would willingly avail themselves; but the fact resulted from the nature of such poetry. The poet found difficulty enough in rendering his far-fetched and elaborate conceits intelligible; and cramp thoughts formed for themselves cramp expressions and dis-jointed verse.

There was another incidental cause, less obvious, but not less certain in its effect. An attempt had been made to introduce the Latin metres into English poetry; not upon a principle of adaptation (which has since so perfectly succeeded among the Germans), but in strict confor-mance to the rules of Latin prosody; and as those rules frequently reversed the common pronunciation, the attempt was necessarily un-successful. Yet earnest endeavours were made for bringing it into use, by men of great ability and great influence; and though it never ob-tained any degree of public acceptance, yet specimens enough of it were published to have the effect of vilifying the art. For in this new versifica-tion nothing could be too bald and beggarly in expression, nothing too harsh in construction, nothing too inharmonious, provided it were forced into the prescribed form of verse; and the license which the metrifiers took in this respect, infected other poets, though not in an equal degree.

. . . when Johnson asserts that before the time of Dryden 'the happy combinations of words which distinguish poetry from prose had been rarely attempted,' and that 'there was no poetical diction, no system of words at once refined from the grossness of domestic use, and free from the harshness of terms appropriated to particular arts,'—Dryden himself never advanced a more inconsiderate assertion. 'From his time,' says Johnson, 'English poetry has had no tendency to relapse to its former savageness.' That it should fall back to the rudeness of an unsettled and rude speech, was impossible; time had polished the language, and the Bible and the liturgy had fixed it; the tendency to degenerate was in another way. Justly as Johnson condemned the metaphysical poets, he saw how superior they were to those who were trained up in the school of Dryden. 'To write on their plan,' he has truly said, 'it was at least necessary to read and think. . . .'.

[He continues the quotation from Johnson's *Life of Cowley*, See No. 90 (iv) (c).]

118. Sir Walter Scott

1808

Scott makes some remarks on metaphysical poetry in the course of an account of the changed temper of Court life following the Restoration (*The Works of John Dryden*, 1808, i, pp. 45–8).

An approaching change of public taste was hastened by the manners of the restored monarch and his courtiers. That pedantry which had dictated the excessive admiration of metaphysical conceits, was not the characteristic of the court of Charles ii, as it had been of those of his grandfather and father. Lively and witty by nature, with all the acquired habits of an adventurer, whose wanderings, military and political, left him time neither for profound reflection, nor for deep study, the restored monarch's literary taste, which was by no means contemptible, was directed towards a lighter and more pleasing style of poetry than the harsh and scholastic productions of Donne and Cowley. The admirers, therefore, of this old school were confined to the ancient cavaliers, and the old courtiers of Charles I; men unlikely to lead the fashion in the court of a gay monarch, filled with such men as Buckingham, Rochester, Etherege, Sedley, and Mulgrave, whose time and habits confined their own essays to occasional verses, and satirical effusions, in which they often ridiculed the heights of poetry they were incapable of attaining. With such men the class of poets, which before the civil war held but a secondary rank, began to rise in estimation. Waller, Suckling, and Denham, began to assert a pre-eminence over Cowley and Donne; the ladies, whose influence in the court of James and Charles I was hardly felt, and who were then obliged to be contented with such pedantic worship as is contained in the 'Mistress' of Cowley, and the 'Epithilamion' [sic] of Donne, began now, when their voices were listened to, and their taste consulted, to determine that their poetical lovers should address them in strains more musical, if not more intelligible. What is most acceptable to the fair sex will always sway the mode of a gay court; and the character of a smooth and easy sonneteer was soon considered as an indispensible requisite to a man of wit and fashion, terms which were then usually synonymous.

To those who still retained a partiality for that exercise of the fancy and memory, afforded by the metaphysical poetry, the style of satire then prevalent afforded opportunities of applying it, the same depth of learning, the same extravagant ingenuity in combining the most remote images, and in driving casual associations to the verge of absurdity, almost all the remarkable features which characterized the poetry of Cowley, may be successfully traced in the satire of Hudibras. The sublime itself borders closely on the ludicrous; but the bombast and extravagant cannot be divided from it. The turn of thought and the peculiar kind of mental exertion, corresponds in both styles of writing; and although Butler pursued the ludicrous, and Cowley aimed at the surprizing, the leading features of their poetry only differ like those of the same face convulsed with laughter, or arrested in astonishment. The district of metaphysical poetry was thus invaded by the satirists, who sought weapons there to avenge the misfortunes and oppression which they had lately sustained from the puritans; and as it is difficult in a laughing age to render serious what has been once applied to ludicrous purposes, Butler and his imitators retained quiet possession of the style which they had usurped from the grave bards of the earlier age.

119. Charles Lamb

1808, ?1820, 1824

Lamb was an early enthusiast for Donne and may have drawn Coleridge to Donne's poetry, for he first defended it in print against Johnsonian assumptions and it was in his copy of Donne's poems that Coleridge scribbled some memorable marginal comments in 1811 (see No. 112). Lamb saw that 'metaphysical' poetry need be neither unnatural nor cold; but he did not develop his insight into an extended commentary on Donne's verse.

(i) From *Mrs Leicester's School and other essays* (1808), 1885, pp. 358–9:

We are too apt to indemnify ourselves for some characteristic excellence we are kind enough to concede to a great author by denying him every thing else. Thus Donne and Cowley, by happening to possess more wit, and faculty of illustration, than other men, are supposed to have been incapable of nature or feeling: they are usually opposed to such writers as Shenstone and Parnell; whereas, in the very thickest of their conceits,—in the bewildering mazes of tropes and figures,—a warmth of soul and generous feeling shines through, the 'sum' of which, 'forty thousand' of those natural poets, as they are called, 'with all their quantity,' could not make up.

(ii) Hazlitt recalls the conversation at Charles Lamb's house, when Lamb enlivened the company with his idiosyncratic enthusiasms ('On the Conversation of Authors', *The Plain Speaker*, 1826, pp. 80–1):

But with what a gusto would he describe his favourite authors, Donne, or Sir Philip Sidney, and call their most crabbed passages *delicious*! He tried them on his palate as epicures taste olives, and his observations had a smack in them, like a roughness on the tongue.

(iii) Hazlitt recounts another conversation, in which Lamb spoke of Fulke Greville's style and said that he would give a great deal 'for the unravelling a passage or two' in Greville ('Persons One Would Wish to have Seen', *Complete Works*, ed. P. P. Howe, 1930–4, xvii, pp. 124–5):

—'I am afraid in that case,' said A——, 'that if the mystery were once cleared up, the merit might be lost;'—and turning to me, whispered a friendly apprehension, that while L—— continued to admire these old crabbed authors, he would never become a popular writer. Dr. Donne was mentioned as a writer of the same period, with a very interesting countenance, whose history was singular, and whose meaning was often quite as *uncomeatable*, without a personal citation from the dead, as that of any of his contemporaries. The volume was produced; and while some one was expatiating on the exquisite simplicity and beauty of the portrait prefixed to the old edition, A—— got hold of the poetry, and exclaiming 'What have we here?' read the following:—

> Here lies a She-Sun and a He-Moon there,
> She give the best light to his sphere,
> Or each is both and all, and so
> They unto one another nothing owe.

There was no resisting this, till L——, seizing the volume, turned to the beautiful 'Lines to his Mistress,' dissuading her from accompanying him abroad, and read them with suffused features and a faltering tongue.

[Hazlitt gives the whole of *Elegie xvi*, 'On his Mistris'.]

(iv) From a letter to Bernard Barton dated 24 March 1824 (*The Letters of Charles Lamb*, ed. F. L. Lucas, 1935, ii, p. 421):

. . . That is the less *light* part of the scruple. It has no darker shade. I put in *darker*, because of the ambiguity of the word light, which Donne in his admirable poem on the Metempsychosis, has so ingeniously illustrated in his invocation,

$$\overset{1\quad 2}{\text{Make my \textit{dark heavy} poem,}}\ \overset{1}{\textit{light}}\ \text{and}\ \overset{2}{\textit{light}}\text{—}$$

where the two senses of *light* are opposed to different opposites.

(v) A footnote in Lamb's *Specimens of English Dramatic Poets, Who Lived About the Time of Shakespeare*, 1808, pp. 363–5. Lamb is commenting on an extract from Beaumont and Fletcher's *Philaster* in which the character Bellario is a woman disguised as a page:

. . . Donne has a copy of verses addrest to his mistress, dissuading her from a resolution which she seems to have taken up from some of these scenical representations, of following him abroad as a page. It is so earnest, so weighty, so rich in poetry, in sense, in wit, and pathos, that I have thought fit to insert it, as a solemn close in future to all such sickly fancies as he there deprecates. The Story of his romantic and unfortunate marriage with the Daughter of Sir George Moore, the Lady here supposed to be addrest, may be read in Walton's Lives.

[Under the title 'Elegy' he gives the whole of Donne's *Elegie xvi*, 'On his Mistris'.]

120. John Aikin

1810

Aikin (1747–1822) was a physician and prolific man of letters. In an anthology of poems for singing he gave an 'altered' version of Donne's 'The Message', which is substantially the one Ritson printed in 1783 (see No. 104), and added a comment on the original (*Vocal Poetry*, 1810, p. 215).

Donne is so rugged a versifier, that scarcely any of his productions are reducible to regular measure without some alteration. His language, also, is generally far from elegant or refined, and his thoughts are extremely strained and artificial. The preceding piece, however, has not required much correction to entitle it to a distinguished place among ingenious songs.

121. Alexander Chalmers

1810

Chalmers (1759–1834), an editor and biographer, reprinted Donne's poetry entire in a twenty-one volume collection of the English poets which included the series edited by Johnson. Donne's poems, and the elegies on his death, are given in volume V together with the poems of Shakespeare, Davies, Hall, Jonson, Carew, Drummond, and others. Chalmers followed the text of the 1719 edition of Donne. He introduced the poems with a brief biographical account of Donne, and some critical comments which are given below (*The Works of the English Poets, from Chaucer to Cowper*, 1810, v, pp. 123–4).

His early years, there is reason to think, although disgraced by no flagrant turpitude, were not exempt from folly and dissipation. In some of his poems we meet with the language and sentiments of men whose morals are not very strict. After his marriage, however, he appears to have become of a serious and thoughtful disposition, his mind alternately exhausted by study, or softened by affliction. His reading was very extensive, and we find allusions to almost every science in his poems, although unfortunately they only contribute to produce distorted images and wild conceits. . . . His sermons have not a little of the character of his poems. They are not, indeed, so rugged in style, but they abound with quaint allusions, which now appear ludicrous, although they probably produced no such effect in his days. With this exception, they contain much good sense, much acquaintance with human nature, many striking thoughts, and some very just biblical criticism. . . .

Dr. Donne's reputation as a poet was higher in his own time than it has been since. Dryden fixed his character with his usual judgment; as 'the greatest wit, though not the best poet, of our nation.' He says afterwards, that 'he affects the metaphysics, not only in his Satires, but in his amorous verses, where nature only should reign, and perplexes the minds of the fair sex with nice speculations of philosophy, when he should engage their hearts, and entertain them with the softnesses of love.' Dryden has also pronounced that if his Satires were to be translated into numbers, they would yet be wanting in dignity of expression. The reader has now an opportunity of comparing the originals and translations in Pope's works, and will probably think that Pope has made them so much his own as to throw very little light on Donne's powers. He every where elevates the expression, and in very few instances retains a whole line.

Pope, in his classification of poets, places Donne at the head of a school, that school from which Dr. Johnson has given so many remarkable specimens of absurdity, in his life of Cowley, and which, following Dryden, he terms the metaphysical school. Gray, in the sketch he sent to Mr. Warton, considers it as a third Italian school, full of conceit, begun in queen Elizabeth's reign, continued under James and Charles I. by Donne, Crashaw, Cleveland, carried to its height by Cowley, and ending perhaps in Sprat.

Donne's numbers, if they may be so called, are certainly the most rugged and uncouth of any of our poets. He appears either to have had no ear, or to have been utterly regardless of harmony. Yet Spenser preceded him, and Drummond, the first polished versifier, was his contemporary; but it must be allowed that before Drummond appeared, Donne had relinquished his pursuit of the Muses, nor would it be just to include the whole of his poetry under the general censure which has been usually passed. Dr. Warton seems to think that if he had taken pains he might not have proved so inferior to his contemporaries; but what inducement could he have to take pains, as he published nothing, and seems not desirous of public fame? He was certainly not ignorant or unskilled in the higher attributes of style, for he wrote elegantly in Latin, and displays considerable taste in some of his smaller pieces and epigrams.

122. Philip Bliss

c. 1810

On the initial leaves of his copy of the 1635 edition of Donne's Poems, the bibliographer Philip Bliss (1787–1857) wrote 'A short account of the life of John Donne D.D.', with a note on the early editions of Donne's poems and on portraits of Donne (the Heathcote-Bliss-Chew copy, now in the Henry Huntington Library, California, acc. no. 59037).

The account of Donne's life succintly summarises Walton. Bliss described quite fully five of the eight editions of the poems up to 1719, but evidently did not know of the other three. He appended some recent sale prices for copies of the 1635 edition:

    at Mr. Steevens's sale 1800 it sold for 0. 1. 0
       Mr. Hunters.   1805 – –   – 0.13. 0
       Mr. Fillinghams.   1805 – –   – 0.11. 6
       M. Heathcotes (this copy. 1805.)   0.17. 0

Cuttings from booksellers' catalogues in the same copy of 1635 show that it sold at Quaritch's in 1892 for seven guineas and was being offered at ten guineas a few years later.

123. Sir Samuel Egerton Brydges

1813, 1814

Brydges (1762–1837), a barrister and sometime M.P., wrote copiously on bibliography and genealogy. In his edition of Raleigh's poems he compared the several variations upon Marlowe's 'Come, live with me and be my love'—Raleigh's 'answer' the anonymous 'Another of the Same Nature Made Since' ('Come, live with me, and be my dear'), and Donne's 'The Baite'. (*The Poems of Sir Walter Raleigh: Now First Collected*, 1813, p. 67 of the 'Notes to Raleigh's Poems'. The 'Biographical and Critical Introduction' is separately paginated.)

Brydges spoke of Donne again in characterising the bad taste of most English poets in the sixteenth and seventeenth centuries (*Restituta; or, Titles, Extracts, and Characters of Old Books in English Literature Revived*, 1814, ii, p. 9, and iii, p. 2).

(i)
[He discusses Raleigh's poem, and then turns to 'Another of the Same Nature Made Since'.]

This being only a Parody of Marlow, is not of so much merit as the other; but it has some beautiful stanzas, particularly the seventh, eighth, and tenth. Dr Donne has also given an imitation of this poem, which he calls 'The Bait', beginning

[he quotes the first stanza].

It is full of pitifull conceits, which shew that Donne had no taste for true poetry, nor any conception wherein the beauty of this piece consisted. A more decisive proof of the superiority of RALEIGH's poetical genius could not have been exhibited!

(ii)
The metaphysical subtlety, and tasteless and unfeeling ingenuity of

Donne, produced execrable distortions in him and his imitators so opposite to all that is attractive or valuable in the Muse, that more than half a century did not rid the common versifiers of its disgusting effects.

[He praises George Wither for 'A freedom from these faults', then praises Milton at the expense of Milton's contemporaries, who merely exhibit the bad taste of their age.]

. . . pure poetry was at that time almost unknown. In Q. Elizabeth's reign it had been occasionally exhibited by Spenser, and in a few songs, such as *Come live with me, and be my love*; and it may be found scattered in detached passages of the dramas of Shakespeare, and Beaumont and Fletcher; and occasionally in the *Shepherd's Pipe* of William Browne, and the *Shepherd's Hunting* of George Wither.

But natural imagery seems in general to have afforded no attraction in itself; and to have been only regarded as the material for figurative language, by which some far-fetched thought might be illustrated, or some absurd flattery conveyed. Donne and Cowley carried this bad taste to the greatest excess.

[He argues that *L'Allegro, Il Penseroso, Lycidas,* and *Comus,* are of 'a different order of beings' from the poetry of Milton's contemporaries, and declares that these poems were not popular while the poetry of Carew, Waller, Suckling, Cleveland, and Cowley, was admired.]

124. John Ferriar

1813

Ferriar (1761–1815) was a physician who worked for many years in Manchester. He published reflections on medical and literary matters. The following is an extract from *An Essay Towards a Theory of Apparitions*, 1813, p. 63.

Unquestionably, the temperament which disposes men to cultivate the higher and graver species of poetry, contributes to render them susceptible of impressions of this nature. Such a temperament, excited by the pathetic circumstances of a story more interesting than any tale of fiction, produced the vision of Dr Donne. When residing in Paris, he saw the figure of his wife, then in London, pass through the room, with her hair hanging loose, and carrying a dead child in her arms. After reading the exquisite poem which he wrote, previous to their separation, it is impossible to wonder at an impression of such a nature.

125. Thomas Park

1813

Park (1759–1834), antiquary and bibliographer, edited Ritson's collection of English songs, adding his own comment on the doctored version of Donne's 'The Message' which Ritson gave (see Nos 104 and 120). (*A Select Collection of English Songs . . . by the late Joseph Ritson Esq.*, ed. T. Park, 1813, i, p. 86.)

A very judicious alteration, and real improvement, of 'The Message', by Dr Donne.

126. Capel Lofft

1813

Capel Lofft the elder (1751–1824), a barrister, translator, and miscellaneous writer, gave three poems by Donne in volume v of *Laura, or An Anthology of Sonnets*, 1813. The poems are the verse letter 'To Mr S.B.' ('O thou which to search out the secret parts'), the sonnet 'To E. of D.' ('See Sir, how as the Suns hot Masculine flame'), and *Holy Sonnet i* ('Thou hast made me').

127. Isaac Disraeli

1814

Disraeli identifies with Donne one of four characters mentioned in a mid-seventeenth-century collection of verses as attackers of Davenant's *Gondibert* (*Quarrels of Authors; or, Some Memoirs For Our Literary History, Including Specimens of Controversy To The Reign of Elizabeth*, 1814, ii, p. 231, fn.). He gives no reason for his opinion.

128. John Fry

1814

Fry (1792–1822), a Bristol bookseller and minor author, commented on a short seventeenth-century poem which imitates Donne's 'Song. Goe, and catche a falling starre'. The poem is called 'On a Womans faith' and opens 'Catch at a starr thats falling from ye skye' (*Pieces of Ancient Poetry, from unpublished manuscripts and scarce books*, Bristol, 1814, p. 76).

These lines would seem to be the germ of a small poem by Dr. Donne, who, although celebrated by his contemporaries, has long been deservedly forgotten; which Mr. Ellis has given as an example of that metaphysical writer's productions, though it be like shewing a single brick as a specimen of a house.

Should it be thought that too strong a censure is here conveyed upon one whom Pope and Cowper have combined to praise, and whose works have been admitted into Mr. Chalmer's *Corpus Poetarum*, still I shall not wish to moderate it. I think that Pope was induced to modernise his Satires, from motives which, although neither honourable to his candour or his love of truth, were quite distinct from any belief in their merit. Cowper, there can be no doubt, was influenced by his relationship to the old Dean; and Chalmers, probably, preserved such worthless trash from deference to the authorities that had preceded him. Donne never can be admired, nor ever obtain a second perusal from any mind imbued with the slightest particle of taste, or fancy, or feeling.

. . . In stating that the pieces of Dr. Donne, selected by Mr. Ellis for his work, would not give a correct idea of his general composition, I did not wish or intend to impute any blame to *him*, whose object it clearly was . . . to collect beautiful blossoms from plantations overrun with weeds of a noxious and imperished existence. . . .

129. 'A.F.G.'

1815

'A.F.G.' listed editions of Donne's poems from 1633 to 1719, with details of their title pages, in his *Bibliotheca Anglo-Poetica; or, a Descriptive Catalogue of a Rare and Rich Collection of Early English Poetry: in the possession of Longmans, Hurst, Rees, Orme, and Browne*, 1815, pp. 78–9 (items 197–204). He omits the editions of 1649 and 1650, of which there were evidently no copies in the collection, but lists two copies each of the editions of 1635 and 1719.

130. Arthur Clifford

1815

Clifford (1775–1830), who had antiquarian interests, lived at Tixall near Stafford, the former seat of Michael Drayton's patron Sir Walter Aston. He edited much seventeenth-century material connected with the house, including poetry and letters. He commented on Donne in an editorial footnote to Catherine Thimelby's letter *c.* 1638–9 (see No. 1), in which she quotes a line from Donne's 'The Legacie' (*Tixall Letters*, 1815, i, p. 147).

Doctor Donne, the famous metaphysical poet and satirist, who died about this time, and whose works were then in the highest reputation. Pope has given some celebrity to his Satires by putting them in a modern dress.

131. Ralph Waldo Emerson

1815–75

Emerson (1803–82) was one of the foremost New England champions of the seventeenth-century English poets. His interest in Donne's poetry appears to have been awakened early, and to have resisted the attitudes to it then current. He was a great admirer and keen student of Coleridge.

(i) In 1815 Emerson, then a very young freshman at Harvard, told his brother in a letter that he had been reading Johnson's *Lives of the Poets*. He quoted from the *Life of Cowley* lines 85–8 of Donne's *An Epithalamion . . . St Valentines day*, with Johnson's comment 'Confusion worse confounded', and added an opinion of his own (letter to William Emerson, 2 and 3 June 1815. *The Letters of Ralph Waldo Emerson*, ed. R. L. Rusk, New York, 1939, i, p. 10):

This is old fashioned Poetry—I should like to see the Poem it was taken from.

(ii) Emerson owned a copy of the 1719 edition of Donne's poems (*The Journals and Miscellaneous Notebooks of Ralph Waldo Emerson*, Cambridge, Mass., vii, ed. A. W. Plumstead and H. Hayford, 1969, p. 5, fn. 3). Over many years he jotted down lines from the poems in his journals and notebooks, and sometimes commented on them or used them as the ground of moral reflections.

1828, Blotting Book ii. He quotes lines 52b–53 of *Elegie xvi*, 'On his Mistris', ascribing them to Donne (*JMN*, vi, ed. R. H. Orth, 1966, p. 88).

1832–4, Blotting Book iva. He quotes lines 48–52 of the epithalamion *Eclogue, 1613. December 26* (Coleridge had quoted these lines in *The Friend*, General Introduction, essay xiv. Emerson also quotes from Herbert's 'Man', which Coleridge had used in the same essay) (*JMN*, vi, p. 103).

1834, Journal A. He adapts line 48 of the epithalamion *Eclogue, 1613. December 26* (Coleridge had adapted lines 48–52 of the poem in *The Friend*, General Introduction, essay xvi) (*JMN*, iv, ed. A. R. Ferguson, 1964, p. 291).

1834, Journal A. He quotes lines 317–18 of *The first Anniversary*, writing them out as prose and ascribing them to Donne (*JMN*, iv, p. 337).

1835, Notebook T. He adapts line 33 of the verse letter 'To the Countesse of Bedford' ('Honour is so sublime perfection') (*JMN*, vi, p. 386).

1837, Journal C. He says that he has been reading Johnson, and mentions Boswell's *Life*, the *Journey to the Western Isles*, and the lives of Pope and Cowley. He remarks that Johnson had strong sense but is no philosopher, and quotes a few things from *Cowley*, with a comment:

Such are the Doctor's poor definitions. His best is that of Wit in Cowley's life. . . . Yet he is a Muttonhead at a definition. Before Coleridge he would be dumb. . . .

He quotes lines 29–32 of Donne's verse letter 'To Mr R.W.' ('If, as mine is, thy life a slumber be') ascribing them to 'Donne p. 154'. Then he quotes a few lines of Cowley, and at once returns to Donne with a series of quotations:

I must quote a few lines from Donne's elegy on Elizabeth Drury.

He gives lines 243–6, 279–80, 288–305 of *The second Anniversary*, and follows it with lines 17–24 of the 'Song. Sweetest love, I do not goe' and a version of line 33 of 'To the Countesse of Bedford' ('Honour is so sublime perfection'), ascribing the last quotation to 'Donne p. 160'.

The next entry in this notebook, written nearly three weeks later, also concerns Donne:

Did I read somewhere lately that the sum of Virtue was to know and dare? The analogy is always perfect between Virtue and genius. One is ethical the other intellectual creation. Whoever creates is God, and whatever talents are, if the man create not, the pure efflux of Deity is not his. I read these Donnes and Cowleys and Marvells with the most modern joy;—with a pleasure, I mean, which is in great part caused by the abstraction of all *time* from their verses. What pleases most, is what is next to my Soul; what I also had well nigh thought and said. . . . Here are things just hinted which not one reader in a hundred would take, but which lie so near to the favorite walks of my imagination and to the facts of my experience that I read them with a surprise and delight as if I were finding very good things in a forgotten manuscript of my own.

Creation is always the style and act of these minds. You shall not predict what the poet shall say and whilst ephemeral poetry hath its form, its contents, and almost its phrase out of the books and is only a skilful paraphrase or permutation of good authors, in these the good human soul speaks because it has something new to say. It is only another face of the same fact to denominate them sincere. The way to avoid mannerism, the way to write what shall not go out of fashion is to write sincerely to transcribe your doubt or regret or whatever state of mind, without the airs of a fine gentleman or great philosopher, without timidity or display, just as they lie in your consciousness, casting on God the responsibility of the facts. This is to dare.

Cowley and Donne are philosophers. To their insight there is no trifle. But philosophy or insight is so much the habit of their minds that they can hardly see as a poet should the beautiful forms and colors of things, as a chemist may be less alive to the picturesque. At the same time their poems like life afford the chance of richest instruction amid frivolous and familiar objects; the loose and the grand, religion and mirth stand in surprising neighborhood and, like the works of great men, without cant (*JMN*, v, ed. M. M. Sealts, Jr, 1965, pp. 339–41).

1838, Journal D. He again adapts line 33 of the verse letter 'To the Countesse of Bedford' ('Honour is so sublime perfection'), ascribing it to Donne (*JMN*, vii, ed. A. W. Plumstead and H. Hayford, 1969, p. 5).

1838, Journal D. Speaking of Providence Library he says that every library ought to hold 'those books in which the English language has its teeth and bones and muscles largest and strongest namely all the eminent books from the accession of Elizabeth to the death of Charles ii'. His list of these books includes Donne (*JMN*, vii, p. 53).

1838, Journal D. He quotes a version of line 17 of Donne's *Goodfriday, 1613. Riding Westward* to bear out his fear of meeting an absolute truth face to face—'I seem to know what he meant who said, "No man can see God face to face and live" ' (*JMN*, vii, p. 151).

1838, Journal D. Under the heading 'Pope's opinion of Herbert' he quotes the remark from Spence—'Crashaw is a worse sort of Cowley . . . and Donne a good deal so'—ascribing it to '*Pope*: in Spence's Table Talk p. 22' (*JMN*, vii, p. 163).

1840, Journal F2. In successive entries he quotes lines 25–6 of *Elegie x*, 'The Dreame', and lines 1–2 of *Elegie ix*, 'The Autumnall' (*JMN*, vii, p. 501).

1846, Journal O. He quotes, without ascribing it to Donne, a version of line 33 of the verse letter 'To the Countesse of Bedford' ('Honour is so sublime perfection'). Then he immediately comments:

Bardic sentences how few! Literature warps away from life though at first it seems to bind it. If now I should count the English Poets who have contributed aught to the bible of existing England and America sentences of guidance and consolation which are still glowing and effective—how few! Milton, Shakespeare, Pope, Burns, Young, Cowper, Wordsworth—(what disparity in the names! Yet these are the authors) and Herbert, Jonson, Donne (*JMN*, ix, ed. R. H. Orth and A. R. Ferguson, 1961, p. 367).

(iii) In his essay 'Love' Emerson quotes lines 202–3 of Donne's epithalamion *Eclogue. 1613. December 26* in describing the effects of love upon lovers. A little later he quotes lines 244b–46 of *The second Anniversary* to show how passion beholds its object as embodied soul and ensouled body (*Essays*: by R. W. Emerson, of Concord, Massachusetts. With a Preface by Thomas Carlyle, 1841, pp. 176 and 185).

(iv) Chapter XIV of Emerson's *English Traits*, 1856, deals with literature. Emerson repeatedly includes Donne when he wants examples of the best English writers in this manner or that. Thus Donne is one of the English authors who have 'A taste for plain strong speech', some of the others being Alfred, Latimer, Hobbes, Bunyan, Milton, Taylor, Swift, and Defoe (p. 131).

Emerson remarks that in his poetry Donne shares with Chaucer, Spenser, Shakespeare, Milton, Herbert, and Browne (among others) the 'national grip and exactitude of mind'. He says that 'This mental materialism' which 'makes the value of English transcendental genius' is 'Saxon materialism and narrowness, exalted into the sphere of intellect' (p. 132).

Donne also figures as one of the British disciples of Plato (p. 134).

(v) According to a contemporary diarist, Annie Fields, Emerson included Donne in programmes of readings he gave at Chickerings Hall. Thus selections from Donne, Daniel, Herrick, Herbert, and Vaughan, were given on 20 February 1869 (*Letters*, vi, pp. 52–3).

(vi) Emerson gave some nine poems or bits of poems by Donne in his anthology *Parnassus*, Boston, 1875, and mentioned Donne in the Preface (p. vi) as a member of Ben Jonson's circle:

His [Ben Jonson's] life interests us from that wonderful circle of companions with whom he lived,—with Camden, Shakespeare, Beaumont, Fletcher, Bacon, Chapman, Herbert, Herrick, Cowley, Suckling, Drayton, Donne, Carew, Selden,—and by whom he was honored.

The extracts from Donne's poetry follow the text of 1719, and are scattered through the collection as follows:

P. 62, under the title 'Love', lines 202–3 of the epithalamion *Eclogue, 1613. December 26*.

Pp. 70–1, 'The Exstasie', complete.

P. 154, 'The Undertaking', complete.

Pp. 180–1, 'A Hymne to Christ, at the Authors last going into Germany', complete.

P. 186, the 'Hymne to God my God, in my sicknesse', complete.

Pp. 273–4, under the title 'Elegy on Mistress Elizabeth Drury', lines 241–470 of *The second Anniversary*, heavily cut.

P. 517, under the general heading 'Oracles and Counsels', lines 48–52 of the epithalamion *Eclogue, 1613. December 26* (given in Coleridge's adaptation, *The Friend*, xvi, see No. 112 (iii)); stanza 3 of the 'Song. Sweetest love, I do not goe'; lines 29–32 of the verse letter 'To Mr R. W.' ('If, as mine is, thy life a slumber be').

132. Henry Austen

Jane Austen's brother used an image from Donne's *The second Anniversary* in paying tribute to his sister after her death ('Biographical Notice of the Author', prefixed to *Northanger Abbey* and *Persuasion*, 1818). Austen dates the notice 13 December 1817.

Her complexion was of the finest texture. It might with truth be said, that her eloquent blood spoke through her modest cheek.

133. William Hazlitt

1818, 1819

Hazlitt had to confess ignorance of Donne's poetry in his *Lectures on the English Poets*, 1818 (*Complete Works*, ed. P. P. Howe, 1930–4, v, p. 83). He seems to have mugged Donne up for his *Lectures on the Comic Writers*, published in the following year (*Complete Works*, vi, pp. 49–53), taking his opinion of the poetry largely from Johnson.

(i)
Of Donne I know nothing but some beautiful verses to his wife, dissuading her from accompanying him on his travels abroad, and some quaint riddles in verse, which the Sphinx could not unravel.

(ii)
The metaphysical poets or wits of the age of James and Charles I. whose style was adopted and carried to a more dazzling and fantastic excess by Cowley in the following reign, after which it declined, and gave place almost entirely to the poetry of observation and reasoning, are thus happily characterised by Dr. Johnson.

[He quotes from Johnson's *Life of Cowley* the two paragraphs beginning 'The metaphysical poets were men of learning . . .', and 'If the father of criticism has rightly denominated poetry . . .', to show that the metaphysical poets were not truly poets at all. See No. 90 (iv)(c).]

The whole of the account is well worth reading: it was a subject for which Dr. Johnson's powers both of thought and expression were better fitted than any other man's. If he had had the same capacity for following the flights of a truly poetic imagination, or for feeling the finer touches of nature, that he had felicity and force in detecting and exposing the aberrations from the broad and beaten path of propriety and common sense, he would have amply deserved the reputation he has acquired as a philosophical critic.

The writers here referred to (such as Donne, Davies, Crashaw, and others) not merely mistook learning for poetry—they thought any thing was poetry that differed from ordinary prose and the natural impression of things, by being intricate, far-fetched, and improbable. Their style was not so properly learned as metaphysical; that is to say, whenever, by any violence done to their ideas, they could make out an abstract likeness or possible ground of comparison, they forced the image, whether learned or vulgar, into the service of the Muses. Any thing would do to 'hitch into a rhyme,' no matter whether striking or agreeable, or not, so that it would puzzle the reader to discover the meaning, and if there was the most remote circumstance, however trifling or vague, for the pretended comparison to hinge upon. They brought ideas together not the most, but the least like; and of which the collision produced not light, but obscurity—served not to strengthen, but to confound. Their mystical verses read like riddles or an allegory. They neither belong to the class of lively or severe poetry. They have not the force of the one, nor the gaiety of the other; but are an ill-assorted, unprofitable union of the two together, applying to serious subjects that quaint and partial style of allusion which fits only what is light and ludicrous, and building the most laboured conclusions on the most fantastical and slender premises. The object of the poetry of imagination is to raise or adorn one idea by another more striking or more beautiful: the object of these writers was to match any one idea with any other idea, *for better for worse*, as we say, and whether any thing was gained by the change of condition or not. The object of the poetry of the passions again is to illustrate any strong feeling, by shew-ing the same feeling as connected with objects or circumstances more palpable and touching; but here the object was to strain and distort the immediate feeling into some barely possible consequence or recondite analogy, in which it required the utmost stretch of misapplied in-genuity to trace the smallest connection with the original impression. In short, the poetry of this period was strictly the poetry not of ideas, but of *definitions*: it proceeded in mode and figure, by *genus* and specific difference; and was the logic of the schools, or an oblique and forced construction of dry, literal matter-of-fact, decked out in a robe of glittering conceits, and clogged with the halting shackles of verse. The imagination of the writers, instead of being conversant with the face of nature, or the secrets of the heart, was lost in the labyrinths of intellectual abstraction, or entangled in the technical quibbles and impertinent intricacies of language. The complaint so often made, and here repeated, is not of the want of power in these men, but of the waste of it; not of the absence of genius, but the abuse of it. They had (many of them) great talents committed to their trust, richness of thought, and depth of feeling; but they chose to hide them (as much as they possibly could) under a false shew of learning and unmeaning subtlety. From the style which they had systematically adopted, they thought nothing done till they had perverted simplicity into affectation, and spoiled nature by art. They seemed to think there was an irreconcileable opposition between genius, as well as grace, and nature; tried to do without, or else constantly to thwart her; left nothing to her outward 'impress,' or spontaneous impulses, but made a point of twisting and torturing almost every subject they took in hand, till they had fitted it to the mould of their self-opinion and the previous fabrications of their own fancy, like those who pen acrostics in the shape of pyramids, and cut out trees into the shape of peacocks. Their chief aim is to make you wonder at the writer, not to interest you in the subject; and by an incessant craving after admiration, they have lost what they might have gained with less extravagance and affectation. So Cowper, who was of a quite opposite school, speaks feelingly of the misapplication of Cowley's poetical genius.

> And though reclaim'd by modern lights
> From an erroneous taste,
> I cannot but lament thy splendid wit
> Entangled in the cobwebs of the schools.

Donne, who was considerably before Cowley, is without his fancy, but was more recondite in his logic, and rigid in his descriptions. He is hence led, particularly in his satires, to tell disagreeable truths in as disagreeable a way as possible, or to convey a pleasing and affecting thought (of which there are many to be found in his other writings) by the harshest means, and with the most painful effort. His Muse suffers continual pangs and throes. His thoughts are delivered by the Cæsarean operation. The sentiments, profound and tender as they often are, are stifled in the expression; and 'heaved pantingly forth,' are 'buried quick again' under the ruins and rubbish of analytical distinctions. It is like poetry waking from a trance: with an eye bent idly on the outward world, and half-forgotten feelings crowding about the heart; with vivid impressions, dim notions, and disjointed words. The following may serve as instances of beautiful or impassioned reflections losing themselves in obscure and difficult applications. He has some lines to a Blossom, which begin thus:

Little think'st thou, poor flow'r,
Whom I have watched six or seven days,
And seen thy birth, and seen what every hour
Gave to thy growth, thee to this height to raise,
And now dost laugh and triumph on this bough,
    Little think'st thou
That it will freeze anon, and that I shall
To-morrow find thee fall'n, or not at all.

This simple and delicate description is only introduced as a foundation for an elaborate metaphysical conceit as a parallel to it, in the next stanza.

Little think'st thou (poor heart
That labour'st yet to nestle thee,
And think'st by hovering here to get a part
In a forbidden or forbidding tree,
And hop'st her stiffness by long siege to bow:)
    Little think'st thou,
That thou to-morrow, ere the sun doth wake,
Must with this sun and me a journey take.

This is but a lame and impotent conclusion from so delightful a beginning.—He thus notices the circumstance of his wearing his late wife's hair about his arm, in a little poem which is called the Funeral:

Whoever comes to shroud me, do not harm
    Nor question much
That subtle wreath of hair, about mine arm;
The mystery, the sign you must not touch.

The scholastic reason he gives quite dissolves the charm of tender and touching grace in the sentiment itself—

For 'tis my outward soul,
Viceroy to that, which unto heaven being gone,
    Will leave this to control,
And keep these limbs, her provinces, from dissolution.

Again, the following lines, the title of which is Love's Deity, are highly characteristic of this author's manner, in which the thoughts are inlaid in a costly but imperfect mosaic-work.

I long to talk with some old lover's ghost,
Who died before the God of Love was born:
I cannot think that he, who then lov'd most,
Sunk so low, as to love one which did scorn.

> But since this God produc'd a destiny,
> And that vice-nature, custom, lets it be;
> I must love her that loves not me.

The stanza in the Epithalamion on a Count Palatine of the Rhine, has been often quoted against him, and is an almost irresistible illustration of the extravagances to which this kind of writing, which turns upon a pivot of words and possible allusions, is liable. Speaking of the bride and bridegroom he says, by way of serious compliment—

> Here lies a she-Sun, and a he-Moon there,
> She gives the best light to his sphere;
> Or each is both and all, and so
> They unto one another nothing owe.

His love-verses and epistles to his friends give the most favourable idea of Donne. His satires are too clerical. He shews, if I may so speak, too much disgust, and, at the same time, too much contempt for vice. His dogmatical invectives hardly redeem the nauseousness of his descriptions, and compromise the imagination of his readers more than they assist their reason. The satirist does not write with the same authority as the divine, and should use his poetical privileges more sparingly. 'To the pure all things are pure,' is a maxim which a man like Dr. Donne may be justified in applying to himself; but he might have recollected that it could not be construed to extend to the generality of his readers, *without benefit of clergy.*

134. Leigh Hunt

1819–67

Hunt (1784–1859) was at Christ's Hospital a little later than Lamb and Coleridge. He shared their interest in old authors, and their feeling that Donne is a poet of strong passions as well as intellectual brilliance. His references to Donne over many years suggest a familiarity with the poetry, though his enthusiasm for it seems to have waned.

(i) In a letter to Percy and Mary Shelley dated 20 September 1819 Hunt spoke of poets who have visited Italy, and included Donne among them. He went on to quote and discuss Donne (*The Correspondence of Leigh Hunt*, ed. Thornton Hunt, 1862, i, pp. 148–9):

There is a fine ghastly image in a poem of Donne's on the subject, which will please you. He is dissuading his wife from going with him (he went on a political mission), and hopes that she will not start in her sleep at night, and fancy him slain.

[He quotes lines 51b–54 of *Elegie xvi*, 'On his Mistris'.]

I am tempted, for other reasons, to copy out the beginning of this poem for you, which, with the exception of a little coarseness which got into the grain of this writer's strong intellect, is very intense throughout.

[He quotes lines 1–17a of *Elegie xvi*.]

She could not accompany him, it seems, openly, and wished to do so in the disguise of a page. Do you know Donne? I should like to have some more talk with you about him. He was one of those over-metaphysical-headed men, who can find out connections between everything and anything, and allowed himself at *last* to become a clergyman, after he had (to my conviction, at least) been as free and deep a speculator in morals as yourself. (I am talking to Shelley, you see, Marina—but you are one flesh.) Are not those three words, 'I calmly beg,' very grave and lovely? And all the rest—is it not fine, and earnest, and 'masculine-persuasive?' [*sic*].

(ii) In reviewing Tennyson's *Poems, Chiefly Lyrical* (1830) Hunt found that one of the poems reminded him of Donne in its manner (*The Tatler*, 26 February 1831. Given in *Leigh Hunt's Literary Criticism*, ed. L.H. and C.W. Houtchens, 1956, p. 358). Tennyson never reprinted the poem in fact:

The 'Tears of Heaven' is a conceit, not founded in natural, and therefore not in poetical truth. 'Love and Sorrow' is a pleasanter one, more wilfully artificial, yet better grounded. The author must have been reading Donne when he wrote it. It might pass for a leaf out of his book.

> Thou art my heart's sun in love's chrystalline:
> Yet on both sides at once thou canst not shine:
> Thine is the bright side of my heart, and thine
> My heart's day; but the shadow of my heart,
> Issue of its own substance, my heart's night,
> Thou canst not lighten even with thy light, &c.

This is the very Analogical Doctor come back again. . . .

(iii) In an essay on 'Epithalamiums' (*The British Miscellany*, April 1841; in *Leigh Hunt's Literary Criticism*, pp. 497–8) Hunt discussed the classical epithalamiums, and then went on to quote some English examples. He came to 'The celebrated Epithalamium of Spenser', which he praised as 'perhaps the best altogether in the language', though he found it 'somehow too stately, and scholar-like'; and he quoted some lines from it:

Next to Spenser's poem, our best Epithalamiums, and the only ones, we fear, worth much remembrance, are those of a great wit and intellect, who is supposed, by some, to be nothing but a bundle of conceits—Dr. Donne. In occasional passages, they are even superior in depth and feeling, though the very audacity of their truthfulness (honest in that depth) hinders them from being quotable to the 'general ear.' One of them is upon the marriage of poor wretched Car, Earl of Somerset, with Lady Essex—singular personages for the feeling and thoughtful Donne to panegyrize. The faith expressed in their love, however, by this good and great child-like man, however startling to us when we know under what circumstances they were married, was, no doubt, as far as regards himself, good and true. Let us hope, therefore, there were more circumstances than we are aware of, to extenuate, if possible, their crimes. One thing there certainly was—they were victims of their own beauty.

(iv) In a critical essay, 'Poems by Alfred Tennyson' (*Church of England Quarterly Review*, October 1842; in *Leigh Hunt's Literary Criticism*, p. 526), Hunt argued for those writers, of whatever standing, who 'are consistent with the truth that is in them', as against some poets of his own day who are 'always provoking and disappointing the degree of expectation which they have undertaken to raise':

We ourselves are adherents to poetry in all its grades, and love the miniatures of Pope, notwithstanding our far greater love and delight in Spenser and Shakspeare, and our admiration of all the genuine intermediate good stuff, whether of thought or feeling, or both, in Beaumont and Fletcher, and Webster, and Marlowe, and Donne, and Daniel, and Drayton; . . .

(v) In an essay 'Donne and his Vision' (*The Town*, 1848, p. 50) Hunt discussed Walton's account of the vision Donne had of his wife when he was in Paris in 1612:

The biographer then presents us with some verses which 'were given by Mr. Donne to his wife at the time he then parted from her,' and which he 'begs leave to tell us' that he has heard some critics, learned both in languages and poetry, say, that 'none of the Greek or Latin poets did ever equal.'

   These lines are full of the wit that Dryden speaks of, horribly misused to obscure the most beautiful feelings. Some of them are among the passages, quoted in Dr. Johnson to illustrate the faults of the metaphysical school. Mr. Chalmers and others have thought it probable, that it was upon this occasion Donne wrote a set of verses, which he addressed to his wife, on her proposing to accompany him abroad as a page; but as the writer speaks of going to Italy, which appears to have been out of the question in this two months' visit to Paris, they most probably belong to some other journey or intended journey, the period of which is unknown. The numbers of these verses are sometimes rugged, but they are full of as much nature and real feeling, as sincerity ever put into a true passion. There is an awfulness in the commencing adjuration—

(vi) In an essay 'Combination of Grave and Gay' (*The Musical Times and Singing Class Circular*, 15 June 1854; in *Leigh Hunt's Literary Criticism*,

p. 562) Hunt cited Swift, Donne and Molière as proof of his thesis that 'no very great wit ever existed who had not an equal fund of gravity'. He said that they were all melancholy men.

(vii) Hunt and S. Adams Lee compiled *The Book of the Sonnet*, which came out in Boston in 1867, eight years after Hunt's death. In his long introduction 'An Essay on the Sonnet', Hunt explained why they had omitted Donne's poetry and expressed an equivocal attitude to Donne's *Divine Poems* (i, pp. 78 and 117):

Learned Ben Jonson's learned friend, Donne, not only wrote some five or six and twenty sonnets, almost all of which are of the legitimate order, but he is the only English poet, as far as I am aware, who has given us a Crown of Sonnets, after the fashion alluded to in the preceding section. It comprises the first seven of his 'Holy Sonnets'; and in reference to the native country of the fashion, he has entitled it *La Corona*. It has fine passages, and I wish I could extract it into this book, as a specimen of the class it belongs to; but Donne's piety, though sincere, was not healthy. It does not do justice to the Divine Goodness. Fortunately the best sonnet he wrote, though it is upon a subject on which, generally speaking, he was in more than one sense of the word least happy,—Death—is equally unexceptionable and noble. . . .
[On the poems of Mr Jones Very.] Mr. Very's tone is deeply devotional. . . . The old metaphysical rhapsodists of the sixteenth and seventeenth centuries, such as Donne, Herbert, Vaugh [*sic*], &c, are evidently his poetic models. He has studied them with faithful attention, and has reproduced their style, more in its faults, however, than in its excellences. Donne, I take it, is his favorite. He could not, in many respects, have chosen a worse master. . . .

135. Thomas Campbell

1819

Campbell gave three of Donne's *Songs and Sonnets*—'Song. Sweetest love, I do not goe', 'Breake of Day', and 'The Dreame' —and some lines from the *Obsequies to the Lord Harrington,* in his *Specimens of the British Poets,* 1819. Campbell commented on Donne as satirist and as love poet (i, pp. 170–1, and iii, p. 73).

Hall was the master satirist of the age; obscure and quaint at times, but full of nerve and picturesque illustrations. No contemporary satirist has given equal grace and dignity to moral censure. Very unequal to him in style, though often as original in thought, and as graphic in exhibiting manners, is Donne, some of whose satires have been modernized by Pope. . . .

Donne was the 'best good-natured man, with the worst-natured Muse.' A romantic and uxorious lover, he addresses the object of his real tenderness with ideas that outrage decorum. He begins his own epithalamium with a most indelicate invocation to his bride. His ruggedness and whim are almost proverbially known. Yet there is a beauty of thought which at intervals rises from his chaotic imagination, like the form of Venus smiling on the waters. . . .

The life of Donne is more interesting than his poetry. . . .

136. Ezekiel Sanford

1819

Sanford (1796–1822), an ambitious young New Englander, brought out in the same year *A History of the United States before the Revolution, with Some Account of the Aborigines,* and the first twenty-two volumes of a fifty-two volume edition of the British poets, expurgated and with biographical prefaces. His health failed before he could tackle the remaining volumes and the project was completed by another editor. Volume iv of Sanford's edition contains select poems of Davies, Donne, Hall, Alexander, Corbet, and Carew. The selection from Donne takes up pages 139–95: there are thirteen *Songs and Sonnets,* four *Epigrams,* six *Elegies,* seven verse letters (one of them not by Donne), one funeral poem, the poem on Coryate, 'Sonnet. The Token', the opening lines of the two epithalamions of 1613 (fourteen lines of one and twelve lines of the other), bits of *Satyres i, iii,* and *iv,* and some other poems not now ascribed to Donne. The arrangement of the poems is haphazard, showing little care or concern for the sense of the writing. Thus *Elegie xvi,* 'On his Mistris', is given the title 'On His Wife' and put with the funeral poems. The life of Donne which precedes the selection of poems contains a few critical comments (*The Works of the British Poets, with Lives of the Authors,* Philadelphia, 1819, iv, p. 137).

Donne is considered a great wit, a tolerable divine, and something of a poet. Poetry, indeed, in the highest sense of the word, we can almost say, he had none. He was more intent upon showing the acuteness of his penetration than the opulence of his fancy; and instead of grouping and describing new objects, he sets himself laboriously at work to refine and analyze the old. What furnishes other poets with a passing metaphorical allusion, would be a sufficient subject of a whole poem to Donne and his followers. It would take them ten centuries to finish the seige of Troy; and the figures of speech in the first book of the Iliad would supply their laboratory with an inexhaustible stock of materials. We are often amused with the brilliancy of their experiments, and with the novelty of their results. They stimulate our reflection, and awaken our memory; but they seldom excite our feelings or give play to the imagination. Of Donne it may be said that he was more witty than learned; and more learned than poetical.

137. John Payne Collier

1820, 1865

Collier (1789–1883), Shakespearean scholar and literary forger, wrote a dialogue in which the three participants debate whether Donne was the first satirist in the language and then discuss at length the text and the texts of Donne's poetry (*The Poetical Decameron or Ten Conversations on English Poets and Poetry, Particularly of the Reigns of Elizabeth and James I*, 1820, i, pp. 153–60). There is an accurate account of the printed texts and of some manuscripts. 'Bourne', who is the scholarly speaker in the dialogue, says that he has done some collating work on the manuscript and early printed versions of the poems; and he gives a good reading or two to replace bad readings in the edition of 1633.

There is mention of poems which were published in Donne's lifetime—the *Anniversaries*, 'Upon Mr Thomas Coryats *Crudities*', and the elegy on Prince Henry. Bourne speaks of the early references to Donne, and quotes those from *Rubbe, and a great Cast,* and *Runne and a great cast.*

The participants show a keen interest in all this, and quote a good deal from the *Satyres*. But there are no critical references as such at all.

Many years later Collier went over the ground again in *A Bibliographical & Critical Account of the Rarest Books in the English Language*, 1865, i, pp. 22–3, and 'Additions, Notes, Corrections' p. 1. This time however his main concern was to give an account of a copy of the first edition (1611) of *The first Anniversary*—one of the 'Rarest Books' of his title. He listed the dates of later editions, related the circumstances of the poem, mentioned the Ellesmere copy, and noted some variant readings between the editions of 1611 and 1633.

138. Lucy Aikin

1822

Miss Aikin (1781–1864) wrote biographies and compiled historical memoirs. In her *Memoirs of the Court of King James the First*, 1822, pp. 74–6, she speaks of the 'taint' given to Elizabethan literature by 'the state of manners and society, a taint which was already turning its beauty to corruption'. She instances the system of patronage, and its effect in producing an art of flattery and compliment.

Nor can any person be widely conversant in the literature of the age of Elizabeth without discovering and deploring numerous similar abuses. Complimentary effusions, commanded strains of congratulation or condolence on subjects then interesting to few, and now to no one, form the larger portion of the occasional pieces of Spenser, of Jonson, of Donne, and of the whole herd of minor poets. Shakespeare alone, preeminent in moral as in intellectual dignity, disdained to prostitute his immortal lines to temporary or selfish purposes. . . .

139. 'M.M.D.'

1822

In an 'Essay on the Genius of Cowley, Donne and Clieveland' in *The European Magazine*, August 1822, pp. 108–12, 'M.M.D.' characterises Cowley, Donne, and Cleveland as poets of a corrupt 'middle stage in the march of intellect' which occurs midway between 'the state of nature' and a condition of 'the most polished refinement'.

These appear to me to be the reasons, why every trace of natural feeling seems to be extinct in the writings of Cowley and his contemporaries.—Perhaps I do not assert more than I could easily prove, when I say, that every line, every idea, every sentiment in Cowley, Donne, Clieveland, &c. can be traced to the philosophy, the metaphysics, or the literature of their predecessors. They never venture to think for themselves, and their highest aim is to present the thoughts of others in a different aspect. They never consult their own feelings: they even address their mistress as if she were totally destitute of all natural feeling,—as if she were an intellectual being, who was not in the least subject to the dominion of the senses; and as if she could only esteem the man, whose love was a mere heterogeneous compound of conceit and wit,—not the man who loved her as a man, and whose love had not the remotest alliance with metaphysical combinations. Who can trace the least spark of natural affection in the following comparison, which Donne makes between himself who travels, and his wife who stays at home, to a pair of compasses?

[He quotes the last five stanzas of 'A Valediction: forbidding Mourning', and approves Dryden's comment that Donne 'affects the metaphysics . . . in his amorous verses'.]

Donne has not confined his metaphysical jargon to his poetical productions.—It is equally characteristic of his prose writings. Even in the

dedication of his poetical works to Lord Craven, where it might naturally be expected he would have laid aside his conceits and witticisms, he
concludes, by representing the collection of his own poems as a pyramid
on which his Lordship's statue might rest secure; in which, by the bye,
the whole compliment is to himself, and not to his Lordship.

[He argues that even Shakespeare shows the corrupt taste of the times in
his indelicacy, which now necessitates an expurgated edition of his
works.]

When the mental powers are once vitiated in any of their functions, and
become subject to an improper or immoral influence, the contagion
becomes, in a manner, universal, and the mind takes a false and distorted view of all its objects. Accordingly, we find that the perversion
of moral sentiment which sacrificed truth and modesty to obscenity and
licentiousness, banished nature altogether from the literary productions
of the time; and servility became the natural consequence of false sentiment and conceit. Cowley, Donne, and Clieveland unite, perhaps, more
than all the rest, this prostrate servility of adulation to a total abandon-
ment of nature, whose modesty they left at an immeasurable distance
behind them. Donne, not satisfied with transforming the Countess of
Bedford into a goddess, endows her with that divinity which is the
object of Christian adoration. In one of his epistles, he addresses her in
the following unintelligible rant:—

[He quotes stanzas 1, 3, and 4 of the verse letter 'To the Countesse of
Bedford', 'Reason is our Soules left hand'.]

Donne's 'Hymn to God in his Sickness,' gives us so clear a portrait
of his manner, his total want of nature, and the length to which he
carried pun and conceit when he could not avoid them, even in so
sacred a subject, that I shall dismiss him with the following quotation
from it:—

[He quotes stanzas 1, 2, and 5 of the 'Hymne to God my God, in my
sicknesse'.]

Were these lines addressed ironically to some Pagan idol, they might
pass for wit: addressed to the God of his faith, they are impious in the
highest degree.

Of Clieveland, little remains to be said, as all our observations on
Donne and Cowley are applicable to him.—He has not a single poem
worthy the attention of a reader of taste; and it is doubtful, whether a

copy either of his or Donne's poems will be extant at the close of the nineteenth century, if nature, united with a correct and elegant taste, continue to be cultivated and progressively improved. At present, indeed, we have so many schools of poetry, so many heresies in matters of taste, that little can be said with certainty with regard to the future; but if false taste, and arbitrary notions of poetic beauty were once exploded, the works of Donne, Clieveland, and their metaphysical contemporaries would soon glide into oblivion. Their names, no doubt, will travel down to posterity, while antiquarian research continues to hoard up the useless lumber of ancient times. But if it ever becomes popular to reject whatever is not stamped with the impress of native excellence,—if it ever be deemed wise not to encumber the mind with useless knowledge, and to pervert the taste by the perusal of false models, we have no hesitation in prophesying the fate of their works. The following lines from Clieveland will shew how exactly his genius and manner correspond with those of Donne and Cowley.

[He quotes Cleveland's lines, 'To Julia, to expedite her marriage', and 'To the Memory of Mr. Edward King'.]

Perhaps it would be wrong to conclude, that Clieveland felt no real sorrow for the loss of his friend; but if the greatest scribbler of the present day wrote such lines, they would be deemed an impious mockery of the dead. It may be safely asserted, that many poets of our own time, whose works never pass beyond one edition, and who are never more destined to be heard of in the lists of fame, are not merely superior to Donne and Cowley, but possess merit which would become the theme and the admiration of future ages, had they lived at the same time.

140. Anon., *The Retrospective Review*

An anonymous reviewer of the 1669 edition of Donne's poems followed Coleridge in taking issue with the eighteenth-century disparagers of Donne (*The Retrospective Review*, viii, 1823, pp. 31–55).

Theobald, in his egregious preface to Shakspeare, calls Donne's Poems 'nothing but a continued heap of riddles.'—We shall presently show that he knew as little about Donne as he himself has shewn that he knew about Shakspeare. If *he* could have written such 'riddles,' or even expounded them, Pope might have put him into the *Dunciad* in vain.

Donne was contemporary with Shakspeare, and was not unworthy to be so. He may fairly be placed, in point of talent, at the head of the minor poets of that day. Imbued, to saturation, with all the learning of his age—with a most active and piercing intellect—an imagination, if not grasping and comprehensive, most subtle and far-darting—a fancy rich, vivid, picturesque, and, at the same time, highly *fantastical*,—if we may so apply the term—a mode of expression singularly terse, simple, and condensed—an exquisite ear for the melody of versification—and a wit, admirable as well for its caustic severity as its playful quickness; all he wanted to make him an accomplished poet of the second order was, sensibility and taste: and both of these he possessed in a certain degree; but neither in a sufficient degree to keep them from yielding to the circumstances in which he was placed. His sensibility was by nature strong, but sluggish and deep-seated. It required to be roused and awakened by the imagination, before it would act; and this process seldom failed to communicate to the action which it created, an appearance of affectation (for it was nothing more than the appearance), which is more destructive to the effect of sentimental poetry than any thing else. We do not mind the images and illustrations of a sentiment being recondite and far-fetched; and, indeed, this has frequently a good effect; but if the sentiment itself has any appearance of being so, we doubt the truth of it immediately; and if we doubt its truth, we are disposed to give it any reception rather than a sympathetic one. The scholastic habits of Donne's intellect also, without weakening his sensibility, contribute greatly to deform and denaturalize its outward manifestations. It was not the fashion of his time for a scholar and a poet to express himself as other people would; for if he had done so, what advantage would he or the world have derived from his poetry or his scholarship? Accordingly, however intense a feeling might be, or however noble a thought, it was to be heightened and illustrated, in the expression of it, by clustering about it a host of images and associations (congruous or not, as it might happen), which memory or imagination, assisted by the most quick-eyed wit, or the most subtle ingenuity, could in any way contrive to link to it: thus pressing the original thought or sentiment to death, and hiding even the form of it, beneath a profusion of superfluous dress. This was the crying fault of all the minor poets of the Elizabethan age; and of Donne more than of any other: though *his* thoughts and feelings would, generally speaking, bear this treatment better than those of any of his rivals in the same class. These persons never acted avowedly, (though they sometimes did unconsciously) on the principle that an idea or a sentiment may be poetical *per se*; for they had no notion whatever of the fact. They considered that *man* was the creator of poetry, not Nature; and that any thing might be made poetical, by connecting it, in a certain manner, with something else. A thought or a feeling was, to them, not a thing *to express*, but a theme to write *variations* upon—a nucleus, about which other thoughts and feelings were to be made to crystallize. A star was not bright to *their* eyes till it had been set in a constellation; a rose was not sweet till it had been gathered into a bouquet, and its hue and odour contrasted and blended with a thousand others. In fact, they had little simplicity of feeling, and still less of taste. They did not know the real and intrinsic value of any object, whether moral or physical; but only in what manner it might be connected with any other object, so as to be made subservient to their particular views at the moment. They saw at once how far it was available *to them*, but nothing whatever of the impression it was calculated to make for itself.

We are speaking, now, of a particular class or school of poets of that day; for they differed as much from all others, and were as much allied by a general resemblance of style among themselves, as the Della Cruscan school in our own day. Indeed, in some particulars, there is no slight resemblance between the two styles; inasmuch, as both are purely artificial, and are dependent for their effect on a particular *manner* of treating their subject: at least, their intended effect is dependent on this—for the school to which Donne belongs often delights us in the highest degree, not in consequence of this manner, but in spite of it. There is also this other grand difference in favour of the latter,—that, whereas the Della Cruscans tried to make things poetical by means of *words* alone, *they* did it by means of thoughts and images;—the one considered poetry to consist in a certain mode of expression; the other, in a certain mode of seeing, thinking, and feeling. This is nearly all the difference between them; but this is a vast difference indeed: for the one supposes the necessity of, and in fact uses, a vast fund of thoughts and images; while the other can execute all its purposes nearly as well without any of these. In short, the one kind of writing requires very considerable talent to produce it, and its results are very often highly poetical; whereas the other requires no talent at all, and can in no case produce poetry, but very frequently covers and conceals it where it is.

But it is not at present our intention to go into a general discussion of that particular school of poetry to which Donne belongs; but merely to bring to light some of the exquisite beauties which have hitherto lain concealed from the present age, among the learned as well as unlearned lumber which he has so unaccountably mixed up with them. We say unaccountably—for it is impossible to give a reasonable account of any poetical theory, the perpetual results of which are the most pure and perfect beauties of every kind—of thought, of sentiment, of imagery, of expression, and of versification—lying in immediate contact with the basest deformities, equally of every kind; each given forth alternately in almost equal proportions, and in the most unconscious manner on the part of the writer as to either being entitled to the preference; and indeed without one's being able to discover that he saw any difference between them, even in kind.

Before doing this, however, it may be well to let the reader know what was thought of Donne in his own day, lest he should suppose that we are introducing him to a person little known at that time, or lightly valued.

If a prophet has little honour in his own time and country, the same can seldom be said of a poet; though *he*, too, is in some sort a prophet. The day in which Donne lived was the most poetical the world ever knew, and yet there can be little doubt, from the evidence of the fugitive literature of the time, that Donne was, upon the whole, more highly esteemed than any other of his contemporaries. We do not, however, mean to attribute all his fame to his published poetry. He was undoubtedly a very extraordinary person in many other respects. He possessed vast knowledge and erudition, and was highly distinguished for the eloquence of his public preaching. But the greater part of the admiration bestowed on him, was avowedly directed to the poetical writings which we are presently to examine.—We shall give a few evidences of the estimation in which Donne was held during his life; taking them, however, (in order to avoid the charge of partiality or flattery) from what was not written till after his death.

[He quotes praises of Donne from the funeral elegies by Hyde (No. 18 (iv) (c), lines 1–8), Walton (No. 18 (iv) (f), lines 19a, 21b–24), and Carew (No. 18 (iv) (g), lines 1–3a, 71–5, 95–8). Carew's lines he calls 'finely thought and nobly expressed'.]

What follows may perhaps, in some degree, account for his popularity. Most of his readers admired him, not *in spite of* his impenetrable obscurity, but *because* of it:

[He quotes lines 20b–21a and 23–8 of Mayne's elegy on Donne (see No. 18 (v) (i)), lines 25–7 of Endymion Porter's elegy (see No. 18 (iv) (l)), and lines 9–12 and 77–80 of the elegy by 'Mr R.B.'].

It is remarkable that the writer, of whom this could be said by persons of repute, (whether truly or not is no matter) in an age which produced Shakspeare and the elder dramatists—besides Spenser, Sydney, Herbert, Raleigh, and a host of minor names—should so long have remained unknown in an after age, one of the distinguishing boasts of which is, that it has revived a knowledge of, and a love for its great predecessor, at the same time that it has almost rivalled it.

In pieces that can be read with unmingled pleasure, and admired as perfect wholes, the poetry of Donne is almost entirely deficient. This may serve, in some degree, to account for the total neglect which has so long attended him. Almost every beauty we meet with, goes hand in hand with some striking deformity, of one kind or another; and the effect of this is, at first, so completely *irritating* to the imagination, as well as to the taste, that, after we have experienced it a few times, we hastily determine to be without the one, rather than purchase it at the price of the other. But the reader who is disposed, by these remarks, and the extracts that will accompany them, to a perusal of the whole of this poet's works, may be assured that this unpleasant effect will very soon wear off, and he will soon find great amusement and great exercise for his *thinking* faculties, (if nothing else) even in the objectionable parts of Donne; for he is always, when indulging in his very worst vein, filled to overflowing with thoughts, and materials for engendering thought.

The following short pieces are beautiful exceptions to the remark made just above, as to the mixed character of this poet's writings. The first is a farewell from a lover to his mistress, on leaving her for a time. For clearness and smoothness of construction, and a passionate sweetness and softness in the music of the versification, it might have been written in the present day, and may satisfy the ear of the most fastidious of modern readers; and for thought, sentiment, and imagery, it might *not* have been written in the present day;—for, much as we hold in honour our living poets, we doubt if any one among them is capable of it. In fact, it is one of those pieces which immediately strike us as being purely and exclusively attributable to the writer of them—which satisfy us, that, *but for him*, we never could have become possessed of them—which bear a mark that we cannot very well expound, even to ourselves, but which we know no one could have placed on them but him: and this, by-the-bye, is one of the most unequivocal criterions of a true poet. Perhaps the piece itself will explain better what we mean, than any thing we could say of it.

[He quotes the whole of 'A Valediction: forbidding Mourning'.]

The simile of the compasses, notwithstanding its quaintness, is more perfect in its kind, and more beautiful, than any thing we are acquainted with. Perhaps the above is the only poem we could extract, that is not disfigured by *any* of the characteristic faults of Donne. Several of them have, however, very few. The following is one of these. It has an air of serious gaiety about it, as if it had been composed in the very bosom of bliss. The versification, too, is perfect. It is called, '*The Good-Morrow*'.

[He quotes the whole of 'The Good-morrow' in the 1669 version.]

The following, though not entirely without the faults of his style, is exceedingly graceful and elegant:

[He quotes the whole of 'The Dreame'.]

What follows is extremely solemn and fine, and scarcely at all disfigured by the author's characteristic faults:

[He quotes the whole of 'The Apparition'.]

329

The next specimens that we shall give of this singular writer will be taken from among those of his poems which unite, in a nearly equal proportion, his characteristic faults and beauties; and which may be considered as scarcely less worthy of attention than the foregoing, partly on account of that very union of opposite qualities, but chiefly on account of their remarkable fullness of thought and imagery; in which, indeed, his very worst pieces abound to overflowing.

Notwithstanding the extravagance, as well as the ingenuity, which characterise the two following pieces, there is an air of sincerity about them, which renders their general effect impressive, and even solemn; to say nothing of their individual beauties, both of thought and expression.

[He quotes the whole of 'The Anniversarie' and of 'Loves Growth'.]

The reader will not fail to observe the occasional obscurities which arise out of the extreme condensation of expression in the foregoing pieces, and in most of those which follow. These passages may always be unravelled by a little attention, and they seldom fail to repay the trouble bestowed upon them. But they must be regarded as unequivocal faults nevertheless.

The following is, doubtless, 'high-fantastical', in the last degree; but it is fine notwithstanding, and an evidence of something more than mere ingenuity.

[He quotes the whole of 'A Valediction: of Weeping'.]

The feelings which dictated such poetry as this, (for it *is* poetry, and nothing but real feelings *could* dictate it,) must have pierced deeper than the surface of both the heart and the imagination. In fact, they wanted nothing but to have been excited under more favourable circumstances, to have made them well-springs of the richest poetry uttering itself in the rarest words.

For clearness of expression, melody of versification, and a certain wayward simplicity of thought peculiarly appropriate to such compositions as these, the most successful of our modern lyrists might envy the following trifle:

[He quotes the whole of 'The Message'.]

Perhaps the two short pieces which follow, include all the characteristics of Donne's style—beauties as well as faults.

[He quotes the whole of 'A Lecture upon the Shadow' and of 'The Expiration'.]

The following piece, entitled, 'The Funeral,' is fantastical and far-fetched to be sure; but it is very fine nevertheless. The comparison of the nerves and the braid of hair, and anticipating similar effects from each, could never have entered the thoughts of any one but Donne; still less could any one have made it *tell* as he has done. The piece is altogether an admirable and most interesting example of his style.

[He quotes the whole of 'The Funerall'.]

As a specimen of Donne's infinite fullness of meaning, take a little poem, called 'The Will'; almost every line of which would furnish matter for a whole treatise in modern times.

[He quotes the whole of 'The Will'.]

The following (particularly the first stanza) seems to us to express even more than it is intended to express; which is very rarely the case with the productions of this writer. The love expressed by it is a love for the passion excited, rather than the object exciting it; it is a love that lives by '*chewing the cud* of sweet and bitter fancy,' rather than by hungering after fresh food—that broods, like the stock dove, over its own voice, and listens for no other—that is all sufficient to itself, and (like virtue) its own reward.

[He quotes the whole of 'Negative Love'.]

What follows is in a different style, and it offers a singular specimen of the perverse ingenuity with which Donne sometimes bandies a thought about (like a shuttle-cock) from one hand to the other, only to let it fall to the ground at last.

[He quotes the whole of 'The Prohibition'.]

The following, in common with many other whole pieces and detached thoughts of this writer, has been imitated by later love-poets in proportion as it has not been read.

[He quotes the 'Song. Goe, and catche a falling starre', putting asterisks in place of line 2.]

The following is to the same purpose, but more imbued with the writer's subtlety of thought and far-fetched ingenuity of illustration.

[He quotes the whole of 'Womans Constancy'.]

The whole of the foregoing extracts are taken from the first department of Donne's poetry—the Love-verses. The only others that we shall choose from these, will be a few specimens of the truth and beauty that are frequently to be met with in Donne, in the shape of detached thoughts, images, &c. Nothing was ever more exquisitely felt or expressed, than this opening stanza of a little poem, entitled 'The Blossom.'

[He quotes the first stanza of 'The Blossome'.]

The admirer of Wordsworth's style of language and versification will see, at once, that it is, at its best, nothing more than a *return* to this.

How beautiful is the following bit of description!

[He quotes lines 21–6 of *Elegy vi*, 'Oh, let me not serve so'.]

The following is exquisite in its way. It is part of an epithalamion.

[He quotes lines 71–8 of the *Epithalamion . . . on the Lady Elizabeth and Count Palatine being Married on St Valentines Day*.]

The simile of the clock is an example (not an offensive one) of Donne's peculiar mode of illustration. He scarcely writes a stanza without some ingenious simile of this kind.

The two first lines of the following are very solemn and far-thoughted. There is nothing of the kind in poetry superior to them. I add the lines which succeed them, merely to shew the manner in which the thought is applied.

[He quotes the first stanza of 'Loves Deitie'.]

Of Donne's other poems, the Funeral Elegies, Epistles, Satires, and what he calls his 'Divine Poems,' particularly the last named, we have little to say in the way of general praise, and but few extracts to offer. We shall, however, notice and illustrate each class briefly, in order that the reader may have a fair impression of the whole body of this writer's poetical works.

The Epistles of Donne we like less than any of his other poems, always excepting the religious ones. Not that they are without his usual proportion of subtle thinking, felicitous illustration, and skilful versification; but they are disfigured by more than his usual obscurity—by a harshness of style, that is to be found in few of his other poems, except the satires—by an extravagance of hyperbole in the way of compliment, that often amounts to the ridiculous—and by an evident want of sincerity, that is worse than all. To whomever they are addressed, all are couched in the same style of expression, and reach the same pitch of praise. Every one of his correspondents is, without exception, 'wisest, virtuousest, discreetest, best.' It is as if his letters had been composed at leisure, and kept *ready cut and dried* till wanted.

Though it will not exactly bear quotation, perhaps the most poetical, as well as the most characteristic, of the Epistles is the imaginary one (the only one of that description) from Sappho to Philænis.

The following is finely thought and happily expressed. It is part of an Epistle to Sir Henry Wotton.

[He quotes lines 47–58 of the verse letter 'To Sir Henry Wotton', 'Sir, more then kisses'.]

We can afford no other extract from the Epistles, although many most curious ones might be found; but pass on to the Funeral Elegies. All Donne's poems, even his best, with one or two exceptions, are laboured in the highest degree; and the Funeral Elegies are still more so than any of the others. They have all the faults of his style, and this one above all. Still they abound in passages of great force, depth, and beauty; but none of them will bear extracting entire—at least, none which are properly included in this class. But there is one poem printed among these, which we shall extract the greater portion of, and which the reader will find to be written in a somewhat different style from that of almost all the others that we have quoted. There is a solemn and sincere earnestness about it, which will cause it to be read with great interest, even by those who may not be capable of appreciating, in detail, the rich and pompous flow of the verse, and the fine harmony of its music; the elegant simplicity of the language; and the extreme beauty of some of the thoughts and images.

The poem seems to have been addressed to his mistress, on the occasion of his taking leave of her, after her having offered to attend him on his journey in the disguise of a page. It is headed strangely enough.

[He quotes lines 1–30 of *Elegie xvi*, 'On his Mistris'.]

He then tells her what ills may befall her in the different countries through which she would have to follow him; and concludes:

[He quotes line 43 to the end of the poem.]

It only remains to speak of Donne's Satires; for his Divine Poems must be left to speak for themselves. General readers are probably acquainted with Donne chiefly as a writer of satires; and, in this character, they know him only through the medium of Pope; which is equivalent to knowing Homer only through the same medium. The brilliant and refined modern attempted to give his readers an idea of Donne, by changing his roughness into smoothness, and polishing down his force into point. In fact, he altered Donne into Pope—which was a mere impertinence. Each is admirable in his way—quite enough so to make it impossible to change either, with advantage, into a likeness of any other.

Donne's Satires are as rough and rugged as the unhewn stones that have just been blasted from their native quarry; and they must have come upon the readers at whom they were levelled, with the force and effect of the same stones flung from the hand of a giant. The following detached character is the only specimen we have left ourselves room to give of them. It strikes us as being nearly the perfection of this kind of writing. He says that, for once in his life, going to court,

[He quotes lines 17–108 of *Satyre iv*, putting asterisks for lines 46–8.]

We had intended to close this paper with a few examples of the most glaring faults of Donne's style; but the reader will probably think that we have made better use of our space. We have endeavoured to describe those faults, and the causes of them; and not a few of them—or of those parts which should perhaps be regarded as *characteristics*, rather than absolute faults—will be found among the extracts now given. Those who wish for more may find them in almost every page of the writer's works. They may find the most far-fetched and fantastical allusions and illustrations brought to bear upon the thought or feeling in question, sometimes by the most quick-eyed and subtle ingenuity, but oftener in a manner altogether forced and arbitrary; turns of thought that are utterly at variance with the sentiment and with each other; philosophical and scholastic differences and distinctions, that no sentiment could have suggested, and that nothing but *searching for* could have found; and, above all, paradoxical plays of words, antitheses of thought and expression, and purposed involutions of phrase, that nothing but the most painful attention can untwist. All this they may find, and more. But, in the midst of all, they not only may, but must find an unceasing activity and an overflowing fullness of mind, which seem never to fail or flag, and which would more than half redeem the worst faults (of mere style) that could be allied to them.

141. Walter Savage Landor

1826, 1836

Landor imagined a mid-seventeenth-century conversation between Walton, Oldways, and Cotton, which turned to a celebration of Donne the lover. Landor supplied some verses,
supposedly Donne's unpublished passions, to suit the amorous
attachment he invented for Donne (*Imaginary Conversations,*
English, xv (1829), in *Complete Works,* ed. T. E. Welby and
S. Wheeler, 1927–36, iv, pp. 164–71). The dialogue was written
in 1826.

Landor expressed a less enthusiastic view of Donne a few years
later when he commented on the *Satyres* in lines 108–11 of *A
Satire upon Satirists,* 1836 (in *Complete Works,* xvi, p. 220).

(i)

WALTON. Oldways, I think you were curate to master Donne?

OLDWAYS. When I was first in holy orders, and he was ready for
another world.

WALTON. I have heard it reported that you have some of his earlier
poetry.

OLDWAYS. I have (I believe) a trifle or two: but if he were living he
would not wish them to see the light.

WALTON. Why not? he had nothing to fear: his fame was established; and he was a discreet and holy man.

OLDWAYS. He was almost in his boyhood when he wrote it, being
but in his twenty-third year, and subject to fits of love.

COTTON. This passion then can not have had for its object the
daughter of Sir George More, whom he saw not until afterward.

OLDWAYS. No, nor was that worthy lady called Margaret, as was
this, who scattered so many pearls in his path, he was wont to say, that
he trod uneasily on them and could never skip them.

WALTON. Let us look at them in his poetry.

OLDWAYS. I know not whether he would consent thereto, were he living, the lines running so totally on the amorous.

WALTON. Faith and troth! we mortals are odd fishes. We care not how many see us in choler, when we rave and bluster and make as much noise and bustle as we can: but if the kindest and most generous affection comes across us, we suppress every sign of it, and hide ourselves in nooks and coverts. Out with the drawer, my dear Oldways; we have seen Donne's sting; in justice to him let us now have a sample of his honey.

OLDWAYS. Strange, that you never asked me before.

WALTON. I am fain to write his life, now one can sit by Dove-side and hold the paper upon one's knee, without fear that some unlucky catchpole of a rheumatism tip one upon the shoulder. I have many things to say in Donne's favour: let me add to them, by your assistance, that he not only loved well and truly, as was proved in his marriage, though like a good angler he changed his fly, and did not at all seasons cast his rod over the same water; but that his heart opened early to the genial affections; that his satire was only the overflowing of his wit; that he made it administer to his duties; that he ordered it to officiate as he would his curate, and perform half the service of the church for him.

COTTON. Pray, who was the object of his affections?

OLDWAYS. The damsel was Mistress Margaret Hayes.

COTTON. I am curious to know, if you will indulge my curiosity, what figure of a woman she might be.

OLDWAYS. She was of lofty stature, red-haired (which some folks dislike), but with comely white eyebrows, a very slender transparent nose, and elegantly thin lips, covering with due astringency a treasure of pearls beyond price, which, as her lover would have it, she never ostentatiously displayed. Her chin was somewhat long, with what I should have simply called a sweet dimple in it, quite proportionate; but Donne said it was more than dimple; that it was peculiar; that her angelic face could not have existed without it, nor it without her angelic face; that is, unless by a new dispensation. He was much taken thereby, and mused upon it deeply; calling it in moments of joyousness the cradle of all sweet fancies, and in hours of suffering from her sedateness, the vale of death.

WALTON. So ingenious are men when the spring torrent of passion shakes up and carries away their thoughts, covering (as it were) the green meadow of still homely life with pebbles and shingle, some colourless and obtuse, some sharp and sparkling.

COTTON. I hope he was happy in her at last.

OLDWAYS. Ha! ha! here we have 'em. Strong lines! Happy, no; he was not happy. He was forced to renounce her by what he then called his evil destiny; and wishing, if not to forget her, yet to assuage his grief under the impediments to their union, he made a voyage to Spain and the Azores with the Earl of Essex. When this passion first blazed out he was in his twentieth year; for the physicians do tell us that where the genius is ardent the passions are precocious. The lady had profited by many more seasons than he had, and carried with her manifestly the fruits of circumspection. No benefice falling unto him, nor indeed there being fit preparation, she submitted to the will of Providence. Howbeit, he could not bring his mind to reason until ten years after, when he married the daughter of the worshipful Sir George More. . . .

OLDWAYS. Izaak! our young friend master Cotton is not sedate enough yet, I suspect, for a right view and perception of poetry. I doubt whether these affecting verses on her loss will move him greatly: somewhat, yet; there is in the beginning so much simplicity, in the middle so much reflection, in the close so much grandeur and sublimity, no scholar can peruse them without strong emotion. Take and read them.

COTTON. Come, come; do not keep them to yourself, dad! I have the heart of a man, and will bear the recitation as valiantly as may be.

WALTON. I will read aloud the best stanza only. What strong language!

> Her one hair would hold a dragon,
>   Her one eye would burn an earth:
> Fall, my tears! fill each your flagon!
>   Millions fall! A dearth! a dearth!

COTTON. The Doctor must have been desperate about the fair Margaret.

WALTON. His verses are fine indeed: one feels for him, poor man!

COTTON. And wishes him nearer to Stourbridge, or some other glass-furnace. He must have been at great charges.

OLDWAYS. Lord help the youth! tell him, Izaak, *that* is poetical, and means nothing.

WALTON. He has an inkling of it, I misgive me.

COTTON. How could he write so smoothly in his affliction, when he exhibited nothing of the same knack afterward?

WALTON. I don't know; unless it may be that men's verses like their knees stiffen by age. . . .

WALTON. Is that between thy fingers, Will, another piece of honest old Donne's poetry?

OLDWAYS. Yes; these and one other are the only pieces I have kept: for we often throw away or neglect, in the lifetime of our friends, those things which in some following age are searched after through all the libraries in the world. What I am about to read he composed in the meridian heat of youth and genius.

> She was so beautiful, had God but died
>   For her, and none beside,
> Reeling with holy joy from east to west
>   Earth would have sunk down blest;
> And, burning with bright zeal, the buoyant Sun
>   Cried thro' his worlds *well done*!

He must have had an eye on the Psalmist; for I would not asseverate that he was inspired, master Walton, in the theological sense of the word; but I do verily believe I discover here a thread of the mantle.

COTTON. And with enough of the nap on it to keep him hot as a muffin when one slips the butter in.

OLDWAYS. True. Nobody would dare to speak thus but from authority. The Greeks and Romans, he remarked, had neat baskets, but scanty simples; and did not press them down so closely as they might have done; and were fonder of nosegays than of sweet-pots. He told me the rose of Paphos was of one species, the rose of Sharon of another. Whereat he burst forth to the purpose,

> Rather give me the lasting rose of Sharon,
> But dip it in the oil that oil'd thy beard, O Aaron!

Nevertheless, I could perceive that he was of so equal a mind that he liked them equally in their due season. These majestical verses——

COTTON. I am anxious to hear the last of 'em.

OLDWAYS. No wonder: and I will joyfully gratify so laudable a wish. He wrote this among the earliest:

> Juno was proud, Minerva stern,
> Venus would rather toy than learn.
> What fault is there in Margaret Hayes?
> Her high disdain and pointed stays.

I do not know whether, it being near our dinner-time, I ought to enter so deeply as I could into a criticism on it, which the Doctor himself, in a single evening, taught me how to do.

WALTON. This is the poetry to reason upon from morning to night.

COTTON. By my conscience is it! he wrongs it greatly who ventures to talk a word about it, unless after long reflection, or after the instruction of the profound author.

OLDWAYS. Izaak, thou hast a son worthy of thee, or about to become so—the son here of thy adoption—how grave and thoughtful!

WALTON. These verses are testimonials of a fine fancy in Donne; and I like the man the better who admits Love into his study late and early: for which two reasons I seized the lines at first with some avidity. On second thoughts, however, I doubt whether I shall insert them in my biography, or indeed hint at the origin of them. In the whole story of his marriage with the daughter of Sir George More there is something so sacredly romantic, so full of that which bursts from the tenderest heart and from the purest, that I would admit no other light or landscape to the portraiture. For if there is aught, precedent or subsequent, that offends our view of an admirable character, or intercepts or lessens it, we may surely cast it down and suppress it, and neither be called injudicious nor disingenuous. . . .

OLDWAYS. . . . Donne fell into unhappiness by aiming at espousals with a person of higher condition than himself.

WALTON. His affections happened to alight upon one who was; and in most cases I would recommend it rather than the contrary, for the advantage of the children in their manners and in their professions.

Light and worthless men, I have always observed, choose the society of those who are either much above or much below them; and, like dust and loose feathers, are rarely to be found in their places. Donne was none such: he loved his equals, and would find them where he could: when he could not find them he could sit alone. This seems an easy matter; and yet, masters, there are more people who could run along a rope from yonder spire to this grass-plot, than can do it.

(ii)

> Churchmen have chaunted satire, and the pews
> Heard good sound doctrine from the sable Muse.
> Frost-bitten and lumbaginous, when Donne,
> With verses gnarl'd and knotted, hobbled on. . . .

142. Augustus William Hare and Julius Charles Hare

1827

The brothers Hare, both in holy orders, quoted lines 5–11a of Donne's *Satyre iii* to support their argument that we must contemplate and practise the virtues of the ancients but, as Christians, strive to surpass them (*Guesses at Truth By Two Brothers,* 1st series (1827), 1847, p. 3).

143. Thomas Phillips

1827

The painter Phillips (1770–1845) was Professor of Painting at the Royal Academy from 1825 to 1832. During a course of ten lectures on painting which he gave in 1827 he spoke of early Italian painting, and especially of Giotto's work in the Cappella degli Scrovegni at Padua (*Lectures on the History and Principles of Painting*, 1833, p. 40).

[He recommends all who go to Italy to see Giotto's frescoes in the chapel of the Annunciata at Padua and]

to make that work an object of particular attention, to endeavour to cast aside its gothic imperfections, and seek, what may undoubtedly be found in it, the real source of pathos in our art. It is as the poetry of Chaucer or of Donne, with their uncouth phraseology, full of sense and sentiment.

144. Thomas Hood

1827

In an account of a mock marriage procession Hood used line 85 of Donne's *An Epithalamion . . . on St Valentine's day* to describe the bride and bridegroom as one normally expects to see them (*Whims and Oddities in Prose and Verse*, 2nd series, 1827, p. 128).

I beheld, not a brace of young lovers—a Romeo and Juliet—not a 'he-moon here, and a she-sun there'—not bride and bridegroom—but the happy *pear*, a solitary Bergamy, carried on a velvet cushion by a little foot-page.

145. James Montgomery

1827

Montgomery (1771–1854), journalist, poet, and hymn writer, included two of Donne's *Holy Sonnets* and 'A Hymne to Christ, at the Authors last going into Germany' in a copious selection of pious verses from Chaucer to his own day. He introduced each new poet with a brief note (*The Christian Poet,* Glasgow, 1827, p. 116).

John Donne. Author of many heterogeneous compositions in verse, so harsh as to be scarcely readable, and so obscure as to be scarcely intelligible, yet abounding with shrewd remarks, elaborate wit, and caustic sarcasm. . . .

146. Thomas de Quincey

1828, 1851

De Quincey shared with Lamb and Coleridge an enthusiasm for seventeenth-century writers and even sought to revive the English prose styles of that time. He spoke memorably of Donne in the course of an analytic account of rhetoric, first printed in *Blackwood's Magazine* in 1828 (*Collected Writings*, ed. D. Masson, 1897, x, pp. 96–102).

Many years later, in tracing the history of satire, he put in another word for Donne ('Lord Carlisle on Pope', first published in *Tait's Magazine*, April to July 1851. *Collected Writings*, xi, p. 110).

(i)

In the Literature of Modern Europe Rhetoric has been cultivated with success. But this remark applies only with any force to a period which is now long past; and it is probable, upon various considerations, that such another period will never revolve. The rhetorician's art in its glory and power has silently faded away before the stern tendencies of the age; and, if, by any peculiarity of taste or strong determination of the intellect, a rhetorician *en grande costume* were again to appear amongst us, it is certain that he would have no better welcome than a stare of surprise as a posture-maker or balancer, not more elevated in the general estimate, but far less amusing, than the acrobat, or funambulist, or equestrian gymnast. No; the age of Rhetoric, like that of Chivalry, has passed amongst forgotten things; and the rhetorician can have no more chance for returning than the rhapsodist of early Greece or the troubadour of romance. So multiplied are the modes of intellectual enjoyment in modern times that the choice is absolutely distracted; and in a boundless theatre of pleasures, to be had at little or no cost of intellectual activity, it would be marvellous indeed if any considerable audience could be found for an exhibition which presupposes a state of tense exertion on the part both of auditor and performer. To hang upon one's own thoughts as an object of conscious interest, to play with them, to watch and pursue them through a maze of inversions, evolutions, and harlequin changes, implies a condition of society either, like that in the monastic ages, forced to introvert its energies from mere defect of books (whence arose the scholastic metaphysics, admirable for its subtlety, but famishing the mind whilst it sharpened its edge in one exclusive direction); or, if it implies no absolute starvation of intellect, as in the case of the Roman rhetoric, which arose upon a considerable (though not very various) literature, it proclaims at least a quiescent state of the public mind, unoccupied with daily novelties, and at leisure from the agitations of eternal change.

Growing out of the same condition of society, there is another cause at work which will for ever prevent the resurrection of rhetoric: viz. the necessities of public business, its vast extent, complexity, fulness of details, and consequent vulgarity, as compared with that of the ancients. The very same cause, by the way, furnishes an answer to the question moved by Hume, in one of his essays, with regard to the declension of eloquence in our deliberative assemblies. Eloquence, or at least that which is senatorial and forensic, the pagan religions did not produce much poetry, and of oratory none at all.

On the other hand, that cause which, operating upon eloquence, has but extinguished it under a single direction, to rhetoric has been unconditionally fatal. Eloquence is not banished from the public business of this country as useless, but as difficult, and as not spontaneously arising from topics such as generally furnish the staple of debate. But rhetoric, if attempted on a formal scale, would be summarily exploded as pure foppery and trifling with time. Falstaff on the field of battle presenting his bottle of sack for a pistol, or Polonius with his quibbles, could not appear a more unseasonable *plaisanteur* than a rhetorician alighting from the clouds upon a public assembly in Great Britain met for the despatch of business.

Under these malign aspects of the modern structure of society, a structure to which the whole world will be moulded as it becomes civilized, there can be no room for any revival of rhetoric in public speaking, and, from the same and other causes, acting upon the standard of public taste, quite as little room in written composition. In spite, however, of the tendencies to this consummation, which have been long ripening, it is a fact that, next after Rome, England is the country in which rhetoric prospered most at a time when science was unborn as a popular interest, and the commercial activities of aftertimes were yet

sleeping in their rudiments. This was in the period from the latter end
of the sixteenth to the middle of the seventeenth century; and, though
the English Rhetoric was less rigorously true to its own ideal than the
Roman, and often modulated into a higher key of impassioned eloquence, yet unquestionably in some of its qualities it remains a monument of the very finest rhetorical powers.

Omitting Sir Philip Sidney, and omitting his friend, Fulke Greville,
Lord Brooke (in whose prose there are some bursts of pathetic eloquence,
as there is of rhetoric in his verse, though too often harsh and cloudy),
the first very eminent rhetorician in the English Literature is Donne.
Dr. Johnson inconsiderately classes him in company with Cowley, &c.,
under the title of *Metaphysical* Poets: metaphysical they were not;
Rhetorical would have been a more accurate designation. In saying *that*,
however, we must remind our readers that we revert to the original
use of the word *Rhetoric*, as laying the principal stress upon the management of the thoughts, and only a secondary one upon the ornaments of
style. Few writers have shown a more extraordinary compass of powers
than Donne; for he combined—what no other man has ever done—the
last sublimation of dialectical subtlety and address with the most impassioned majesty. Massy diamonds compose the very substance of his
poem on the Metempsychosis, thoughts and descriptions which have
the fervent and gloomy sublimity of Ezekiel or Æschylus, whilst a
diamond dust of rhetorical brilliances is strewed over the whole of his
occasional verses and his prose. No criticism was ever more unhappy
than that of Dr. Johnson's which denounces all this artificial display as
so much perversion of taste. There cannot be a falser thought than this;
for upon that principle a whole class of compositions might be vicious
by conforming to its own ideal. The artifice and machinery of rhetoric
furnishes in its degree as legitimate a basis for intellectual pleasure as
any other; that the pleasure is of an inferior order, can no more attaint
the idea or model of the composition than it can impeach the excellence
of an epigram that it is not a tragedy. Every species of composition is
to be tried by its own laws; and, if Dr. Johnson had urged explicitly
(what was evidently moving in his thoughts) that a metrical structure, by
holding forth the promise of poetry, defrauds the mind of its just
expectations, he would have said what is notoriously false. Metre is
open to any form of composition, provided it will aid the expression of
the thoughts; and the only sound objection to it is that it has *not* done
so. Weak criticism, indeed, is that which condemns a copy of verses
under the ideal of poetry, when the mere substitution of another name

and classification suffices to evade the sentence, and to reinstate the composition in its rights as rhetoric. It may be very true that the age of Donne gave too much encouragement to his particular vein of composition. That, however, argues no depravity of taste, but a taste erring only in being too limited and exclusive.

(ii)
In Marston and in Donne (a man yet unappreciated) satire first began to respire freely, but applying itself too much, as in the great dramatists contemporary with Shakespeare, to the exterior play of society.

147. Robert Browning

c. 1828–86

Browning succeeded Coleridge as Donne's leading advocate in the nineteenth century, and his continuing admiration for Donne's poetry became notorious. The two poets were often compared, and there seems no doubt that Browning himself felt a degree of artistic kinship with Donne (see J. E. Duncan, 'The Intellectual Kinship of John Donne and Robert Browning', *S.P.*, L, 1953, pp. 81–100).

(i) As a boy, *c.* 1828, Browning 'wrote music for songs which he himself sang: among them Donne's "Goe, and catche a falling starre" . . . and his settings, all of which he subsequently destroyed, were, I am told, very spirited . . .' (Mrs A. Orr, *Life and Letters of Robert Browning*, 1908, p. 41).

(ii) Browning told a correspondent that he had dreamed of Donne when he had a bad sore throat in 1835, immediately before writing *Paracelsus* (letter to Julia Wedgwood, 17 October 1864. In *Robert Browning and Julia Wedgwood*, ed. R. Curle, 1937, p. 102):

I remember I was a little lightheaded one long night, and fancied I had to go through a complete version of the Psalms by Donne, Psalm by Psalm! Fact!

(iii) In 1842 an admirer presented Browning with a copy of the 1719 edition of Donne's poems, inscribing it 'To Robert Browning, Esq. from Thos. Powell, June 12, 1842'. The book came up for auction at Sotheby's in May 1913 among the effects of R. W. Browning, who had just died, and was sold to Elkin Matthews for £2. It is listed in the catalogue of the sale, *Catalogue of The Browning Collections*, 1913, p. 94 (given in *Sales Catalogues of Libraries of Eminent Persons*, vi, ed. J. Woolford, 1972, p. 121).

(iv) Elizabeth Barrett several times spoke of 'your Donne' in her early letters to Browning, quoting *Satyre ii* and 'The Will'; and Browning, replying, aptly wove in quotations from a verse letter, the *Epithalamion . . . St Valentines day*, and 'A Valediction: forbidding Mourning' (*The Letters of Robert Browning and Elizabeth Barrett Browning 1845–6*, ed. R. B. Browning, 1899, i, pp. 27, 145, 196, 420, 440; ii, p. 116).

In this famous correspondence Browning used Donne at times to suggest a motive he could not explicitly avow. There is an interesting instance in a letter written on 11 September 1845, the day before the meeting in which they declared their love to each other for the first time. Miss Barrett had been talking of a trip to Italy she might make with some of her family, and Browning urged her to go. He returned to the subject a little later, saying that another of his wishes had just come true—he had found out the pet name by which her family knew her:

So, wish by wish, one gets one's wishes—at
least I do—for one instance, you will go to Italy

Why, 'lean and harken after it' as Donne says—

The musical phrase, which Browning closes with a large question mark, is the opening of an aria from Gluck's *Orpheus and Euridice*—'*Che Farò . . .?*', 'What shall I do without you, Euridice?'; and the quotation replies that he will 'lean and hearken after' her, as the separated lovers respond to each other in Donne's poem. It amounts to a discreet avowal, preparing the way for the open declaration of love that ensued.[1]

(v) Sir John Simeon presented Browning with a copy of his 'Unpublished Poems of Donne' (see No. 187) which came out in 1856–7. Browning wrote on the title page 'Robert Browning from Sir John Simeon'. The copy was sold to Elkin Matthews for £3 10s. at Sotheby's in May 1913. (See the *Catalogue of the Browning Collections*, 1913, p. 94, in *Sale Catalogues of Libraries of Eminent Persons*, vi, ed. J. Woolford, 1972, p. 121.)

(vi) Sir Sidney Colvin, looking back to the acquaintance of his early manhood, *c.* 1865, recalled Browning's 'coming out once with a long crabbedly fine screed from John Donne'. It was the Elegie on M[ris] Boulstred (*Memories and Notes of Persons and Places, 1852–1912*, 1921, p. 82).

(vii) William Rossetti made an entry in his diary for 1869 (W. M. Rossetti, *Rossetti Papers 1862–70*, 1903, p. 378):

Thurs. 7 January. Browning and others came to Euston Square. B. speaks with great enthusiasm of a poem by Donne named *Metempsychosis*.

(viii) A. B. Grosart dedicated to Browning his edition of Donne's poems, 1872–3, with an acknowledgment of Browning's particular interest in Donne:

TO

ROBERT BROWNING,

THE POET OF THE CENTURY FOR THINKERS,

I DEDICATE

THIS FIRST COMPLETE EDITION OF THE POEMS OF

JOHN DONNE

(BORN 1573, DIED 1631);

KNOWING HOW MUCH HIS POETRY,

WITH EVERY ABATEMENT,

IS VALUED AND ASSIMILATED BY HIM:

RIGHT FAITHFULLY,

ALEXANDER B. GROSART.

[1] Mrs K. Tillotson takes the quotation itself for a neutral inquiry—'he asks her why she should lean and hearken after Italy' ('Donne's Poetry in the Nineteenth Century', in *Elizabethan and Jacobean Studies*, ed. Herbert Davis and Helen Gardner, Oxford, 1959, p. 324). I do not see that this is a possible reading of the passage.

Browning owned and signed his name in a copy of Grosart's edition, which was sold for £3 5s. at Sotheby's in May 1913. He also owned and signed a copy of volume i of the edition which was sold on the same occasion for £2 15s. (See the *Catalogue of the Browning Collections*, 1913, p. 94, in *Sales Catalogues of Libraries of Eminent Persons*, vi, ed. J. Woolford, 1972, p. 121.)

(ix) Browning quoted and praised Donne's *Metempsychosis* in stanza 114 of his *The Two Poets of Crosic*, published in 1878:

> *He's greatest now and to de-struc-ti-on*
> *Nearest.* Attend the solemn word I quote,
> O Paul! *There's no pause at per-fec-ti-on.*
> Thus knolls thy knell the Doctor's bronzed throat!
> *Greatness a period hath, no sta-ti-on!*
> Better and truer verse none ever wrote
> (Despite the antique outstretched *a-i-on*)
> Than thou, revered and magisterial Donne!

(x) In another poem, 'Epps', dated 1886, Browning describes a heroic episode in the siege of Ostend and has Donne and Dekker writing verses to celebrate it. (The poem was printed posthumously in *The Cornhill Magazine* and *The New York Outlook* in October 1913, and has never appeared in a collected edition of Browning's poems. It is given in *New Poems by Robert Browning and Elizabeth Barrett Browning*, ed. F. G. Kenyon, London, 1914, pp. 56–9.)

Browning describes how one Epps, a Kentishman, took the flag from its staff and wrapped it round his own body, then 'shot and slashed' to the point of death, staggered back to save it:

> And die did Epps, with his English round:
> Not so the fame of the feat:
> For Donne and Dekker, brave poets and rare,
> Gave it honour and praise: and I join the pair
> With heart that's loud though my voice compete
> As a pipe with their trumpet-sound!

Dekker does in fact tell the story of '*William Eps his death*' in prose, otherwise just as Browning describes it, in *A Knights Coniuring. Donne in earnest: Discovered in Iest*, 1607, 14^r–K1^v. Possibly Browning had the epigram on Wingfield in mind when he coupled Donne with Dekker here.

148. Mrs Anna Murphy Jameson

1829

Mrs Jameson (1794–1860) wrote essays on art, on famous women, and the like, and devoted much time to sick nursing. In a sentimental account of Donne's marriage and married life she made a few comments on his poetry (*Memoirs of the Loves of the Poets*, 1829, pp. 94–109).

CONJUGAL POETRY CONTINUED.
STORY OF DR. DONNE AND HIS WIFE.

My next instance of conjugal poetry is taken from the literary history of our own country, and founded on as true and touching a piece of romance as ever was taken from the page of real life.

Dr. Donne, once so celelebrated as a writer, now so neglected, is more interesting for his matrimonial history, and for one little poem addressed to his wife, than for all his learned, metaphysical, and theological productions. As a poet, it is probable that even readers of poetry know little of him, except from the lines at the bottom of the pages in Pope's version, or rather translation, of his Satires, the very recollection of which is enough to 'set one's ears on edge,' and verify Coleridge's witty and imitative couplet.—

> Donne—whose muse on dromedary trots,—
> Twists iron pokers into true love knots.

It is this inconceivable harshness of versification, which has caused Donne to be so little read, except by those who make our old poetry their study. One of these critics has truly observed, that 'there is scarce a writer in our language who has so thoroughly mixed up the good and the bad together.' What is good, is the result of truth, of passion, of a strong mind, and a brilliant wit: what is bad, is the effect of a most perverse taste, and total want of harmony. No sooner has he kindled the fancy with a splendid thought, than it is as instantly quenched in a

351

cloud of cold and obscure conceits: no sooner has he touched the heart with a feeling or sentiment, true to nature and powerfully expressed, than we are chilled or disgusted by pedantry or coarseness.

[She quotes in full *Elegie xvi*, 'On his Mistris', in the 1669 version.]

I would not have the heart of one who could read these lines, and think only of their rugged style, and faults of taste and expression. The superior power of truth and sentiment have immortalised this little poem, and the occasion which gave it birth. The wife and husband parted, and he left with her another little poem which he calls a 'Valediction, forbidding to mourn.'

Among Donne's earlier poetry may be distinguished the following little song, which has so much more harmony and elegance than his other pieces, that it is scarcely a fair specimen of his style. It was long popular, and I can remember when a child, hearing it sung to very beautiful music.

[She quotes 'The Message' in full.]

Perhaps it may interest some readers to add, that Donne's famous lines, which have been quoted *ad infinitum*,—

> The pure and eloquent blood
> Spoke in her cheeks, and so distinctly wrought,
> Ye might have almost said her body thought!

were not written on his wife, but on Elizabeth Drury, the only daughter of his patron and friend, Sir Robert Drury.

149. William Godwin

1831

Godwin (1756–1836), radical thinker, essayist, novelist, was a sometime associate of Coleridge and Shelley, and the father of Mary Wollstonecraft Shelley. He spoke of Donne in his *Thoughts on Man, His Nature, Productions, and Discoveries*, 1831, pp. 3–4 and 83.

What a miraculous thing is the human complexion! We are sent into the world naked, that all the variations of the blood might be made visible. However trite, I cannot avoid quoting here the lines of the most deep-thinking and philosophical of our poets . . .

[He quotes lines 243b–46 of *The second Anniversary*.]

[Later in the book Godwin writes of European poets.] One of the most admired of our English poets about the close of the sixteenth century was Donne. Unlike many of those trivial writers of verse who succeeded him after an interval of forty or fifty years, and who won for themselves a brilliant reputation by the smoothness of their numbers, the elegance of their conceptions, and the politeness of their style, Donne was full of originality, energy, and vigour. No man can read him without feeling himself called upon for earnest exercise of his thinking powers, and even with the most fixed attention and application, the student is often obliged to confess his inability to take in the whole of the meaning with which the poet's mind was perceptibly fraught. Every sentence that Donne writes, whether in verse or prose, is exclusively his own. In addition to this, his thoughts are often in the noblest sense of the word poetical; and passages may be quoted from him that no English poet may attempt to rival, unless it be Milton and Shakespeare. Ben Jonson observed of him with great truth and a prophetic spirit: 'Donne for not being understood will perish'. But this is not all. If Waller and Suckling and Carew sacrificed every thing to the Graces, Donne went into the other extreme. With a few splendid

353

and admirable exceptions, his phraseology and versification are crabbed and repulsive. And, as poetry is read in the first place for pleasure, Donne is left undisturbed on the shelf, or rather in the sepulchre; and not one in an hundred even among persons of cultivation, can give any account of him, if in reality they ever heard of his productions.

150. Alexander Dyce

1833, ?1850

Dyce (1798–1869), a clergyman, was a prolific editor of old texts. He included Donne's *Holy Sonnet x*, 'Death be not proud', in his *Specimens of English Sonnets*, 1833, p. 108, and commented on the poem in the Notes, p. 214. Dyce owned a copy of the 1633 edition of Donne's poems, and some time later than 1833 he made several pages of notes in the endpapers. This copy is now in the Dyce Collection of the Victoria and Albert Museum, press mark D.25.D15.

(i) *Sonnet by John Donne*, p. 108] Deep-thoughted, and forcible—from the first edition of his *Poems*, 1633.

(ii) One page of the notes Dyce made in his copy of Donne's poems, 1633, is taken up with a list of the unusual words and phrases which Donne uses. On another page Dyce records his observations as he read through the volume from beginning to end. He notes some words omitted or misprinted in the 1633 edition and supplies or corrects them from a later seventeenth-century text of the poems. He recalls Wordsworth's high opinion of *Holy Sonnet x*, 'Death be not proud' (see No. 151). He lists some phrases which Milton and Pope seem to have imitated from Donne, giving reference to Pope's *Eloisa to Abelard* and *The Rape of the Lock*. And he indicates passages he admired—' "her pure and eloquent blood," &c' (*The second Anniversary*, line 244), ' "And, though thou beest," &c. A grand passage' ('Elegie on Mris Boulstred', line 31).

354

151. William Wordsworth

1833

Wordsworth wrote to Alexander Dyce early in 1833 advising him on the choice of poems for an anthology, *Specimens of English Sonnets*, which came out later in that year. (*The Letters of William and Dorothy Wordsworth: The Later Years*, ed. E. de Selincourt, Oxford, 1939, ii, p. 652. The text given below is reproduced from the manuscript in the Dyce collection, Victoria and Albert Museum.) Dyce included Donne's *Holy Sonnet x*, 'Death be not proud', at Wordsworth's suggestion, and noted Wordsworth's regard for this sonnet in a copy of the 1633 edition of Donne's poems now in the Dyce collection, Victoria and Albert Museum: 'When I was preparing my *Specimens of English Sonnets*, Wordsworth wrote to me to request that I would not overlook this one, which he thought very fine.'

. . . It should seem that the best rule to follow, would be, first to pitch upon the Sonnets which are best *both* in kind and perfectness of execution, and next those, which, although of a humbler quality, are admirable for the finish and happiness of the execution, taking care to exclude all those which have not one or other of these recommendations, however striking they might be as characteristic of the age in which the author lived, or some peculiarity of his manner.— The tenth sonnet of Donne, beginning 'Death be not proud', is so eminently characteristic of his manner, and at the same time so weighty in thought and vigorous in the expression that I would entreat you to insert it, though to modern taste it may be repulsive or quaint and laboured. . . .

152. James Augustus St John

1835

St John (1801–75) was a traveller, journalist, and historian, who sometimes tried his hand at fiction. For his exotic tales he took mottoes from the English poets, and twice used lines by Donne. He gave lines 91b–92 of *Satyre iv* as the former of two mottoes to chapter XLVII of *Tales of the Ramad'han*, 1835, iii, p. 17, and lines 53–4 of *Elegie xvi*, 'On his Mistris', as the motto of a story called 'Hell's Hollow' which appeared in the periodical *Friendship's Offering*, 1835, pp. 321–45. Donne's lines aptly introduce 'Hell's Hollow', which is a Gothic melodrama about banditry in the French Alps and describes a murderous attack in a narrow precipitous place.

153. Richard Cattermole and Henry Stebbing

1836

The compilers of an anthology of seventeenth-century religious poetry, both clergymen-authors, devoted some twenty-three pages of it to Donne's verse. They give one stanza from the *Metempsychosis*, a sonnet from *La Corona*, six *Holy Sonnets*, the funeral elegy 'Death I recant', the verse letter to Goodyer 'Who makes the Past, a patterne for next yeare' (retitled 'Improvement'), an excerpt from *The Lamentations of Jeremy*, a long excerpt from *The second Anniversary*, and 'A Hymne to Christ, at the Authors last going into Germany'.

The extracts that follow are taken from the essay which introduces the volume, and the brief life of Donne prefixed to the selection of his poems (*Sacred Poetry of the Seventeenth Century*, 1836, ii, pp. xi and 53).

(i)
It may appear paradoxical, to say of the poets of the Seventeenth Century that they were not artificial. They were so, in style and manner; not in sentiment and opinion. From the most fanciful of the school of Donne and Cowley it is easy to strip off the out-growth of affectation and conceit; and discover the opinions and feelings of the writer in all their plainness and genuine simplicity beneath. . . .

(ii)
He was the first, and certainly the most vigorous of that poetical school which the critics have held up to ridicule under the character of 'metaphysical',—a term sufficiently alarming to modern ears to have had the effect of limiting the popularity of those writers who have been assigned to the class so stigmatized. Another inexpiable offence of

Donne is the harshness of his versification. Admitting that he is frequently rugged and sometimes obscure, the judicious critic will yet not deny to this once favourite writer, the praise of a true and often a delightful poet; nor will it surprise him, that more than is needful has been said on both points, in times which abound with readers more capable of relishing voluptuous sweetness of language than of appreciating depth of sentiment and originality of thought; and ignorant that it is necessary to reflect on what is read, if we would correctly judge and effectually profit. There is much, undoubtedly, in the volume of Donne's Poems, which cannot be more fitly disposed of, than as 'Alms for Oblivion'; but there is also much, for the sake of which it is worth while making one more attempt to avert the fulfilment of Ben Jonson's prediction that 'for want of being understood he would perish'.

154. Samuel Carter Hall

1836

Hall, expatriate Irish author and editor, gave eight of Donne's *Songs and Sonnets* and an excerpt from the verse letter 'The Storme' in an anthology of English verse. The *Songs and Sonnets* are 'The Good-morrow', 'The Will', 'The Baite', 'Loves Deitie', 'Breake of Day', 'The Legacie', 'Song. Sweetest love, I do not goe', 'Song. Goe, and catche a falling starre'. In a brief biographical notice of Donne which precedes the poems, Hall spoke of Donne's marriage and its consequences for his poetry (*The Book of Gems*, 1836, p. 122).

. . . we have a beautiful though a mournful picture of the struggle of a high and generous mind against the most galling of all troubles. . . . His Poems . . . appear rather as outbreaks of deep feeling, or reliefs to pressing troubles, than the produce of any settled purpose. His name as a poet is, however, largely known and esteemed—notwithstanding his perpetual affectations and the occasional unmeasured harshness of his verse.

[He quotes Dryden on Donne's *Satyres*.]

Pope acted upon this hint; but while he gave them roundness and polish, he lessened the value of the rough and rugged masses which the Poet had heaved from the quarry of human life.

The specimens we have given will abundantly prove that all the compositions of Donne were not careless and uncouth. Some of them indeed are, by comparison, smooth even to elegance. His faults are, that he has made the natural subordinate to the artificial—that he has little of simplicity and less of taste—that he has laboured to render himself obscure rather than intelligible;—and, although his productions are liable to any complaint but that of poverty, that he has crowded thought upon thought and image upon image, with so little skill or care to effect—has, in fact, so mingled beauties with deformities, that those who look with but a casual glance perceive only objects that dishearten them from desiring a nearer and more scrutinizing view. He was absolutely saturated with learning—his intellect was large and searching—his fancy rich, although fantastic—and his wit playful yet caustic. At times he is full of tenderness; and in spite of himself submits to the mastery of nature.

[He alludes to Drummond's claim that Ben Jonson knew some of Donne's verses by heart.]

. . . and other readers will at least agree with 'Old Ben' in his admiration of a passage in which a Calm is described as so perfect, that

in one place lay
Feathers and dust today and yesterday.

155. Edgar Allan Poe

1836

Poe reviewed S. C. Hall's *The Book of Gems* (see No. 154) and took the opportunity to characterise the 'Old English Muse', by which he seems chiefly to have meant the seventeenth-century poets. In the course of the brief review he quotes Wotton's 'You meaner beauties of the night' and attacks it savagely as naked, awkward, threadbare, without fancy, without a jot of imagination. He praises Corbet's 'Farewell Rewards and Fairies'; and he enthuses over Marvell's 'The Nymph complaining for the death of her Faun' as redolent with poetry of the very loftiest order, in which every line is an idea and there is great variety of truth and delicate thought. (*The Southern Literary Messenger*, August 1836. In *The Complete Works of Edgar Allan Poe*, ed. J. A. Harrison, New York, 1902, pp. 94–6.)

. . . the general character of the old English Muse. She was a maid, frank, guileless, and perfectly sincere, and although very learned at times, still very learned without art. No general error evinces a more thorough confusion of ideas than the error of supposing Donne and Cowley metaphysical in the sense wherein Wordsworth and Coleridge are so.

With the two former ethics were the end—with the two latter the means. The poet of *The Creation* wished, by highly artificial verse, to inculcate what he considered moral truth—he of the *Ancient Mariner* to infuse the *Poetic Sentiment* through channels suggested by mental analysis. The one finished by complete failure what he commenced in the grossest misconception—the other by a path which could not possibly lead him astray, arrived at a certainty and intensity of triumph which is not the less brilliant and glorious because concentrated among the very few who have the power to perceive it. It will now be seen that even the 'metaphysical verse' of Cowley is no more than the evidence of the straight-forward simplicity and single-heartedness of the man. And he was in all this but a type of his school—for we may as well designate in this way the entire class of writers whose poems are bound up in the volume before us, and throughout all of whom runs a very perceptible general character. They used but little art in composition. Their writings sprang immediately from the soul—and partook intensely of the nature of that soul. It is not difficult to perceive the tendency of this glorious *abandon*. To elevate immeasurably all the energies of the mind—but again—so as to mingle the greatest possible fire, force, delicacy, and all good things, with the lowest possible bathos, baldness, and utter imbecility, as to render it not a matter of doubt, but of certainty, that the average results of mind in such a school, will be found inferior to those results in one (ceteris paribus) more artificial: Such, we think, is the view of the older English Poetry, in which a very calm examination will bear us out. The quaintness in manner of which we were just speaking, is an adventitious advantage. It formed no portion of the poet's intention. Words and their rhythms have varied. Verses which affect us to-day with a vivid delight, and which in some instances, may be traced to this one source of grotesqueness and to none other, must have worn in the days of their construction an air of a very commonplace nature. This is no argument, it will be said, against the poems *now*. Certainly not—we mean it for the poets *then*. The notion of *power*, of excessive *power*, in the English antique writers should be put in its proper light. This is all we desire to see done.

We cannot bring ourselves to believe that the selections made use of in the *Book of Gems*, are such as will impart to a poetical reader the highest possible idea of the beauty of the *school*. Better extracts might be made. Yet if the intention were merely to show the *character* of the school the attempt is highly successful. There are long passages now before us of the most utterly despicable trash, with no merit whatever beyond their simple antiquity. And it is almost needless to say that there are many passages too of a glorious strength—a radiant loveliness, making the blood tingle in our veins as we peruse them. The criticisms of the Editor do not please us in a great degree. He seems to have fallen into the common cant in such cases. . . .

156. George Godfrey Cunningham

1836

Cunningham (*fl.* 1829–68), a Scottish writer and compiler, gave a Life of Donne in a collection of English Lives. He makes a few remarks on Donne's poetry (*Lives of Eminent and Illustrious Englishmen*, Glasgow and Edinburgh, 1834–7, iii, pp. 240–2). He republished the life in *The English Nation; or A History of England in the Lives of Englishmen*, 1863–8, ii, pp. 428–30.

. . . he gave up close study for a season, and betook himself to the easier and pleasanter task of inditing amorous verses. For a time this employment satisfied him, and his poetry, though often grossly indelicate in language and ideas, became highly popular, and introduced him to the company of the young men of fashion of the day, with whom he launched out into such extravagances as quickly dissipated his fortune.

Donne's mind, however, was naturally of a studious and contemplative cast, and he soon recovered himself from the temporary delusion into which he had allowed himself to be betrayed. . . .

[He quotes Dryden on Donne's poetry, then adds]

His satires are pungent and forcible, but exceedingly rugged and uncouth in their versification.

[He quotes Pope's remark that Donne's satires would be generally admired if they were translated into numbers and English.]

157. Alfred John Kempe

1836

Kempe (?1785–1846) was an antiquary, and sometime civil servant at the state paper office, who wrote books and articles on ancient monuments and other antiquarian matters. His description of the papers at Loseley House, Surrey, included an account of Donne's marriage and career. Loseley House was the home of the More family into which Donne married; and among the documents preserved there were the pleading letters Donne wrote from confinement to Sir George More and Sir Thomas Egerton after the disclosure of the clandestine marriage, and his own draft of the epitaph for his wife. Kempe printed a number of Donne's letters for the first time, from the holographs, introducing them with some observations on Donne's writings (*The Loseley Manuscripts*, 1836, pp. 325–6).

His poetry abounds with figures suggested by an imagination of the brightest class; but it is greatly deteriorated, and rendered perhaps altogether unpalatable to the reader of the modern school, by the vice of his day, the sedulous pursuit of far-fetched quaint conceits.

158. Anon., *The Quarterly Review*

1837

From an anonymous review of H. N. Coleridge's *The Literary Remains of Samuel Taylor Coleridge* (see No. 112), in *The Quarterly Review*, lix, no. xviii, July and October 1837, p. 6.

The framework of the course of lectures delivered in 1818 has enabled the editor to find a place for numerous scattered criticisms upon books or authors mentioned by Mr Coleridge as he went along; and some of these are among the most agreeable things he ever wrote. On Donne's poetry he says

[The reviewer quotes Coleridge's quatrain on Donne, 'With Donne, whose muse on dromedary trots . . .', the description of 'The wit of Donne' which Coleridge wrote in Gillman's copy of Chalmers's *English Poets*, (see No. 112(xi)), and Coleridge's marginal reply to Theobald's note on *Hamlet*, Act 2, Scene 2 (see No. 112(ix)). He then raises Coleridge's question—'Why are not Donne's volumes of sermons reprinted at Oxford?']

Surely the character of some of his juvenile *poems* cannot be the reason! Donne's Life is placed in a cheap form in the catalogue of the Society for Promoting Christian Knowledge, and deservedly so in every respect. Why does Oxford allow one hundred and thirty sermons of the greatest *preacher*, at least, of the seventeenth century—the admired of all hearers—to remain all but totally unknown to the students in divinity of the Church of England, and to the literary world in general? Would we could hope to see Donne and Field, and some others of our old divines, edited in succession with the judgment and learning which distinguish the late Clarendon Hooker?

159. Anon., *The Penny Cyclopaedia*

1837

The following is an extract from an anonymous essay entitled 'John Donne' in *The Penny Cyclopaedia of the Society for the Diffusion of Useful Knowledge,* 1837, ix, p. 85.

As a poet, Donne was one of those writers whom Johnson has (to use Wordsworth's expression) 'strangely' designated metaphysical poets; a more infelicitous expression could not well have been devised.

In the biography of Cowley, Johnson has committed an unintentional injustice towards Donne. By representing Cowley's faults as the faults of a school, he brings forward parallel passages from other authors containing like faults, and Donne is one of them. He has previously described the school as a set of unfeeling pedants, and hence the reader finding Donne's worst lines cited in illustration of that remark, may easily imagine that he never did anything better, and set him down as a mere pedantic rhymer.

The fact is, that 'quaint conceits' are only the deformities of Donne's poetical spirit: the man himself had a rich vein of poetry, which was rarely concealed even when most laboriously encumbered, while some of his pieces, both for thought and even melody, are absolute gems. His fault, far from being coldness, is too much erotic fervour: he allows his imagination to run loose into the most prurient expressions; and on some of his amatory pieces, the conceits stand as a corrective to their excessive warmth. His satires, though written in a measure inconceivably harsh, are models of strength and energy. Their merits were discovered by Pope, who (to use his own odd phrase) translated them into English. . . .

We beg leave to call the attention of those readers who study the progress of their own language to one fact, and that is, that whilst many of the pieces of Donne, written in lyric measures, are absolute music, what he has composed in the heroic measure is painfully uncouth and barbarous. Thus, though the invention of heroic verse took place at an early period (it is attributed to Chaucer), we find that a language must be in a highly cultivated state before this kind of verse can be written in perfection.

160. George Henry Lewes

1838

Lewes is almost certainly the author of an unsigned magazine article entitled 'Donne's Poetical Works', the seventh of a series of 'Retrospective Reviews', published in *The National Magazine and Monthly Critic*, ix, April 1838, pp. 374–8. The 'L.H.' whose marginalia he quotes must be Lewes's friend Leigh Hunt.

Honest John Donne—rough—hearty—pointed and sincere, well worthy art thou to be placed in this retrospective gallery! Donne was in every sense a *man*, and though tinged with the pedantic *concetti* of his time, humanity with its still strength pushed aside the silken cords of affectation.

'Literature,' says Goëthe, profoundly, 'is a fragment of fragments; the least part of that which has happened and has been said (*thought* had been the better term, for little that is said is time-worthy) has been written: of what has been written, the least part has survived.' Deeply impressed with the truth of this remark, we are anxious that the best part of this wondrous mind-fragment should be preserved, and for this purpose use our endeavours to recal attention to what was once justly prized.

In Donne's poetry there is much to delight, and much food for thought; but it is also liable to much censure considered as art. Let us briefly glance at his faults, and then turn our attention to the beauties, for he is one of those nuts under whose rough exterior lies a kernel worth cracking for.

At ingenium ingens inculto latet hoc sub corpore;

as Horace says of another (what he could hardly say of himself, since the outward form is his peculiar charm.)

That Donne's, 'poems' are not poems at all, may be very readily granted; but they are a very pleasant repertory of thought, wit, fancy and conceits, and therefore worthy to be read. As we dismiss the idea altogether of considering them as poems, it will be merely necessary to state that his poetical sins are *concetti*; ruggedness of versification, which is indeed nothing but measured prose, and very bad prose, as far as relates to style; want of consistency and harmony, nay, even truth, in his illustrations; and an almost total deficiency of imagination, or any feeling of art. Yet is he full of wit, subtlety, and fancy. Thus he calls 'night,'

> *Time's dead low-water.*

And he says of a strange animal that ran to him,

> A thing which would have posed Adam to name,
> Stranger than seven antiquaries studies;
> Stranger than strangers.

Again,—

> He rushes in as if 'Arm, arm,'
> He meant to cry; and though *his face be as ill*
> *As theirs, which in old hangings whip Christ*, still
> He strives to look worse.

The image in the third line is very expressive. You see the rustling arras, and on it worked the figures of men, the malignity of whose faces, tells us how a strong feeling in the worker's mind has risen into art, which is but its realization.

In his beautiful eclogue, he has a fine Shaksperian conceit,—

> May never age nor error overthwart
> *With any West those radiant eyes—with any North this heart.*

And in the next stanza,—

> Every part to dance and revel goes;
> They tread the air, and fall not where they rose,
> Tho' six hours since the sun to bed did part,
> The masks and banquets will not yet impart
> *The sunset to these weary eyes, a centre to this heart.*

His idea of absence being love-peopled, as conveyed in the two following lines, is eminently poetical,—

Thou art not gone, being gone; where'er thou art
Thou leavest in him thy watchful eyes, in him thy loving heart.

A dear friend, (L.H.) whose volume we quote from, and who has marked these passages, writes at the conclusion of his eclogue, 'The burden of this ode has a fine earnest sound of enthusiasm—a rushing fire. But what an ode when we think on the history of the parties! Donne's faith, however, was no doubt, good and true; and let us hope that there were more circumstances than we are aware of to extenuate, if possible, the crimes of Carr and his wife; one there certainly was— they were victims of their own beauty'. . . .

To return to Donne. That *man is a microcosm* we have repeatedly endeavoured to enforce; he is, indeed, the world's epitome. His struggles are the struggles of the world—his elements are the elements of the world—his physical revolutions are the physical revolutions of the world—and what is more, the soul is supreme in both! Thus tersely and finely does Donne express it,—

> *I am a little world, made cunningly*
> *Of elements and an angelic sprite.*

But he is not equally Platonic when he says—

> Nor hours, days, months, which are the *rags of Time.*

He has been accused of mixing his love poetry with laboured conceits, and we must say is in general open to the imputation; but it was the fault of the age, and even Shakspeare often destroys a passage by it; and Petrarch is far more culpable in this respect; indeed, all the Italian love poetry has the same blemish. But we suspect that there exists a great confusion abroad between conceits and extravagance; and while it is admitted that the true language of Passion can never translate itself into conceits, yet there is a law in Nature, and consequently it becomes a canon in criticism, that the *language of passion is ever extravagant,* and when *Guarini* says in the *Pastor Fido*—

> S'io miro il tuo bel viso
> Amore è un paradiso.

Which may be rendered—

> When I see those soul-lit eyes,
> Love becomes my Paradise.

it is evident that he is guilty of hyperbole, but not the less natural for

369

all that;★ and the following passage from Donne is the true language of passion, which will appear unnatural only to those who never felt *une grande* passion—

[He quotes the first stanza of 'The Good-morrow'.]

'*The Will*' is an exquisite piece of wit—out of which we extract some couplets, by way of a taste, 'I give,' says he—

[He quotes 'The Will', lines 5–6, 10–11, 28–31, 38–9.]

The poem called 'Metempsychosis,' is considered by the friend, before alluded to, to be spurious. 'From the versification of this poem,' says he on a most niggardly margin, 'I do not believe it to be Donne's. It has the tone and measure of a later age, and might have been written by Sedley or Buckingham. Somebody has ignorantly attributed it to Donne, from meeting with similar opinions in some of his poems; but Donne has always the weight and imagery of old plate in him, compared with this smoother metal.'—With this we entirely agree—Long live *marginalia*!

We shall now quote two more beauties, and then leave the reader to seek the rest with a whetted appetite.—

> And my head
> With *Care's harsh sudden hoariness* o'erspread.

A superb image! and the next, though not so concentrated, has a fine thought of poetry in it—

> *Her pure and eloquent blood*
> *Spoke in her cheeks, and so distinctly wrought,*
> *That one might almost say her body thought.*

Now, reader, render up thy thanks—for, *Parbleu! vous avez mangez des Fleurettes.*

★ Donne himself says,
> 'A naked, thinking heart, that makes no show,
> Is to a woman but a kind of ghost.'

161. Elizabeth Barrett

1838, 1842, *c.* 1844

Miss Barrett evidently read and admired Donne before she met Robert Browning in 1845. She owned a copy of the 1639 edition of Donne's poems and herself inscribed it on the fly leaf 'Elizabeth B. Barrett, from her very dear Stormie'; it was sold for £7 at Sotheby's in 1913 as part of 'The Browning Collections' (see *Sales Catalogues of Libraries of Eminent Persons*, vi, ed. J. Woolford, 1972, p. 121).

Her references to Donne, reproduced below, suggest that at this time she took a romantic view of his writings.

(i) Miss Barrett used lines from Donne's *Holy Sonnets* as mottoes for two poems in her *The Seraphim, and Other Poems*, 1838. She gives lines 3b–5 of 'What if this present' before her poem 'The Weeping Saviour' (Hymn III of a set of four hymns, p. 342), and line 9 of 'Why are wee by all creatures waited on?' before the poem 'The Weakest Thing'. The latter motto was dropped from the edition of *The Seraphim* published in 1888 and from subsequent editions of Mrs Browning's poems.

(ii) Miss Barrett reviewed *The Book of the Poets* (see No. 169) anonymously in successive numbers of *The Athenaeum* in 1842. She commented on Donne in no. 763, 11 June 1842, p. 522:

Honor to the satirists! to Marston . . . Hall . . . and to Donne, whose instinct to beauty overcame the resolution of his satiric humour.

Honor, again, to the singers of brief poems, to the lyrists and sonnetteers! . . . Shakespeare . . . Ben Jonson . . . Fletcher . . . Sidney . . . Raleigh . . . Marlowe . . . Drummond . . . Lyly . . . and Donne, who takes his place naturally in this new class, having a dumb *angel*, and knowing more noble poetry than he articulates. . . .

In no. 771, 6 August 1842, p. 707, she speaks of the seventeenth-century poets from Donne to Cowley, first disclaiming Johnson's title for them:

We have said nothing of 'the metaphysical poets' because we disclaim the classification, and believe with Mr Leigh Hunt, that every poet, inasmuch as he is a poet, is a metaphysician. . . .

The review was reprinted verbatim as 'The Book of the Poets' a section of Mrs Browning's *The Greek Christian Poets and the English Poets*, 1863, pp. 105–211. The references to Donne are on pp. 143–5 of this volume.

(iii) Some time in 1843 or 1844 Miss Barrett and Robert Browning, still strangers to each other, independently supplied mottoes for a work of literary criticism called *A New Spirit of the Age,* 1844, edited by R. H. Horne with Miss Barrett's help. One of the mottoes was from Donne; it consists of lines 47–50 of *Elegie iv*, 'The Perfume'. The variant reading 'sweets' instead of 'good' in line 50 shows that the quotation was taken from either the 1669 edition of Donne's poems or the 1719 edition (see R. H. Horne, *Letters of Elizabeth Barrett Browning addressed to R. H. Horne*, 1877, p. 134). Robert Browning possessed a copy of the 1719 edition (see No. 147 (iii)).

162. Robert Bell

1839

Bell (1800–67) was an Irish journalist who settled in London and devoted himself to occasional literary enterprises, including a vast edition of the English poets of which twenty-four volumes appeared. He followed Johnson in deeming Donne worthy of only passing discussion in the course of a life of Cowley, one of his *Lives of the Most Eminent Literary and Scientific Men of Great Britain*, 1839, i, pp. 49–53.

If the final test of a poet's excellence be the duration of his works in the affectionate regards of posterity, it must be admitted that the claims of Cowley, and others of his class, are not of the highest order. They have long since lost their popularity, and the few amongst whom they are still cherished, render but a conditional allegiance to their genius. The reason of this, however, is not because they were not poets in the exact sense of the term, but because they mixed up with what was beautiful and true much that was fantastical and false. They were perpetually going out of their way in search of the extravagant and the uncommon, and were never content, when they got hold of a natural image, to treat it naturally, as if they believed that it was necessary to embellish or disguise nature herself to make her agreeable and attractive. They had no conception of the universality and permanence of nature, and almost invariably expressed themselves as if they had discovered a train of existences and associations independent of the living world, which it became their province, as well as their delight, to explore throughout its remotest links. Thus dwelling in an artificial region of thought and fancy, they produced a species of double-natured poetry, which has been conventionally, but, perhaps, not very felicitously, designated the metaphysical.

Donne, who lived in the age which produced Shakespeare, and the great dramatists, Sydney, Raleigh, Herbert, Spenser, and a crowd of

JOHN DONNE

other distinguished men, was the patriarch of this class of poets. To profound and extensive erudition, he united a subtle intellect, and a vivid
imagination; but these advantages, which, otherwise employed, or
subjugated by a just taste, would have been of inestimable value, only
had the effect of infusing an air of supreme affectation into his poetry,
and diverting his genius into tangled labyrinths in pursuit of chimeras
and phantoms, disdainful of the simple truths that lay close at hand.
The art of clustering an enormous variety of illustrations together,—
of heaping up a fatiguing quantity of distant and startling analogies,—
of detecting the invisible particles of which all objects were composed,
which required apparently the most painful search to find, and which
were useless for all moral and poetical purposes when found,—of
hunting down a thought, and then anatomising it, until in the length-
ened process the original form was utterly annihilated, and its application forgotten,—of following out the finest threads of suggestions
which could be drawn from the web and woof of a given texture, until
the design was lost at a thousand vanishing points,—of exhibiting a
perverse ingenuity in bandying a subject, like a shuttlecock, from hand
to hand, and then, in a fit of caprice or weariness, suffering it to fall to
the ground,—and of lavishing alike upon the meanest or most exalted
theme, all the flowers of wit or stores of learning which genius and
inexhaustible resources of knowledge could command—seems to have
constituted the aim and triumph of the metaphysical poets. Yet, in the
midst of this wilderness of deformities and faults, there is such a luxu-
riant growth of fancy, and there are so many detached beauties of the
most exquisite cast, that while we are suspended in wonder at the
marvellous heresies and obscurities to which these writers committed
themselves, we cannot withhold our admiration of those transcendent
passages in which they open to us glimpses of an elysium of poetry
which none but themselves were fitted to penetrate. That the hyperbolical turn of such poems, considered entire, should have subjected
them to sweeping and indiscriminate censures, is not surprising. Commentators will not always incur the severe labour of rendering justice
in detail. It is easier and more plausible to generalise the language of
criticism, which carries weight with the multitude in proportion to its
decisiveness, than to examine the evidence with patience, and deliver an
analytical judgment. Thus Theobald pronounced Donne's poetry to be
'nothing but a continued heap of riddles,' and Rochester said of Cowley's, that 'not being of God, it could not stand.' But Theobald was a
driveller, and Rochester a ribald jester, and neither of them were quali-

374

fied to appreciate, even assuming that they could understand, Donne and Cowley. Dr. Johnson's estimate of the metaphysical poets is, as might be anticipated, more just and comprehensive: he exposes their prevailing faults, but acknowledges their particular merits.

[He gives some of Johnson's criticisms.]

The popularity of Donne and Cowley during their own lives must be admitted as a proof that, whatever may be thought of them now, they once filled a large space in the world's applause. The age in which Donne lived gave birth to the richest poetry in our language; yet Donne was as highly esteemed as any of his contemporaries. He asserted, no doubt, other claims to the admiration of his countrymen. He was a profound scholar, a brilliant wit, and an eloquent preacher; but we must trace chiefly to his poetry the influence he exercised.

[He quotes some lines from the funeral elegies for Donne first given in the 1633 edition of Donne's poems.]

Cowley, without imitating, followed in the track of Donne, and excelled him in the grasp and earnestness of his writings. He is more real and less fantastic, and, although not much closer to nature, nor much farther removed from the extravagant in art, he gains something each way, which is considerable in the aggregate.

163. Henry Alford

1839

Alford (1810–71), Dean of Canterbury from 1857, published an edition of the *Works of Donne* in six volumes. In the prefatory *Life of Donne* he speaks of the work as an edition of the sermons. But he gives the *Devotions* in volume iii, and the prose letters and some poems in volume iv. The selection of poems is such as fitly accompanies the sermons: chiefly verse letters, funeral elegies, and *Divine Poems*. But there are three *Songs and Sonnets* ('The Baite', 'A Valediction: forbidding Mourning', and 'The Will'), one *Elegie* and one *Epithalamion*.

An account of Donne's writing given in the course of the life plainly has the sermons in view first and foremost, but sometimes bears on the verse too (*The Works of John Donne, D.D., Dean of Saint Pauls 1621–1631*, 1839, i, pp. xix–xxiv).

. . . we never find in him poverty of thought, but are rather sensible (as generally in reading the most eminent of human writings, and always in the Scriptures) that the store has been but sparingly dealt out, and that much more remained, if he would have said it. Having shone as a wit in an age of wit, and an age when wit was not confined to ludicrous associations, but extended to a higher skill of point and antithesis, and cunning inter-weaving of choice words, he gained his hearers by flattering their discernment; and served up to the English Solomon and his court, dark sentences, which, in these days, when we have levelled our diction for convenience, and use language as a mere machine, require some thoughtful unravelling before their meaning is detected. That he should have gained among the moderns the reputation of obscurity is no wonder; for, on the one hand, the language of one age will always be strange to those who live in, and are entirely of, another of a totally different character; and again, this intricacy of words, frequently accompanies subtle trains of thought and argument, which it requires some exertion to follow. But it must be remembered that obscurity is a subjective term, that is, having its place in the estimation of him who judges, and not necessarily in the language judged of; and is therefore never to be imputed to an author without personal examination of his writings. . . . A man is obscure, either from his thoughts being confused and ill-arranged; or from his language being inadequate to express his meaning; or because he affects obscurity. Neither of these three was the fault of Donne. Precision and definiteness of thought, and studied arrangement of the steps of an argument, are to be found in all his sermons; and it is always more evident what he is proving, than whether his premises legitimately belong to that conclusion. 'Whereunto all this tendeth' is a note which never need be placed in his margin, as far as the immediate subject is concerned. Again, his power over the English language, one rarely surpassed in its capabilities of ministering to thought, was only equalled by one or two of his great contemporaries. And the affectation of obscurity, (the resource of weakness and ignorance, and the greatest of crimes in a literary, much more in an ecclesiastical writer,) can hardly be laid to the charge of one so single-hearted in his zeal, and so far above such a meanness, both from his learning and genius. His faults in this matter are the faults of his time, somewhat increased by a mind naturally fond of subtilty and laborious thought. And even the real difficulties of his style will soon give way and become familiar to the reader, who is capable of discovering and appreciating the treasures which it contains. . . .

In illustration by simile or allusion, Donne shows the true marks of great genius. The reader of the following Sermons will find sentences and passages which he will be surprised he never before had read, and will think of ever after. In depth and grandeur these far surpass (in my judgment) the strings of beautiful expressions to be found in Jeremy Taylor; they are the recreations of a loftier mind; and while Taylor's similes are exquisite in their melody of sound, and happy in external description, Donne enters into the inner soul of art, and gives his reader more satisfactory and permanent delight. Sir Thomas Browne is, perhaps, the writer whose style will be most forcibly recalled to the mind of the reader by many parts of these Sermons; but here again Donne has immeasurably the advantage. While the one is ever guessing at truth, the other is pouring it forth from the fulness of his heart. While the one in his personal confessions keeps aloof and pities mankind, the other is of them, and feels with them. . . .

His poems were mostly written in his youth; his satires, according to one of the panegyrics on him, before he was twenty. It has been re-marked, that the juvenile poems of truly great men are generally dis-tinguished by laborious condensation of thought; and the remark is amply borne out in this instance. This labour of compression on his part has tended to make his lines harsh and unpleasing; and the corres-ponding effort required on the reader's part to follow him, renders most persons insensible to his real merits. That he had and could turn to account a fine musical ear, is amply proved by some of his remaining pieces.* Why Dr. Johnson should have called him a metaphysical poet, is difficult to conceive. What 'wittily associating the most discordant images' has to do with metaphysics is not very clear; and Johnson, per-haps, little thought that the title which he was giving to one of the most apparently laboured of poets, belonged of all others to his im-mortal contemporary, who is recorded 'never to have blotted a line'. A greater man than Dr. Johnson, even Dryden, has said in his dedica-tion of Juvenal to the Earl of Dorset, that Donne 'affects the meta-physics;' probably meaning no more than that scholastic learning and divinity are constantly to be found showing themselves in his poems.

The personal character of Donne is generally represented to us to have undergone a great change, between his youth and the time when he entered holy orders. This representation is countenanced by the uniform tenor of deep penitence with which he speaks in his Sermons of his former life; and by the licentiousness of some of his poetical pieces. It would be wrong, however, to infer moral depravity solely from the latter circumstance, as this strain was in keeping with the prevalent taste of the times; and the object addressed in the Love-poems of the day, and the circumstances introduced, were often both equally imaginary. That his manners were the manners of the court and the society in which he lived, is the most reasonable and the most charitable sentence; . . .

* See especially the piece, 'Come live with me and be my love;' that written to his wife on parting from her to go into France, (vol. VI, p. 554), and the opening of his Epithala-mion on the marriage of the Princess Elizabeth.

164. Henry Hallam

1837-9

The historian Hallam (1777-1859) attempted to characterise Donne and his supposed followers in an *Introduction to the Literature of Europe*, 1837-9, ii, p. 316, iii, pp. 124 and 488-95.

[On Donne's *Satyres*]

With as much obscurity as Hall, he has a still more inharmonious versification, and not nearly equal vigour.

[On Donne's sermons]

In their general character, they will not appear, I think, much worthy of being rescued from oblivion. The subtlety of Donne, and his fondness for such inconclusive reasoning, as a subtle disputant is apt to fall into, runs through all of those sermons. . . . His learning he seems to have perverted in order to cull every impertinence of the fathers and schoolmen, their remote analogies, their strained allegories, their technical distinctions; and to these he has added much of a similar kind from his own fanciful understanding.

Notwithstanding the popularity of Spenser, and the general pride in his name, that allegorical and imaginative school of poetry, of which he was the greatest ornament, did not by any means exclude a very different kind. The English, or such as by their education gave the tone in literature, had become, in the latter years of the Queen, and still more under her successor, a deeply thinking, a learned, a philosophical people. A sententious reasoning, grave, subtle and condensed, or the novel and remote analogies of wit, gained praise from many whom the creations of an excursive fancy could not attract. Hence much of the poetry of James's reign is distinguished from that of Elizabeth, except perhaps her last years, by partaking of the general character of the age; deficient in simplicity, grace and feeling, often obscure and pedantic, but impressing us with a respect for the man, where we do not recognise the poet. From this condition of public taste arose two schools of poetry, different in character, if not unequal in merit, but both appealing to the reasoning more than to the imaginative faculty as their judge.

[He says that one of these is an 'argumentative school of verse' founded by Sir John Davies, continued by Daniel, Giles Fletcher, and Fulke Greville—'of all our poets he may be reckoned the most obscure'—and culminating in Denham.]

Another class of poets in the reigns of James and his son were those whom Johnson has called the metaphysical; a name rather more applicable, in the ordinary use of the word, to Davies and Brooke. These were such as laboured after conceits, or novel turns of thought, usually false, and resting upon some equivocation of language, or exceedingly remote analogy. This style Johnson supposes to have been derived from Marini. But Donne, its founder, as Johnson imagines, in England, wrote before Marini. It is in fact, as we have lately observed, the style which, though Marini has earned the discreditable reputation of perverting the taste of his country by it, had been gaining ground through the latter half of the sixteenth century. It was, in a more comprehensive view, one modification of that vitiated taste which sacrificed all ease and naturalness of writing and speaking for the sake of display. The mythological erudition and Grecisms of Ronsard's school, the Euphuism of that of Lilly, the 'estilo culto' of Gongora, even the pedantic quotations of Burton and many similar writers, both in England and on the continent, sprang like the concetti of the Italians, and of their English imitators, from the same source, a dread of being over looked if they paced on like their neighbours. And when a few writers had set the example of successful faults, a bad style, where no sound principles of criticism had been established, readily gaining ground, it became necessary that those who had not vigour enough to rise above the fashion, should seek to fall in with it. Nothing is more injurious to the cultivation of verse, than the trick of desiring, for praise or profit, to attract those by poetry whom nature has left destitute of every quality which genuine poetry can attract. The best, and perhaps the only secure basis for *public* taste, for an æsthetic appreciation of beauty, in a court, a college, a city, is so general a diffusion of classical knowledge, as by rendering the finest models familiar, and by giving them a sort of authority, will discountenance and check at the outset the vicious novelties which always exert some influence over uneducated minds. But this was not yet the case in England. Milton was perhaps the first writer who eminently possessed a genuine discernment and feeling of antiquity; though it may be perceived in Spenser, and also in a very few who wrote in prose.

Donne is generally esteemed the earliest, as Cowley was afterwards the most conspicuous model of this manner. Many instances of it, however, occur in the lighter poetry of the Queen's reign. Donne is the most inharmonious of our versifiers, if he can be said to have deserved such a name by lines too rugged to seem metre. Of his earlier poems many are very licentious; the later a chiefly devout. Few are good for much; the conceits have not even the merit of being intelligible; it would perhaps be difficult to select three passages that we should care to read again.

The second of these poets was Crashaw, a man of some imagination and great piety, but whose softness of heart, united with feeble judgment, led him to admire and imitate whatever was most extravagant in the mystic writings of Saint Teresa. He was more than Donne a follower of Marini, one of whose poems, The Massacre of the Innocents, he translated with success. It is difficult, in general, to find any thing in Crashaw that bad taste has not deformed. His poems were first published in 1646.

In the next year, 1647, Cowley's Mistress appeared; the most celebrated performance of the miscalled metaphysical poets. It is a series of short amatory poems, in the Italian style of the age, full of analogies that have no semblance of truth, except from the double sense of words, and thoughts that unite the coldness of subtlety with the hyperbolical extravagance of counterfeited passion. . . . Cowley, perhaps, upon the whole has had a reputation more above his deserts than any English poet; yet it is very easy to perceive that some who wrote better than he, did not possess so fine a genius.

165. Anon., *Selections from the Works of John Donne D.D.*

1840

A volume of *Selections from the Works of John Donne, D.D.* was published by Talboys at Oxford in 1840. The greater part of it consists of a series of short passages from the sermons; but there are some eleven pages of poetry too. Seven poems are given entire: five *Holy Sonnets*, 'To Mr Tilman', and 'A Hymne to Christ, at the Authors last going into Germany'. Otherwise there are some bits of the verse letters and of *The second Anniversary*.

All the extracts, in prose and in verse, bear pious titles; those from *The second Anniversary*, for example, are headed 'Human Ignorance'. The volume seems to be laid out as a source book for clergymen.

166. J. C. Robertson

1841

A contributor who signed himself J. C. Robertson of Boxley, Maidstone, published 'Notes on the Life and Works of Dr Donne', a long essay in double columns in *The Gentleman's Magazine*, xvi, n.s., July 1841, pp. 25–32. Robertson corrects many errors in Walton and Alford, and shows a minute and scholarly grasp of the circumstances of Donne's life and writings. He notes that Walton's image of Donne's preaching as 'an angel from a cloud' comes from Donne's own poem 'To Mr Tilman after he had taken orders'. Robertson's piece invites more scholarly work on Donne's writings and in all, well demonstrates by its professional rigour the kind of interest now being taken in Donne.

The contributor may have been James Craigie Robertson (1813–82), a church historian who became Canon of Canterbury in 1859.

167. Evert Augustus Duyckinck

1841

Duyckinck (1816–78) was an American editor, biographer, and book-collector. He knew J. R. Lowell. The following is an extract from an essay entitled 'Dr Donne' which appeared over the signature 'D' in a journal he edited with Cornelius Mathews, *Arcturus, A Journal of Books and Opinions,* New York, June 1841, pp. 19–26.

[The writer extols Walton's *Life of Donne* and expresses his admiration for Donne's nobility of soul and thoroughly furnished mind, as Walton displays them. Then he turns to Donne's writings and sets out to undermine Johnson's criticism of them:]

The literary standing of Donne has for a long time been merely that of the leader of the metaphysical poets skilfully analyzed by Johnson in the life of Cowley. The faults of that school, after the lapse of several new eras of taste and criticism, are transparent to the most careless reader of the present day: its virtues need a keen philosophical spirit of sympathy to be felt. The censure of the so-called metaphysical poets, has been too indiscriminate; they were not wholly given up to affectation or conceit; Donne and Cowley were too honest, too poetical by nature, to practice exclusively the forced tricks of art. We must not judge of them by the literary habits of our own times; but, looking at them as foreign authors, so to speak, translate them out of the seventeenth century into the nineteenth.

We have no intention of palliating the censure of Donne in common with the other perverse writers of his times. They mistook the true laws of poetry, for they failed in the universality of style, nature's own simplicity, by which Homer and Shakspeare are to be intelligible for ever. They are not read, and never can be again, in the spirit in which they were written. But we must not forget that below the pure unvarying Parnassian heights there is a changing atmosphere, that still protects the

384

houses and haunts of men, though it is fickle and inconstant. The metaphysical poets were no unprofitable writers in their own day and gener-
ation; they were understood by their contemporaries; and in their own
way the most ingenious and wire-drawn of their conceits, at which our
modern smooth taste looks with pain, drew forth hidden and deep
ecstacies of feeling. . . . There are many avenues to the heart. To a
class of readers already bent upon subtleties by a scholastic education and
studies, the toughest of these old metaphysical conceits may have conveyed as gently the whispers of affection, as the harmonious lines of
Thomas Moore to modern ears. It is unfair to say, as Johnson has concluded, that these intellectual writers had no heart. There never was a
good head, without the capacity of a liberal, generous heart. The very
titles of the poems, and their personal character—treating of love and
friendship—might have prevented this remark; which, it must be said,
comes with an ill grace from the author of the vague generalities of
Irene, and the satirical imitation of Juvenal. A generous man gives such
offerings as he has:—the whole intellectual wealth of these poets was
offered up at the shrine of love and friendship. . . .

Many of the strange conceits might be philosophically defended.
Some of them are successful even with modern readers, by their very
acuteness and corresponding nicety of truth: others, that have been
abused for their remoteness, when we look at them, are very good
poetry after all. Johnson, in his examples, ridicules a passage of Donne,
in which Death is compared to a Voyage,

> No family
> E'er rigg'd a soul for Heaven's discovery,
> With whom more venturers might boldly dare
> Venture their stakes, with him in joy to share;

but this is a natural, even a fine conception, if we look at it by the light
of the times in which it was written. There could then be no more
poetical idea than that of voyaging and discovery, (not stripped of all
romance yet), when Raleigh and Essex were setting forth on the ocean
in the faith of unknown wonders, and gallant spirits flocked around
them to venture forth in a new world. It is probable that many pious
Christians have at this day a less imaginative idea of Heaven, than was
then held of America by those chivalrous adventurers.

A list of choice happy passages may easily be given to counteract
Johnson's catalogue of defects. There is a joyous burst of fanciful illustrations in the Epithalamium on the marriage of the celebrated queen of

Bohemia, the idol of the court of James I., which Charles Lamb has imitated in his Valentine's day. 'Hail to thy returning festival, old Bishop Valentine,' &c.

[He quotes lines 1–8 of *An Epithalamion . . . St Valentines day*.]

This musical passage ought to neutralize the celebrated metaphysical puzzle that occurs in the same poem.

[He quotes lines 85–8 of the same poem, beginning 'Here lies a She Sun, and a He Moon there'.]

In spite of this, Donne, in many poems, deserves to be studied for his grace and ease. His mind was full of poetic impulses, 'reaching from earth to heaven;' he frequently commences with ardor and beauty, and then falls away into a train of poor conceits. Had he understood the laws of true poetry as well as Milton, he might have equalled the beauty of Lycidas and the minor poems.

Here is a rapid beginning in one of the amatory poems, a choice prelude hastily struck on the lyre: [he quotes lines 1–4 of 'Loves Deitie'] and then follows a table of Actives and Passives, Correspondency and Subject.

In some respects the genius of Donne resembled that of his friend Ben Jonson; amid the constant rugged style of each, there were flowers of strange beauty found growing in the clefts of the rock. A writer in Dr. Hawks' Church Record, in an article upon Donne's Sermons, says, that among the divines, Donne resembled Jeremy Taylor, as Ben Jonson resembled Shakspeare. There is much truth in the parallel; perhaps better sustained by Donne's sermons than his poetry. In his early poems, Donne reminds us of Suckling, in a gay airy vein, which the latter appears to have imitated, especially from the following

[He quotes the whole of 'Song. Goe, and catche a falling starre'.]

Jonson heartily admired Donne, and used to quote, among other passages, one from the Calm, as perfect in its effect.

> And in one place lay
> Feathers and dust, to day and yesterday.

Equally grave and picturesque, is the following single line:

> The deep,
> Where harmless fish monastique silence keep.

In the sermons of Donne, there are instances of a remarkable fineness and strength of fancy: chiefly confined to thoughts of death, and kindred topics. . . .

We like to read the theology of Donne, by the light of his early love poems. The sincerity of his affection, is remarkable in both. It is not long since we met with a bigotted, ungenerous use of some passages of his early life. In his youth, Donne was a gay, ardent lover, and committed some passages to paper, for the printing of which, after his death, we are indebted to his scape-grace son, who followed the worst manners of the court of Charles II.; but Donne was never a profligate, or a libertine. He had an ardent imagination, and was a hearty lover; and was sometimes so natural in his poetry, as to address his wife as his mistress. The history of his love and marriage, is one of the purest and most touching stories of affection superior to trial and misfortune. His friendships were with the best men of his day. To hold his life up to the vulgar sot or rake, as an illustration of the converting power of religion, is to misunderstand not only Donne, but the spirit of Christianity itself. If Donne had not been a very devoted lover, he would not have been the same zealous Dean of St. Paul's. Donne repented, aye, bitterly; he felt the sorrow which haunts every man of true feeling in this world, in every fibre of his sensitive heart; his later writings are filled with painful contrition: a contrition too sacred to be impertinently spoken of by a mere critic, or hastily quoted even in a sermon. If sinners are to be reclaimed only by coarse appeals and examples of penitent men, let other subjects be selected for anatomy. Do not torture the fine harmony of Donne's spiritual life, to give forth those warnings to the profligate, which may be drawn, if need be, from meaner natures.

168. Anon., *Gems of Sacred Poetry*

1841

The anonymous editor of an anthology of religious verse set out 'to draw from their undeserved obscurity' some of the seventeenth-century poets it had lately been the fashion to deride. He gives six poems by Donne—the *Holy Sonnets* 'Thou hast made me', 'This is my playes last scene', 'At the round earths imagin'd corners', and 'Death be not proud'; 'A Hymne to Christ, at the Authors last going into Germany'; and the 'Hymne to God my God, in my sicknesse'. There is also an introductory comment on Donne's religious poetry (*Gems of Sacred Poetry*, ?Oxford, 1841, p. 86).

Without being in the strictest sense of the word a sacred poet, Donne is one of those writers who have shown their reverence of religion with the warmth and sincerity of genuine feeling. He is frequently rugged and obscure, yet he displays a depth of sentiment and an originality of thought, which contain the germs of true poetry.

169. Anon., *The Book of the Poets*

1842

An anonymously edited anthology of English poetry gave three poems by Donne, *Elegie v*, 'His Picture'; 'The Dissolution'; and *Holy Sonnet xiii*, 'What if this present were the worlds last night?'. It gave one poem by Marvell, four poems each by Quarles, Crashaw, and Carew, five poems each by Herbert and Suckling, six poems by Cowley, and ten poems or extracts by Milton. Donne is mentioned in an introductory survey, and a brief account of him precedes his three poems. The survey distinguishes between 'the Metaphysical' poets of the Court of Charles I, and 'the Classical' poets of the Court of Charles II, but Donne is not included in either class. The anthology was reissued in 1844. (*The Book of the Poets* (1842), 1844, pp. xxiii–iv and 49.)

(i) From the Introduction, after mention of the great poets of the turn of the century, Drayton, Daniel, the Fletchers, Sir John Davies:

Dr Donne also, who was contemporary with Davies, was a poet of great strength and deep piercing wit, but of studied obscurity, who seems to have delighted in puzzling his readers, and setting all their faculties upon the stretch.

(ii) From the account of Donne which precedes his three poems:

John Donne, who has been so highly eulogised by Dryden, Pope, and our most eminent poets. . . .

. . . His poems, which are of a miscellaneous character, suggested by the impulse of the moment rather than the result of systematic study, consist chiefly of satires, elegies, songs, and sonnets; and although his versification is frequently harsh, and his language pedantic, yet his productions possess an innate vigour which will always secure them a high rank in our English poetry.

389

170. Hartley Coleridge

c. 1843

Hartley Coleridge, S. T. Coleridge's son, referred to Donne in some marginal comments he wrote against poems by Carew in a copy of *Anderson's British Poets* (1793 edition) which his father had bequeathed to him (they were printed in *Essays and Marginalia*, ed. Derwent Coleridge, 1851, ii, pp. 7 and 10).

On a blank sheet at the end of volume iv of this copy Hartley Coleridge wrote some lines beginning 'Brief as the reign of pure poetic Truth' which contain a reference to Donne and quotes the epigram his father had written in Charles Lamb's copy of Donne in 1811 (it had been published in Coleridge's *Literary Remains*, 1836. See No. 112 (iv)). Hartley's poem was transcribed by E. H. Coleridge when the book passed down to his sister Christabel; the lines referring to Donne were printed in W. Davenport Adams, *A Dictionary of English Literature*, 1878, p. 182.

(i) A marginal comment on Carew's poem 'Upon the Kings Illness':

Sir Thomas More died with a jest, and he was a martyr, at least to his own sincerity. Men may joke and quibble till they cannot do otherwise, and yet not have joked away all feeling. To come nearer the point. Is there any difference in style between Donne's Sacred Poems and his wildest love riddles? . . .

A marginal comment on Carew's 'A Fancy':

He seems to have made Donne his ideal. He is far smoother; but where is the strength, the boundless wealth of thought, the heart beating beneath its twisted mail?

(ii)

> Thus Donne—not first—but greatest of the line—
> Of stubborn thoughts, a garland thought to twine;

To his fair maid brought cabalistic posies,
And sung fair ditties of metempsychosis:
Twists iron pokers into true love knots,
Coining hard words not found in polyglots.

171. Henry David Thoreau

1843, 1849

Thoreau grew up in Concord, Massachusetts, where Emerson
lived for much of his life. The two men became friendly in 1841,
and Thoreau lived in Emerson's house for a time, having the run
of the large library there. In the 1840s Thoreau seems to have
read Donne on two distinct occasions, without acquiring Emerson's or Lowell's enthusiasm for him.

(i) Thoreau's *Journal* for 1843 shows that he had been reading the
Elizabethan and Jacobean poets in a New York Library. He noted down
an opinion of Donne among others (it is quoted here from F. B.
Sanborn, *The Life of Henry David Thoreau*, Boston and New York,
1917, p. 274):

Donne was not a poet, but a man of strong sense,—a sturdy English
thinker, full of conceits and whimsicalities; hammering away at his
subject, be it eulogy or epitaph, sonnet or satire, with the patience of a
day-laborer; without the least taste, but with an occasional fine distinction and poetic utterance of a high order. He was rather Doctor
Donne than the poet Donne. He gropes, for the most part; his letters
are perhaps best.

(ii) Thoreau several times quotes Donne in *A Week on the Concord and
Merrimack Rivers*, 1849, pp. 137, 281, 310–11, 352. He seems to have
been reading a complete Donne and not some anthologised snippets.

He gives lines 129–30 of 'To the Countesse of Huntington' ('That unripe side of earth'), line 464 of *The second Anniversary*, and lines 355–6 of *The first Anniversary*, which he uses as the epigraph for the 'Friday' chapter of his book.

172. Barron Field

c. 1844

Field (1786–1846) was a lawyer, and sometime friend of Lamb, Coleridge, Wordsworth, Hazlitt, and Leigh Hunt. He was theatre critic of *The Times,* edited Elizabethan plays, and wrote poetry; he served as a judge in Australia for some years, and became Chief Justice of Gibraltar.

Late in life Field prepared to publish an edition of Donne's *Songs and Sonnets* for the Percy Society, with Coleridge's notes. The project failed and the work remained in manuscript. Field introduced the notes as a transcript he had made some thirty years before of Coleridge's jottings in Lamb's copy of Donne; but he added a comment of his own (R. F. Brinkley, *Coleridge on the Seventeenth Century*, Durham, N.C., 1955, pp. 519–20).

. . . the Poems of Donne are so little read, that there will be no harm in affording Members of the Percy Society with opportunity of refreshing their acquaintance with this learned and fanciful poet. . . .

173. Richard Cattermole

1844

Cattermole (?1795–1858) was an Anglican clergyman who wrote on literary and religious matters and was secretary of the Royal Society of Literature for many years. He devoted a chapter to 'Dr Donne' in *The Literature of the Church of England*, 1844, i, pp. 118–27, following it with Donne's sermon on St Paul at Malta (*Sermons*, viii, pp. 312–34).

The chapter amounts to a summary of Walton's *Life of Donne*, with some incidental observations on Donne's poetry which I give below. A list of Donne's works includes the 1633 edition of the poems but is largely taken up with the sermons.

[On Donne's early career and marriage.] But the prospect thus opened before him, was quickly clouded by the occurrence of an incident rather indicative of the youthful poet's ardent feelings,—for a poet he truly was,—than of his prudence. . . .

[On Donne's departure for the continent in 1611.] Donne and his wife had parted with affectionate regret, expressed on her side by 'forebodings of ill in his absence', on his by a 'valediction' in verse, which, though censured by Johnson for absurd ingenuity, well denoted, in the quaint manner of its author, his struggles to repress a concentrated tenderness.

Finding death approach, he took leave of his friends in a manner which savoured of that serious ingenuity which characterized his mental efforts: he caused the figure of our Saviour, represented as crucified upon an anchor, to be engraved on blood-stones and set in gold, for seal-rings, which he presented as memorials to his surviving benefactors and friends. . . .

Wisdom is justified of all genuine sons; and if a few solitary readers have been carried away with an excessive admiration of the brilliant dean of St Paul's, is it an adequate excuse for others who depreciate his great powers, that the literary faults of his age, finding in him a soil of prodigious richness, grew up and flourished together with his excellencies? His subtlety and ingenuity are certainly extreme, and the discursive affluence of his thoughts unchecked by the niceness of modern taste; but he is strictly logical and profoundly learned; always earnestly, if sometimes fancifully, pious; very often pathetically eloquent. . . .

Those writings of Donne's, however, by which he is, and will ever be, the best, most honourably, and most beneficially known, are his noble sermons; viz. . . . [he lists Donne's sermons].

174. Robert Chambers/Robert Carruthers

1843, 1876

An account of the 'Third Period' of English literature, that between 1558 and 1649, includes an article 'John Donne' which comments closely on Donne's poetic manner (*Chambers Cyclopaedia of English Literature* (1843), 1858, i, pp. 114–15). In the third edition of the *Cyclopaedia*, which was revised by Robert Carruthers over thirty years later, the remarks on Donne's poetry are subtly modified and the account of the onset of 'metaphysical' decadence is omitted, so that a far less Johnsonian picture of Donne emerges (1876, i, pp. 97–9).

(i) From the article as it appeared in the first and second editions of *Chambers Cyclopaedia*, 1843 and 1858:

John Donne. . . . His reputation as a poet, great in his own day, low during the latter part of the seventeenth, and the whole of the eighteenth centuries, has latterly in some degree revived. In its days of abasement, critics spoke of his harsh and rugged versification, and his leaving nature for conceit. It seems to be now acknowledged that, amidst much rubbish, there is much real poetry, and that of a high order, in Donne. He is described by a recent critic as 'imbued to saturation with the learning of his age', endowed 'with a most active and piercing intellect—an imagination, if not grasping and comprehensive, most subtile and far-darting—a fancy, rich, vivid, and picturesque—a mode of expression terse, simple, and condensed—and a wit admirable, as well for its caustic severity, as for its playful quickness—and as only wanting sufficient sensibility and taste to preserve him from the vices of style which seem to have beset him'. Donne is usually considered as the first of a series of poets of the seventeenth century who, under the name of the Metaphysical Poets, fill a conspicuous place in English literary history. The directness of thought, the naturalness of description, the rich abundance of genuine poetical feeling and imagery, which distinguish the poets of Elizabeth's reign, now begin to give way to cold and forced conceits, elaborate exercises of the intellect, a kind of poetry as unlike the former as punning is unlike genuine wit. To give an idea of these conceits—Donne writes a poem on a familiar subject, a broken heart. Here he does not advert to the miseries or distractions which are presumed to be the causes of broken hearts, but starts off into a play of conceit upon the phrase. He entered a room, he says, where his mistress was present, and

> Love, alas!
> At one first blow did shiver it [his heart] as glass

Then, forcing on his mind to discover by what means the idea of a heart broken to pieces, like glass, can be turned to account in making out something that will strike the reader's imagination, he proceeds thus:

[He quotes the whole of the last stanza of 'The Broken Heart', italicising everything from 'broken glasses' to 'ragges of heart'.]

There is here, certainly, analogy, but then it is an analogy which altogether fails to please or move: it is a mere conceit. Perhaps we should not be far from the truth, if we were to represent this style as a national symptom of the decline of the brilliant school of Sackville, Spenser, and Shakspeare. All the recognised modes, subjects, and phrases of poetry introduced by them and their contemporaries, were in some degree exhausted, and it was deemed necessary to seek for novelty of style and manner. This was found, not in a new vein of equally rich ore, but in a continuation of the workings through adjoining veins of spurious metal.

This peculiarity, however, did not characterise the whole of the writings of Donne and his followers. They are often direct, natural, and truly poetical in spite, as it were, of themselves. Donne, it may be here stated, is usually considered as the first writer of satire, in rhyming couplets, such as Dryden, Young, and Pope carried to perfection. . . . They are greatly deficient, like all this poet's work, in metrical harmony, which some of the minor poets carried to such perfection.

The specimens which follow are designed only to exemplify the merits of Donne, not his defects. . . .

[He gives the first stanza of *An Epithalamion* . . . *St Valentines day,* the whole of 'A Valediction: forbidding Mourning' and 'The Will', and a long extract from *Satyre iv*.]

(ii) Revisions in the 1876 version of the article:

has latterly in some degree revived.] has latterly revived.

amidst much rubbish,] amidst much bad taste,

Donne is usually considered as the first . . . unlike genuine wit.] *three sentences omitted.*

Donne writes a poem on a familiar subject, a broken heart.] Donne writes a poem on a broken heart.

Here he does not advert to . . . a play of conceit upon the phrase.] He does not advert to the miseries or distractions which are presumed to be the causes of the calamity, but runs off into a play on the expression 'broken heart'.

the reader's imagination, he proceeds thus:] the reader's imagination, he adds:

Perhaps we should not be far from the truth . . . veins of spurious metal.] *Three sentences omitted.*

did not characterise the whole of the writings] does not characterise the bulk of the writings

truly poetical—in spite, as it were, of themselves.] truly poetical—abounding in rich thought and melody.

They are greatly deficient . . . the merits of Donne, not his defects] *Two sentences omitted.*

There are two additional extracts from Donne's verse, with comments:

One of the earliest poetic allusions to the Copernican system occurs in Donne:

[He quotes lines 37–8 of 'To the Countesse of Bedford' ('To have written then, when you writ,').]

The following is a simile often copied by later poets:

[He quotes lines 231–7a of the *Metempsychosis.*]

175. George Lillie Craik

1845

Craik (1798–1866), journalist and literary historian, became Professor of English Literature and History at Belfast in 1849. He gave an account of Donne's poetry in *Sketches of the History of Literature and Learning in England*, 1845, pp. 168–72. It was reprinted verbatim in *A Compendious History of English Literature*, 1861, pp. 552–6.

DONNE.

The title of the metaphysical school of poetry, which in one sense of the words might have been given to Davies and his imitators, has been conferred by Dryden upon another race of writers, whose founder was a contemporary of Davies, the famous Dr. John Donne, Dean of St. Paul's. Donne, who died at the age of fifty-eight, in 1631, is said to have written most of his poetry before the end of the sixteenth century, but none of it was published till late in the reign of James. It consists of lyrical pieces (entitled Songs and Sonnets), epithalamions or marriage songs, funeral and other elegies, satires, epistles, and divine poems. On a superficial inspection, Donne's verses look like so many riddles. They seem to be written upon the principle of making the meaning as difficult to be found out as possible—of using all the resources of language, not to express thought, but to conceal it. Nothing is said in a direct, natural manner; conceit follows conceit without intermission; the most remote analogies, the most far-fetched images, the most unexpected turns, one after another, surprise and often puzzle the understanding; while things of the most opposite kinds—the harsh and the harmonious, the graceful and the grotesque, the grave and the gay, the pious and the profane—meet and mingle in the strangest of dances. But, running through all this bewilderment, a deeper insight detects not only a vein of the most exuberant wit, but often the sunniest and most delicate fancy, and the truest tenderness and depth of feeling. Donne, though in the latter part of his life he became a very serious and devout poet as well as man, began by writing amatory lyrics, the strain of which is anything rather than devout; and in this kind of writing he seems to have formed his poetic style, which, for such compositions, would, to a mind like his, be the most natural and expressive of any. The species of lunacy which quickens and exalts the imagination of a lover, would, in one of so seething a brain as he was, strive to expend itself in all sorts of novel and wayward combinations, just as Shakespeare has made it do in his Romeo and Juliet, whose rich intoxication of spirit he has by nothing else set so livingly before us, as by making them thus exhaust all the eccentricities of language in their struggle to give expression to that inexpressible passion which had taken captive the whole heart and being of both. Donne's later poetry, in addition to the same abundance and originality of thought, often running into a wildness and extravagance not so excusable here as in his erotic verses, is famous for the singular movement of the versification, which has been usually described as the extreme degree of the rugged and tuneless. Pope has given us a translation of his four Satires into modern language, which he calls The Satires of Dr. Donne Versified. Their harshness, as contrasted with the music of his lyrics, has also been referred to as proving that the English language, at the time when Donne wrote, had not been brought to a sufficiently advanced state for the writing of heroic verse in perfection. That this last notion is wholly unfounded, numerous examples sufficiently testify: not to speak of the blank verse of the dramatists, the rhymed heroics of Shakespeare, of Fletcher, of Jonson, of Spenser, and of other writers contemporary with and of earlier date than Donne, are, for the most part, as perfectly smooth and regular as any that have since been written; at all events, whatever irregularity may be detected in them, if they be tested by Pope's narrow gamut, is clearly not to be imputed to any immaturity in the language. These writers evidently preferred and cultivated, deliberately and on principle, a wider compass, and freer and more varied flow, of melody than Pope had a taste or an ear for. Nor can it be questioned, we think, that the peculiar construction of Donne's verse in his satires and many of his other later poems was also adopted by choice and on system. His lines, though they will not suit the see-saw style of reading verse,—to which he probably intended that they should be invincibly impracticable,—are not without a deep and subtle music of their own, in which the cadences respond to the sentiment, when enunciated with a true feeling of all that they convey. They are not smooth or luscious verses, certainly; nor is it contended that the endeavour to raise them to as vigorous and impressive a tone as possible, by depriving them of all over-sweetness or liquidity, has not been carried too far; but we cannot doubt that whatever harshness they have was designedly given to them, and was conceived to infuse into them an essential part of their relish.

Here is one of Donne's Songs:—

[He quotes the whole of the 'Song. Sweetest love, I do not goe'.]

Somewhat fantastic as this may be thought, it is surely, notwithstanding, full of feeling; and nothing can be more delicate than the execution. Nor is it possible that the writer of such verses can have wanted an ear for melody, however capriciously he may have sometimes experimented upon language, in the effort, as we conceive, to bring a deeper, more expressive music out of it than it would readily yield. We add one of his elegies as a specimen of his more elaborate style:—

[He quotes in full the 'Elegie. Death' ('Language thou art too narrow, and too weake').]

176. James Russell Lowell

1845–95

Lowell (1819–91) was another nineteenth-century poet who made no secret of his lifelong devotion to Donne and championed Donne's poetry strenuously. As Professor of Literature at Harvard from 1855 he plainly had much to do with the interest New England writers then began to show in Donne.

C. E. Norton's Grolier Club edition of Donne's poems, 1895, was intended partly as a tribute to Lowell's memory. In his Preface Norton remarked that 'Donne's Poems were, from an early period of his life, among Mr Lowell's favorite books', and ascribed to Lowell's prompting the Boston edition of 1855. Norton spoke of the 'many hundreds' of marginal emendations, mainly of the punctuation, which Lowell had made in a copy of that edition and commented: 'It seemed a pity that this work should be lost, and the Grolier Club undertook the present edition for the sake of preserving it.' The Grolier Club edition was described on its title page as 'Revised by James Russell Lowell'. (*The Poems of John Donne*, New York, 1895, i, pp. vii–viii.)

(i) From *Conversations on Some of the Old Poets* (1845), 1893, p. 159. Lowell is speaking of Chapman's section of *Hero and Leander*:

. . . If there be a few blurs in it, it is yet one of the clearest and most perfect crystals in the language, an entire opal, beautiful without the lapidary's help; but it will shine with true pureness only in

> the nunnery
> Of a chaste breast and quiet mind

like some of Donne's more private and esoteric poems. The same candle may light the soul to its chapel of devotion or its bed of harlotry:—. . . .

(ii) From 'The Life and Writings of James Gate Percival', 1867 (*The Writings of James Russell Lowell*, Cambridge, Mass., 1890, ii, p. 160):

. . . He discovered his own genius, as he supposed,—a thing impossible had the genius been real. Donne, who wrote more profound verses than any other English poet save one only, never wrote a profounder verse than

> Who knows his virtue's name and place, hath none

(iii) From 'Dryden', 1868 (*Writings*, iii, pp. 107 and 170–1). He is speaking of Dryden's poetic career:

The earliest of his verses that have come down to us were written upon the death of Lord Hastings, and are as bad as they can be,—a kind of parody on the worst of Donne. They have every fault of his manner, without a hint of the subtle and often profound thought that more than redeems it. As the Doctor himself would have said, here is Donne out-donne. . . .

Dryden, I suspect, was not much given to correction, and indeed one of the great charms of his best writing is that everything seems struck off at a heat, as by a superior man in the best mood of his talk. Where he rises, he generally becomes fervent rather than imaginative; his thought does not incorporate itself in metaphor, as in purely poetic minds, but repeats and reinforces itself in simile. Where he *is* imaginative, it is in that lower sense which the poverty of our language, for want of a better word, compels us to call *picturesque*, and even then he shows little of that finer instinct which suggests so much more than it tells, and works the more powerfully as it taxes more the imagination of the reader. In Donne's 'Relic' there is an example of what I mean. He fancies some one breaking up his grave and spying

> A bracelet of bright hair about the bone,—

a verse that still shines there in the darkness of the tomb, after two centuries, like one of those inextinguishable lamps whose secret is lost.★

(iv) From 'Shakespeare Once More', 1868 (*Writings*, iii, p. 35):

Donne is full of salient verses that would take the rudest March winds of criticism with their beauty, of thoughts that first tease us like

---

★ Dryden, with his wonted perspicacity, follows Ben Jonson in calling Donne 'the greatest wit, though not the best poet, of our nation.' (Dedication of *Eleonora*.) Even as a poet Donne
> 'Had in him those brave transulunary things
> That our first poets had.'

To open vistas for the imagination through the blind wall of the senses, as he could sometimes do, is the supreme function of poetry.

charades and then delight us with the felicity of their solution; but these have not saved him. He is exiled to the limbo of the formless and the fragmentary.

(v) From 'Wordsworth', originally given on 10 May 1884 as the presidential address to the Wordsworth Society (*Writings*, vi, pp. 107–8):

. . . What are the conditions of permanence? Immediate or contemporaneous recognition is certainly not dominant among them, or Cowley would still be popular,—Cowley to whom the Muse gave every gift but one, the gift of the unexpected and inevitable word. Nor can mere originality assure the interest of posterity, else why are Chaucer and Gray familiar, while Donne, one of the subtlest and most self-irradiating minds that ever sought an outlet in verse, is known only to the few?

(vi) From an unpublished lecture on poetic diction, quoted in *The Love Poems of John Donne*, ed. C. E. Norton, Boston, 1905, p. 85, note. Lowell comments on 'A Valediction: forbidding Mourning':

This poem is a truly sacred one and fuller of the soul of poetry than a whole Alexandrian library of common love verses.

(vii) From a letter to Mrs W. K. Clifford, 16 November 1884 (*The Letters of James Russell Lowell*, ed. C. E. Norton, 1894, ii, p. 319):

Could I have been such an ass as to ask if I was charming? It is out of the question. Even if I thought I was, I should be too clever to inquire nicely about it, for I hold with my favorite Donne that

Who knows his virtue's name and place hath none

(viii) From a letter to C. E. Norton, 22 December 1887 (*Letters*, ii, pp. 385–6):

I have finished the 'Epistle to Curtis' after a fashion, well or ill is hard to say. The measure is so facile that one soon loses one's sense of the difference between what sounds like something and what really is something. One needs to brace one's self with a strong dose of Dr. Donne. . . .

(ix) From a letter to Mrs W. E. Darwin, 13 September 1889 (*Letters*, ii, p. 430):

[Speaking of robins.] What is it Donne calls them? 'The household bird with the red stomacher,' or something prettier. I am doubtful about 'household'.

(x) From a letter to the Misses Lawrence, 18 December 1890 (*Letters*, ii, p. 480):

I had forgotten Dean Church's death, a great loss to friendship and to literature, one of the few men worthy to sit in Donne's stall. . . .

177. Anon., *Lowe's Edinburgh Magazine*

1846

The first number of *Lowe's Edinburgh Magazine* inaugurated a *Gallery of Poets* in which 'We intend to exhibit from time to time, such specimens of the less familiar, but worthy English poets, as, along with a few biographical and critical remarks, may introduce many of our readers to a new and engaging literary field, and recall pleasing recollections to those of them who are already familiar with it'. Specimen no. 1, anonymously written, was John Donne (*Lowe's Edinburgh Magazine* i, 1846, pp. 228–36).

For every individual reader of the poems of John Donne, there have probably been a hundred readers of the exquisite 'Life' of him, by Izaak Walton. Unprefaced by this 'Life,' no edition of Donne's poems ought ever to have appeared. Not only is the memoir itself in every respect worthy of its subject—executed *con amore*—coming, paragraph after paragraph, like a succession of 'meadow-gales in spring,' over the heart of the habitual wanderer in the arid wastes of modern biographical literature; touching the souls of men with a tender sorrow for the noble days gone by—a sorrow which hardly subsides at thought of the nobler, but far different days to come: not only has it all these and many similar merits, but it moreover supplies a commentary upon the writings of our poet which could ill have been dispensed with. To the fact that 'his father was masculinely and lineally descended from a very ancient family in Wales,' and that 'by his mother he was descended of the family of the famous and learned Sir Thomas More, some time Lord Chancellor of England,' we may trace the lofty self-possession which breathes through all his writings, and which, in literature as in manners, is almost invariably the result of lofty extraction. In the circumstance, that although 'his friends were of the Romish persuasion,' young Donne would not receive their, or any creed implicitly; but 'about the nineteenth year of his age, he being then unresolved what religion to adhere to, and considering how much it concerned his soul to choose the most orthodox, did therefore (though his youth and health promised him a long life), to rectify all scruples that might concern that, presently lay aside all study of the law, and of all other sciences that might give him a denomination, and began seriously to survey and consider the body of divinity, as it was then controverted betwixt the Reformed and the Roman Church,' we find an explanation of the peculiar vent of thought and imagination which characterizes all his writings, but particularly the first, namely, the 'Satires,' and 'Funeral Elegies.' In his deep and various acquaintance with the physical, mathematical, and metaphysical sciences, as they then existed, we discover the origin of many of his far-fetched, and often painfully-ingenious illustrations. In his travels and his troubles, we find him undergoing the true poet-education, an experimental knowledge of men and sorrows. Finally, in his latterly blameless and holy life, we behold his defence against those who might otherwise have been inclined to infer, from the wonderful subtlety of his religion, an absence of a great sincerity in its pursuit.

Though too often neglected, it is one of the first duties of the critic, in his estimation of the merits and demerits of a literary production, to point out, as far as may be in his power, what of those merits and demerits belong to the author, and what to the time he wrote in. An endeavour to do this in a general manner shall be our first step in criticizing the poems of Donne.

His death occurred in 1631, when he was 58 years old. Shakspeare died in 1616. Therefore English intellect was at its height in the age Donne wrote. Mental philosophy was profounder and purer than it had ever been before; but it was occasionally wronged by an attempt to wed it with physical science: a marriage of which the times forbade the bans, because the latter was as yet unripe. Philosophy being profound and pure, so was religion; and in the midst of a vigorous and flourishing philosophy and of a true religion, what could poetry be but vigorous, flourishing, and true?

Religion, also, in various ways, enhanced the poetic liberty of the time: especially it extinguished that false shame which Romanism had attached to the contemplation of the sexual relations. The purity of these relations had been for long ages lied away by the enforcement, *as a permanent doctrine,* of what St. Paul had advised merely as '*good for the present distress,*' (I Cor. vii. 26) caused by the persecutions in his day. But the Reformation had arisen, and commanded, that what God had declared to be clean, no man should call common. The command had been received with an obedience which had not, in Donne's time, been deadened or destroyed by the poisonous taint of Romanism, which yet lurked in the doctrine, and afterwards developed itself in the life-blood of the new era. The consequence was, that the sphere of nature was yet widened to the rejoicing poet, who now revered true chastity all the more that he was no longer obliged to bow down to the really unchaste mockeries of her 'unblemished form,' which had been set up for his worship by the harlot, Rome.

Again, a true philosophy gave birth to powers of the subtlest perception; which it did by inducing a faith in those powers. A good, perhaps the best, test of the subtlety of a poet's perception, is his appreciation of the female character; which, presenting, as it does, an endless series of contradictions to the understanding, thus declares itself to be the subject of a wholly different tribunal. Poets, whose powers of perception have fallen short of the highest, have made endless unavailing attempts to *solve* the character of woman. The subtle singers of Donne's time knew that they might as well endeavour to solve an irrational equation, or to express, in terminated decimals, a 'surd quantity.' But they knew that a comprehension of her character was no indispensable qualification for depicting it; and accordingly, and *therefore,* they have depicted it, as no poets had ever done before, or have done since.

In Donne's day, the faith in instinctive immediate perception was not a thing merely to talk about and admire, or to act upon within due and decent limitation, as it is with our living poets; it was a thing to possess and act upon *unconsciously,* and without limits imposed by the logical faculty, or by the hyperbole-hating decencies of flat conventionality. Our modern carpet-poets tread their way upon hyperbole as nicely as they would do over ice of an uncertain strength, dreading every moment to be drowned by ridicule, or sucked into some bottomless abyss, by an 'Edinburgh' or 'Quarterly' 'Attack.' Not so in Shakespeare's time:—

> Tempests themselves, high seas, and howling winds,
> The gutter'd rocks, and congregated sands,—
> Traitors ensteep'd to clog the guiltless keel,
> As having sense of beauty, did omit
> Their mortal natures, letting go safely by
> The divine Desdemona.

So much, then, for the qualities of the period; qualities which Donne, as a poet, must necessarily participate in, and represent. We now proceed to name and illustrate some of his peculiarities. To begin with censure, and to prepare our readers for the quotations we shall make, let us state our conviction, that Donne's ordinary *versification* is about the very ruggedest that ever has been written. We shall not extract any particular lines to prove this assertion, since we shall make few quotations which will *not* prove it. This defect will always prevent Donne from becoming popular: fit and few will be his audience as long as poetry is read.

Another quality, equally against his popularity, is his profundity of thought, and the constant attention which is therefore required in order to understand him. Though his poems may be read once through, as a kind of disagreeable duty, by the professed student of English literature, they will be pored over, again and again, as true poetry should be, only by the most faithful and *disciplined* lovers of the muse. With these latter, however, Donne will always be a peculiar favourite. By them his poems will be valued as lumps of precious golden ore, touched, here and there, with specks of richest gold, and almost everywhere productive of the shining treasure, when submitted to the operation of affectionate reflection. By such readers even his worst versification will be pardoned, since no sacrifice of meaning is ever made to it,—it thus becoming so much more palatable to the truly cultivated taste than the expensive melody of some modern versifiers.

Donne's Poems seem to divide themselves naturally into three classes:—I. His early 'Songs and Sonnets' and 'Elegies,' chiefly love-poems, and his 'Epithalamions.' II. His 'Satires,' 'Letters,' and 'Funeral Elegies.' III. His 'Divine Poems.' We will notice the contents of each class in its order.

The love-poems seem rather to be inspired by *a love of love*, than by any very powerful passion for the object of whom they chiefly discourse. Most lovers love their object because they confound her with their ideal of excellence. Donne seems ever aware that his is the mere suggestion of that ideal which he truly loves. His love is a lofty and passionate, but voluntary, contemplation, deriving its nourishment mainly from the intellect, and not a fiery atmosphere, in which he lives and moves always, and whether he will or no.

On the whole, this class of his poems is greatly inferior to the second order. It is much more deformed by the intrusion of 'conceits,' and its general lack of spontaneous feeling is compensated by no general profundity of thought. Here and there, however, we find gems of admirable and various lustre, though no one, of any magnitude, without defect. We give the following noble poem entire. It is, perhaps, the most perfect thing of its length in Donne's whole volume. Its versification is generally good, and, sometimes, exquisite. It is called,

A VALEDICTION, FORBIDDING TO MOURN

[He quotes the whole of 'A Valediction: forbidding Mourning'.]

Old Izaak Walton mentions this poem in his 'Life,'—'a copy of verses given by Mr. Donne to his wife at the time he then parted from her (to spend some months in France.) And I beg leave to tell, that I have heard some critics, learned both in languages and poetry, say, that none of the Greek or Latin poets did ever equal them.'

The above is the only entire poem, and indeed the only considerable passage of continuous beauty in the love-poems. There are indeed little exquisite touches without number, starting up here and there, like violets in the rough and, as yet, leafless woods. Of these we will give only as many as we think may be sufficient to sharpen the appetite of the lover of poetry, and send him to their source for more. This is from a little poem, called 'The Good-morrow:'

[He quotes the first stanza.]

Here is a pretty sigh:—

> Ah, what a trifle is a heart
> If once into love's hands it come!

The following passages are from 'The Ecstasy':—

[He quotes lines 1–4 and 17–28.]

From 'The Blossom':—

[He quotes lines 1–8 and 27–8.]

The only lines which we shall quote from the 'Epithalamions, or Marriage Songs,' are, perhaps, unsurpassed in descriptive poetry:—

[He quotes lines 1–10 of the *Epithalamion . . . St Valentines day*.]

Unfortunately, (or shall we say, fortunately?) the best thing in a true poet is that which it is impossible to convey any fit notion of, by a few and limited extracts. 'Every great poet has, in a measure, to create the taste by which he is to be enjoyed.' The divine *aura* that breathes about his works, is not to be found by the chance reader in any particular passage or poem. This only reveals itself to the loving *student* of the Muses, and departs from him who departs from them, or endeavours to *a*-muse himself by carelessly attending to their songs. The longest and most famous of these 'Epithalamions,' has scarcely a quotable passage. Its whole merit lies in this inexplicable, incommunicable *aura*.

The 'Elegies,' which we have classed with the early poems, and 'Epithalamions,' form rather, indeed, a link between these and the second class. We give the following passage, which seems to illustrate our assertion, combining, as it does, the fantastic beauty of the former, the maturer thought of the latter, and the faults of both:—

[He quotes lines 21–34 of *Elegie vi*, 'Oh, let mee not serve so'.]

Donne's 'Satires,'—to speak of which we now come—are, to our mind, the best in the English language. A satirist should never get into a passion with that which he is satirizing, and call names, as Dryden and Pope do; it is totally inconsistent with the dignity of the *judicial* position he assumes. To be sure, a lofty indignation may sometimes be allowed, but only on great occasions, and not against such petty-larceny practices and people as are, for the most part, the objects of satire. This was fully felt by the gentlemanly Donne, who, in his satires, resorts more often to the simple and the crushing strength of truth, than to the 'cat-o'-nine-tails' of invective. We quote largely from Satire III; it is upon the adoption of a religion—a subject which, as we have seen, had engaged our author's deepest thoughts.

[He quotes *Satyre iii*, lines 40–52, 62–79, 93–102.]

Throughout all our former quotations, there was a tolerable smoothness of versification: sometimes there was the sweetest music; but they were, in this, exceptions to the rule. The above passage is a good specimen of the *average* flow (!) of Donne's verses. But who, that, loving best of course the marriage of sound and meaning, would not yet prefer climbing, with Donne, these crags, where all the air is fresh and wholesome, to gliding, with Thomas Moore, over flats, from beneath the rank verdure of which arises malaria and invisible disease?

Pope took it upon himself to 'improve' some of Donne's Satires; and he did it, but in much the same style as the sailor who, having obtained a curiosity in the form of the weapon of a sword-fish, 'improved' it by scraping off, and rubbing down, all the protuberances by which it was distinguishable from any other bone. Fortunately, however, in most editions of Pope's writings, the original crudities are printed side by side with the polished improvement upon them; as sometimes we see, uphung in triumph at the doors of writing-masters, pairs of documents to some such effect as this:—I. 'This is my handwriting *before* taking lessons of Mr. Pope. *Signed*, John Donne.' II. 'This is my handwriting *after* taking lessons of Mr. Pope. *Signed*, John Donne.' Let us, however, give specimens of those so-different handwritings. The theme is the appearance of a reduced courtier.

I. *This is Donne, before being improved by Pope:*—

[He quotes *Satyre iv*, lines 17–29.]

II. *This is Donne, after being improved by Pope:*—

[He quotes Pope's version of the same lines.]

Oh, wonderful Mr. Pope! powerful to knock off *such* excrescences as,

> *Stranger than seven antiquaries' studies.*

and, '*Stranger than strangers;*' powerful to introduce *such* improvements as,

> Nay, all that *lying* travellers can *feign*!

We had marked many more passages for quotation from the 'Satires,' but we must, for want of space, hurry on, skipping the 'Letters,' which are crowded with gems of purest ray serene, and give a sweet word or two from the 'Funeral Elegies,' which contain more wisdom and poetry in the same space, than almost anything out of Shakspeare. We will take only one of the Elegies, and string some of its gems together without remark,—

[He quotes *The second Anniversary*, lines 244–6, 417–24, 69–70, 380–2, 110–12, in that order.]

The 'Divine Poems' are, for the most part, very poor, compared to these 'Elegies;' but here, as everywhere, splendid thoughts and splendid words abound. One instance or two is all we can give. Here is a description of Leviathan in the style of Milton, who made him 'swim the ocean *stream.*'

[He quotes the *Metempsychosis*, lines 311–15.]

To his soul,—

> Oh make thyself with holy mourning black,
> And red with blushing as thou art with sin.

Of a repentant sinner,—

> Tears in his eyes quench the amazing light.

With these extracts we conclude, hoping that we shall have introduced many of our readers to hundreds more like them, by having sent them to the volume out of which we have copied.

178. Henry Wadsworth Longfellow

1846

Longfellow (1807–82) preceded J. R. Lowell as Professor of Literature at Harvard. The following is an entry in his journal for 1846 (S. Longfellow, *The Life of Henry Wordsworth Longfellow*, Boston, 1886, ii, p. 40).

May 29th 1846. Called to see Lowell this morning. . . . Read Donne's poems, while he went down to feed his hens and chickens. . . .

179. Anon., *Lectures on the English Poets*

1847

An anonymous author read to his children some lectures on English poets which he later published. He mentioned Donne in speaking of the writers of the reign of Elizabeth, and of the seventeenth century. (*Lectures on the English Poets,* 1847, pp. 27–8 and 30.)

Towards the end of this queen's reign and during that of her immediate successor, a class of poets arose to whom the name of philosophical didactic, or, according to Dr. Johnson, metaphysical poets, has been given; such as Donne, who, though highly esteemed in his day, fell into disrepute in the last century, but whose works, harsh and full of conceits as they are, have recently been praised, as displaying much learning and caustic wit, with a rich and picturesque fancy. . . .

. . . Milton appears to have been free from the affectation of language and metaphysical jargon, which were the characteristic of the age. . . .

180. Edward Farr

1847

Farr (*fl.* 1836–76) wrote on religious topics and compiled books for children. He included some seventeen poems or bits of poems by Donne in an anthology of Jacobean religious verse: there are seven *Holy Sonnets*, three sonnets from *La Corona*, 'A Hymne to God the Father', 'A Hymne to Christ, at the Authors last going into Germany', 'Upon the Annunciation and Passion', 'Good-friday, 1613. Riding Westward', the 'Elegie on M^ris Boulstred' ('Death I recant'), an excerpt from *The Lamentations of Jeremy*, and one stanza from the *Metempsychosis*. Farr gives a brief biographical notice of Donne, from which the following item is an extract (*Select Poetry Chiefly Sacred of the Reign of King James the First*, 1847, p. xii).

This celebrated poet and preacher of the reign of King James was the first and most vigorous of that poetical school, which critics have held up to ridicule under the character of 'metaphysical'. . . . His great offence appears to be harshness of versification; but admitting that he is frequently rugged and sometimes obscure, this once favourite writer may nevertheless be pronounced to be a true and often a delightful poet.

181. Augustus Jessopp

c. 1847, 1855

Jessopp (1823–1914), headmaster and clergyman, was another lifelong student of Donne though it was Donne's religious prose which attracted him. In a book on Donne he brought out in 1897 at the age of seventy-four he recalled his undergraduate interest in Donne's writings (*John Donne: Sometime Dean of St Paul's* (1897), 1905, p. vii).

In 1855 Jessopp published a reprint of Donne's *Essays in Divinity*, with notes, and a 'Notice of the Author and his Writings' in which he made a few scattered observations on Donne's poetry (*Essays in Divinity by John Donne D.D.*, 1855, pp. xvii–xviii, xxxvii–xxxix, lvi–lvii, lxix–lxx).

(i)
It is fifty years since, as an undergraduate at Cambridge, I projected and began to make collections for a complete edition of the works of Dr. Donne.

In those days there was a great revival of the study of our seventeenth-century divinity, the result of the great Oxford Movement. Young men were told that the great teachers of that period were the safest and wisest guides to follow. Certainly we knew none better. The Textual Criticism of the New Testament was then in its infancy, and the New Theology was not yet born.

Perhaps it was just as well that publishers shrank from embarking in so ambitious a venture as I had contemplated; and soon circumstances intervened which took from me 'the dream of doing and the other dream of done'. . . .

(ii) [Of Donne's student days at Lincoln's Inn:] During his leisure hours he amused himself with occasional exercise of composition, in prose and verse, mere trifles for the most part—clever sallies flowing out from an exuberant wit,—the prose nervous and dexterous, the verse occasionally rugged, but both one and the other characterized by a vigour and grasp of mind which in so young a man is truly wonderful; and though open to the charge of being occasionally obscure (though this is true only of the poems) yet, the very faults are those of a man who has more power than he knows how to manage, certainly not those of one who is aiming at an originality which he does not possess.

It was at this time that he wrote his Satires, the earliest efforts at this branch of poetry written in our language; they are valuable not only for their poetical merit, which earned for them the warm praise of Suckling, Ben Jonson and Dryden, and even induced Mr. Pope to 'versify' (!) them—but they are historically interesting, as picturing the habits and tone of feeling among the upper classes, and especially the frequenters of the court, in the latter part of Queen Elizabeth's reign. . . .

[On *The first Anniversary*; after relating the circumstances.] It is written as might be expected, in a strain of extravagant panegyric, and though Donne had never seen his heroine, yet this by no means hindered his imagination from doing its part or made his task at all more difficult. . . . If Donne had no better motive in writing this elegy than that he might be taken into the favour of Sir Robert Drury, he succeeded completely. The compliment was too delicate, and the flattery too eloquent not to be appreciated very highly. . . . But the time was drawing near when Donne was to begin a life of more seriousness and more usefulness. The courtier and poet and wit, whose splendid powers had hitherto been comparatively trifled away, or turned to wholly unworthy purposes, was to be called on to dedicate them to a nobler end,—God had work for him to do; . . .

[On 'An hymne to the Saints, and to Marquesse Hamylton'.] Though confessing it to be 'reasonably witty, and well done', Mr. Chamberlain was scandalised that a man of Donne's 'years and place' should not 'give over versifying'. As if poetry had no higher mission than to please the ear; as if the 'sphere-born harmonious sisters' were only well employed, when they were ministering to folly and frivolity and sin!

[On the edition of Donne's poems published in 1633.] . . . a collection of his Poems, huddled together without any pretence of arrangement or the least discrimination in their selection.

[On a collection of Latin epigrams and poems ascribed to Donne, and translated into English by John Donne the younger in 1653.] . . . The epigrams and poems were written in Donne's boyhood. The wretched man who would not even leave them in their Latin dress, could not see that there was anything disgraceful in putting forth this obscene trash in the meretricious garb of a jingling English rhyme, and attaching to the unworthy rubbish his father's revered name:—On the son, not father, the scandal of their publicity must rest.

182. Charles Dexter Cleveland

1850

Cleveland (*fl.* 1836–68), a Pennsylvanian, edited Milton and produced compendia, literary histories, and Latin grammars. He spoke of Donne's poetry in *A Compendium of English Literature*, 1850, p. 165.

Donne's poems . . . procured for him among his contemporaries an extraordinary share of reputation, but now he is almost entirely forgotten. Either extreme does him injustice. Though he has not much harmony of versification, and but little simplicity and naturalness in thought and expression, yet he exhibits much erudition, united to an exuberance of wit, and to a fancy, rich, vivid, and picturesque, though at the same time, it must be confessed, not a little fantastical. Dr. Johnson, in his life of Cowley, considers him as the founder of the metaphysical school of poets; meaning, thereby, the faculty of wittily associating the most widely discordant images, and presenting ideas under the most remote and fanciful aspects. . . .

The following presents a very fair specimen of his poetry; indeed, it is more simple and natural than the greater part of it. The simile of the compasses, whatever may be thought of its beauty or fitness, is certainly original.

[He gives the whole of 'A Valediction: forbidding Mourning'.]

[In a footnote] . . . an article in the *Retrospective Review* gives to his poetry higher praise than we think it deserves. . . .

183. John Alfred Langford

1850

One of a series of 'evenings with' great writers in a periodical for the self-improvement of working men was devoted to Donne. Its author was J. A. Langford, described at the head of the essay as 'Chairmaker, Birmingham'. Langford (1823–1903) had in fact just then given up his trade of chairmaking to become a professional journalist; and he went on to establish himself as a commentator on the affairs of the day and as a local historian. There were 'evenings with' Herbert and other seventeenth-century poets in subsequent numbers of the journal. ('An Evening with John Donne', *The Working Man's Friend and Family Instructor*, supplementary number for December 1850, pp. 18–21.)

Among the many glories of English literature, not the least is her possession of so long a list of truly religious poets. In this, the highest order of poetry, we have names unsurpassed by those of any nation, or of any time. Setting aside the matchless glory of Milton, we have the quaint song of the pious old George Herbert; the epigrammatic force of the 'Night Thoughts' of Young; the genial, warm-hearted homeliness of the strains of Cowper; the child-like lyrics of the ever-loved Watts; the smooth, streamlike flow of Montgomery; the soul-raising thought of the nature-loving Wordsworth; and not to mention others of high and lofty fame, whose works the world will not willingly let die, we have him with whom we propose to spend the present evening— the old, antiquated, and venerable DONNE.

Dr. Johnson has offered some very curious reasons why religious poetry has not been successful in attaining a very high state of excellence. We venture to opine that in this respect the Doctor has committed himself, by giving a verdict which posterity will not confirm. We could select from our religious writers passages unequalled, in all that constitutes high poetry, by any equal number of passages from the greatest bards who have not especially devoted their talents to religion, such as Byron and Shelley, for instance. It is curious to think that the Doctor should fall into such a mistake; and it is still more curious to think of the numbers who have since re-echoed the opinion, considering that all the facts are against them. Why, the greatest of every land, and of every faith, are the religious ones, whether we look at the sublime old Hebrew bards, with 'the fires of Sinai, and the thunders of the Lord!' or at the poets of classic Greece, or at their numerous successors, who have drawn their inspiration from the Christian faith, the fact is the same. Well has a modern poet said,

> The high and holy works, mid lesser lays,
> Stand up like churches among village cots:
> And it is joy to think that in every age,
> However much the world was wrong therein,
> The greatest works of mind or hand have been
> Done unto God. So may they ever be!
> It shows the strength of wish we have to be great,
> And the sublime humility of might.—FESTUS.

But now to Donne. He was born in London in the year 1573. His parents were of the Roman Catholic faith, but their son, convinced of the truth of Protestantism, early declared himself a proselyte to the doctrines of the Reformation. He studied, and successfully, at both the Universities, and became, as one of the critics well observes, 'completely *saturated* with the learning of his times.' His works are rather voluminous, filling six goodly sized volumes, and consist of satires, ejaculations, occasional poems, elegies, and devotional pieces.

There is a class of poets known as the metaphysical. Of these Donne is perhaps the first in point of time, though some give 'rare old Ben,' the precedence. Their chief characteristic is their intellectualism. Forsaking the pure and genial naturalness of the Elizabethan poets, they seek by strange and far-fetched allusions, similes, and figures, to clothe a simple thought in party-coloured garments; and to offer it to the reader in as many varied aspects as the most violent twistings and torturings of this brave English language would allow. Extremely learned, in whatever was considered learning in their day, they ransacked all their store in the search for refined, *recherché*, and difficult analogies. Physics, metaphysics, scholastic literature, were made to bear tribute to their love of 'the blue-eyed maid' chimera. 'The metaphysical poets,' says Dr. Johnson, 'were men of learning; and to show their learning was their whole endeavour, but, unluckily, resolving to show it in rhyme, instead of writing poetry, they only wrote verses, and very often such verses as stood the trial of the finger better than of the ear, for the modulation was so imperfect, that they were only found to be verses by counting the syllables. Such is sure to be the case, when men sit down to put thoughts into verse, instead of waiting till the divine afflatus compels them to utter their feelings, which necessarily take the form of song; as different a thing from verse as light is from darkness. Goethe has well said in one of those world-famous *Xenien* of his,

> What many sing and say,
> Must still by us be borne!
> Ye worthy—great and small—
> Tired you sing yourselves and lorn;
> And yet let no one tune his lay
> Except for what he has to say.

But of these poets, if we except Cowley, Donne holds the highest place. He had much wit, in which gift Dryden confesses himself and his cotemporaries to be inferior. He had, as we have seen, a vast erudition, some fancy and elegance, together with strong piety. These combined must surely make a poet of no ordinary power. His satires are strong, vigorous, and masculine. Compared with Pope his verses would certainly want smoothness, but Pope himself would have been a much greater poet, had he possessed some of the wholesome roughness, and known that amidst a profusion of sweets that a bitter is often welcome and good. It is true that Donne is very capricious about the place of accent; but few readers would have to count the fingers to tell whether it were verse or no. Certain we are, if much of his writing be not verse, there is much of it that is poetry. Take the following lines on the 'Last Night of the Year':—

[He quotes lines 1–10 of the verse letter 'To the Countesse of Bedford At New-yeares Tide'.]

The critic we have quoted above as saying that Donne was saturated with all the learning of his times, also says of him 'That he was endowed with a most active and piercing intellect—an imagination, if not grasping and comprehensive, most subtle and far-darting—a fancy rich, vivid and picturesque—and a wit admirable as well for its caustic severity as for its playful quickness.' This is particularly applicable to his satires, which are the precursors of Dryden and Pope's. It would be useless to select from these, as it is but by examination of them as a whole that their force, their truthfulness, and their caustic severity and playful quickness can be felt. To take a passage from any, at all adapted to the limits of this paper, in order to show their quality, would be about as wise as the man who having a house to sell, carried a brick with him as a specimen. We may say of them, what can be said of but few satires, that they possess more than a temporary interest, and may be read with profit and advantage at the present time.

The following piece illustrates pretty well the best and worst qualities of Donne:—

[He quotes the whole of 'A Valediction: forbidding Mourning'.]

A strange analogy this; but yet not so absurd as at first reading it may appear. It is true it may need reading over more than once clearly to seize its hidden meaning; but what then, shall we turn aside from every one 'who does not wear his heart upon his sleeve for daws to peck at?'

One more extract, and we bid our poet good night. It is on the littleness of temporal existence, compared with the great, solemn eternity beyond. The lines are quaint, but their spirit fine.

[He quotes lines 173–84 of *The second Anniversary*.]

184. George Gilfillan

Gilfillan (1813–78), a Presbyterian minister, was an industrious author of moral works and editor of the poets. In an anthology of British poetry he gave two poems by Donne—'A Valediction: forbidding Mourning', and 'The Will'—as against two each by Carew and Suckling, three by Beaumont, four each by Jonson, Drummond, Herbert, and Harington, five by Herrick and nine extracts by Shakespeare. He spoke of Donne in his prefatory 'Essay on British Poetry', making a bad start by giving Donne's dates as 1570–1630 (*The Book of British Poesy*, 1851, pp. xx and 147–51).

Gilfillan launched an assault on Johnson's account of the metaphysical poets in an essay on 'The Life and Poetry of Richard Crashaw' which introduces *The Poetical Works of Richard Crashaw and Quarles' Emblems*, Edinburgh, 1857, pp. xiv–xviii.

In a three-volume collection of verses by some less familiar British poets Gilfillan included all sixteen *Holy Sonnets* then known and the whole of the *Metempsychosis*, prefacing these poems with a brief account of Donne from which the third extract is taken (*Specimens with Memoirs of the Less-Known British Poets*, 1860, i, pp. 203–4).

(i)
Drayton, Donne, Withers, Quarles, Cowley, and Herbert, all belong to what Dr Johnson called the 'metaphysical', or elaborately ingenious school of poetry. They twist their gold into the most formal and fantastic chains; they cut their gardens, trees, and hedges into the most singular shapes; but how rich the 'greenery' of the gardens, and how pure and massive the gold! 'Holy' George Herbert's 'Temple' is quiet and cool, as the temple of Jerusalem on the evening after the buyers and sellers were expelled. . . .

(ii)

Crashaw, at least, has never mingled metaphysics with his poetry, although here and there he is as fantastic as Donne or Cowley, or any of the class. . . .

. . . Johnson valued himself on his brief but vigorous account of the 'Metaphysical Poets', in his Life of Cowley. We think, however, with all deference to his high critical authority, that not only has he used the word 'metaphysical' in an arbitrary and inapposite sense, but that he has besides confounded it with perverted ingenuity, and very much underrated the genius of the men. He calls them, after Dryden, 'wits, not poets, but if wit is almost always held to signify a *sudden perception of analogies more or less recondite*, along with a TENDENCY *to the ludicrous*, then these writers have very little of the quality indeed. They see and shew remote analogies, but the analogies are too remote or too grave to excite any laughable emotion. Coming from far—coming as captives—and coming violently chained together in pairs, they produce rather wonder, tinctured with melancholy, than that vivid delight which creates smiles, if it does not explode into laughter. Sometimes, indeed, the conceits produce a ridiculous effect, but this arises rather from their absurdity than their wit. . . . But apart from their perverted ingenuity, their straining after effect, their profusion of small and often crooked points, and their desire to shew their learning, these writers had undoubtedly high imagination. . . .

[He gives some examples from Cowley, and comments on them.]

These are bold metaphors, but they are not conceits. We feel them to rise naturally out of, and exactly to measure the majesty of the theme, not like conceits, to be *arbitrarily embossed* upon the shield of a subject, without any regard to its size, proportions, or general effect. We are happy to find De Quincy coinciding in part with our opinion of Johnson's criticism.

[He quotes de Quincey's criticism of Johnson's remarks on Donne. See No. 146.]

Here it would be noticed that De Quincy takes somewhat different ground from what we would take in reply to Johnson. He seems to think that Johnson principally objected to the *manner* of these writers, and he argues, very justly, that as professed rhetoricians they had a right to use the artifices of rhetoric, and none the less that they wrote in metre; and he might have maintained, besides, that finding a peculiar

mode of writing in fashion, they were quite as justifiable in using it, IF
they did not caricature it, as in wearing the bag, sword, and ruffles of
their day. But Johnson, besides, denied that these men were poets; he
objected to the *matter* as well as the manner of their song; and here we
join issue with him, nay, are ready to admit that they were often
rhetorically faulty, even by their own standard, if it be granted that
they possessed a real and sublime poetic genius. That De Quincy agrees
with us in this belief, we are certain, but it was his part to defend them
upon another and a lower basis of assault. . . .

[He quotes Johnson's denial of their claims to sublimity—'The sublime
was not within their reach. . . '.]

In these remarks there is much truth as well as splendour; but Dr
Johnson seems to forget that with all the elaborate pettiness of much
in their writings—Cowley . . . 'Davideis'; 'Donne in his 'Metempsychosis'; Crashaw . . . 'Sospetto d'Herode'; Quarles . . . *Emblems*; Herbert in certain parts of his 'Temple', [they] have, perhaps *in
spite* of their own system, attained a rare grandeur of thought and
language.

[He says that Jeremy Taylor and Sir Thomas Browne show the same
characteristics in prose—'yet both have passages unsurpassed for sublimity of imagination'.]

[He goes on to attack Johnson for saying that 'Great things cannot
have escaped their former observation']—surely, although all men in all
ages have seen the sun, the ocean, the earth, and the stars, new aspects
of them are often presenting themselves to the poetic eye. . . .

The truth is, Dr Johnson had great sympathy with the broad—the
materially sublime and the colossally great; but, from a defect in eye-
sight and in mind, had little or none with either the beautiful or the
subtle, and did not perceive the exquisite effects which a minute use of
the knowledge of both these often produces. . . .

[He exemplifies from Milton, and then Crashaw.]

(iii)
[He quotes de Quincey's admiring comments on Donne in the essay on
Rhetoric—see No. 146:]

We beg leave to differ, in some degree, from De Quincey in his estimate
of the 'Metempsychosis,' or 'The Progress of the Soul,' although we

have given it entire. It has too many far-fetched conceits and obscure allegories, although redeemed, we admit, by some very precious thoughts, such as

> This soul, to whom Luther and Mahomet were
> Prisons of flesh.

Or the following quaint picture of the apple in Eden—

> Prince of the orchard, fair as dawning morn,
> Fenced with the law, and ripe as soon as born.

Or this—

> Nature hath no jail, though she hath law.

If our readers, however, can admire the account the poet gives of Abel and his bitch, or see any resemblance to the severe and simple grandeur of Æschylus and Ezekiel in the description of the soul informing a body, made of a '*female fish's sandy roe*' '*newly leavened with the male's jelly,*' we shall say no more.

Donne, altogether, gives us the impression of a great genius ruined by a false system. He is a charioteer run away with by his own pampered steeds. He begins generally well, but long ere the close, quibbles, conceits, and the temptation of shewing off recondite learning, prove too strong for him, and he who commenced following a serene star, ends pursuing a will-o'wisp into a bottomless morass. Compare, for instance, the ingenious nonsense which abounds in the middle and the close of his 'Progress of the Soul' with the dark, but magnificent stanzas which are the first in the poem.

In no writings in the language is there more spilt treasure—a more lavish loss of beautiful, original, and striking things than in the poems of Donne. Every second line, indeed, is either bad, or unintelligible, or twisted into unnatural distortion, but even the worst passages discover a great, though trammelled and tasteless mind; and we question if Dr Johnson himself, who has, in his 'Life of Cowley,' criticised the school of poets to which Donne belonged so severely, and in some points so justly, possessed a tithe of the rich fancy, the sublime intuition, and the lofty spirituality of Donne. How characteristic of the difference between these two great men, that, while the one shrank from the slightest footprint of death, Donne deliberately placed the image of his dead self before his eyes, and became familiar with the shadow ere the grim reality arrived!

Donne's Satires shew, in addition to the high ideal qualities, the rugged versification, the fantastic paradox, and the perverted taste of their author, great strength and clearness of judgment, and a deep, although somewhat jaundiced, view of human nature. That there must have been something morbid in the structure of his mind is proved by the fact that he wrote an elaborate treatise, which was not published till after his death, entitled, 'Biathanatos,' to prove that suicide was not necessarily sinful.

185. The Boston edition of Donne's poems

1855

An unnamed scholar edited Donne's poems in New England, producing a text based in a fresh collation of some of the early printed versions: *The Poetical Works of Dr John Donne, With a Memoir*, Boston, 1855. The edition is volume xxxix of *The Complete Collection of British Poets*, general editor F. J. Child. In the same year it appeared as the second part of *The Poetical Works of Skelton and Donne* published at Riverside, Cambridge, Mass., a press associated with the New England school of writers headed by Emerson and J. R. Lowell. There is a 'Life of Donne' abridged from Walton. The poems are given in a curious order—verse letters; *Anniversaries* and funeral elegies; *Divine Poems*; *Metempsychosis*; 'Miscellaneous Poems' (i.e., the *Songs and Sonnets*); *Epigrams*; *Elegies*; *Epithalamions*; *Satyres*; Latin poems.

In his Preface to the Grolier Club edition of Donne's poems C. E. Norton spoke of Lowell's part in this Boston publication. He said that 'Donne's Poems were, from an early period of his life, among Mr Lowell's favorite books. In 1855 an edition of them was included, I believe at his instance, in the series of "British Poets" then in course of publication by Little, Brown and Company in Boston. It was, apparently, a reprint, without material change, from one of the later English editions, and, like all previous editions, it stood greatly in need of editorial revision. . . .' Norton went on to say that Lowell had scored his copy of the 1855 edition with textual emendations. (*The Poems of John Donne, From The Text of The Edition Of 1633*. Revised by James Russell Lowell . . ., With A Preface, An Introduction, And Notes By Charles Eliot Norton, New York, 1895, i, pp. vii–viii.)

Sir Geoffrey Keynes ascribes to Lowell himself the editing of the Boston edition of 1855 (*A Bibliography of Dr John Donne*, Oxford

1973, p. 211). He cites a copy of it unearthed some years ago which carries a pencil note in Lowell's hand saying that he edited it. But possibly Lowell was referring to the textual emendations Norton noted.

186. Anon., *Putnam's Monthly Magazine*

1856

An anonymous contributor to a monthly journal made what was then becoming a standard comparison of Browning with some seventeenth-century poets ('Robert Browning', *Putnam's Monthly Magazine of American Literature, Science, and Art*, vii, April 1856, pp. 372–81). He was reviewing Browning's published poems up to *Men and Women*, 1856.

Robert Browning's poetry is certainly very hard reading, like Cowley's and Dr. Donne's. But the difference between him and such obscurists is, that with the earlier poets, both the style and the sentiment were equally conceits—while Browning's style is the naturally quaint form of a subtle or sinewy thought. In any general classification of English poetry, Browning must be ranked with the modern school for his profound reality and humanity and faithful reliance upon nature. . . .

187. Sir John Simeon

1856-7

Simeon (1815–70) was for many years M.P. for the Isle of Wight. He edited a number of texts for the Philobiblon Society, among them a collection of twenty poems which he claimed to be hitherto unpublished pieces by Donne. Only two of the poems have been generally accepted as Donne's—*Elegie xx*, 'Loves Warre', and the epigram 'The Lier'. *Elegie xx* had in fact been published by F. G. Waldron in 1802. Simeon introduced the poems with some comments on Donne ('Unpublished Poems of Donne', in *Miscellanies of the Philobiblon Society*, iii, 1856–7, pp. 8–9).

He presented a copy of the collection to Robert Browning (see No. 147 (v)).

In conclusion, I venture to express my entire conviction, which will, I think, be borne out by the opinion of all who are conversant with the very peculiar style and versification of Donne, that the transcribers of these MSS have not erred in assigning these poems to him. The least works of an author who, though little appreciated in our day, ranked among the choice luminaries of his own, are worth preserving; and some of the verses now printed may challenge comparison with the best of the poems hitherto published as his. I therefore trust that they will be acceptable as a not uninteresting contribution to the works of a poet, who, whatever may have been his faults, and however he may have been deficient in some of the highest characteristics of the poetic mind, will always deserve attention for the keenness of his wit, and the exuberance of his fancy,—a quality in which he is perhaps without a rival, even among those Italians upon whose fantastic conceits he seems to have modelled his style.

188. *Notes and Queries*

1856–80

From the mid-1850s *Notes and Queries* frequently carried contributions concerning Donne, many of which were preparing
the way for an edition of his poems. There were eight such notes
on Donne in 1863 alone, and at least eight in 1880. The correspondent in the 1860s who signs himself 'Cpl' was probably the
Rev. T. R. O'Flaherty of Capel, near Dorking, the possessor of
the invaluable manuscript of Donne's poems which is now known
by his name. O'Flaherty had long been collecting material towards
an edition of Donne's poems but it was Grosart who edited
Donne in the end. The following are some of the references to
Donne's poetry.

---

n.s. ii, ii, 1856, p. 205. W. S. Simpson wrote about the tomb of Elizabeth Drury in Hawsted Church and the epitaph it bears, which is
ascribed to Donne. He quoted lines 244b–6 of *The second Anniversary*.

n.s. iii, iii, 1863, pp. 308 and 336. 'Chessborough' asked the date of the
first collected edition of Donne's poems and the editor replied at once.
J. P. Collier replied later.

n.s. iii, iv, 1863, p. 150. 'Cpl.' asked who Mrs Bulstrode was, and the
editorial reply mentioned a surmise 'that she may have been the concealed subject of much of Donne's lighter verse'.

n.s. iii, iv, 1863, pp. 198–9. J. A. Harper wrote on the identity of Mrs
Bulstrode and referred to the poems by Donne in the Farmer-Chetham
manuscript.

n.s. iii, vii, 1865, pp. 84–5, 145, 439. 'Cpl.' asked for 'a construe' of the
macaronic poem to Coryate, and 'RSQ' gave him his construe with a
comment that Donne's verses are not strictly macaronic, for 'Donne's
set all principles of prosody at defiance, as completely as most of the
modern attempts at English hexameters. It does not, however, require

any extraordinary effort to relieve "Cpl." from his real or pretended difficulty'. Later in the same issue 'Cpl.' asked for the identities of people addressed in Donne's verse letters, and suggested some possibilities.

n.s. iv, ii, 1868, pp. 35, 483, 614. 'Cpl.' asked the whereabouts of a copy of the 1635 edition of Donne's poems from a recent library sale. W. C. Hazlitt listed some variant readings between an unnamed manuscript of Donne's poems and the 1669 edition, and gave 'The Message' entire from the manuscript. He added that 'A good edition of Donne may be worth a place in the *Library of Old Authors*, if some competent person could be found to undertake such a task *con amore*. All the old copies would require collation with each other, and with any existing manuscripts, notably with Harl. MS. 5110, which contains *Ihon Donne his Satires, Anno Domini 1593*, and with the present little collection.'

'Cpl.' replied—'I quite agree with your correspondent Mr W. Carew Hazlitt, that a good edition of Donne is a desideratum, and I have made large collections for his life [Walton's] and works, but I cannot find time or courage to carry out my intentions'. He went on to discuss Hazlitt's list of variant readings, and asked if 'your learned correspondent Dr Rimboult' knows 'anything of these "certaine aires" to which Donne's songs were written'.

n.s. iv, vii, 1871, p. 494. A. B. Grosart asked for help in identifying the people addressed by their initials in Donne's verse letters. He added that his Fuller Worthies edition of Donne's complete poems was well advanced, 'with numerous additions from MSS of rare value and interest'.

n.s. v, iii, 1875, pp. 382, 433, 472–3, 494–5; n.s. v, v, 1876, p. 313 et seq. A correspondence developed over a quatrain on the Real Presence sometimes attributed to Donne and sometimes to Queen Elizabeth. The chief contributors were J. H. Friswell, E. Solly, and S. H. Harlowe. The debate prompted discussion of several matters concerning Donne's poems—which poems were included in the early editions, variant readings as between those editions, the circumstances in which particular poems or bodies of poems were written, Donne's epigram style, and so on.

n.s. v, v, 1876, pp. 242–3. 'A.R.B.' gave 'A Poem by Dr Donne', a long (and spurious) verse letter with an eighteenth-century note declaring it to be by Donne. 'A.R.B.' quoted de Quincey's praise of Donne (see No. 146(i)).

n.s. vi, ii, 1880, pp. 8 and 190–1. J. Dixon asked 'Will any reader of
N. & Q. who has Donne's *Satires* at hand, kindly tell me whether the
word "glare" occurs at line 8 of *Satire iv*? I have a copy of Pope in
which his paraphrase is printed along with Donne's original doggerel . . .'. This note drew eight replies, most of them beside the point
since the readers assume that any edition is authoritative and give
readings from texts published in 1669, 1795, 1810, and so on. But E.
Solly and A. Jessop show a sound enough knowledge of editions of
Donne to trace the reading back to its source in the 1650 text. Jessop
asks 'But what can Mr Dixon mean by talking of "Donne's original
doggerel"?'

189. Adolphus William Ward

1858

Ward (1837–1924) had a very distinguished academic career at
Manchester and Cambridge, and was knighted in 1913. He became
editor-in-chief of the *Cambridge Modern History*, and co-editor of
the *Cambridge History of English Literature*. As a young man he
edited the Globe *Pope*, and introduced Pope's version of Donne's
Satyre ii and *Satyre iv* with some remarks on Donne (*The Poetical
Works of Pope* (1858), 1956, pp. 324–5).

Donne has been, in deference to Pope's classification of poets, regarded
as the father of the metaphysical, or fantastic school of English poets,
which reached its height in the reign of Charles I. His poetry divides
itself into two distinctly marked divisions—profane and religious. The
former must be in the main regarded as consisting of purely intellectual
exercitations; nor should the man be rashly confounded with the writer,
or the Ovidian looseness of morals which he affects be supposed to have
characterised his life. His *Songs* are full of the conceits criticised by Dr

Johnson; some of his *Epigrams* are very good; his *Elegies* are most offensively indecent; and the *Progress of the Soul* is a disgusting burlesque on the Pythagorean doctrine of metempsychosis. The *Funeral Elegies* already show the transition to sacred poetry; and it is on these and the *Holy Sonnets* that rests Donne's claim to be called a metaphysical poet.

Yet he states that he affected the metaphysics in his *Satires* and amorous verses as well. The former were first published, with the rest of his works, in 1633. In Dryden's opinion, quoted by Chalmers, the *Satires* of Donne, even if translated into numbers, would yet be found wanting in dignity of expression. It has however been doubted whether the irregularity of Donne's versification in the *Satires* was wholly undesigned. His lyrical poetry is fluent and easy; and the *Satires* of Hall, which preceded those of Donne by several years, show a comparative mastery over the heroic couplet which could surely have been compassed by the later Satirist. Pope has treated Donne's text with absolute freedom.

190. Francis Turner Palgrave

1858–89

Palgrave quoted Donne's poetry pseudonymously in 1858 but omitted Donne from his *Golden Treasury of Songs and Lyrics*, 1861, a collection which aimed 'to include in it all the best original Lyrical pieces and Songs in our language, by writers not living,— and none beside the best'. He gave poems by Herbert, Vaughan, and Marvell, as well as by such lesser poets as Barnefield, Lodge, Dekker, Drummond, and Wotton.

In an essay he published in the same year as the *Golden Treasury* Palgrave expressed a low opinion of Donne's poetry which sufficiently explains why he did not represent it in the anthology. Nearly thirty years later however he had come to take Donne more seriously.

(i) Under the pseudonym 'Henry J. Thurston', Palgrave published a perfervid account of a lifelong but hopeless love for one Désirée. He adapted lines 61–2 of 'A Funerall Elegie' (the tailpiece to *The first Anniversary*) to describe the 'community more than commonly complete in Désirée between Spirit and Body'. The reference is unascribed in the text, but the list of 'References and Translations' notes it as 'DONNE: *A Funeral Elegy*'. (*The Passionate Pilgrim or Eros and Anteros*, 1858, pp. 68 and 241.)

(ii) From 'The Growth of English Poetry', an unsigned review of the first twenty-nine volumes of Bell's *Annotated Series of British Poets*, *The Quarterly Review*, 110, October 1861, pp. 449–50 and 455–6:

Readers who have heard our early poetry specially noted for the qualities of freshness and simplicity, and are familiar with the common specimens, will have been often surprised when they turned to the original authors in their integrity. The style which Shakespeare has dramatised in 'Love's Labour's Lost,' the far-sought conceits and allusions, the strange contorted phraseology, are no peculiarities of Donne and Cowley, but more or less mark English poetry from Surrey to Herbert and Crashaw. The powerful effort which freed our literature from a disguise above all others fitted to conceal want of thought and poetic fancy (although worn by many who needed no such disguise), has been but scantily appreciated in modern times, and a great deal of criticism, often unjust, has been directed against the poetry of the hundred years following 1660. But of the meaning and the results of the change begun by Dryden and consummated in Gray we hope to speak hereafter. Reverting, meanwhile, to the antecedent period,—there is a sense in which it is characterized by simplicity, though not the pure simplicity of the ancients. It is a simplicity less of words than of ideas. For the subjects then treated are not only limited in range, but in conception; it is in the drama only that a wider sweep is taken, and there, obviously, under very different conditions. Love, as the passion best suited for song, is of course prominent; but it is love in its elementary aspects, and rarely carried into any subtlety of analysis. We have despair and triumph and jealousy, passionate pleading, and proud renunciation; but except in Shakespeare's sonnets we look in vain for those finer aspects and remoter links of feeling which Wordsworth, Shelley, and Tennyson have in our own days shown in co-existence with a simplicity and natural strength rarely found in their predecessors.

[He compares verse by Oxford and Habington with bits of Words-worth's 'Lucy' poems and develops a lengthy comparison between the old writers and the new, always much preferring nineteenth-century poetry for its greater depth, finish, compass, art, and the like.]

Meanwhile the Muses of England were learning modes of expression hitherto scarcely attempted. Comic songs and satire on subjects of the day, before almost confined to the drama, became the separate pursuit of Corbet, Suckling, Cartwright, Donne, and Jonson. And, as in the days of Horace, in connection with satire, appear poetical epistles (the first specimen of which is stated to be one given by Hall in 1613) on a vast variety of subjects. Few of these forms of poetry produced much that is valuable except historically, yet it would be an unjust opinion which, from the nature of their themes, ranked them below the narra-tives and pastorals, in which so much ordinary verse under Elizabeth displayed itself. Their aim indeed is less distinctly poetical; but their result was to bring poetry into vital connection with real life in all its phases; thus commencing those lessons of sobriety and simplicity in thought which the English mind so eminently needed. Even the rank luxuriance then displayed in the qualities most opposed to these—conceit and affectation—of which Johnson, in his Life of Cowley, has given excellent specimens, tended in the same direction. For the earlier conceits lie more in imaginative embroidery—those of Cowley, Donne, and Cartwright in fanciful and overstrained thought. By this change the disease reached the last stage of its career, and, by seizing on the intellect rather than the imagination, worked itself out of poetry. Compare two imitations of Marlowe's well-known song:—

[He gives the first four stanzas of 'Come live with me, and be my dear', which he ascribes to Raleigh, and the first four stanzas of Donne's 'The Baite'.]

Here the fancies of Raleigh, his nymphs and satyrs, his 'summer's green' for the girl's complexion, and 'eternal ditties' for the spring, are all imaginative conceits and fallacies; Donne's the frostwork ingenuities of the intellect. Lodge's noble *Description of Rosaline*, glowing with the colours of Tintoret or Veronese, might be similarly compared with Cowley's *Clad all in White*.

(iii) About 1888 Palgrave marked a copy of Grosart's edition of Donne's poems which is now in the British Museum (press mark 2326.d.3). The marks suggest that he was chiefly concerned to select poems for his *The Treasury of Sacred Song*, which came out in 1889, but he may also have had in mind the second series of his *Golden Treasury*, 1896. Palgrave gave three of the *Holy Sonnets* in *The Treasury of Sacred Song*, but he never did admit Donne to the *Golden Treasury*.

Volume i of Palgrave's copy of the Grosart edition appears to be quite unmarked. In volume ii there are light crosses, in pencil, on the 'Song. Sweetest love, I do not goe' and 'The Anniversarie'. The first stanza of 'The Anniversarie' is marked out by a vertical line, and Palgrave has written '*Si sic omnia*' alongside it in pencil. Lines 13–20 of 'The Exstasie' have a vertical line drawn alongside them. Palgrave makes brief notes against poems which have been printed among the writings of other authors, to indicate that they may not be by Donne.

Palgrave has ticked five of the *Holy Sonnets*—i, ii, vi, vii, and x; and he has put a small circle against a further eleven—iii, iv, v, viii, ix, xi, xii, xiii, xiv, xv, xvi. He has marked several places in 'The Crosse' and has written alongside the whole poem 'Spoiled by its own cleverness'.

A Litanie carries a small circle against the title and vertical lines against stanzas 3 and 5, and the last two lines of stanza 7. Alongside 'A Hymne to Christ, at the Authors last going into Germany' Palgrave has written 'fine and pathetic'. There is a cross against the title of 'A Hymne to God the Father'.

The copy is not catalogued as Palgrave's. It was identified by Mrs Kathleen Tillotson ('Donne's Poetry in the Nineteenth Century (1800–72)' in *Elizabethan and Jacobean Studies Presented to F. P. Wilson*, ed. H. Davis and H. Gardner, Oxford, 1959, p. 323).

(iv) Palgrave included three of Donne's *Holy Sonnets* in *The Treasury of Sacred Song*, Oxford, 1889, and gave a brief account of Donne's career and poetry from which the following extract is taken (p. 333):

. . . Donne's poems . . . cover an extraordinary range in subject, and are throughout marked with a strange originality almost equally fascinating and repellant. It is possible that his familiarity with Italian and Spanish literatures, both at that time deeply coloured by fantastic and far-fetched thought, may have in some degree influenced him in that direction. His poems were probably written mainly during youth. There is a strange solemn passionate earnestness about them, a quality which underlies the 'fanciful conceits' of all his work. Donne, like Herbert and Vaughan, who show the same intensity and quaintness, was of Welsh descent. . . .

191. Samuel Austin Allibone

1859

Allibone (1816–89) was a Philadelphian writer of biographies and of commentaries on literature and scripture. He gave a brief life of Donne in *A Critical Dictionary of English Literature*, Philadelphia, 1859, pp. 512–13, and made one comment on Donne's poetry.

He enjoyed great reputation as a poet, being placed at the head of the Metaphysical School; and after long neglect has received some attention within the last four years; but his poetry is not of a character calculated to gain extensive popularity. He excelled in complimentary addresses, epigrams, satires, elegies, and poems of a theological character.

192. Anne Charlotte Lynch Botta

1860

Mrs Botta (1815–91), whose parents were Irish, was a poetess, translator, and compiler. For years she presided over a noted literary salon in Boston. In a general history of literature she characterised the reign of James I as a time when 'English writing began to be infected with pedantic affectations' and spoke of Donne as one of the chief offenders (*A Handbook of Universal Literature* (1860), Boston, 1885, pp. 452–3, 476, and 483).

. . . the poet Donne introduced fantastic eccentricities into poetical composition. . . .

. . . Cowley now closed with great brilliancy the eccentric and artificial school of which Donne had been the founder. . . .

[On the lyrical poems of the time.] . . . In those of Donne, in spite of their conceits and affectations, are many passages wonderfully fine. . . .

. . . The sermons of Donne, while they are superior in style, are sometimes fantastic like his poetry, but they are never coarse, and they derive a touching interest from his history.

193. Alfred, Lord Tennyson

In a memorial volume published five years after Tennyson's death F. T. Palgrave recalled some of Tennyson's favourite poets and poems. He mentioned poems by Clough, Rogers, and Moore, among others, and gave lines which Tennyson was in the habit of quoting, from Marvell, Milton, Sidney, Petrarch, Pope, Chaucer, and Donne ('Personal Recollections by F. T. Palgrave', in Hallam Tennyson, *Alfred Lord Tennyson: A Memoir by his Son*, 1897, ii, p. 503).

From Donne he would quote the 'Valediction, forbidding Mourning', the last four stanzas:

> Our two souls . . .

where the poet compares himself to the moving leg, his love to the central, of the compass when describing a circle: praising its wonderful ingenuity. . . .

194. Edward FitzGerald

1861

FitzGerald published translations of Calderon in 1853. He compared Donne and the metaphysical poets with Calderon in a letter to E. B. Cowell dated 7 December 1861 (*The Letters and Literary Remains of Edward FitzGerald,* ed. W. A. Wright, 1902–3, ii, pp. 132–3).

I always said about Cowley, Donne, etc. whom Johnson calls the metaphysical Poets, that their very Quibbles of Fancy, showed a power of Logic which could follow Fancy through such remote Analogies. This is the case with Calderon's conceits also. . . .

195. William Francis Collier

1861

Collier (*fl.* 1861–91) was a grammarian, historian, and writer for schools. He gave a slipshod account of Donne in *A History of English Literature in a Series of Biographical Sketches*, 1861, p. 168. He declares, among other things, that Donne was buried in Westminster Abbey.

John Donne . . . He deserves remembrance as a very learned man, who began the list of what critics call the Metaphysical poets. Beneath the artificial incrustations which characterize this school, Donne displays a fine vein of poetic feeling. He is also noted in our history as the first writer of satire in rhyming couplets. . . .

196. Mrs Katharine Thomson

1861

Mrs Thomson (1797–1862) wrote anecdotal biographies and historical novels. She spoke of Donne's poetry in an account of his friendships with patronesses and others (*Celebrated Friendships*, 1861, pp. 305–7).

Donne was eccentric through life. A picture of him at Lincoln's Inn is mentioned by Grainger. . . .

[She describes, accurately, the Lothian portrait.]

. . . of his poems it has been said:

> 'Twas then plain Donne in honest vengeance rose,
> His wit harmonious, but his rhyme was prose.

Satire was Donne's forte; but, as Dryden observed, his 'thoughts were debased by his versification'. . . .

Notwithstanding the wit and knowledge of the human mind displayed by Dr. Donne, he was, during the whole of his life, an eccentric being.

197. Anon., *Temple Bar*

1861

The following is an extract from an anonymous essay which gives a dramatic account of Donne's life and work ('Donne the Metaphysician', *Temple Bar*, iii, 1861, pp. 78–89).

. . . Donne had already distinguished himself as a wit who wrote excellent verses, and his genius found a liberal patron in Sir Francis Wooley, a distant kinsman. I am afraid that Master Donne toadied at this time about the crowded ante-chambers of the rich, in the common but vain expectation of Court preferment. Literature was a hired jester, not a lady, in those days. She jingled a cap and bells, and received chance halfpence.

. . . The great secret of the merits and demerits of Donne's poetry is partly to be found in the insatiable desire for book-knowledge which at this period distinguished his genius, in common with that of Cowley and the other metaphysical poets. Almost unconsciously, he became pedantic. Pedantry, coming into contact with a metaphysical habit of thought, soon made his language a puzzle to vulgar comprehensions. 'He dealeth so profoundly,' said Harrison of John Heywood's *Spider and Fly*, 'and beyond all measure of skill, that neither he himself that made it, neither any one that readeth it, can reach unto the meaning thereof.' And much the same criticism might be applied to Donne's writings. He had always a meaning, sometimes a beautiful one, but it was too subtle to be easily detected. So with the rest of the metaphysicians,

> Wha ding their brains in college classes,
> And syne expect to climb Parnassus,
> By dint o' Greek.

. . . Add to all this, that he was a wild dreamer, and saw apparitions. He had imaginary conflicts with Satan, during which he fortified himself with quotations from Scripture. *Satius est supervacua discere quam nihil.* A superfluity of knowledge is better than noodledom. The intense thirst for knowledge which distinguished Donne and the other metaphysical poets served at least one purpose, if it did not improve their verses. It elevated them above the follies and meannesses of the idle Court butterflies, it kept their blood cool and sober, and it taught one or two of them to meditate divinely on themes beyond the sunset. They busied their brains with book-lore, they lived exemplary lives, and they left poems which are often unintelligible.

. . . 'The metaphysical poets were men of learning,' says Johnson in one of his just fits; 'and to show their learning was their whole endeavour; but, unluckily, resolving to show it in rhyme, instead of writing poetry, they only wrote verses, and very often such verses as stood the trial of the finger better than of the ear; for the modulation was so imperfect, that they were only found to be verses by counting the syllables.' This is as true as any criticism Johnson ever penned; still, like all his criticisms, it is only half true. The metaphysical poets were for the most part men of genius as well as learning; and their whole endeavour was not so much to show their learning, as to gratify their love for quaint fancies. The form was in their eyes so subservient to the substance, that they neglected the form of their poems altogether; yet they now and then touch a key-note of melody which has a deeper and more lingering effect than the music of the more finished verse-writers. They were addicted to what Dryden calls 'the fairy kind of writing.' They lost sight of nature while racking their learned heads for queer images. Their pictures, though essentially poetical, were proportionally false; yet they limned them with an honest desire to benefit their fellow mortals. They paint at second-hand, taking as models those vague hypothetical memories which, through a long sojourn in the domains of the fancy, have been distorted into a picturesqueness not their own. They are lavish of metaphor, generally far fetched, but seldom more than pretty. All these faults were most prominent in their love-verses,—a kind of composition which ought to be peculiarly free from such affectations. But, you see, ever since Queen Elizabeth (whom Mr. Froude has, on the no-evidence of a Spanish prelate, just turned traitor to) taught her maids of honour to study Greek, in which language she herself was a proficient,—ever since Queen Elizabeth had studied Plato, and grown jealous of Amy Robsart,—the fine ladies had become very learned and clever. The poets, therefore, saddled their Pegasi, placed their mistresses on the crupper, and, to the astonishment of worthy burghers, who could not read Marino, galloped away into the cloud-land of metaphysics. It is rather amusing to see these clever scholars

443

cutting Cupid's bowstring into infinitesimal conceits, and hashing the whole up into philosophical mince-meat. If a fly flew into your sweet-heart's eye, reader, what could you say on the subject? Nothing, I suppose; yet the metaphysicians were at no loss. They would tell you that the fly, after winging about in the sun for some time, was attracted by a still brighter luminary,—an eye so bright that it made the sun appear a shadow; that, flying about cheek and lip, it sucked thence such sweets as converted it into a bird of paradise; that, phaeton-like, it flew into her eye at last, was scorched in flames; and that, when it fell, a tear fell with it, which tear straightway changed into a pearl in which the poor fly was embalmed! If your sweetheart sang to you, would you swear that, listening to her voice, the wind ceased, the panther became tame, the rugged rocks were dissolved to tears; and further, that, because she frowned while singing, the melted rocks were frozen to stone again by her disdain? This was rather conceit than metaphysics; but it is im-possible to illustrate the more characteristic writing, save by quotation. Only let me state here, that under all this affectation, all this false orna-ment, and all this absurdity, there lay in the verses of these poets a vein of deeper and profounder meaning than many give them credit for. Once make yourself master of their involved diction, once crack the kernel of their quaint inverted style, and you will arrive at a clearer perception of their real merits. One has to grope about some time before he finds the silken clue which leads the true lover to their Rosamond's bower; but when he has caught the clue, and followed it boldly, ten to one he will be brought face to face with a blushing beauty, powerful to soften the heart of the sternest critical Eleanor that ever raised dagger and poisoned bowl. The best of the poets I speak of erred almost uncon-sciously. You must approach them with no timorous and mincing tread, if you desire to touch their depths. Don't stand shivering on the brink of beauty. There is Hippocrene; no shallow and noisy stream in which you can see the pebbles glistening, but a deep quiet pool,—so deep as to be almost without music,—so deep that you cannot catch a glimpse of the bottom. What then?—what then? Off with your straight laces, and plunge in head foremost. You will not only find the good old English bath refreshing, but if you are an expert diver in such waters, you may bring up some of the jewels good men left there for your benefit two or three hundred years ago. To pursue the metaphor, you may, if you please, place the jewels in your own setting, sell them as your own at modern value, and very few (with the exception of such ancient jewellers as myself) will be able to detect you in the theft.

You must not confound Donne and his imitators with that other metaphysical school of which Sir John Davies was the author. Davies . . . expressed nice simple philosophy in melodious and elegant language. He is never deep, but he is always readable, and his style is wonderfully well sustained. His great poem is rather superior to that portion of the *Mirror for Magistrates* which the vigorous pen of Thomas Sackville did not endeavour to immortalise.

Dryden, who went deep into the Elizabethan gold-mines, styles Donne 'the greatest wit, but not the greatest poet, in our language,'— praise which would hold truer in Dryden's time than it possibly can in the present day. At all events, Donne is the first of his class in point of merit, as well as in point of time. He is deeper, profounder, and more original than any of his imitators. He is never shallow, as Cowley often is; and he has more common sense than Cowley.

. . . Donne's prose is fully as involved and metaphysical as his poetry.

198. W. Harry Rogers

1861

Rogers (*fl.* 1859–71), an illustrator and engraver, gave Donne's *Holy Sonnet v* ('I am a little world'), to exemplify *The Present*, and lines 15–22 of 'The Crosse', in an anthology of religious extracts with strange emblematic pictures. He added a brief note on Donne's poetry. (*Spiritual Conceits, Extracted from the Writings of the Fathers, the old English Poets, &c. and Illustrated by W. Harry Rogers* (1861), 1862, pp. 26, 128, 208.)

Donne (John). The 'founder of the Metaphysical School of Poetry', as he has been termed by Dr Johnson, was born in London, A.D. 1573. His early works had little of serious sentiment, but his talents flowed into a genuine religious channel after his ordination. He became Dean of St Paul's, and died A.D. 1631, leaving a crowd of enthusiastic admirers.

199. Thomas Arnold

1862

Arnold (1823–1900), younger son of Arnold of Rugby, went over to the Church of Rome and held chairs of English in several Irish universities. He wrote of Donne and his followers in *A Manual of English Literature* (1862), 1867, pp. 131–2, 189–91, 393.

. . . when we come to speak of John Donne, the image of a strange wayward life, actuated evermore by a morbid restlessness of the intellect, rises to our thoughts. This man, whose youthful *Epithalamia* are tainted by a gross sensuality, ended his career as the grave and learned Dean of St. Paul's, whose sermons furnish the text for pages of admiring commentary to S. T. Coleridge. One fancies him a man with a high forehead, but false wavering eye, whose subtlety, one knows, will make any cause that he takes up seem for the moment unimpeachable, but of whose moral genuineness in the different phases he assumes,—of whose sincere love of truth as truth,—one has incurable doubts. As a writer, the great popularity which he enjoyed in his own day has long since given way before the repulsive harshness and involved obscurity of his style. The painful puns, the far-fetched similes, the extravagant metaphors, which in Shakspeare occur but as occasional blemishes, form the substance of the poetry of Donne; if they were taken out, very little would be left. He is the earliest poet of the fantastic or metaphysical school, of which we shall have more to say in the next chapter. The term metaphysical, first applied to the school by Johnson, though not inappropriate, is hardly distinctive enough. It is not inappropriate, because the philosophising spirit pervades their works, and it is the activity of the intellect, rather than that of the emotions, by which they are characterised. The mind, the nature of man, any faculty or virtue appertaining to the mind, and even any external phenomenon, can hardly be mentioned without being analysed, without subtle hairsplitting divisions and distinctions being drawn out, which the poet of feeling could never stop to elaborate. But this is equally true of a great deal that Shakspeare (especially in his later years), and even that Milton has written, whom yet no one ever thought of including among the metaphysical poets. It is the tendency to conceits,—that is, to an abuse of the imaginative faculty, by tracing resemblances that are fantastic, or uncalled for, or unseemly,—which really distinguishes this school from other schools. This point will be further illustrated in connexion with the poetry of Cowley.

Donne's poems are generally short; they consist of elegies, funeral elegies, satires, letters, divine poems, and miscellaneous songs. Besides these, he wrote *Metempsychosis, or the Progress of the Soul*, a poem published in 1601; 'of which,' Jonson told Drummond, in 1618, 'he now, since he was made Doctor, repenteth highlie, and seeketh to destroy all his poems.' In a man of so much mind, it cannot be but that fine lines and stanzas occasionally relieve the mass of barbarous quaintness. Take, for instance, the following stanza from the *Letter to* Sir H. Wotton:—

> Believe me, Sir, in my youth's giddiest days,
> When to be like the court was a player's praise,
> Plays were not so like courts, as courts like plays;

or this, from the letter to R. Woodward:—

> We are but farmers of ourselves, yet may,
> If we can stock ourselves and thrive, up-lay
> Much, much good treasure 'gainst the great rent day.

The younger race of poets belonged nearly all to what has been termed by Dryden and Dr. Johnson the Metaphysical school, the founder of which in England was Donne. But in fact this style of writing was of Italian parentage, and was brought in by the Neapolitan Marini. Tired of the endless imitations of the ancients, which, except when a great genius like that of Tasso broke through all conventional rules, had ever since the revival of learning fettered the poetic taste of Italy, Marini resolved to launch out boldly in a new career of invention, and to give to the world whatever his keen wit and lively fancy might prompt to him. He is described by Sismondi as 'the celebrated innovator on classic Italian taste, who first seduced the poets of the seventeenth century into that laboured and affected style which his own richness and vivacity of imagination were so well calculated to recommend. The most whimsical comparisons, pompous and overwrought descriptions, with a species of poetical punning and research, were soon esteemed, under his authority, as beauties of the very first order.' Marini resided for some years in France, and it was in that country that he produced his *Adone*. His influence upon French poetry was as great as upon Italian, but the vigour and freedom which it communicated were perhaps more than counterbalanced by the glaring bad taste which it encouraged. The same may be said of his influence upon our own poets. Milton alone had too much originality and inherent force to be carried away in the stream; but the most popular poets of the day,—Donne, Cowley, Crawshaw, Waller, Cleveland, and even Dryden in his earlier efforts— gave in to the prevailing fashion, and, instead of simple, natural images, studded their poems with *conceits* (concetti). This explains why Cowley was rated by his contemporaries as the greatest poet of his day, since every age has its favourite fashions, in literature as in costume; and those who conform to them receive more praise than those who assert their independence. Thus Clarendon speaks of Cowley as having 'made a flight beyond all men.' A few specimens will, however, better illustrate the Metaphysical, or, as we should prefer to term it, the Fantastic school, than pages of explanation. The first is from Donne's metrical epistles: describing a sea-voyage, he says:—

> There note they the ship's sicknesses,—the mast
> Shaked with an ague, and the hold and waist
> With a salt dropsy clogged.

Cleveland compares the stopping of a fountain to a change in the devolution of an estate:

> As an obstructed fountain's head
>   Cuts the entail off from the streams,
> And brooks are disinherited;
>   Honour and beauty are mere dreams,
>   Since Charles and Mary lost their beams.

Cowley talks of a trembling sky and a startled sun: in the *Davideis*, Envy thus addresses Lucifer:—

> Do thou but threat, loud storms shall make reply,
> And thunder echo to the *trembling* sky;
> Whilst raging seas swell to so bold a height,
> As shall the fire's proud element affright.
> Th' old drudging sun, from his long-beaten way,
> Shall at thy voice *start* and misguide the day, &c.

Dryden, in his youthful elegy on Lord Hastings, who died of the small-pox, describes that malady under various figures:—

Blisters with pride swelled, which through 's flesh did sprout
Like rose-buds, stuck in the lily-skin about.
Each little pimple had a tear in it,
To wail the fault its rising did commit.

To such a pitch of extravagance did talented men proceed in their endeavour to write in the fashion, in their straining after the much-admired *conceits*!

. . . The satires of Donne and Hall (the first of which received the honour of modernisation from Pope) are too rough and harsh to have much poetical value.

200. Henri Taine

1863-4

In his great history of English literature Taine described a rapid degeneration in English life after the 'unique and admirable epoch' of Elizabeth's reign. In his view the seventeenth-century poets signal the decline of 'The Pagan Renaissance' (*Histoire de la littérature anglaise*, Paris, 1863–4, trans. H. van Laun, Edinburgh (1871), 1872, pp. 201–5).

Meanwhile the literature undergoes a change; the powerful breeze which had guided it, and which, amidst singularity, refinements, exaggerations, had made it great, slackened and diminished. With Carew, Suckling, and Herrick, prettiness takes the place of the beautiful. That which strikes them is no longer the general features of things; that which they try to express is no longer the inner character of things. They no longer possess that liberal conception, that instinctive penetration, by which man sympathised with objects, and grew capable of creating them anew. They no longer boast of that overflow of emotions, that excess of ideas and images, which compelled a man to relieve himself by words, to act externally, to represent freely and boldly the

interior drama which made his whole body and heart tremble. They
are rather wits of the court, cavaliers of fashion, who wish to try their
hand at imagination and style. In their hands love becomes gallantry;
they write songs, fugitive pieces, compliments to the ladies. Do their
hearts still prick them? They turn eloquent phrases in order to be
applauded, and flattering exaggerations in order to please. The divine
faces, the serious or profound looks, the virgin or impassioned expressions which burst forth at every step in the early poets, have dis-
appeared; here we see nothing but agreeable countenances, painted in
agreeable verses. Blackguardism is not far off; we meet with it as early
as in Suckling, and crudity to boot, and prosaic epicurism; their sentiment is expressed before long, in such a phrase as: 'Let us amuse ourselves, and a fig for the rest.' The only objects they can paint, at last, are
little graceful things, a kiss, a May-day festivity, a dewy primrose, a
marriage morning, a bee. Herrick and Suckling especially produce little
exquisite poems, delicate, ever laughing or smiling like those attributed to Anacreon, or those which abound in the *Anthology*. In fact,
here, as at the time alluded to, we are at the decline of paganism; energy
departs, the reign of the agreeable begins. People do not relinquish the
worship of beauty and pleasure, but dally with them. They deck and fit
them to their taste; they cease to subdue and bend men, who sport and
amuse themselves with them. It is the last beam of a setting sun; the
genuine poetic sentiment dies out with Sedley, Waller, and the rhy-
mesters of the Restoration; they write prose in verse; their heart is on a
level with their style, and with an exact language we find the com-
mencement of a new age and a new art.

Side by side with prettiness comes affectation; it is the second mark
of the decadence. Instead of writing to say things, they write to say them
well; they outbid their neighbours, and strain every mode of speech:
they push art over on the side to which it had a leaning; and as in this
age it had a leaning towards vehemence and imagination, they pile up
their emphasis and colouring. A jargon always springs out of a style. In
all arts, the first masters, the inventors, discover the idea, steep themselves in it, and leave it to effect its outward form. Then come the
second class, the imitators who sedulously repeat this form, and alter it
by exaggeration. Some nevertheless have talent, as Quarles, Herbert,
Habington, Donne in particular, a pungent satirist, of terrible crude-
ness,* a powerful poet, of a precise and intense imagination, who still

* See in particular, his satire against the courtiers. The following is against imitators:
[He quotes lines 25–30 of *Satyre ii*.]

preserves something of the energy and thrill of the original inspiration.★
But he deliberately abuses all these gifts, and succeeds with great difficulty in concocting a piece of nonsense. For instance, the impassioned
poets had said to their mistress, that if they lost her, they should hate all
other women. Donne, in order to eclipse them, says:

[He quotes the first stanza of 'A Feaver'.]

Twenty times while reading him we rub our brow, and ask with
astonishment, how a man could so have tormented and contorted himself, strained his style, refined on his refinement, hit upon such absurd
comparisons? But this was the spirit of the age; they made an effort to
be ingeniously absurd. A flea had bitten Donne and his mistress. He
says:

[He quotes lines 12–18 of 'The Flea'.]

The Marquis de Mascarille never found anything to equal this. Would
you have believed a writer could invent such absurdities? She and he
made but one, for both are but one with the flea, and so one could not
be killed without the other. Observe that the wise Malherbe wrote very
similar enormities, in the *Tears of St. Peter*, and that the sonneteers of
Italy and Spain reach simultaneously the same height of folly, and you
will agree that throughout Europe at that time they were at the close
of a poetical epoch.

[He goes on to speak of Cowley, describing him as a poet of total
decadence in whom 'Literary exhaustion has seldom been more mani-
fest. He possesses all the capacity to say whatever pleases him, but he has
just nothing to say. The substance has vanished, leaving in its place a
hollow shadow'.]

★ [He quotes lines 21–34 of *Elegie vi*, 'Oh, let mee not serve so'.]

201. Anon., *The Leisure Hour*

1864

The anonymous author of an essay on Donne mentions Donne's poetry only in passing but declares that it is widely known ('Dr Donne', *The Leisure Hour*, xiii, 1864, p. 555).

The writings of Dr. Donne as a poet, and as the founder of what Dr. Johnson called the metaphysical school of poetry, are familiar to all who have diligently studied English literature. . . .

202. Henry Hart Milman

1868

Milman (1791–1868), a copious poet and historian, was Professor of Poetry at Oxford, 1821–31, and Dean of St Paul's from 1849. He gave an account of his predecessor 'Dean John Donne' in his *Annals of S. Paul's Cathedral*, 1868, pp. 323–30, and commented on Donne's poetry.

[He speaks of Walton's *Life* and of Donne's life.]

That life was a singular combination of romance and of poetry in its beginning, of grave and solemn wisdom and holiness at its close. . . .

Donne is the only Dean of S. Paul's, till a very late successor, who was guilty of poetry. Mr Campbell has justly said that Donne's life is more poetical than his poetry. As a poet, he has in a high degree the faults and but a few of the beauties of his age. I give one graceful sample of his lighter pieces, if that word may fairly be used, of the generally hard, harsh, inharmonious lyrics, crowded with incongruous, laborious conceits, with here and there a stanza gleaming out in rare fancifulness and sweetness:—

[He quotes the whole of 'The Message'.]

His rough satires needed the clear style of Pope to make them, not pleasing only but even intelligible. One poem, however, was unearthed by the fine judgment of Charles Lamb, though rough, of great beauty. . . .

[He refers in a footnote to Lamb's *Specimens of English Dramatic Poets*. In the text he gives an account of *Elegie xvi*, 'On his Mistris', and then quotes the poem, omitting 'a few lines, which, too much in the spirit of the age, mar the exquisite delicacy as well as feeling'. In fact he omits lines 31–43a.]
[He speaks of Donne as a preacher, finding him interminable, full of laboured obscurity, false and misplaced wit, fatiguing antitheses. Then he notes Coleridge's taste for Donne.]

In one of his caprices of orthodoxy . . . he sets Donne above one of his great quaternion of English writers, Shakespeare, Hooker, Bacon, Jeremy Taylor. . . .
[Milman goes on to allow that he does find fine qualities in Donne]

a wonderful solidity of thought, a sustained majesty, an earnest force, almost unrivalled, with passages occasionally of splendid, almost impassioned devotion. . . . Even what in those days was esteemed wit, which ran wild in his poetry, and suffocated the graceful and passionate thoughts, is in his prose under control and discipline.

203. Richard Chenevix Trench

Trench (1807–86) became Archbishop of Dublin in 1863. He was a poet, and wrote copiously on religious, philological, and literary matters. He included three poems by Donne in an anthology—'A Lecture upon the Shadow' and two *Holy Sonnets*—and commented on one of these, the *Holy Sonnet ii*, 'As due by many titles' (*A Household Book of English Poetry*, 1868, pp. 403–4).

A rough rugged piece of verse, as indeed, almost all Donne's poetry is imperfect in form and workmanship; but it is the genuine cry of one engaged in that most terrible of all struggles, wherein, as we are winners or losers, we have won or lost all. There is indeed much in Donne, in the unfolding of his moral and spiritual life, which often reminds us of St. Augustine. I do not mean that, noteworthy as on many accounts he was, and in the language of Carew, one of his contemporaries,

> A king, that ruled as he thought fit
> The universal monarchy of wit

he at all approached in intellectual or spiritual stature to the great Doctor of the Western Church. But still there was in Donne the same tumultuous youth, the same entanglement in youthful lusts, the same conflict with these, and the same final deliverance from them; and then the same passionate and personal grasp of the central truths of Christianity, linking itself as this did with all that he had suffered, and all that he had sinned, and all through which by God's grace he had victoriously struggled.

204. Edward FitzGerald

1868

In the second edition of his translation of the *Rubáiyát* FitzGerald added a note on stanza 58 (*Rubaiyat of Omar Khayyam, The Astronomer Poet of Persia*, 1868, p. 28, note 19).

A curious mathematical Quatrain of Omar's has been pointed out to me; the more curious because almost exactly parallel'd by some Verses of Doctor Donne's, and quoted in Izaak Walton's Lives! Here is Omar: 'You and I are the image of a pair of compasses; though we have two heads (sc. our *feet*) we have one body; when we have fixed the centre for our circle, we bring our heads (sc. feet) together at the end'.

[FitzGerald then quotes the last three stanzas of Donne's 'A Valediction: forbidding Mourning'.]

205. John Chippendall Montesquieu Bellew

1868

Bellew (1823–74), a clergyman, was converted to Roman Catholicism in 1868 and then devoted himself to writing on literary matters and giving public readings. In a manual for students he introduced a selection from Donne's verse with a brief account of the poet's life and writings (*Poet's Corner. A Manual for Students in English Poetry*, 1868, p. 189).

Donne was a man of most sincere piety and of the truest affection. The deep love which ever existed between him and his wife may be traced in his poetry, as it adorned their lives. Despite the deformities of style, common to the pedantry of the age, which encumber both his verses and also his sermons, Donne was a man possessed of genuine poetic fire. He has left behind him real gems of poetry; and although it is a fact that in his earlier works, and long before he was induced to enter holy orders, he gave too loose a rein to his imagination, nevertheless, as we read them now, the faults of excess can be pardoned and overlooked, whilst we are often startled and delighted by the energy and power which he displays. Dryden styled him 'the greatest wit, though not the greatest poet of our nation.' Ben Jonson held his genius in the highest estimation.

[He quotes Drummond's report of Jonson's estimation of Donne. See No. 3 (ii).]

The student who desires a genuine intellectual entertainment in seeking knowledge regarding the poets of his country cannot have a greater treat than in reading the lives of Sir Henry Wotton and Dr. Donne, as written by Isaac Walton.

206. George MacDonald

1868

MacDonald (1824–1905) was highly esteemed in his own day as poet and novelist, and published much. He devoted to 'Dr Donne' chapter VII of a book on the English religious poets. After getting Donne's dates wrong he moves on to characterise Donne's poetry (*England's Antiphon*, 1868, pp. 113–24).

We now come to Dr. John Donne, a man of justly great respect and authority, . . .

. . . But, although even Ben Jonson addresses him as 'the delight of Phœbus and each Muse,' we are too far beyond the power of his social presence and the influence of his public utterances to feel that admiration of his poems which was so largely expressed during his lifetime. Of many of those that were written in his youth, Izaak Walton says Dr. Donne 'wished that his own eyes had witnessed their funerals.' Faulty as they are, however, they are not the less the work of a great and earnest man.

He is represented by Dr. Johnson as one of the chief examples of that school of poets called by himself the *metaphysical*, an epithet which, as a definition, is almost false. True it is that Donne and his followers were always ready to deal with metaphysical subjects, but it was from their mode, and not their subjects, that Dr. Johnson classed them. What this mode was we shall see presently, for I shall be justified in setting forth its strangeness, even absurdity, by the fact that Dr. Donne was the dear friend of George Herbert, and had much to do with the formation of his poetic habits. Just twenty years older than Herbert, and the valued and intimate friend of his mother, Donne was in precisely that relation of age and circumstance to influence the other in the highest degree.

The central thought of Dr. Donne is nearly sure to be just: the subordinate thoughts by means of which he unfolds it are often grotesque, and so wildly associated as to remind one of the lawlessness of a dream, wherein mere suggestion without choice or fitness rules the sequence. As some of the writers of whom I have last spoken would play with words, Dr. Donne would sport with ideas, and with the visual images or embodiments of them. Certainly in his case much knowledge reveals itself in the association of his ideas, and great facility in the management and utterance of them. True likewise, he says nothing unrelated to the main idea of the poem; but not the less certainly does the whole resemble the speech of a child of active imagination, to whom judgment as to the character of his suggestions is impossible, his taste being equally gratified with a lovely image and a brilliant absurdity: a butterfly and a shining potsherd are to him similarly desirable. Whatever wild thing starts from the thicket of thought, all is worthy game to the hunting intellect of Dr. Donne, and is followed without question of tone, keeping, or harmony. In his play with words, Sir Philip Sidney kept good heed that even that should serve the end in view; in his play with ideas, Dr. John Donne, so far from serving the end, sometimes obscures it almost hopelessly: the hart escapes while he follows the squirrels and weasels and bats. It is not surprising that, their author being so inartistic with regard to their object, his verses themselves should be harsh and unmusical beyond the worst that one would imagine fit to be called verse. He enjoys the unenviable distinction of having no rival in ruggedness of metric movement and associated sounds. This is clearly the result of indifference; an indifference, however, which grows very strange to us when we find that he *can* write a lovely verse and even an exquisite stanza.

Greatly for its own sake, partly for the sake of illustration, I quote a poem containing at once his best and his worst, the result being such an incongruity that we wonder whether it might not be called his best *and* his worst, because we cannot determine which. He calls it *Hymn to God, my God, in my Sickness*. The first stanza is worthy of George Herbert in his best mood.

> Since I am coming to that holy room,
>> Where with the choir of saints for evermore
> I shall be made thy music, as I come
>> I tune the instrument here at the door,
>> And what I must do then, think here before.

To recognize its beauty, leaving aside the depth and truth of the phrase, 'Where I shall be made thy music,' we must recall the custom of those days to send out for 'a noise of musicians.' Hence he imagines that he has been summoned as one of a band already gone in to play before the king of 'The High Countries:' he is now at the door, where he is listening to catch the tone, that he may have his instrument tuned and ready before he enters. But with what a jar the next stanza breaks on heart, mind, and ear!

> Whilst my physicians by their love are grown
>   Cosmographers, and I their map, who lie
> Flat on this bed, that by them may be shown
>   That this is my south-west discovery,
>   *Per fretum febris*—by these straits to die;—

Here, in the midst of comparing himself to a map, and his physicians to cosmographers consulting the map, he changes without warning into a navigator whom they are trying to follow upon the map as he passes through certain straits—namely, those of the fever—towards his southwest discovery, Death. Grotesque as this is, the absurdity deepens in the end of the next stanza by a return to the former idea. He is alternately a map and a man sailing on the map of himself. But the first half of the stanza is lovely: my reader must remember that the region of the West was at that time the Land of Promise to England.

> I joy that in these straits I see my West;
>   For though those currents yield return to none,
> What shall my West hurt me? As west and east
>   In all flat maps (and I am one) are one,
>   So death doth touch the resurrection.

It is hardly worth while, except for the strangeness of the phenomenon, to spend any time in elucidating this. Once more a map, he is that of the two hemispheres, in which the east of the one touches the west of the other. Could anything be much more unmusical than the line, 'In all flat maps (and I am one) are one'? But the next stanza is worse.

> Is the Pacific sea my home? Or are
>   The eastern riches? Is Jerusalem?
> Anyan, and Magellan, and Gibraltar?
>   All straits, and none but straits are ways to them,
>   Whether where Japhet dwelt, or Cham, or Sem.

The meaning of the stanza is this: there is no earthly home: all these places are only straits that lead home, just as they themselves cannot be reached but through straits.

Let my reader now forget all but the first stanza, and take it along with the following, the last two:

We think that Paradise and Calvary,
    Christ's cross and Adam's tree, stood in one place:
Look, Lord, and find both Adams met in me;
    As the first Adam's sweat surrounds my face,
    May the last Adam's blood my soul embrace.

So, in his purple wrapped, receive me, Lord;
    By these his thorns give me his other crown;
And as to others' souls I preached thy word,
    Be this my text, my sermon to mine own:
    Therefore, that he may raise, the Lord throws down.

Surely these are very fine, especially the middle verse of the former and the first verse of the latter stanza. The three stanzas together make us lovingly regret that Dr. Donne should have ridden his Pegasus over quarry and housetop, instead of teaching him his paces.

The next I quote is artistic throughout. Perhaps the fact, of which we are informed by Izaak Walton, 'that he caused it to be set to a grave and solemn tune, and to be often sung to the organ by the choristers of St. Paul's church in his own hearing, especially at the evening service,' may have something to do with its degree of perfection. There is no sign of his usual haste about it. It is even elaborately rhymed after Norman fashion, the rhymes in each stanza being consonant with the rhymes in every stanza.

[He quotes the whole of 'A Hymne to God the Father'.]

In those days even a pun might be a serious thing: witness the play in the last stanza on the words *son* and *sun*—not a mere pun, for the Son of the Father is the Sun of Righteousness: he is Life *and* Light.

What the Doctor himself says concerning the hymn, appears to me not only interesting but of practical value. He 'did occasionally say to a friend, "The words of this hymn have restored to me the same thoughts of joy that possessed my soul in my sickness, when I composed it".' What a help it would be to many, if in their more gloomy times they would but recall the visions of truth they had, and were assured of, in better moments!

Here is a somewhat strange hymn, which yet possesses, rightly understood, a real grandeur:

[He quotes in full 'A Hymne to Christ, at the Authors last going into Germany'.]

To do justice to this poem, the reader must take some trouble to enter into the poet's mood.

It is in a measure distressing that, while I grant with all my heart the claim of his 'Muse's white sincerity,' the taste in—I do not say *of*—some of his best poems should be such that I will not present them.

Out of twenty-three *Holy Sonnets*, every one of which, I should almost say, possesses something remarkable, I choose three. Rhymed after the true Petrarchian fashion, their rhythm is often as bad as it can be to be called rhythm at all. Yet these are very fine.

[He quotes in full *Holy Sonnets i, viii*, and *x*—'Thou hast made me', 'If faithfull soules be alike glorifi'd', and 'Death be not proud'.]

In a poem called *The Cross*, full of fantastic conceits, we find the following remarkable lines, embodying the profoundest truth.

> As perchance carvers do not faces make,
> But that away, which hid them there, do take:
> Let crosses so take what hid Christ in thee,
> And be his image, or not his, but he.

One more, and we shall take our leave of Dr. Donne. It is called a fragment; but it seems to me complete. It will serve as a specimen of his best and at the same time of his most characteristic mode of presenting fine thoughts grotesquely attired.

[He quotes in full the 'imperfect' poem 'Resurrection'.]

What a strange mode of saying that he is our head, the captain of our salvation, the perfect humanity in which our life is hid! Yet it has its dignity. When one has got over the oddity of these last six lines, the figure contained in them shows itself almost grand.

As an individual specimen of the grotesque form holding a fine sense, regard for a moment the words,

> He was all gold when he lay down, but rose
> All tincture;

which means, that, entirely good when he died, he was something yet greater when he rose, for he had gained the power of making others good: the *tincture* intended here was a substance whose touch would turn the basest metal into gold.

Through his poems are scattered many fine passages; but not even his large influence on the better poets who followed is sufficient to justify our listening to him longer now.

207. John Forster

1869

Forster commented on the *Imaginary Conversation* between Walton, Cotton, and Oldways (see No. 141), in his *Walter Savage Lander. A Biography*, 1869, ii, p. 183. He mentioned the pastiche verses in a footnote.

The style of Donne is so happily caught in one of these pieces, not its extravagance only but its genius, that I cannot resist quoting it here.

[He quotes the six lines beginning 'She was so beautiful, had God but died/for her. . . .'.]

208. Edwin Percy Whipple

1869

Whipple (1819–86) was a Bostonian essayist, reviewer, literary historian, and public lecturer. In *The Literature of the Age of Elizabeth*, Boston, 1869, pp. 230–7, Whipple placed Donne among the 'Minor Elizabethan Poets' and gave an account of his writings, opening it with Coleridge's lines 'With Donne, whose muse on dromedary trots', and the anonymous sequel 'See lewdness and theology combin'd' (see No. 112 (xi)).

John Donne, the heterogeneous qualities of whose intellect and character are thus maliciously sketched, was one of the strangest of versifiers, sermonizers, and men.

. . . It was probably during the period between his twentieth and thirtieth years that most of his secular poetry was written, and that his nature took its decided eccentric twist. An insatiable intellectual curiosity seems, up to this time, to have been his leading characteristic; and as this led him to all kinds of literature for mental nutriment, his faculties, in their formation, were inlaid with the oddest varieties of opinions and crotchets. With vast learning, with a subtile and penetrating intellect, with a fancy singularly fruitful and ingenious, he still contrived to disconnect, more or less, his learning from what was worth learning, his intellect from what was reasonable, his fancy from what was beautiful. His poems, or rather his metrical problems, are obscure in thought, rugged in versification, and full of conceits which are intended to surprise rather than to please; but they still exhibit a power of intellect, both analytical and analogical, competent at once to separate the minutest and connect the remotest ideas. This power, while it might not have given his poems grace, sweetness, freshness, and melody, would still, if properly directed, have made them valuable for their thoughts; but in the case of Donne it is perverted to the production of what is *bizarre* or unnatural, and his muse is thus as hostile to use as to beauty.

464

The intention is, not to idealize what is true, but to display the writer's skill and wit in giving a show of reason to what is false. The effect of this on the moral character of Donne was pernicious. A subtile intellectual scepticism, which weakened will, divorced thought from action and literature from life, and made existence a puzzle and a dream, resulted from this perversion of his intellect. He found that he could wittily justify what was vicious as well as what was unnatural; and his amatory poems, accordingly, are characterized by a cold, hard, labored, intellectualized sensuality, worse than the worst impurity of his contemporaries, because it has no excuse of passion for its violations of decency.

But now happened an event which proved how little the talents and accomplishments of this voluptuary of intellectual conceits were competent to serve him in a grapple with the realities of life.

[He gives an account of Donne's marriage and subsequent hardships, then comments on Donne's scruples when he was first asked to enter the Church.]

It is probable that his habits of intellectual self-indulgence, while they really weakened his conscience, made it morbidly acute. He would not adopt the profession of law or divinity for a subsistence, though he was willing to depend for subsistence on the charity of others. Izaak Walton praises his humility; but Donne's humility was only another name for indisposition to practical labor,—a humility which makes self-depreciation an excuse for moral laziness, and shrinks as nervously from duty as from pride. Both law and divinity, therefore, he continued to make the luxuries of his existence.

In good time this selfish intellectuality resulted in that worst of intellectual diseases, mental disgust. . . . Sickness and affliction and comparative poverty came to wake him from his dream and reveal him to himself. . . .

[He quotes from Donne's letters with their 'moans over his moral inefficiency' and desire to escape to the next life 'from the perplexities of this'.]

And this was the mental state to which Donne was reduced by thirty years of incessant study,—of study that sought only the gratification of intellectual caprice and of intellectual curiosity,—of study without a practical object. From this wretched mood of self-disgust and disgust with existence, this fret of thought at the impotence of will, we may date Donne's gradual emancipation from his besetting sins; for life, at such a point of spiritual experience, is only possible under the form of a new life. . . .

Donne's published sermons are in form nearly as grotesque as his poems, though they are characterized by profounder qualities of heart and mind. It was his misfortune to know thoroughly the works of fourteen hundred writers, most of them necessarily worthless; and he could not help displaying his erudition in his discourses. Of what is now called taste he was absolutely destitute. . . .

209. George Eliot

1871–2

George Eliot used stanzas from two of the *Songs and Sonnets* as chapter mottoes in *Middlemarch*. Chapter XXXIX has at its head the last three stanzas of 'The Undertaking'; chapter LXXXIII has lines 8–11 of 'The Good-morrow'. Both quotations are ascribed to 'Dr Donne'.

210. Francis Cunningham

1872

Cunningham (1820–75) served for some years in India, and in his fifties took to editing Elizabethan and Jacobean dramatists. In his edition of Ben Jonson he annotated the 'Conversations with Drummond' and commented on Jonson's remarks about Donne (*The Works of Ben Jonson*, 1872, iii, pp. 471–4).

[On the remark that 'Done for not keeping of accent deserved hanging'.]

It is impossible to read Donne's 'Anatomie of the World. The first Anniversary', and 'The Progress of the Soul. The second Anniversary', without admitting the truth of Jonson's criticism. . . .

[On Jonson's esteeming Donne 'the first poet in the World in some things'.]

Any reader who struggles manfully to understand Donne, will certainly endorse Jonson's 'censure'. When he says afterwards that 'Donne from not being understood would perish,' he shows that the difficulty of reading him was hardly less in his own time than in ours. Coleridge has, both in rhyme and prose, described his style. . . . [He quotes Coleridge's quatrain on Donne, and a general comment from the marginalia in Lamb's copy.]

[On the 'verses of the Lost Chaine'.]

Some vigorous and humorous objurgation at the end of this piece is much in Jonson's own style. . . . Any person who has been becalmed in the Tropics, or voyaged in an iron boat in the Red Sea in the month of September, will acknowledge the extraordinary force and truth of Donne's picture. . . .

[On Donne's alleged remark that he wrote the epitaph on Prince Henry 'to match Sir Ed: Herbert in obscurenesse'.]

It would require a subtle critic to distinguish between Donne's natural and simulated 'obscurenesse'. . . .

211. Alexander Ballock Grosart

1872–3

Grosart (1827–99), one of the most indefatigable of Victorian editors, was Vicar of Blackburn from 1868 to 1892. Among many similar enterprises he essayed a scholarly edition of Donne's poems for the Fuller Worthies Library, the first English attempt since the seventeenth century to re-edit all the poems from the early manuscripts. A hundred and six copies of the two-volume edition were printed, for private circulation. Grosart dedicated the edition to Browning, and expressed in a Preface the scruples of a Victorian clergyman who set himself to edit Donne. He opened the second volume with a long 'Essay on the Life and Writings of Donne' (*The Complete Poems of John Donne, D.D.*, 1872–3, i, title page, Dedication, and p. ix; ii, pp. xxvii–xlviii).

(i) The title page:

THE COMPLETE POEMS

OF

JOHN DONNE, D.D.
DEAN OF ST. PAUL'S.

FOR THE FIRST TIME FULLY COLLECTED AND COLLATED WITH THE ORIGINAL AND EARLY EDITIONS AND MSS.
AND ENLARGED
WITH HITHERTO UNPRINTED AND INEDITED POEMS FROM MSS. ETC.
AND PORTRAITS, FACSIMILES, AND OTHER ILLUSTRATIONS
IN THE QUARTO FORM.

Edited

WITH PREFACE, ESSAY ON LIFE AND WRITINGS, AND NOTES,

(ii) From the Preface:

I do not hide from myself that it needs courage . . . to edit and print the Poetry of Dr. JOHN DONNE in our day. Nor would I call it literary prudery that shrinks from giving publicity to such sensuous things (to say the least) as indubitably are found therein. . . . I deplore that Poetry, in every way almost so memorable and potential, should be stained even to uncleanliness in sorrowfully too many places. . . .

(iii) In his 'Essay on the Life and Writings of Donne' Grosart strings together many of the notable opinions of Donne's poems from Coleridge to his own day. But he has some comments of his own too:

[He speaks of Donne's *Satyres*, after quoting George MacDonald's remarks in *England's Antiphon*—see No. 206.]

Looking into Donne's specially, they have their blots in provocative allusions; but substantially they seem to us eminently *judicial* and justi-fied. He does not simply scold and call it invective, or give nicknames, or 'report' scandals that have reached him, or hold-up physical or mental infirmities to ridicule; but, fixing his eye keenly on the wicked-ness he is roused to expose, he does it with a crashing destructiveness, a bearing-down *momentum* of indignation, a sad passionateness of scorn, an honest, unfearing, unsparing striking at the highest-seated wrong-doers, and a felicitous realism of word-painting, that to our mind makes these first of English Satires very notable indeed. O' times there are solemnities of emotion, as in the Third Satire on 'Religion,' unspeakably pathetic in so young a man as Donne in 1592–3 was, and warranting us to believe that in those early 'Divine Poems', already noticed, he uttered out the innermost convictions of his soul, and consequently that in ceasing to be a Roman Catholic, he reached his new standing-ground through an agony of spiritual experience. Our Satirist is pun-gent, yet never in a fury. He is proportioned too in his noble rage: *e.g.* he does not treat follies and vanities as if they were vices, any more than he does vices as if they were merely follies and vanities. He has vehemence for vices with no lightness; he has lightness for follies and vanities without vehemence and without malice. And again, 'weighing' the large actions condemned against the petty actors of them he has a fine gentlemanliness of rebuke; contemptuous, dainty of touch, yet penetrative as a Toledo-blade. As pictures of the age, in its manners and usages and morals, these Satires are inestimable. Without a superfluous epithet, though I dare not say without coarseness, you have the whole moving panorama of 'high and low' presented. Occasionally you catch the sound of musical, joyous laughter, and anon the awful tears consecrated to outrages too deep for words. To me these 'Satires' are not so much a given number of printed lines and part of a book, as a man's living heart pulsating with the most tragical reality of emotion. Bishop Hall's 'Satires' placed beside them look thin and empty, and painfully envious of contemporaries. Marston and Wither are worthier to be associated with Donne. I have no room for confirmatory quotations. I write for those only who mean to 'study' the Poetry now furnished: and I promise every painstaking Reader reward for his pains.

One of the 'Curiosities of Literature' more fantastically curious than any in D'Israeli, is, that Pope and Parnell re-versified the Satires of Donne. I know not that I can do better than allow here an open eyed Writer (the late Dr. Samuel Brown of Edinburgh, I believe) to put this thing as follows:

[He quotes from the anonymous article in *Lowe's Edinburgh Magazine*, i, 1846, the whole of the comparison between some of Donne's lines in *Satyre iv* and Pope's version of the same lines. See No. 177.]

Few will differ from this drastic verdict; and, indeed, apart from Elwin's demonstration of the rottenness of Pope as a man, it were easy to prove, by the 'improvements' on Donne and the like, that, while a matchless Verser, he was no Poet in any deep sense of the much-abused word. Parnell could not be expected to succeed where Pope failed; and he fails egregiously.

The Biographers of Donne must discuss fully the place of his Satires in our Literature, as having been the first in English.

[He pays tribute to J. P. Collier's discussion, in the *Poetical Decameron*, of the rival claims of Donne and Hall to be the first English satirist—see No. 137. Then he reviews the evidence of dates of publication, contemporary references, manuscripts and the like, demonstrating his close work on the primary sources.]

The Thinker and Imaginator

[He quotes George MacDonald on Johnson's classification of the metaphysical poets by mode and not by subject. See No. 206.]

By the 'Thinker' I intend not the mode but the 'subjects' (=objects) of much of Donne's poetry; and I pronounce it *thoughtful* in the highest and subtlest region of speculative thought. Thomas Carew, in his very remarkable Elegy, recognises this intellectual power and *momentum*, as thus:

[He quotes lines 45–53 of Carew's 'An Elegie upon the death of . . . Dr John Donne'. See No. 18(iv)(g).]

Sidney Godolphin too, in his Elegy discerned it:

[He quotes lines 36–40 and 47–8 of Godolphin's 'Elegie on D.D.'. See No. 25.]

In our own day, across the Atlantic, Professor Lowell ('Among my Books') puts it even finelier:

[He quotes the praises of Donne from Lowell's essay on Dryden. See No. 176(iii).]

To appropriate a familiar word from our English Bible, Donne 'intermeddled' with problems and started inquiries uncommon in the period; Sir John Davies and Abraham Cowley being earlier and later fellow-thinkers. His verse-letters to the (then) Countess of Bedford—a lady of whom the world ought to know more, and I trust will ere very long, from the Bedford MSS., and so I put past my own gatherings on her—and to Herbert Lord Cherbury, are laden with profound speculative and imaginative thought. They will abundantly recompense the most prolonged study. One characteristic of this thinking is its sudden outflashing from the common level of the subject in hand—a characteristic common to all Donne's poetry. Shakespeare describes it memorably in the 'dolphin,' which 'shows its back *above the element*' in which it moves (Ant. and Cleo. v. 1), all lustrous and iridescent. So in this Poetry, even in the Satires, and indeed notably there, you are arrested by some quaint image or allusion, that, when you come to dwell on it, is found to carry in its heart some splendid thought altogether out of the beaten track, and which comes with absolute surprise in the place. In Donne's (prose) 'News from the very Country' (1669, pp. 395–6) he says, 'Sentences in Authors, like haires in horse-tails, concur in one root of beauty and strength; but being pluckt out one by one, serve only for springes and snares:' and I quote the Fullerian gnome because I cannot tarry (even if it were desirable) to quote illustrative and confirmatory passages from Donne's poetry; but at hap-hazard take these half-dozen 'haires' out of the 'root of beauty and strength.' First, in the

471

'Relique,' what a strange quaint 'fancy' to enter the poet's brain of the 'bracelet of bright hayre about the bone,' is this—

> think that there a lovinge couple lyes
> Who hopte that this device might be a way
> *To make their sowles at the last busye daye*
> *Meete at this grave, and make a little stay.*

Second: what fantastic, almost grotesque, grandeur is there in this measurement of a young human life by an 'angel's flight'—

> As when an angell downe from heaven doth flye,
> Our quick thought cannot keep him company;
> Wee cannot think, *now he is at the sunne,*
> *Now through the moone, now through the aire doth runn;*
> Yet when hee's come, *we know he did repaire*
> *To all'twixt heav'ne and earth, sunn, moone, and aire.*

The whole 'Obsequies' of Lord Harrington, in which these lines occur, is packed-full of the like unique thoughts, worked-out with lustrous imaginative edges. Third: there is profound truth in this 'fancy,' if it be fancy, in 'The Cross'—

> As perchance carvers do not faces make,
> *But that away which hid them there do take;*
> Let crosses so take what hid Christ in thee,
> And be His image, or not His, but He.

Fourth: let the reader turn to the 'Fragment,' as it is called, of 'The Resurrection.' Here are two of its thought-laden lines—

[He quotes lines 13–14 of 'Resurrection', and gives George MacDonald's account of the poem in *England's Antiphon*—see No. 206.]

Fifth: speaking of closing the eyes of the dead, how arresting is this—

> O, they confess much in the world amiss
> Who dare not trust a dead-man's eyes with that
> Which they from God and angels cover not.

Sixth: six, and four, and two, and single lines and half-lines, you are perpetually marking in the margin as you read Donne: *e.g.*

> her pure and eloquent blood
> Spoke in her cheeks, and so distinctly wrought,
> That one might almost say her body thought:

—and

in all she did
Some figure of the golden times was hid:

—and

Tears in his eyes quench *the amazing light:*—

and this Wordsworthian touch, of the 'Robin Redbreast,'

The household bird, with the red stomacher.

Whoso reads 'The Blossom' and 'The Primrose' will understand the delicate praise of Arthur Wilson in his Elegy:

Thou sweetly didst contrive
To Beautie's elements, and thence derive
Unspotted lillies white; which thou didst set
Hand in hand with the vein-like violet,
Making them soft and warm, and by thy power
Couldst give both life and sense unto a flower. (1669, p. 389.)

But while I thus make the supremest claims for Donne as a Thinker and Imaginator, I must, at the same time, in measure assent to Dr. Macdonald's criticism on Donne's *mode* as distinguished from his '*subjects*'—highest and deepest problems of thought and experience—and so I give it:

[He quotes George MacDonald's general estimation of Donne's poetry, from 'The central thought of Dr Donne is nearly sure to be just' down to 'squirrels and weasels and bats'. See No. 206.]

Coleridge (*the* Coleridge) has, almost to superlative, marked out the greatness of Donne's thought:

[He quotes Coleridge's comments on 'Womans Constancy' in Lamb's copy of Donne's poems. See No. 112(iv).]

Even the light-hearted Carew saw the gleam of the kingly crown on his associate's brow, when he celebrated him dead as

A king that rul'd as he thought fit
The universal monarchie of wit.

Let the reader give a month to the Verse-Letters and Elegies and Funeral Elegies, and he will find how noble o' times is Donne as a Thinker. Nor will he then gainsay our characteristic of surprise and suddenness in the nobleness. As already indicated, in the most unsuspected places a grand thought will be come on. Thus it is of the 'Progress of the Soul'—flagrantly faulty though it be—that such a one as Thomas De Quincey said:

[He quotes de Quincey's comments on the *Metempsychosis* in the essay on 'Rhetoric'. See No. 146.]

In truth, what Milman affirms of his Prose holds largely of Donne's Poetry: 'a wonderful solidity of thought . . . an earnest force almost unrivalled, with passages occasionally of splendid, almost impassioned devotion' ('St. Paul's,' p. 329).

As an Imaginator it is impossible to place Donne too high. The light of his imagination lies goldenly over his thinking. Granted to Dr. Macdonald (as above) that a 'shining potsherd' takes him now and again away from the main line of his thought; but it is not the potsherd that does it, but the 'shining,' and the 'shining' is not from the 'potsherd,' but from above in the glory of the sun. Two farther examples must suffice to confirm our estimate of Donne's imaginative faculty. The first occurs in a 'Valediction, forbidding to mourn'—on parting from his young wife; and of the entire poem even placid Izaak Walton is quickened to say in the 'Life:'

[He quotes Walton's praise of the poem. See No. 27(vi).]

We ask the reader to turn now to the poem in its completeness (see vol. ii. pp. 210–12), and in so doing ask him to pass from it to the Elegy, 'Refusal to allow his young Wife to accompany him abroad as a Page' (vol. i, pp. 161–4), whose 'exquisite delicacy as well as feeling' 'took' even his, in this case, frigid successor at St. Paul's (pp. 325–6).

The metaphor of the 'compasses' in the 'Valediction' only so daring an Imaginator as Donne would have attempted; and the out-of-the-wayness of it is not more noticeable than the imaginativeness which glorifies it. It is used elsewhere by the poet, and with equal success, viz. in the 'Obsequies of the Lord Harrington.' The touches of imaginativeness are also the more noticeable in that the image was fetched from a family-fact: for in the 'Extracts from the Hawthornden MSS.' (as before) we read that the 'Impressa' of old John Heywood—Donne's maternal grandfather—was 'a compass *with one foot in center*, the other broken, the words *Deest quod duceret orbem*' (p. 101). Here, no doubt, was the source of the quaint but really magnificent simile. Of the 'Valediction' Coleridge (as before) writes,

[He quotes Coleridge's comments on 'A Valediction: forbidding Mourning' from the marginalia in Lamb's copy of Donne's poems. See No. 112(iv).]

The second example is found in 'The Anniversary' (vol. ii, p. 181), another commemoration of his Wife. I ask the student similarly to turn to it, and read and re-read it in full, and mark the greatness of the close:

> Let us live nobly, and live and add again
> Years and years unto years, till we attain
> To write threescore: this is the second of our reign.

[He quotes J. C. M. Bellew's opinion of 'The Anniversarie', in *Poet's Corner*. See No. 205.]

It were easy to multiply proofs of the highest claim possible to be made for Donne as Thinker and Imaginator. In the spirit of our quotation from 'News from the Country,' I prefer sending the reader to the complete poems for himself; for Coleridge speaks truly on 'Canonization' when he thus remarks:

[He quotes Coleridge's comment on 'The Canonization' in the margin of Lamb's copy of Donne's poems. See No. 112(iv). And he gives a paragraph from the article in *Lowe's Edinburgh Magazine*, i, 1846, which he again ascribes to Dr Samuel Brown, to confirm the impossibility of doing justice to a great poet by 'a few and limited extracts'.]

The Artist

[He opens this section by playing off George MacDonald's low opinion of Donne's artistry against Coleridge's remarks—which he considers 'more deeply and truly' said—on the way Donne's poems move and are to be read; and he chides Coleridge for his silent emendations of Donne's text, such as reveal the corrupt state of the text until the present edition.]

But, after all, I fear it must be conceded that it is as Thinker and Imaginator, and Artist of ideas rather than words in verse, we have to assert Donne's incomparable genius. He has nothing of the 'smoothness' of various contemporaries, and very little of the ever-changing music of *the* Poet of 'all time.' Nevertheless, the various-readings and perpetual fluctuations of text in the MSS. lift up a united protest against any such charge as that of 'indifference.' He must have worked laboriously even in his versification. What satisfied Ben Jonson ought to be sympathetically studied by us. Instead of quoting, I ask the student to read all of Jonson on Donne, specially on the 'Calme,' as given in the 'Conversations.' One line in one of the 'Holy Sonnets' (IX.) tells us that Milton read Donne; as thus,

if that tree,
Whose fruit threw death on else immortal us.

Even to the rhythm this recalls the opening of 'Paradise Lost.' In Milton's immortal lines on Shakespeare we read:

> Thou, in our wonder and astonishment,
> Hast built thyself a livelong monument;
> And there sepulchred in such state dost lie,
> *That kings for such a tomb might wish to die.*

Coleridge has written these lines on the margin of one of Donne's letters to the Lady G., where is this: 'No prince would be loath to die that were assured of so fair a tomb to preserve his memory' (as before, p. 258). There are other Miltonic parallels. When Wordsworth's reading, as reflected in his greatest poetry, comes to be adequately traced in its influence on him, Donne will yield not a few *memorabilia*; and so with other singers, from Addison to Robert Browning—who has wealth of admiration for Donne. Even prosaic Benjamin Franklin seems to have turned to him, as Notes and Queries on his famous 'Epitaph' would suggest. 'Cato' drew its almost single *quick* line, that everybody knows, from Elegy xx., 'Opinion' (l. 36); and another line of it keeps ringing through our memory, though we cannot fix it on a great or any name.

We should have liked to trace the influence of Shakespeare on Donne, although, sooth to say, considering the subtlety common to both, that influence is less marked than might have been expected. A poor anecdote of 'gentle Will,' given in 'Wit's Interpreter' and elsewhere, on the authority of Donne, and other data, assure us that Donne and he knew each other, and met (probably) at 'The Mermaid.' Apart from this, on reading the Verse-Letters, and Elegies, and Funeral Elegies, and the class entitled 'Lyrical,' there reach my ear occasionally Shakespearean melody, and now and again as I study I am conscious of an indefinable something suggestive of Shakespeare. In its place I have pointed-out that the song, 'Break of day,' has a flavour of 'Romeo and Juliet;' and similarly you chance on Shakespeare's very own way of starting, pursuing, and illumining a fancy. . . .

Glancing back on our Essay, I feel how very much remains unsaid; how I must return on the great subject, and especially on certain things in the Life that give significance to the writings, verse and prose. Meanwhile, in the absence of anything approaching a worthy edition of Donne as a poet, or so much as an attempt to vindicate his peculiar claims or to mark his characteristics, even our inadequate words may be acceptable. With every abatement, I re-assert that Donne was not over-estimated in his lifetime; and that it was no 'glamour' of personal love which drew out the wonderful Elegies by his greatest compeers; neither is it asking too much for such an absolute and unique genius, that the reader will master his language and methods, and with all reverence and humility sit at his feet, and look, if not with shut, yet shaded eyes on poems and lines one must wish he had blotted. Let 'Elia's' wise as brave verdict be pondered by all who accept traditional criticism:

[He quotes Charles Lamb's comment on Donne and Cowley in *Mrs Leicester's School*—see No. 119. And he concludes his essay with some remarks on the elegies on Donne's death and a reference to Ben Jonson's 'singularly reverent admiration towards Donne, as man and poet', as it is demonstrated in Jonson's epigram 'Donne, the delight of Phoebus, and each Muse'.]

212. A correspondence in *The Athenaeum*

1873

A. B. Grosart's edition of Donne's poems called forth an article by Augustus Jessopp ('Donne's Epigrams', *The Athenaeum*, 1873 (2), pp. 81–2). The article raised the question of the authenticity of some Latin epigrams attributed to Donne and translated into English by Jasper Mayne. It started up a hot controversy in *The Athenaeum*, which shows professional scholarship already getting to work on the circumstances of the writing and publishing of Donne's poems.

Correspondents concentrated on the identification of persons named in the epigrams. Grosart retorted vehemently upon Jessopp, Jessopp replied, and 'R.D.' and B. Nicholson joined in. In the end they all agreed that the epigrams are not Donne's anyway (pp. 148, 179–80, 210–11).

213. Thomas Corser

1873

Corser (1793–1876), a clergyman, was an amateur bibliographer and antiquary. In his *Collectanea Anglo-Poetica*, 1873, pp. 223–7, he gave an account of the 1633 edition of Donne's poems and made some comments on Donne and his poetry.

It is probable that after he turned his mind to more serious thoughts and pursuits he neglected the further cultivation of the Muses. . . .

Donne was at the head of a particular class or school of poetry, which had many imitators; but it has been well observed that his life is more interesting than his poetry; that his name rather than his works may be said to survive; and that he left English poetry worse than he found it. The Editor is free to confess, along with many others, that Donne as a writer of poetry is no favourite of his. When he considers the pedantry, obscurity and metaphysical conceits introduced into his lighter poetry, the rugged and discordant diction, and inharmonious versification of his Satires, and the dulness and utter want of sensibility in his Elegies and religious Poems, as compared with the beauty, the tenderness and graceful simplicity of many of the writers of his own age, he is immediately struck with the contrast they exhibit, and is filled with wonder and surprise that he should have found so many imitators in his own style.

[He gives some extracts from Donne's poems 'to show the peculiarities of his style', and comments briefly on the poems:]

['The Baite'] . . . is one of the smoothest, although somewhat fantastical. . . .

['The Message'] The following light and pleasing song, expressed with much playful simplicity, affords one of the most favourable examples of Donne's style. . . .

['The Funerall'] . . . highly characteristic of Donne's peculiar and fantastic style of thought and expression. . . .

There is a long and highly eulogistic article on Donne's poetry in the *Retrosp. Rev.*, vol. viii. p. 31, in which the writer has laboured to bring into prominence the beauties and merits of his poetry, and to throw into shade his numerous and important defects; but the whole article is overwrought, and we doubt whether it has done much in the half century which has since elapsed to revive a love of this Author, or to remove the neglect which has so long attended his poetical works, in spite of the zealous efforts of a few respectable remonstrants.

[He refers to the 1719 edition of Donne's poems.]

It contains a Poem addressed 'To his Mistress,' p. 90, which is omitted in most of the other editions, and which, with one or two others disfigured by their grossness, it would have been better also to have omitted. Donne lived at a period when great licentiousness was tolerated, and when much more coarseness and vulgarity was allowed in speaking than at present, and in his younger days he was not free from those defects which he afterwards repudiated and abhorred. But had he lived to correct and edit his own early Poems these blemishes would certainly have been corrected.

214. Anon., *Temple Bar*

1876

The following are extracts from an anonymous article on Donne entitled 'The First of the English Satirists', *Temple Bar*, xlvii, 1876, pp. 337–9 and 350.

In the following lines, which open the general prologue to his satires, Bishop Hall claims to be the first of the English satirists.

> I first adventure with foolhardy might,
> To tread the steps of perilous despight;
> I first adventure, follow me who list,
> And be *the Second English Satirist*.

And, upon this assertion, his claims are usually admitted by literary historians. But although Hall's 'Toothless Satyrs' were printed in 1597, Donne had written his first two, and perhaps his third satire, as early as 1593. He did not deem it prudent to print them, however; and considering that those of his rival were publicly burned, we cannot but approve his forbearance.

Both of these fine, vigorous old writers, in whose works we see 'the very age and body' of their time reflected as in a mirror, have fallen into oblivion. A little ruggedness of metre, a few archaisms in spelling and expression, repel the indolent readers of the present day, who pronounce such books to be unintelligible. Johnson's shallow criticism, which clung to Shakespeare, obscuring his beauty and his art, so many years, is much to blame for the neglect of Donne's poetry. In his essay 'On Cowley and the Metaphysical Poets,' he has dwelt so minutely upon those forced metaphors and similes, those strained conceits and that pedantry of learning, which disfigured all the compositions of the Elizabethan age, even those of Shakespeare himself, he has so industriously collected specimens of his faults, and so carefully omitted all examples of his beauties, that few people would have the courage, after reading that essay, to even glance at a page of Donne's poetry. The

480

falseness of the great Aristarch's criticism, or we should rather say his lack of appreciative sympathy with the subtle spirit of pure poesy, is well exemplified in his remarks upon this writer. We will contrast them by some notices of other and, in our opinion, far higher authorities.

Ben Jonson told Drummond that he esteemed Donne 'the first poet in the world in some things.' Dryden called him 'the greatest wit, though not the best poet of our nation.' A modern critic writes thus:—

[He quotes George MacDonald's account of Donne in *England's Antiphon*, from 'The central thought of Dr Donne is nearly sure to be just' down to 'squirrels, and weasels, and bats'. See No. 206.]

And here, highest of all, we have Coleridge's opinion:—

[He quotes, not from Coleridge but from de Quincey's essay on 'Rhetoric', the praises of Donne which begin 'Few writers have shown a more extraordinary compass of powers than Donne', and conclude 'by conforming to its own ideal'. See No. 146.]

Coleridge has also suggested that read with a due regard to time, that is to say, giving *each thought* its due proportion in the utterance, the inharmoniousness of Donne's verses will disappear. We have ourselves tried to experiment, and must confess that attention to that rule has greatly smoothed their apparent ruggedness. How tender he could be in his quaint conceits is evidenced by the following verse, selected from many such, of a poem called 'The Relique;' the lines in italics are exquisitely pathetic:—

[He quotes the first stanza of 'The Relique'.]

Here is a powerful description of the condition of a crew on board a becalmed ship in the Red Sea:—

[He quotes lines 27–32 of the verse letter 'The Calme', which refers not to the Red Sea but to an episode in the 'Islands Expedition' to the Azores in 1597.]

Noble images, forcible lines, passages of surpassing power and pathos, are to be found in all his poems, although at times we have to wade through much that is tedious and pedantic, and wander through regions of almost hopeless obscurity before we come to these gems. Even to his contemporaries he appears to have been almost equally unintelligible, and Jonson prophesied that from that fault his works would perish. Coleridge has very aptly described his style in this witty quatrain:—

[He gives Coleridge's lines on Donne, 'With Donne, whose muse on dromedary trots'.]

The day after his burial some unknown friend wrote this epitaph with a coal upon the wall over his grave:—

> Reader! I am to let thee know
> Donne's body only lies below;
> For, could the grave his soul comprise,
> Earth would be richer than the skies.

. . . The satires display much humour, and a great knowledge of the men and women of his age. Pope versified two of them, and his attempt, like a similar one on the part of Dryden to modernise Chaucer, has been to emasculate and almost destroy the rugged force of the original. . . .

215. Algernon Charles Swinburne

1876, 1889, 1916

Swinburne's several references to Donne suggest that Donne's poetry loomed large in his mind. He sometimes develops a critical comment by way of championing the 'magisterial Donne' of the long poems. A copy of Grosart's edition of Donne's poems, 1872, went for 12s. at the sale of Swinburne's library in June 1916 (see *Sale Catalogues of Libraries of Eminent Persons*, vi, ed. J. Woolford, 1972, p. 279.)

(i) From Letter v, to Theodore Watts-Dunton, 15 March 1876 (*The Swinburne Letters*, ed. C. Y. Lang, New Haven, 1960, iii, p. 152):

I have just read through carefully for the first time Donne's 'Anniversaries'. What a magnificent and enthralling poem! how overflowing with glories of thought and word like a phosphoric sea by night with crossing and breaking flames, and how rich in deep grave harmonies of splendid and sonorous sadness! How did he for once learn such music, and then return to his habitual discords 'like the sow that is washed to her wallowing in the mire'?

(ii) From *A Study of Ben Jonson*, 1889, pp. 99, 129, 142. [He denies the appropriateness of Macaulay's term 'rugged rhymes' to Jonson's verse:]

Donne is rugged: Jonson is stiff. And if ruggedness of verse is a damaging blemish, stiffness of verse is a destructive infirmity. Ruggedness is curable; witness Donne's *Anniversaries*: stiffness is incurable; witness Jonson's *Underwoods*.

On Jonson's *Discoveries*:

That chance is the ruler of the world I should be sorry to believe and reluctant to affirm; but it would be difficult for any competent and careful student to maintain that chance is not the ruler of the world of letters. Gray's odes are still, I suppose, familiar to thousands who know nothing of Donne's *Anniversaries*; and Bacon's Essays are conventionally if not actually familiar to thousands who know nothing of Ben Jonson's *Discoveries*. And yet it is certain that in fervour of inspiration, in depth and force and glow of thought and emotion and expression, Donne's verses are as far above Gray's as Jonson's notes or observations on men and morals, on principles and on facts, are superior to Bacon's in truth of insight, in breadth of view, in vigour of reflection and in concision of eloquence. . . .

On Jonson's remarks to Drummond:

. . . the great writer whom 'he esteemed the first poet in the world in some things', but upon whom he passed the too sweeping though too plausible sentence 'that Donne, for not being understood, would perish. . . .'

216. Henry Morley

?1877

Morley (1822–94) was a Professor of Literature, and later principal
of a college, in the University of London. In his *Illustrations of
English Religion*, undated but ?1877, pp. 235–6, he gave a brief
account of Donne's later life and writings, asserting that some of
Donne's *Divine Poems* were certainly written while the poet was
still a Catholic. He quoted two of the *Divine Poems* entire, 'A
Hymne to God the Father', and the 'Hymne to God my God, in
my Sicknesse'.

217. Joseph Barber Lightfoot

1877

Lightfoot (1828–89) was a Professor of Divinity at Cambridge who became Bishop of Durham in 1879. He published much in the field of biblical criticism, and on Christian history and literature. The following extracts are taken from a chapter 'Donne, the poet-preacher' in his *The Classic Preachers of the English Church*, 1877, pp. 10–11 and 21.

[He discusses the way Donne's life bore upon his art, and especially upon his religious writings.]

This moral experience was the complement of his intellectual experience. It taught him to feel and to absorb into himself, as the other taught him to understand and to reason about, the doctrine of Christ's atoning grace. What penitence, what tears, what merits of his own *could* wash out the stains with which such a life as his was imbrued? . . .

[He quotes 'A Hymne to God the Father', minus the first two lines, with Walton's account of how Donne had it set to music.]

. . . Of Donne's romantic career it has been said, that his life is more poetical than his poetry. . . .

[He attributes this remark to Campbell, as reported by Milman. And he quotes Campbell's comment that 'the life of Donne is more interesting than his poetry'. See No. 135.]

. . . If, then, I were asked to describe in a few words the secret of his power as a preacher, I should say that it was the contrition and the thanksgiving of the penitent acting upon the sensibility of the poet. [In a footnote he adds] Donne seems to have the best right to the title of the poet-preacher—a designation which has sometimes been given to another.

[He speaks of Donne's style in the sermons, comparing it with the style of the poems.]

Moreover, the taste of the age for fantastic imagery, for subtle disquisition, for affectations of language and of thought, exercised a fascination over him. Yet even here he is elevated above himself and his time by his subject. There is still far too much of that conceit of language, of that subtlety of association, of that 'sport with ideas,' which has been condemned in his verse compositions; but, compared with his poems, his sermons are freedom and simplicity itself. And, whenever his theme rises, he rises too; and then in the giant strength of an earnest conviction he bursts these green withes which a fantastic age has bound about him, as the thread of two snaps at the touch of fire. Nothing can be more direct or more real than his eager, impetuous eloquence, when he speaks of God, of redemption, of heaven, of the sinfulness of human sin, of the bountifulness of Divine Love.

At such moments he is quite the most modern of our older Anglican divines. He speaks directly to our time, because he speaks to all times. . .

218. William Henry Davenport Adams

1878

Adams (1828–91), a journalist and miscellaneous writer, gives Hartley Coleridge's lines on Donne (see No. 170) and makes one comment of his own on Donne's poetry in his *A Dictionary of English Literature*, 1878, p. 182.

Funeral Elegies by Dr. John Donne. These exhibit all his subtlety of thought and ruggedness of versification, and many passages have a sonorous dignity, like the prose of Bacon or Sir Thomas Browne.

219. John Wesley Hales

1880

Hales (1836–1914), a literary historian, editor, and essayist, held for many years the Chair of English at King's College, London. The following extracts are taken from an essay 'John Donne' which he contributed to *The English Poets*, ed. T. H. Ward, 1880, i, pp. 558–61.

Donne's contemporary reputation as a poet, and still more as a preacher, was immense; and a glance at his works would suffice to show that he did not deserve the contempt with which he was subsequently treated. But yet his chief interest is that he was the principal founder of a school which especially expressed and represented a certain bad taste of his day. Of his genius there can be no question; but it was perversely directed. One may almost invert Jonson's famous panegyric on Shakespeare, and say that Donne was not for all time but for an age.

To this school Dr. Johnson has given the title of the Metaphysical; and for this title there is something to be said. 'Donne,' says Dryden, 'affects the metaphysics. . . .' [He completes the quotation. See No. 49.] Thus he often ponders over the mystery of love, and is exercised by subtle questions as to its nature, origin, endurance. But a yet more notable distinction of this school than its philosophising, shallow or deep, is what may be called its fantasticality, its quaint wit, elaborate ingenuity, far-fetched allusiveness; and it might better be called the Ingenious, or Fantastic School. Various and out-of-the-way information and learning is a necessary qualification for membership. Donne in one of his letters speaks of his 'embracing the worst voluptuousness, an hydroptic immoderate desire of human learning and languages.' Eminence is attained by using such stores in the way to be least expected. The thing to be illustrated becomes of secondary importance by the side of the illustration. The more unlikely and surprising and preposterous this is, the greater the success. This is wit of a kind. From one point of view, wit, as Dr. Johnson says, 'may be considered as a kind of *discordia concors*; . . .'.

[He completes Johnson's definition of metaphysical wit; cites the Dedication to Lord Craven in the 1650 edition of Donne's poems—which he takes for the poet's—to show that Donne identified 'wit' with 'poetry'; and quotes Dryden's estimate of Donne as 'the greatest wit though not the best poet of our nation'.]

The taste which this school represents marks other literatures besides our own at this time. It was 'in the air' of that age; and so was not originated by Donne. But it was he who in England first gave it full expression—who was its first vigorous and effective and devoted spokesman. And this secures him a conspicuous position in the history of our literature when we remember how prevalent was the fashion of 'conceits' during the first half of the seventeenth century, and that amongst those who followed it more or less are to be mentioned, to say nothing of the earlier poems of Milton and Waller and Dryden, Suckling, Denham, Herbert, Crashaw, Cleveland, Cowley.

This misspent learning, this excessive ingenuity, this laborious wit seriously mars almost the whole of Donne's work. For the most part we look on it with amazement rather than with pleasure. It reminds us rather of a 'pyrotechnic display,' with its unexpected flashes and explosions, than of a sure and constant light (compare the *Valediction* given in our selections). We weary of such unmitigated cleverness—such ceaseless straining after novelty and surprise. We long for something simply thought, and simply said.

His natural gifts were certainly great. He possesses a real energy and fervour. He loved, and he suffered much, and he writes with a passion which is perceptible through all his artificialities. Such a poem as *The Will* is evidence of the astonishing rapidity and brightness of his fancy.

He also claims notice as one of our earliest formal satirists. Though not published till much later, there is proof that some at least of his satires were written three or four years before those of Hall. Two of them (ii. and iv.) were reproduced—'versified'—in the last century by Pope, acting on a suggestion by Dryden; No. iii. was similarly treated by Parnell. In these versions, along with the roughness of the metre, disappears much of the general vigour; and it should be remembered that the metrical roughness was no result of incapacity, but was designed. Thus the charge of metrical uncouthness so often brought against Donne on the ground of his satires is altogether mistaken. How fluently and smoothly he could write if he pleased, is attested over and over again by his lyrical pieces.

[He goes on to give examples of Donne's verse—four of the *Songs and Sonnets* and some lines from a verse letter to Wotton.]

220. Dante Gabriel Rossetti

1880

Rossetti praised Donne in a letter which he wrote to his brother, W. M. Rossetti, on Sunday, 22 February 1880. (In *Dante Gabriel Rossetti: His Family-Letters, with a Memoir by William Michael Rossetti*, 1895, ii, p. 356.)

. . . I have been much enjoying Donne, who is full of excellences, and not brimming but rather spilling with quaintnesses.

221. Sir Henry Taylor

1885

Taylor (1800–86) was a civil servant with literary interests. In his autobiography he several times quoted Donne to illustrate observations or attitudes of his own. Commenting on a lady his mother had once praised for her beauty he says that he could now almost say it all again, and he quotes lines 1–2 of *Elegie ix*, 'The Autumnall'. He describes his 'strong leaning towards youthfulness' as he approached the age of forty, and says that this feeling defied his reason; he quotes lines 47–50 of *Elegie ix*, 'The Autumnall' and adds 'But I am not sure that Donne did actually feel as he saw reason to feel; and neither did I.' Referring to his marriage in October 1839 he says that marriage leaves nothing more to be said of a man, and quotes a version of lines 5–8 of 'A Valediction; forbidding Mourning', which he describes as some stanzas Donne addressed to his wife when about to depart for the Continent. (*The Autobiography of* [*Sir*] *Henry Taylor, 1800–75*, 1885, pp. 183, 272–3, 288.)

222. Sarah Orne Jewett

1889

Miss Jewett (1849–1909) was a New England novelist and essayist. She corresponded with the leading women writers of her day, knew Emerson, Whitman, and C. E. Norton, and became an intimate friend of J. R. Lowell. Her correspondent Mrs Annie Fields was the diarist who reported on Emerson's poetry readings at Chickerings Hall, when he included Donne in the programmes (see No. 131(v)). The following is an extract from an undated letter to Mrs Fields written in autumn 1889 (*Letters of Sarah Orne Jewett*, ed. Annie Fields, 1911, p. 60).

I have been reading an old copy of Donne's poems with perfect delight. They seem new to me just now, even the things I knew best. We must read many of them together. I must have my old copy mended; it is quite shabby, with its label lost and leaves working out from the binding.

APPENDIX A

The publication of Donne's poems down to 1912

Important appearances of Donne's poems are listed below. Many editors of poetical miscellanies included a few pieces by Donne, especially nineteenth-century editors. These reprints are described in the main body of documents but not mentioned here unless the publication is of special note.

1609   The first stanza of 'The Expiration' given with a musical setting in A. Ferrabosco, *Ayres*.

1611   'Upon Mr Thomas Coryats *Crudities*' given as one of the mock-panegyrical poems which introduced *Coryats Crudities*, and reprinted with the rest of the panegyrics in *The Odcombian Banquet*, 1611.

1611   *An Anatomie of the World* (*The first Anniversary*) published separately.

1612   *Of the Progresse of the Soule* (*The second Anniversary*) published with a fresh edition of *The first Anniversary*.

1612   The first stanza of 'Breake of Day' given with a musical setting in W. Corkine, *The Second Booke of Ayres*.

1613   'Elegie upon the untimely death of the incomparable Prince Henry' given with other elegies on Prince Henry's death in the third edition of J. Sylvester, *Lachrymae Lachrymarum*.

1621   *The first Anniversary* and *The second Anniversary* republished together in a fresh edition.

1625   *The first Anniversary* and *The second Anniversary* republished together in a fresh edition.

1630   'The Broken Heart' and part of the 'Song. Goe, and catche a falling starre' given in *A Helpe to Memory and Discourse*.

1633   *Poems, by J.D.* (publisher Marriot). The first collected edition of Donne's poems.

1635   *Poems, by J.D.* (Marriot). Adds a number of poems, and titles, and first groups the poems in their familiar order.

1639   *Poems, by J.D.* (Marriot).

1649   *Poems, by J.D.* (Marriot). Several poems added.

1650   *Poems, by J.D.* (Marriot). The first edition supervised by Donne's son, John Donne D.C.L. About a dozen pieces added, and the younger Donne's dedication to Lord Craven substituted for 'The Printer to the Understanders'.

1654   *Poems, by J.D.* (Sweeting).

1654   *Elegie xviii*, 'Loves Progress', and *Elegie xix*, 'To his Mistris Going to Bed', published for the first time in *The harmony of the Muses: or, The Gentlemans and Ladies Choisest Recreation.*
        Elegie xviii was given again in *Wit and Drollery. By Sir J.M., J.S., Sir W.D., and the most refined Wits of the Age*, 1661.

1669   *Poems, &c. By John Donne late Dean of St Pauls* (Herringman). Several pieces added, including the full version of *Elegie xii*, 'His parting from her', and *Elegies xviii* and *xix*.

1719   *Poems on Several Occasions. Written by the Reverend John Donne, D.D. Late Dean of St Paul's* (Tonson).

1779   *The Poetical Works of Dr John Donne, Dean of St Paul's.* Volumes xxiii–v of *The Poets of Great Britain Complete from Chaucer to Churchill*, ed. J. Bell, Edinburgh.

1793   *The Poetical Works of Dr John Donne.* In volume iv of *A Complete Edition of the Poets of Great Britain*, ed. R. Anderson, Edinburgh.

1802   *Elegie xx*, 'Loves Warre', published for the first time by F. G. Waldron in his *A Collection of Miscellaneous Poetry* and *The Shakespearean miscellany*.

1810   *Poems by John Donne.* In volume v of *The Works of the English Poets*, ed. A. Chalmers.

1819   Nearly forty poems by Donne, or excerpts from poems, given in volume iv of *The Works of the British Poets, with Lives of the Authors*, ed. E. Sanford, Philadelphia.

1839   A selection of Donne's poems given in volume iv of *The Works of John Donne, D.D., Dean of Saint Paul's 1621–1631*, ed. H. Alford.

1840   A selection of Donne's poems, and excerpts from poems, given in *Selections from the Works of John Donne, D.D.*, Oxford.

1855   *The Poetical Works of Dr John Donne*, Boston. A new edition from the early printed texts.
        Also issued as the second part of *The Poetical Works of Skelton and Donne*, Boston, 1855.

1864   Reissue of the Boston edition of *The Poetical Works of Dr John Donne.*

1866   Reissue of the Boston edition of *The Poetical Works of Dr John Donne.*

1872–3   *The complete poems of John Donne D.D., Dean of St Paul's*, ed. A. B. Grosart. Fuller Worthies Library, two volumes.

1895   *The Poems of John Donne*, ed. C. E. Norton and J. R. Lowell, New York, Grolier Club, two volumes.

1896   *The Poems of John Donne*, ed. E. K. Chambers. The Muses Library, two volumes. Prints for the first time the verse letter by Donne and Goodyer written 'alternis vicibus'.

1905   *The Love Poems of John Donne*, selected and edited C. E. Norton, Boston.

1905   *Poems of John Donne selected from his Songs, Sonnets, Elegies, Letters, Satires, and Divine Poems*, ed. F. L. Babbott, New York.

1912   *The Poems of John Donne*, ed. H. J. C. Grierson, Oxford. Two volumes.

Poems by Donne which are known to have been set to music down to the nineteenth century

---

'The Expiration' (i) Set for voice and lute by Alfonso Ferrabosco, *First Booke of Ayres*, 1609.

(ii) Set for voice and lute, anonymously. In MS.

'Breake of Day' Set for voice and bass-viol by William Corkine, *Second Booke of Ayres*, 1612.

'The Message' Set for voice and lute by Giovanni Coperario (John Cooper, *c.* 1575–1626). In MS.

'Song. Goe, and catche a falling starre'

(i) Set for voice and lute, anonymously. In MS.

(ii) Set (and sung) by Robert Browning as a boy, in the 1820s. Setting subsequently destroyed by Browning himself.

'Song. Sweetest love, I do not goe' (given as 'Deerest love I doe not goe') Set for voice and bass, anonymously. In MS.

'The Apparition' A three-part setting by William Lawes (1602–45). In MS (incomplete).

['The Primrose' A piece of music in the Fitzwilliam Virginal Book entitled 'The Primerose', by Martin Peerson (?1590–?1651), has a theme which may be a setting of the opening of Donne's poem. But there is nothing that specifically connects the music with Donne.]

The Lamentations of Jeremy A three-part setting by Thomas Ford (*c.* 1580–1648). In MS.

'A Hymne to God the Father' (i) Set for voice and bass by John Hilton (1599–1657). In MS.

(ii) According to Walton, set 'to a most grave and solemn tune' which was commissioned by Donne himself and 'often sung to the Organ by the Choristers of St Paul's Church'. This setting is probably not Hilton's but another one, now lost.

(iii) Set by Pelham Humfrey in *Harmonia Sacra*, 1688.

Bibliography

The following are the chief works which list references to Donne's poetry or trace the currency of his poems.

BRYAN, R. A., 'A Sidelight on Donne's Seventeenth Century Reputation', *Seventeenth-Century News*, summer 1954, p. 21.

BRYAN, R. A., 'John Donne's Poems in Seventeenth-Century Commonplace Books', *English Studies*, 43, 1962, pp. 170–4.

DUNCAN, J. E., 'The Revival of Metaphysical Poetry, 1872–1912', *PMLA*, 68, 1953, pp. 658–71.

DUNCAN, J. E., *The Revival of Metaphysical Poetry: The History of a Style*, Minneapolis, 1959.

ELDREDGE, F., 'Further Allusions and Debts to John Donne', *ELH*, 19, 3, 1952, pp. 214–28.

HOWARTH, R. G., 'References to John Donne', *NQ*, n.s., 5, 1958, p. 43.

HOWARTH, R. G., Addenda to the *Biography and Criticism* section of the 3rd ed. of Keynes's *A Bibliography of Dr John Donne*, Cambridge, 1958.

KEYNES, SIR GEOFFREY L., *A Bibliography of Dr John Donne*, 4th ed., Oxford, 1973.

MACCOLL, A., 'The Circulation of Donne's Poems in Manuscript', in *John Donne: Essays in Celebration*, ed. A. J. Smith, 1972, pp. 28–46.

MILGATE, W., 'The Early References to John Donne', *NQ*, cxcv, 1950, pp. 229–31, 246–7, 290–2, 381–3.

MILGATE, W., 'References to John Donne', *NQ*, cxcviii, 1953, pp. 421–4.

MUNBY, A. N. L. (general editor), *Sale Catalogues of Libraries of Eminent Persons*, 1971– (continuing; eight volumes by 1974).

NETHERCOTT, A. H., 'The Term "Metaphysical Poets" before Johnson', *MLN*, xxxvii, 1922, pp. 11–17.

NETHERCOTT, A. H., 'The Reputation of John Donne as Metrist', *Sewanee Review*, xxx, 1922, pp. 463–74.

NETHERCOTT, A. H., 'The Reputation of the "Metaphysical Poets" during the Seventeenth Century', *JEGP*, xxiii, 2, 1924, pp. 173–98.

NETHERCOTT, A. H., 'The Reputation of the "Metaphysical Poets" during the Age of Pope', *PQ*, iv, 1925, pp. 161–79.

NETHERCOTT, A. H., 'The Reputation of the "Metaphysical Poets" during the Age of Johnson and the "Romantic Revival" ', *SP*, 22, 1925, pp. 81–132.

TILLOTSON, K., 'Donne's Poetry in the Nineteenth Century (1800–72)' in *Elizabethan and Jacobean Studies presented to F. P. Wilson*, ed. Herbert Davis and Helen Gardner, Oxford, 1959, pp. 307–26.

Index

II GENERAL INDEX